BOLLINGEN SERIES LIX · 1

PAUL FRIEDLÄNDER

PLATO

1

AN INTRODUCTION

TRANSLATED FROM THE GERMAN
BY HANS MEYERHOFF

BOLLINGEN SERIES LIX

PRINCETON

THIS IS THE FIRST OF THREE VOLUMES
CONSTITUTING THE FIFTY-NINTH PUBLICATION
IN A SERIES SPONSORED BY
BOLLINGEN FOUNDATION

First Princeton/Bollingen Paperback Edition, 1973

Originally published in German as
Platon: Seinswahrheit und Lebenswirklichkeit
2d edn., 1954; 3d edn., 1964
by W. de Gruyter & Co., Berlin

LIBRARY OF CONGRESS CATALOGUE CARD NO. 57–11126
ISBN 0–691–01795–6 (paperback edn.)
ISBN 0–691–09812–3 (hardcover edn.)
MANUFACTURED IN THE U. S. A.

UDALRICO · DE · WILAMOWITZ-MOELLENDORFF

OCTOGENARIO

HOC · OPUS · OLIM · INSCRIPSI

DEINDE · RENOVATUM · ET · AUCTUM

EIUSDEM · MEMORIAE · REDEDICAVI

TUNC · DENIQUE · ANGLICE · VERSUM

BENIGNE · ACCEPIT · OBLATUM

VIR · NONAGENARIUS

ET · DE · LITTERIS · ET · DE · PACE

MERITISSIMUS

GILBERTUS · MURRAY

Preface

This second edition of the introductory volume of my work on Plato does not differ basically from the first edition. Only chapter XI, "*Aletheia*, A Discussion with Martin Heidegger," has undergone substantial revision. My opposition to Heidegger's interpretation of the Platonic concept of truth remains unchanged. Yet, recent extensive analysis of the meaning of *aletheia* in the older literature has more clearly brought out the various early meanings of the concept. It has become clear that the aspect of unhiddenness most stressed by Heidegger was present very early, but so were the elements which later combined in Plato's lofty concept of *aletheia*.

"Plato as Geographer and Geophysicist" would be a more adequate title for chapter XV; only technical reasons prevented the change. The text of the chapter is unaltered except for a postscript on page 285.

The notes have been revised and supplemented, in accord with the German third edition published in 1964. These revisions, and a few completely new notes, are presented here in a separate section as Addenda to the Second Edition. For explanation of the use of an asterisk, see page 339.

P.F.

Los Angeles, California
November, 1968

Preface to the First Edition

The first German edition of the present volume, published in 1928, contained chapters I to IX, and as an appendix, the two chapters that are now XV and XVII. The second German edition, revised and enlarged, appeared in 1954; six chapters were added, of which the first three relate Platonic problems to modern philosophy. The present English translation is again a revision throughout. Mr. Huntington Cairns, moreover, has allowed the reprinting of his paper on Plato as jurist. This chapter, the two chapters preceding, and the one following combine to give a notion of Plato's universality. Two volumes devoted to the interpretation of the single dialogues will complete this work.

The preparation of the present edition is being supported by grants from the Reserve, the Johnson, and the Penrose Funds of the American Philosophical Society. A fellowship from Bollingen Foundation has made it possible for me to devote my time to scholarly work.

P.F.

[*Los Angeles, 1958*]

Translator's Note

I am indebted to Miss Helen Caldwell, Mr. Johnny Christensen, Miss Friedl Ekart, Mrs. Vivien d'Estournelles de Constant, Professor B. Q. Morgan, Dr. David Sachs, and Dr. Bertha Stenzel for help at various stages in the making of this translation. Dr. Stenzel also translated the notes. Chapters XIV, XVI (by Mr. Huntington Cairns), and XVII appeared originally in English. Thanks are due also to the editors of Bollingen Series for helpful suggestions and corrections made in preparing the manuscript for print. Throughout the various phases of this work, I have been able to consult constantly with the author himself in order to bring the English version as closely as possible into line with the German original.

The translation of passages from the works and authors cited follows in general the German text. In the case of translations from Plato, however, I have used English versions of these passages as models for the translation.

H.M.

Acknowledgment is made to The Johns Hopkins Press and the *Harvard Law Review* for permission to reprint, with slight modifications, Huntington Cairns' chapter on Plato as jurist.

Table of Contents

Plato's autobiography ⌊ 9 – 9 ⌋, the only document we
have about his intellectual development, reveals a person
destined to pursue a political career, but thwarted by
the political disintegration of the age and by the fate of
Socrates. The postulate of the philosopher-kings is an
epigrammatic formulation of the goal of a radical
restoration [9]. Plato's written works and his active
participation in politics confirm the priority of the political
domain in his life [9 – 10]. The Greek state, originally
built on religious foundations, had succumbed to arbitrary
rule and thought [10 – 12]. The Socratic method and the
death of Socrates are counterweights against the political
disintegration [12]. In the encounter with Socrates,
Plato's inner eye [13 – 14] beholds the eternal Forms
[14 – 19]. The new state is to be built around this central
vision [19 – 20]. To translate this vision into conceptual
language Plato falls back upon Parmenidean ontology
[21 – 25]. The Herakleitean world view presents itself
as the opposite pole to that of Parmenides, and both,
again, are fused in Plato [25 – 26]. Pythagoras helps to
expand this realm into cosmology [26 – 28]; and the
Pythagorean-Orphic myth of the soul serves as a vehicle

PART II

CHAPTER X: *Intuition and Construction*   213

A PATH TO BERGSON AND
SCHOPENHAUER

Bergson distinguishes between the intuitive origin and
the systematic construction of a philosophy and asks that
historians of philosophy observe this distinction [*213 –*

CHAPTER XI: *Aletheia*   221

A DISCUSSION WITH MARTIN HEIDEGGER

CHAPTER XV: *Plato as Geographer*   261

THE BEGINNINGS OF SPHERICAL GEOGRAPHY

notion of the philosopher-king is modified by Polybios
who looks upon himself as a combination of statesman,
historian, and philosopher [*329 – 30*]. Since philosophy
for him is synonymous with *paideia*, he criticizes Rome,
which he admired, for its lack of culture and education.
He transmits the Socratic-Platonic influence to the circle
of the Scipios [*330 – 31*]. Polybios was well acquainted
with the dialogue *Alcibiades;* and the first conversation
with the young Scipio, in particular, is written most of all
under the influence of this dialogue [*332*].

List of Illustrations

PART I

CHAPTER ONE

Eidos

W HEN I was young," Plato writes in his mid-seventies in the manifesto *To the Friends and Associates of Dion*, "my experience was the same as that of many others. I thought that as soon as I became my own master I would immediately enter into public life. But it so happened that fateful changes occurred in the political situation.

"In the government then existing, hated as it was by many, a revolution took place. The revolution was headed by fifty-one leaders, of whom . . . thirty formed the highest political authority with unlimited powers. Of these some were relatives and acquaintances of mine, and they invited me to join their administration as if I were entitled to do so. What I then experienced was not surprising considering my youth; for I imagined that they would administer the state by leading it out of an unjust way of life into a just way, and consequently I paid close attention to see what they would do. What I saw in fact was that these men within a short time caused us to look back upon the former government as a golden age. Above all, they tried to send my aged friend Socrates—whom I would, without scruple, call the most just of men then living—along with others after one of the citizens to take him by force so that he might be put to death, their object being apparently that Socrates, whether he wished to or not, should be made to participate in their political actions; he, however, refused to obey and risked the worst penalties rather than be a participant in their unholy practices. So when I saw these things and others of a similar serious nature, I was revolted and I withdrew from

3

these evils. Not long afterward the power of the Thirty was
overthrown together with the whole of the government which
then existed. And once again, though less urgently, I was
seized with a desire to take part in public affairs. Many deplor-
able events were still happening in those troubled times, and it
was not surprising that, in the course of the revolution, some
people took violent revenge on their enemies, although the
party returning to power exercised, on the whole, considerable
moderation. Yet, as misfortune would have it, certain men of
authority summoned our companion Socrates before the law
courts, raising against him a most criminal charge, one that
Socrates, of all men, least deserved. For the indictment was
based on the charge of impiety against the gods of the city;
and the judges upheld the indictment and put to death the man
who, at the very time when they themselves had the misfortune to be in exile, refused to take part in the criminal arrest of a
friend of the exiled party.

"When, therefore, I considered all this, and the type of men
who were administering the affairs of the state, and the laws and
customs too—the more I considered all this, and the more I
advanced in years myself, the more difficult appeared to me the
task of managing the affairs of the state rightly. For it was impossible to take action without friends and loyal companions,
and these it was not easy to find among my acquaintance, since
our city no longer lived according to the custom and principles of
our forefathers; yet to acquire other, new friends was impossible
without great difficulties. Moreover, the corruption in legislation and customs increased to a surprising degree. Thus it
happened that I, who was at first filled with an ardent desire to
engage in public affairs, finally became dizzy when I viewed all
this and saw everything disintegrating around me. Still, not
only did I continue to consider what sort of improvement might
be made with regard to these matters and with regard to the
government as a whole, but also as regards political action I
kept constantly waiting for an opportune moment—until,
finally, looking at all the states that now exist, I came to the
conclusion that one and all they were badly governed. For the
state of their laws is such as to be almost incurable, unless,

perchance, some action of an astonishing sort coincides with good luck. So I was compelled, praising true philosophy, to declare that she alone enables men to discern what is justice in the state and in the lives of the individuals. The generations of mankind, therefore, would have no cessation from evils until either the class of those who are true and genuine philosophers came to political power or else the men in political power, by some divine dispensation, became true philosophers. This was the conviction I held when I came to Italy and Sicily, at the time of my first arrival." [1]

This is Plato's view in retrospect, as an old man, upon the period of his growth between the ages of eighteen and forty. According to Goethe, nobody can share the peculiar way in which an individual looks back upon his past life; and one would be grateful for additional evidence that might complement Plato's testimony or permit us to look upon this testimony from a different perspective. But, for an understanding of how Plato came to be what he finally was, there remains only this fragment of an autobiography. To be sure, it must stand up against the view of many who have denied the Platonic authorship of the manifesto, and against the skepticism of Nietzsche, who "would give no credit to a history of Plato's life written by himself, as little as to Rousseau's, or to the *Vita Nuova* of Dante." [2]

The autobiographical testimony runs counter to most of the prevalent conceptions about Plato. He has come to occupy his place in the history of Western philosophy. Under the influence of Parmenides, Herakleitos, and Socrates, he is viewed as having discovered philosophical truths; and later philosophers continued to work on his problems. "After the systems we have named came the philosophy of Plato, which in most respects followed these thinkers, but which had peculiarities that distinguished it from the philosophy of the Italians" (Pythagoreans). Creative power can hardly be more narrowed down to the dimension of doctrinal history than it is in this passage by Aristotle (*Metaphysics* I 6). Indeed, it is he who is primarily responsible for this kind of theoretical construction; though it may be questioned whether Plato, at times, could not see himself in such a perspective, if we take what Socrates, in the *Phaedo*, says about the stages of his own philosophical growth as being somehow autobiographical on Plato's part. We do not know the answer, and there is no hint of it in the letter.

The retrospect of the letter, to be sure, is not complete, as is quite evident from the reference to the term "philosophy" at the end of the passage just cited. Nothing is said about how Plato came to this philosophy. He is conscious of having discovered a metaphysical world, and the true philosophy of which he speaks in the letter is the knowledge of the eternal forms and their true being. But Plato did not set out in quest of this world. He set out in quest of the best state, and on this quest he discovered the world of forms.

How this is meant may be seen more clearly when we consider the historical conditions under which Plato grew up. He was not destined, either by the place and time of his birth or by virtue of the social class to which he belonged, to lead the life of the philosopher in the manner in which for centuries now—and partly through Plato's own influence—a person is born into the mainstream of philosophy in the Western world. "When I *entered* into philosophy . . . " wrote Wilhelm Dilthey in a manner characteristic of a modern philosopher. Plato could not have used such an expression; for the intellectual position of a person born of a noble family in Athens at the beginning of the great war was altogether different.

At a time when the sun of Homer had already risen over the Ionian shores, Attica—a small country of landed proprietors, farmers, and seamen—still slumbered at the dawn of a new era. The waves of science and philosophy rising in Miletus and spreading to the colonial settlements in southern Italy did not touch Athens. While in the colonies minds were busy calculating solar eclipses or drafting maps of the earth or inquiring into the basic structure of the universe, Solon and Peisistratos were building the state of Athens and opening its doors to the rich arts of the East. While in Ionia and Magna Graecia the system of pure being competed with the law of opposites hidden in the eternal flux, and while other thinkers carried further the research into the order and basic stuff of the physical world, Athens founded the state of free citizens, defeated the Persians, and created tragic poetry. To be sure, Anaxagoras came to Athens as the first great representative of the Ionian philosophy of nature and won the statesman Perikles as well as the poet Euripides to his new doctrines. But he was a stranger, and so were the younger "physiologists" who in Athens met with applause, ridicule, or enmity. And soon skeptical conclusions began to appear as a result of the contradictions inherent in these philosophies of nature and of the epistemological inquiries of the older thinkers.

Gorgias and Protagoras, the Sophists, also came to Athens as visitors. The Athenian youth ran after them because they offered a new kind of contest and new weapons in the struggle for power. But while the vendors of these novel products were received with honors, no Athenian citizen would have cared to share their trade. "Would you not be ashamed of yourself to appear as a Sophist before the Hellenes!" Socrates asks a young Athenian rushing out to become a pupil of Protagoras. "Yes, by Zeus, Socrates, to confess the truth, I should be," (*Protagoras* 312A). This reply of the young man might have been the confession of every well-bred Athenian.

Aristotle reports, in the same passage where he places the philosophy of his teacher in the history of metaphysical systems, that Plato, when young, had become familiar with the Herakleitean Kratylos and had learned from him the doctrine of eternal flux and the impossibility of true knowledge. Socrates, however, had shown him that ethical concepts contained a common element not found in the world of sensible things, and Plato had called this element an *Idea*. It would be a misunderstanding of Aristotle if this account, which makes sense only in so far as it points in the direction of his own problems, were to be taken as a historical account of Plato's intellectual growth. If that were the case, it would even be possible to assume that the skeptical period in Plato's life was preceded by a materialistic one. One would have only to take Socrates' description, in the *Phaedo*, of his own philosophical development as a biographical account applying to Plato.[3] But aside from modern reconstructions of this kind, we do not know in the least how deeply Plato was affected by "philosophical" ideas to which he was exposed through Kratylos and others. And even if this influence did lead him to the point of despairing of all knowledge—which, incidentally, sounds more like the case of Doctor Faustus than that of a man in classical antiquity—there was always practical reality. If he had been able to act, speculative broodings of this kind might have vanished as they did in the case of the young Bismarck, who overcame Byronic world-weariness and Feuerbach's skepticism once he plunged into the world of action.

No, an Athenian citizen tracing his genealogy to Solon would wish, even at the end of the fifth century, only to enter upon a political career. "To become a leading man in the city"—that is the aspiration of every young man, of Alkibiades in Plato's dialogue of the same name, of Plato's brother Glaukon in Xenophon's *Memorabilia*, of Plato himself, according to the retrospect of the great letter. However, there was one fundamental difference between him and the others: for him this career raised deep personal and intellectual problems leading to the turning point in his life.

The more a person's life is concerned with the quest for the essential, the more likely he is to perceive a symbolic meaning in what is happening before his eyes. Plato saw the disintegration of Athens in the fate of Socrates. If Athens could no longer tolerate its most loyal servant, who was always ready to die for the city and finally did die for its laws, if the aristocratic revolutionaries wanted to involve him in the moral responsibility for their misdeed—involve Socrates, who had always opposed the arbitrary rule of momentary majorities and who had always pleaded for a government of the "best"; if, finally, the democratic restoration condemned this very man who had refused to become a partner of the oligarchy in criminal proceedings against a member of the democratic party—then, Plato felt, the city created and made great by the ancestors had deteriorated to a level of meaningless political drifting.

To be a statesman or politician was not yet a separate profession when Plato considered such a career seriously. For when Aristotle defined man as a "political animal," he expressed conceptually what was tacitly taken for granted in real life. How to win *Arete* and how to become a statesman were questions facing every young man, and both questions were ultimately one and the same. If he could not become a political man, this did not mean, as it does today, that he would have to choose a different profession: it meant that the essential part of man's existence was denied, since the time of the Stoic Sage or the Christian Saint had not yet come. Thus the impossibility of a political career—symbolized in the fate of Socrates— meant for Plato either the destruction of one's own life or the demand to build a new life on an entirely different foundation for both the individual and the state. And had not Socrates shown how this was to be done? It was no longer a question of patching up old institutions: it was a question of the remaking of man. Without making man "virtuous," it was impossible to conceive of the *Arete* of the city. Socrates, by constantly asking the question, What is virtue?, had already begun the work of restoration. He alone knew what was necessary: he was the only Athenian practicing the true art of politics. When Plato, through the mouth of Socrates, presented the challenge that philosophers should be rulers or the rulers of the city philosophers, this was not a manifestation of an "excess of philosophical pride," as Jacob Burckhardt [4] called it; it was rather an epigrammatic formulation of a profound insight dawning upon the statesman in Plato as a result of his personal experience at that moment in history and as a result of his encounter with Socrates.

In the last analysis, we cannot but "share with Plato the peculiar way in which he looked back upon his past life." [5] To be sure, this life is too rich to be described by a simple formula, however general. Yet he undoubtedly saw what was the most essential aspect of it, and this is confirmed by his own writings. The *Republic* and the *Laws* by far surpass, in size alone, any other work of Plato's. A survey of the total body of his writings must place the *Republic* in the center of his entire literary production. In fact, it is legitimate to consider most of the earlier dialogues as a preparation directly leading to the *Republic*. The inner structure of the *Republic*, in turn, is deter-

mined by the thesis that the true rulers and the true philosophers are identical; it contains, at its very center (473CD,
499B), the pointed epigram of the *Seventh Letter* about the
philosopher-kings. Finally, Plato's own life shows repeated
attempts to realize this apparent paradox in the political
events of his own times. What, then, does the paradox mean?
This question may be answered by a brief digression on the
nature of the Greek state.

Originally the Greek state is firmly based on a divine or
religious foundation. In Homer, it is Zeus who grants scepter
and ruling power to the kings. In Hesiod, Themis is the wife of
Zeus; both have, besides the Fates, which bring good and evil
to mortals, three other daughters, the Horai: their names—
Eunomia, Dike, and Eirene—represent the basic principles
underlying all human or "political" communities. Even a
criminal or a tyrant who violated the law of the state acknowledged its divinity when he used the terms Themis or Dike.
Later, when this original stability was subjected to questions
and doubts, Herakleitos secured the foundations of the state in
the order of the cosmos. Why "should the people fight for the
law as for their city wall?" Because the order of the state is
part of the larger order of the world. "For all human laws are
nourished by one which is divine. It governs as far as it will, and
is sufficient for all, and more than sufficient." [6]

The line of thought expanding the rule of Dike to the universe
may be found in most of the earlier thinkers. Anaximander
looked upon the destruction of existing things as a giving of
justice and reparation for the "injustice" of their coming into
being. Parmenides entrusted into the hands of Dike the keys to
the gate through which the paths of day and night cross and,
also, the chains binding together the One Being. For Herakleitos, too, Dike was a symbol of universal necessity. "The sun
will not transgress his measures; otherwise the Furies, con-
stables of Dike, will find him out." And when Herakleitos
identifies the contrary powers of "law" and "strife," this
mythical expression reveals quite transparently his primary
vision of the universal principle of the "hidden harmony of
opposites." Thus the legal order of the state was raised to the

metaphysical order of the universe, and the city and its laws recaptured in thought some of the sublimity they lost when the religious foundations were dissolving.[7]

For those foundations were not so secure but that they disintegrated within the span of a few generations. The separation of the individual from the community grew rapidly both in the lives and thoughts of men. A survey of other peoples and different customs led to a comparison with one's own norms; and this comparison, in turn, shook the conviction of the uniqueness of one's own beliefs and institutions as well as the faith in their necessity. The fate of the great individuals of the tragic age had already shown the concept of justice, heretofore firmly grounded in the city and religion, in a problematic light. Now the "Twofold Speech" (Δισσοὶ Λόγοι) of the Sophists taught that just and unjust were one and the same: what was just at one time might be unjust at another, or the unjust might be as good as the just, even better. Kritias constructed a theory of human civilization—similar to that of Demokritos and Epicurus and the philosophers of the eighteenth-century Enlightenment—according to which a few wise individuals set up social laws to conquer man's bestial inclinations in the state of nature "in order that Dike might be the ruler and have Insolence as her slave." Just as human or all-too-human was Antiphon's conception of *Nomos* as artificially constructed and practiced, and the result of a social contract. What for Herakleitos had been a part of the universal order of nature now became its counterpart, a hostile opponent. "What is just according to the laws of the city is, in most cases, hostile to nature," and "what the laws lay down as useful puts nature into chains."[8] Pindar had hailed *Nomos* as "king of all gods and men"; the Sophist Hippias, as he appears in Plato, hates *Nomos* as a "tyrant who coerces contrary to nature."

Other sources reveal the gradual breakup of the old structure joining city and universe. One of the hostile brothers confronting each other in Euripides' *Phoenician Women*[9] still claims his power in the name of the law; but the law is no longer divine for him. The other openly acknowledges "tyranny as the greatest of goddesses." The mother fails to reconcile the fraternal strife, for she has only the goddess "Equality" (Isotes) to call upon for help. Isotes has decreed measure and balance for man. According to her law it comes to pass that the "night's lusterless eye and the sun's light move in the perennially equal circle of the year." In the same manner, it is said, she also governs men and cities and "joins together friend with friend, city with city, and comrade with comrade in battle." But when the divinity of Dike is forgotten, Isotes reveals herself as a verbal ghost without power over men's souls. The sacred bond is dissolved and disrupted, arbitrariness is let loose in the world, and the "tyrannical man" is set free from the bonds of Dike.

The moment of history into which Socrates was born confronted him with the task of searching for Dike, who had all but disappeared from the sight of men. He "discovered the inductive method and definition," he "founded science"—in so far as he did [10]—because he searched, through the *Logos*, through continuous dialogical or dialectical inquiry, for the true meaning behind words, for "what is," for the meaning of "justice," of the "virtues," and of the one and only "virtue." He embarked upon this quest because, since Dike once ruled over the city and state of his forefathers, she might be found again, however hidden. He even died for this "justice," according to the command of the city; the city, despite its disintegration, for him still bore witness to the supremacy of Dike.

Plato met Socrates. He heard him inquiring into the meaning of justice and the other "virtues." And this inquiry gave direction to his own, as yet vague, inclination "to strive after the commonweal." "There is nothing more urgent to me than to become as virtuous as possible. And for this, I believe, no one can be of more decisive help to me than yourself." This is Alkibiades speaking to Socrates in the *Symposium* (218D), and Plato must have spoken to him or felt toward him similarly. And from Socrates he either heard or thought he heard the words that, in *Alcibiades Major* (105D) he put into the mouth of Socrates speaking to the young Alkibiades: "None of your plans can find fulfillment without me; for so strongly do I prevail over you and your affairs." Thus Plato came to acknowledge the life and death of the master as his own fate.

Plato possessed what Socrates did not seem to need: the plastic eye of the Greeks, an eye akin to that by which Poly-kleitos perceived the "canon" in the runners and javelin throwers of the palaestra, Pheidias envisaged Homer's picture of Zeus in the "Zeuslike men" (δῖοι ἄνδρες), and also to the eye by which Greek mathematicians looked at the pure geometric forms. Plato seems to have been aware of this gift, stronger in him than in any other thinker. Or is it an accident that we first find in him the metaphor "eye of the soul"? [11]

Before Plato we find similarly daring formulations in poetry: Aeschylus speaks of an "understanding endowed with eyes" (φρένα ὠμματωμένην) and Pindar conversely, of a "blind heart" (τυφλὸν ἦτορ). Moreover, poet-philosophers like Parmenides, Empedokles, and Epicharmos raise the demand that we must "see with our minds," an expression, partly poetical, partly epistemological, which stands in contrast to physical vision. This is echoed in Sophistic literature, for example, when Gorgias speaks about the "explorers of the above" (μετεωρολόγοι) who "make the incredible and the hidden clear to the eyes of the imagination" (τοῖς τῆς δόξης ὄμμασιν); and similarly, when the Sophistic author of a Hippokratean work contrasts, in the case of a physician, the eye of the body with the vision of the mind (ἡ τῆς γνώμης ὄψις).[12] All this is quite Greek, however different in its various formulations; but it is still far from the plasticity and systematic meaning of the Platonic image.

Not so far from the last examples is the statement in the *Symposium* (219A) that "the mind's vision begins to perceive critically and distinctly as the bodily eye fails in strength." Yet Plato goes much farther than that. While in a beautiful allegory in the *Alcibiades Major* he compared the process of knowledge with the vision of the human eye, he carried this parallelism to its ultimate stage in the allegory of the cave in the *Republic*.[13] Comparing the world of the soul and the world of the body, or "the organ in the soul by which we learn the truth" and the eye of the body (518C), Plato refers to the leaden weights of sensuality, which turn the "vision of the soul" (τὴν τῆς ψυχῆς ὄψιν) downward and away from true reality (519B). Later the mathematical sciences and astronomy are said to "purify and rekindle an organ in every soul (ὄργανόν τι ψυχῆς) when its light is dimmed or extinguished by other interests, an organ better worth saving than a thousand eyes because it is our only means of seeing the truth." (527DE) From here it is only a small step to calling this "organ" the "eye of the soul" (τὸ τῆς ψυχῆς ὄμμα, 533D). Buried in mud, it is gradually drawn and led upward by the dialectical method to the highest intelligible forms. These forms had just been compared again to the noblest vision of the visible world (532B). Thus, after a long preparation, the final picture, closely connected with a metaphysical theory of illumination and the intuition of forms, at last emerges: the soul, interpreted after the model of the body, has eyes to see; but these eyes look upon the eternal forms.

Plato is a poet-philosopher who does not repeat himself without purpose in his choice of images. The myth of the soul in the *Phaedrus* visualizes the chariot, the charioteer, and the plumage of the soul; the image of the eye would not quite fit into this context. But we are tempted to think of the allegory in the *Republic* as we encounter, again and again, expressions from the world of vision. The immortal souls see what is beyond the heavens. The mind (διάνοια) of the god, in his journey through the heavens, sees justice itself, sees measure, sees truth; and after it has seen the world of true being and has nourished itself, it returns home. As far as human souls are concerned, the best of them can just reach with the head of the charioteer into the outer regions and barely see true being. But it is part of the nature of human souls that they once beheld the essences; and whenever man's mind grasps the one form in the midst of many appearances, this is due to remembering what the soul beheld while following the god. Here one could often substitute the phrase "eye of the soul." It is almost like the solution to a riddle when, in the *Symposium*, Diotima shows Socrates what he will learn at the end of his ascent to beauty. Pure, unmixed, and unaffected by any mortal triviality, one of a kind (μονοειδές), the divinely beautiful becomes visible. He "perceives it with that by which it can be perceived" (ὁρῶντι ᾧ ὁρατόν, 212A)—we add, readily, with the eye of the soul. And, for the last time, the same image reappears in the *Sophist*: the philosopher, it is said, resides with the archetypes of being, but because of the splendor of this place he is not easily seen, for the "eyes of the soul" of most people are incapable of looking at the divine. Only once, in the *Nicomachean Ethics*,[14] does Aristotle call thinking (φρόνησις) the "eye of the soul"; and this image is so strange in the midst of the matter-of-factness of Aristotle's style that the reference to Plato cannot be missed. Even the stories according to which the Cynics ridiculed the eye by which we see "horseness" and the mind by which we see "tableness" may go back to Plato's own lifetime. Later, Epicurus or one of his pupils, while attacking the Platonic cosmology, satirizes the "eyes of the mind" with which Plato had viewed the workshop of the world.[15] Apparently the inevitable chatter had seized upon the great image quite early. In later periods, the image is usually found in the writings of Platonists: Philo, Plotinos, Proklos, and St. Augustine; when it occurs in other authors, it is apparent in one way or another that the flower was picked from Plato's garden.

It is no accident that Plato, as far as we know, was the first to speak of the eye of the soul, and that he does so especially in those passages where he envisages the highest stages of his philosophy; or that, even if he does not use the phrase, his language of myth and allegory belongs in the same area. How he found his own way to this vision he suggests in the dialogues by making Socrates lead the way to this goal. Even the man who in the allegory of the cave succeeds in throwing off the chains and making the ascent bears marks of Socrates. For when this man returns to those still in chains to "free them and to lead them upward," they "would kill him if only they could lay their hands on him." Plato could not have said more clearly who was responsible for his own conversion and ascent to that region where he first learned to see the real shadows of real things, then their mirror images, and finally the "things themselves" and the "sun." Thus it was through and, as it were, in Socrates that he beheld with the eye of the soul the "just itself" and likewise "the courageous," or "the temperate" and "the wise"; in general, "the virtues" or "the virtue." To be sure, everybody was talking about virtue, whether it was teachable or not, and everybody meant something else by the threadbare name, preferably what pleased him at the moment. Socrates was the only one who not only tried to clarify the meaning of the word— although he did this too, more seriously and more persistently than anybody else—but who bore witness, through his life and death, to the existence of "virtue"; through his presence Plato's "eye of the soul" gained access to the world of forms.[16]

For what is *Eidos* and *Idea?* [17] Something to which we gain access through sight. Possibly the word *Idea* originally referred more to "sight" itself, in which the act of seeing and the visible object are combined; the word *Eidos* more to what is seen, the image, form, *Gestalt* as the object of vision. At any rate, the two words became practically synonymous. Their meaning is generally believed to have been worn down with time; it might be more correct to say that this meaning was transferred from an outward appearance to inner form and structure. Herodotos says "leaves of such a form or kind" (φύλλα τοιῆσδε ἰδέας) and means the corrosive effect of juice, i.e., nothing concretely, or immediately visible, or he has somebody "think in a twofold form" (ἐφρόνησαν διφασίας ἰδέας). Ionian physicians deny, against the claim of the natural philosophers, "that there is such a thing as something warm or cold or dry or wet by itself, which has nothing in common with any other form of being" (μηδενὶ ἄλλῳ εἴδει κοινωνέον, Π. ἀρχ. ἰητρ., I 605L); [18] they speak of the "four kinds of wet" (τέσσαρες ἰδέαι τοῦ ὑγροῦ, Περὶ γονῆς, VII 474; Περὶ νούσων, VII 542), i.e., phlegm, gall, water, blood; of the "sweet juice," which is transformed into another "kind" (εἰς ἄλλο εἶδος, Π. ἀρχ. ἰητρ., I 635); of the many "forms" of diseases (πολλαὶ ἰδέαι τῶν νουσημάτων, Π. φύσ. ἀνθρ., VI 36), to which correspond the various types of medicine; or of the "kinds" of bandages, fever, and medication. These expressions have the character of classifications; but it is the concept of "form" that determines the classification—just as in other classifications it is the concept of origin (γένος, ἔθνος) or of direction (τρόπος). The same writers speak of the "knobby form" (εἶδος κονδυλῶδες) of the thigh bone, of the kidney as having the "shape" of the heart, or again, even more symbolically, of the "nature of man, his age and form" (τήν τε ἡλικίην καὶ τὸ εἶδος, VII 52), to which the physician must pay attention. Aristophanes puts something "always newly formed" on the stage (ἀεὶ καινὰς ἰδέας εἰσφέρων), and his chorus sings in a "different hymnic form" (ἑτέραν ὕμνων ἰδέαν). Thucydides, according to his interpreters, is supposed to have used the word ἰδέα in the weakened meaning of "kind" or "manner." [19] Now we might speak of "many kinds of war," "every kind of death," or the "manner of escape or destruction"; but we need not assume that for the Greeks these words lacked precise plasticity as they do for us. Even we speak of the "picture of an illness" (εἶδος τῆς νόσου, τὸ νόσημα τοιοῦτον ἦν ἐπὶ πᾶν τὴν ἰδέαν); and where we "translate" the "visible form" into a pale general concept, a language much more sensitive to sensuous meanings than ours might well have envisaged something much more plastic and visible.

Plato shares the ordinary use of the words *Eidos* and *Idea*; but in his case, too, we must not give a general and colorless meaning to words that in Greek are much more sharply stamped. He might say the syllable arises out of its component sounds as a unity; but he does say: as a unitary form, as a unitary structure (μία ἰδέα ἐξ ἑκάστων τῶν συναρμοττόντων στοιχείων ἡ συλλαβή, *Theaetetus* 204A), something that "catches the eye." Plato does not ask whether the soul is dual or triple, whether it has two or three parts; but whether it has two or three "forms," meaning, as it were, the complete shape and visually apparent structure of each. If, finally, he also gives the name *Eidos* or *Idea* to the "truly just," "the beautiful as truly existent," "the good itself," we must be careful not to substitute for it the worn-out notion "idea." We must also be careful in speaking about a "theory of *Ideas*"—except in the case of the old Plato who once used this somewhat rigid conceptual scheme (τῇ τῶν εἰδῶν σοφίᾳ τῇ καλῇ ταύτῃ, *Letter VI* 322D). Ultimately, it means very little to know what Plato's sources for the term were, whether he took it from the physicians, the natural philosophers, or the rhetoricians—who used the words "form" and "structure" with reference to the over-all picture of an illness, the basic elements of the body (phlegm, gall, blood), the basic qualities of nature ("warm and cold, dry and moist"), the physical "atoms," the figures of speech—or whether he took it from another field of current language. "Visible forms" he called the invisible eternal essences—without trying to aim at terminological precision, but perhaps not without a sense for the paradox contained in the expression—because the term seemed to convey better than any other that the "just as truly existent" or the "courageous itself" was to him something that he was able to see with the eyes of his soul.

Socrates was, so it is said since the days of Aristotle, the discoverer of the concept and the definition, and Plato made the *Idea* out of the concept.[20] What does the reality look like that is here projected onto a plane of conceptual abstraction? To be sure, Socrates asked indefatigably: What is justice? What is the good? What is *techne* or *sophia* or anything else you talk about all the time? But his final purpose was not the discovery of a concept, just as he was never satisfied with any definition he reached. Behind every and any question raised there was the final question: How should man live in the service of the city, which requires the virtuous man, and in the service of God, who requires the good man in a well-ordered city? Socrates knew that there was an answer to this question because he was that kind of man; and that knowledge determined the form of his dialogues. In and through his inquiries he turned to where an answer might be found. He asked: What is . . . ? Hence there must be something that *is*. But only Plato's eyes saw it, and in the *Eidos* he found what Socrates had taught his students to seek and what Socrates himself had lived.

It is not a matter of biographical curiosity if we try to understand tentatively how Plato grasped the *Idea*. It must also be apparent by now that we are not dealing with a subject that might be important from a historical or biographical point of view but is philosophically insignificant. *Idea* has a history of more than two thousand years, and there is no other word in the philosophical vocabulary that is so heavily weighted down by the conceptual labors of centuries. Plato's *Eidos* alone is not a philosophical concept derived from earlier philosophies—as is every inquiry made into the status of ideas since and because of Plato. This is precisely the reason why we should try to lay bare the original sense of the term. To be sure, there is no historical tradition about Plato's primary experience. We must not be misled, however, by a view still sometimes found plausible, that the visible, aesthetic, and intuitive component of the *Idea*—which could hardly be overlooked entirely—is a contamination, pardonable perhaps, because so characteristically Greek, but still a contamination of the intellectual purity of the concept, an "intellectual fall from grace." On the contrary, we must try to take the term that Plato used to describe his experience, simply and concretely, and to see it within the context of his myths and allegories. Precisely because it has an intuitive origin, we must not begin by defining conceptually what the *Idea* is; for Plato himself, the *Idea*, though the highest object of knowledge, is never entirely definable in conceptual terms.[21] We must also be careful not to identify Plato's "intuition" with an ecstatic act in the ordinary sense of the word. We shall attempt to focus upon the point where Plato, in quest of the true city, encountered that dimension for the designation of which he used the words *Eidos* and *Idea*. From here we must then try to penetrate the whole structure of his work.

For one whose inner eye had seen the eternal forms with the same, or rather with an incomparably greater, certainty than bodily eyes see the visible shapes, the eristic "double talk" of the Sophists made no sense at all. To say that good and bad were one and the same, or that one and the same thing might be good for this person or bad for that person, or for the same person now good and now bad; and that this was also true of beautiful and ugly, just and unjust, true and false—all these statements were like a play with empty words for one who had seen "the beautiful," "the just," and "the true." He could no longer ask whether there was such a thing as justice, or whether the word was useful in a public contest but otherwise meaningless. He could not doubt that justice could be taught. If there was such a thing as justice, if it was an *Eidos*, then a person became just when he looked at justice. "Or do you consider it possible," says Socrates in the *Republic* (VI 500c), "that a man would not imitate that with which he lives in admiring companionship? So the philosopher, in constant companionship with the divine order of the world, will reproduce that order in his soul and, as far as man may, become godlike." But if this was valid, then the task was clear: to open the eyes of others to what he himself had seen. Not only the education of the individual was at stake. If the city disintegrated because Themis and Dike were no longer honored at its hearth, it was necessary to found a new state around the *Eidos* of justice, around the *Eidos* in general, and, eventually, around the *Idea* of the Good at its center as the divine principle of order and stability. This and nothing else is meant by Plato's epigram according to which there will be no end to evils unless philosophers become rulers or the rulers genuine seekers after the truth. It is just another expression of that "systematic" connection which always existed for him between *Eidos* and *Polis*, not because of any conceptual construction, but because of an experienced necessity.

How could others be taught to see what only Plato's inner eye saw, what, according to Schopenhauer, "is only attainable by the man of genius, and . . . is therefore not absolutely but only conditionally communicable"? [22] How could one be sure at all that this was knowledge and truth—the only kind of knowledge and highest truth? Indeed, as the *Seventh Letter* (341c) has it, "it cannot be put into words like other studies"; and Plato always talked about the eternal forms in suggestions only. But he knew that "mere opinions run out of the human soul, so that they are not worth much until they are fastened by conceptual ties of the understanding of their cause" (ἕως ἂν τις αὐτὰς δήσῃ αἰτίας λογισμῷ, *Meno* 98A). Even if what he had glimpsed was unspeakably far removed from opinion and appearance, it was necessary to use the support of words in order to make the intuition last for himself and others. To discover these intellectual ties became the content of his philosophical inquiry. To lead men "through a long communion" to a point "where a light is kindled in the soul by a leaping spark" (*Letter VII* 341c)—this is the basis of all his teaching.

What has just been said may perhaps be further clarified by a brief digression. [23] When Goethe, at the memorable meeting with Schiller, on July 14, 1794, "vividly developed his metamorphosis of plants and created before Schiller's eyes, with a few characteristic pen strokes, a symbolic plant," Schiller shook his head and said: "That is not experience, that is an Idea." He meant, of course, an Idea in the Kantian sense as a necessary concept of reason for which there is no corresponding object of the senses. Goethe, somewhat annoyed, hesitated. This difference between experience and idea, introduced by a speculative mind, was incomprehensible and annoying to him, the "intuitive mind," as Schiller was to call him shortly later, at the beginning of their correspondence. "That's a strange business," he replied, "that I have ideas without knowing it, and *that I even see them with my own eyes.*" Not a Kantian Idea, but a Platonic *Idea* in its original meaning—this was Goethe's *Urpflanze* (plant archetype). Goethe knew "that there is a difference between seeing and seeing, that the eyes of the mind must constantly co-operate with the eyes of the body in a living bond, because otherwise there is a danger that we see and still miss seeing" (*weil man sonst in Gefahr kommt zu sehen und doch vorbeizusehen*).[24] He saw "with his own eyes"—with the eyes of his soul, Plato would have said—the *Urpflanze* in the palm tree in the botanical gardens of Padua; he hoped to "discover" it among the plants of the public gardens at Palermo; and if, according to his own words, "he completely understood the original identity of all parts of plants in Sicily and now tried to trace and rediscover this identity everywhere," this kind of understanding is in the last analysis the intuitive grasp, and what follows is an attempt to recapture the original vision through the power of the *Logos*.

To return to Plato, when one speaks about the conceptual ties with which he captured and communicated his intuition, one should be warned, to begin with, that this cannot be done in the form of tracing a gradual historical development. An apparently genetic approach is used only in order to disclose the structure of his thought, not unlike the method Plato himself used in the *Timaeus* when he told the myth of the creation of the world, but warned his readers not to take the successive stages of the creation literally. Plato may have been well versed in the systems of earlier thinkers. According to ancient tradition he was well acquainted with the Herakleitean Kratylos, so we can assume that he was at least familiar with this trend of thought.[25] One thing is certain, though invariably ignored: his philosophy did not grow out of earlier systems. Only after his eyes had been opened to the *Eidos* did he turn the energy of his being, with enormous intensity, in this one direction. Only then did Plato become—in an entirely new sense—a "philosopher." What one must try to find is the law according to which the substance of his thinking was focused around this point rather than the historical order in which this may have taken place.

If Plato wished to preserve his intuition for himself and others, he had to use the materials of language. "The just" or "the beautiful," which he perceived with the eyes of his soul, alone bore the mark of true being. If he wished to avoid confusion between "the beautiful" and a beautiful girl—and this was at times necessary, as is shown in the *Hippias Major* (287ε)—he might add "the beautiful-itself" (αὐτὸ τὸ καλόν). In addition, he had another phrase at his disposal, a newly coined expression bandied about during the time of the Sophists: the phrase "being," or "in existence" (ὄντως, τῷ ὄντι), used in contradistinction from mere appearance or the unreal, is known from Euripides and Aristophanes.[26] Thus Plato referred to the "good-as-being" or the "beautiful-as-being" (τὰ ὄντως ἀγαθὰ ἢ καλά, *Phaedrus* 260a); or he enlarged this expression to: "the knowledge of the equal-itself, what it [really] is" (ἐπιστήμην αὐτοῦ τοῦ ἴσου ὅτι ἔστιν, *Phaedo* 75b), and even gave this phrase a slightly terminological shade: "all upon which we stamp that name: 'what it [really] is' or 'that which [really] is' " (περὶ ἁπάντων οἷς ἐπισφραγιζόμεθα τοῦτο "ὃ ἔστι,"*Phaedo* 75d).[27]

These expressions which Plato took from the current language of his age and developed further had important consequences. For they placed him in the tradition of the search for the true being, which extended from Gorgias, Melissos, and Zeno back to the great Parmenides, the discoverer of the one eternal, immutable being. Plato did not have to be conscious of this historical context, and perhaps was not conscious of it, just as people today are not aware of using the language of St. Paul when they say "all in all" or the language of Comte when they say, "I am positive." Yet it was not accidental that Plato turned in the direction of the most original and powerful inquiry into being.

The prevailing history of philosophy gives a somewhat wrong

impression about who Socrates really was. He is generally
considered the one who—as Cicero puts it—brought philosophy
down from the heavens to earth. It is difficult indeed to find any
connection between the early scientific thinking and Socrates'
method of never-ending questions. Would it be possible at all
to place the elenctic thinker and the philosophers of nature in
one and the same "history of philosophy"—possible without
Plato, who in his own person combined the critical and educational power of Socrates with the speculations of the earlier
thinkers? This question does not seem to be recognized. Yet
there is a hidden connection. Socrates lived and taught among
the Sophists; for the majority of the people he was indistinguishable from them; for Aristophanes, literally their representative. To see the profound difference required the keen eye
of Plato. Sophistic speculation still retained, in its legerdemain
with being and not-being, Parmenidean elements, though these
had become not much more than verbal exercises. Now the
contrast to the Sophists, while not determining the nature of
Socrates, did influence the kind of question he asked. When he
asked, "What is justice?" and knew that "justice is," he did not
have to know that, although pursuing a different goal, he still
followed the kind of inquiry originally posed by Parmenides.

With the Socratic question and with every attempt to name
the newly perceived forms and to demarcate them from that
with which they must not be confused, Plato took over current
linguistic and conceptual terms, which ultimately owed their
origin to Parmenides. But Plato could not be satisfied with
these watered down expressions, especially not as far as his
highest intuitions were concerned. Departing from the deriva-
tive speculations, he returned to their origin. As a philosopher
he did not inherit—as Aristotle did from him or Kant from the
English empiricists—certain problems that his predecessors
had failed to solve. Rather, the Parmenidean philosophy of
being provided him with the means to anchor his intuition in
permanent thoughts and words. Now it is true that, in place
of the simple, immutable, spherical being that the intuitive
fantasy of this first ontologist, this awkward yet great poet,
had also "perceived with his mind," Plato knew an abundance

of visions, which were increased and enlarged with every new perception and, even though they drove toward unity, never again achieved the lonely rigidity of Parmenides' being. However, despite this contrast, we can see a remarkable agreement down to the level of language. It is the very predicates of the Parmenidean being—whole, simple, immutable—that Plato transferred to his archetypes.[28] While Zeno proved the sole existence of the Parmenidean being from the contradictions resulting from postulating the existence of many things, Plato pointed to the contradictions resulting from thinking of the just, beautiful, or pious in their multiple appearances, instead of in their uniqueness of ideal being.[29] But more than that. The entire structure of his world of being and of the corresponding stages of knowledge, as shown most clearly in the *Republic* (476E *et seq.*), is strictly Parmenidean. For both thinkers, being is diametrically opposed to absolute not-being. For both, not-being is unknowable. "How could not-being be known?" asks Glaukon in the *Republic*. "Not-being can neither be known nor named," says the goddess to Parmenides.[30] Complete being (παντελῶς ὄν), on the other hand, is for Plato completely knowable (παντελῶς γνωστόν), just as there is only one path of knowledge for Parmenides, namely, that which leads to pure being and which bears the characteristics of this being as marks (σήματα). For both, the world in which we live lies between these two poles; it is both being and not-being.[31] To this world belongs, according to Plato, the particular form of knowledge that he calls opinion or *Doxa*. Correspondingly, the intermediary world is called by Parmenides the world according to *Doxa* (κατὰ δόξαν ἔφυ τάδε); only in his case the word refers inseparably both to confused opinion of the subject and confused appearance of the object. This is the point of difference between these two similar structures of thought. For Parmenides, who ultimately knows only pure being and nothing else, "being and thinking are one and the same," just as in the intermediary world of *Doxa* the ontological status of the object and the mode of knowledge are fused with each other.[32] Plato, who incorporates the abundance of intuited forms into his world of being and for whom, because of Socrates, man or the "soul"

is one of the highest experiences, could no longer envisage so
simple a construction. He adopted the basic plan. Yet he envisaged different degrees of reality precisely corresponding to
different degrees of knowledge. Eventually, far transcending
Parmenides, he constructed a harmonious system of being and
knowledge. But this cannot be treated here, where we are
concerned only with what he adopted from previous thinkers
in order to give conceptual firmness to his own intuition.

Even today it is still seriously believed (a view that, at least
in tendency, is reminiscent of Aristotle) that Plato constructed
his "system" by adding the Herakleitean world of becoming to
the Parmenidean world of being. But no organic system of
thought results from mere addition, and Plato was concerned
with other things than a place in the history of ideas. He had
caught sight of the *Eidos*, and was then confronted with the
task of making his intuition permanently visible through the
Logos. Now it is certain that permanent being can be posited
only in contrast to some other mode of existence. Thus the
Indian thinkers also gave different names, such as inconstancy,
change, suffering, not-self, to the world that is opposed to the
eternal *atman*. Plato did not have to search for new words.
Parmenides did not desert him when he looked for terms to
designate "that which we (ordinarily, in everyday life) call
'being.' " [33] The Parmenidean formulation "being as well as
not-being" (εἶναί τε καὶ μὴ εἶναι) serves in the ontological
system of the *Republic* to refer our world of becoming to the
world of true being and, paradoxically, at the same time to
mark the eternal distance of the former from the latter. Parmenides, moreover, had separated pure being from unreality,
the world of becoming and passing away, growth and decay.
Plato adopted these words because they corresponded precisely
to his own view, and because he was not so dependent that he
had to give the appearance of originality. [34] At that very moment, it may be supposed, he saw Herakleitos and Parmenides in
conjunction. Perhaps the comrade of Kratylos did not at first see,
as did no one in his age, that Herakleitos had a central element in
common with Parmenides, if one did not emphasize becoming
and change, but rather the dialectical law of becoming and the

permanence of change. But with that power of analysis and synthesis, by which he also distinguished Socrates from the Sophists despite everything they had in common, he pulled apart the Herakleitean and Parmenidean world views—much as the creator of the Sistine ceiling divides day and night—and then yoked them together again as a symbol of the opposition between the world of being and the world of becoming, as was required by his discovery of the eternal forms.

But there was still a higher perspective in which this duality was rounded again into a unity. "One is all." "Conjoined-disjoined, consonant-dissonant, from all one and from one everything": thus spoke Herakleitos. For Plato, the one *Eidos* gives to the many individual things a share in true being; the things, in turn, strive for the completeness of the *Eidos*. Only if the one is not without the other is "the cosmos joined together with itself." Was this not the Herakleitean world view, more genuine than the watered down, sophistically abused doctrine of the flux of all things? [35] Plato formulated this "harmony of opposites" (παλίντονος ἁρμονίη), which is alive everywhere in his construction of the world, most elaborately in the *Parmenides*, where it has, as it were, been crystallized in the precise dialectics of the "one" and the "other." Paradoxical as it may sound, the dialogue *Parmenides* is the most strongly Herakleitean among Plato's writings, and the philosopher Parmenides, in this work, just as much a Herakleitean as an Eleatic. Here the point is reached where the forces of the two great old masters are united in Plato, as "the beginning and end of the circumference of a circle are one and the same." The "one wise" of Herakleitos, which expressly contains manyness, even allness, and the "one being" of Parmenides, which is meant to exclude not-being and the multitude of things—without being able to do so; for even of being, one speaks with "names" derived from this world of "being and not-being," and being is present in the world of appearance—these two perspectives coincide in Plato's world where being penetrates not-being and unity becomes visible through multiplicity.

Besides Parmenides and Herakleitos Pythagoras was the third among the great early thinkers whose influence reached

Plato in the Pythagorean circles of Magna Graecia,[36] and perhaps still earlier in the company of Socrates. What did Pythagoras—this intellectual force effective through the ages and constantly attracting and permeating new elements—mean to Plato? The one passage in which Plato mentions Pythagoras by name makes him a successor of Homer, the "leader of *paideia*."

Let us remember that Plato, in his formative years, was most profoundly stirred and shocked by the chaos in the city to which he thought he belonged, and by the disintegration of the men who ruled this city. His final goal was to put order in place of disorder. Just as the artisan and artist join pieces to form a well-ordered object (τεταγμένον τε καὶ κεκοσμημένον πρᾶγμα), so must order (τάξις καὶ κόσμος) prevail in body and soul, family and state, for therein consists the value and perfection of every structure. Thus Plato teaches at the summit of his *Gorgias* (503E, 507E *et seq.*), after the protagonists of Sophistic oratory, lust, and caprice, in other words, of disorder, have been vanquished. Nothing is farther removed from Plato than Goethe's remark that he could tolerate injustice rather than disorder. For to Plato injustice is disorder. Wherever the hateful transgression into someone else's function, into a foreign field of action, is avoided, there Plato finds measure, temperance, and justice. If artisans and artists create order out of perishable material, how much more must this order suit the invisible model "to which they look" in their creations! Thus the world of forms, the realm of perfection, cannot be anything but a world of "unchanging and harmonious order, where nothing can do or suffer wrong, where all is in order according to reason" (*Republic* 500C). The cosmos of numbers, the harmony and proportion of musical strings and, on a larger canvas, the cosmos of the starry sky were replicas of perfect being; they pointed upward to a place beyond the heavens. It is, therefore, the sciences of this order, and, above all, their unity and integration in the Pythagorean system, that moved Plato and seem to have revealed to him in an entirely different realm what he could not find in the states of his time. Cosmos is the structure of the world as it is of the state and of the soul. Geometry binds heaven and earth together. "The wise men tell us, Kallikles, that communion and friendship and orderliness and temperance and justice bind together heaven and earth; and that this universe is therefore called cosmos or order, not disorder or misrule, my friend. But although you are a wise man you seem to me never to have observed that geometrical equality [proportion] is mighty both among gods and men. You think you ought to strive ruthlessly after power and excess (πλεονεξίαν ἀσκεῖν), for you do not care about geometry" (*Gorgias* 507E *et seq.*).

Now it is apparent what the contact with Pythagoras meant for Plato. Socrates restricted himself to man and the state, and so did Plato by virtue of his origin and the example of his teacher. But while Socrates claimed not to understand anything about "the things above" (τὰ μετέωρα), there was something in Plato's soul akin and open to the cosmos that, as the outermost homocentric sphere, surrounds man and state. Plato owed to the great Italian philosopher, and the force that still radiated from him, his transcending the state by a search into the cosmos and, conversely, his conceiving of man and state as beings of "cosmic" rank. That is why Plato has the Pythagorean Timaios present his view of the universe after he had Socrates found the ideal state.

There was something else that made the Pythagoreans indispensable to Plato. This was the seriousness with which they approached the human soul. Herakleitos had penetrated into his own soul without ever reaching definite limits. The Pythagoreans and "those around Orpheus" spoke in vivid myths about the nature and fate of the human soul. Plato's written work shows a strong interest in these messages about the soul—so strong, in fact, as to suggest the view that, besides everything else, he was also an "Orphic theologian." The doctrine of the eternal life and permanence of the individual soul, it is said, can hardly be reconciled with the "theory of *Ideas.*" Plato, in fact, is supposed to have borrowed this article of faith concerning the soul ready-made from the Orphics.[37] But even if a contradiction in Plato's system were to appear, it would be wrong to explain the contradiction as a combination of originally separate doctrines. Plato undoubtedly listened whenever he could hear familiar tones, but he was the last person to fit foreign doctrines arbitrarily into his own system. It is not sufficiently recognized that Plato does not, in the strict sense of the word, "teach" anything at all about the fate of the human soul. Socrates speaks about it in myths, which are part of the dramatic structure in Plato's works. Plato's references to the authority of the priests and theologians of the mystery religions are undoubtedly an indication of the origin of these mythological symbols, but are in no way an indication of what they meant to Plato himself. For him they contained a profound symbolic reality; they were venerable allegories, images, and phrases for something that he preferred not to express in his own language. It is a mistake to use them as evidence for a Platonic theory or history of the soul.

If Plato had been Parmenides, all of his thinking might have fused in the intuition of the power, immediacy, and, as it were, consistency of the *Agathon*, and the result might have been a doctrine of all-in-one. But Plato was much too conscious of his own humanity, had had, through Socrates, much too powerful an experience of the other human being, of the *Eros*, who leads one person to another and both to the *Idea*, to be satisfied with the Parmenidean identification of thought and being. Since his world fell apart into the realm of not-being, perpetual becoming and passing away, and into the realm of eternal being, custodian of every value, the question arose: Where does man belong? This question did not arise for him from a theoretical or systematic interest, but because of the necessity of forming a new type of man and of placing him in a new kind of state. In the *Alcibiades Major*, during a discussion of the Delphic pronouncement "Know thyself," the question is raised: What is this self? The answer is paradoxical, for a Greek much more so than for a citizen of the Christian world: man is soul. This means that the soul is that which characterizes man intrinsically, is his "existence," constitutes his essence. To use the language of Plotinos: "The idea of man is formed after that which is the prevailing and best element in him" (κατὰ δὲ τὸ κρεῖττον τὸ ὅλον εἶδος ἄνθρωπος, *Enneads* III 4 2). Once Plato has discovered the world of eternal being, man is part of both worlds and of neither; he is between both worlds, belonging to the world of becoming and passing away because of his body and the "lower parts of his soul," belonging to the world of being because of the eternal part of his soul. Thus it is the discovery of the world of ideas that no longer permits man to be altogether a member of one undivided world and forces upon him the separation into "body and soul."

Plato's "doctrine" of the eternal and immortal soul is not accepted as a ready-made theology, nor is it proved on the basis of theoretically conclusive arguments. The *Phaedo* clearly shows two things: Plato considered the belief in an immortal soul justified because of Socrates' victory over death. There was something untouched by the fact of the man "Socrates," as he was called, lying dead and about to be buried. "I cannot make Kriton believe that I am the Socrates who is now speaking and conducting these arguments; he believes that I am the one whom he will soon see as a dead body—and he asks, how to bury *me?*" But the arguments for the immortality of the soul— of which none, for good reasons, has been ultimately conclusive —show something else. The eternity of the soul is justified for Plato because of the existence of the *Idea*. To speak of the undyingness of the soul makes sense only for the "friends of the *Ideas*." If the human soul is by nature of such a kind that it knows eternal being, then it must itself—for like can only be known by like—have being after the manner of the eternal forms. Just as the arguments for immortality are not accidentally placed within the frame of the story about the death of Socrates, so these two justifications for the eternal existence of the human soul are not juxtaposed accidentally. For Plato had perceived the eternal forms in and through Socrates. Thus "Socrates," "*Eidos*," and "immortality" are, as it were, three different aspects of the same reality.

Man in the city: this was the fact with which Plato, as every Greek, began. The old unquestioned unity was dissolved. But from disunity and the struggle for a new order there arose in Plato his own vision: on the one hand, man or his soul as an "inner *politeia*"; on the other, the state as an expanded soul. Soul and state, then, are units with the same structure, in a necessary mutual relation, both oriented toward the *Eidos* and ultimately to the "*Idea* of the Good."

Man in the cosmos: this was the realization to which Pythagoras helped Plato. The vision to which Plato himself progressed was as follows: he saw the small cosmos included in the large cosmos, and both of them as "living souls," again in necessary mutual relation, since the stars and the universe possess soul, and the perfect human soul reflects the ordered movement of the universe.[38] Their common principle of order is the *Agathón*.

Man and the *Eidos:* this was Plato's own experience, which he owed to Socrates, but which he did not share with anyone. The soul received eternal being from the *Eidos*, which it perceived intuitively. The *Eidos* became, or rather was from the beginning, of the nature of "soul." For the just, the courageous, the pious, the good were *Ideas* which Plato first perceived in the soul of Socrates. In his later period, it was inconceivable to him how anyone could deny that "complete being" (τὸ παντελῶς ὄν) had communion with movement, life, thought, or kinship and similarity with mind.[39]

Soul and *Eidos*, therefore, of necessity refer to each other. Just as the eye of the soul first envisioned the eternal forms, and Plato's subsequent philosophy was an ever-repeated effort to hold fast to the world he had discovered, so do the Platonic dialogues mirror these two modes of knowledge in the two movements which lead to the *Eidos:* mania and dialectics.

CHAPTER TWO

Demon and Eros

THE PLATONISTS of antiquity assign to demonology a definite place in the structure of the master's thought.[1] Modern interpreters are too enlightened to take Plato's statements on this subject very seriously. But how are we justified in regarding as mere play what is said about the demons if we consider the physical and physiological "doctrines" of the *Timaeus*, or the "philosophy of language" of the *Cratylus*, as integral parts of Plato's system? By the mere fact that we have a contemporary science of nature and language, but none of demons? The *Cratylus* is much more like a medley of merry pranks than a scientific treatise in linguistics. And the mixture of myth and natural science in the *Timaeus* might have caused a scientist like Demokritos to shake his head. As a matter of fact, there should be no doubt that, in his writings, Plato does not teach a science in our sense of the word. And while what the characters in his dramas say about the world of demons is certainly "play," it is—like all play in Plato's works—of a deeply serious nature. If anyone, however, should venture to express this underlying element of seriousness in his own words, Plato would probably protest: "This much I know: if it ought to be written or said at all, it had better be said by me in my own words" (*Letter VII* 341D).

Plato encountered the demonic dimension when he encountered Socrates. For this man, who, more than any other, proposed to clarify by the power of his intellect what was unclear and ambiguous, recognized mysterious forces, which he obeyed without examining their claim. He liked to talk—and often did

—about his "daimonion," a peculiarity that was so well known that the authorities used it as a basis for the indictment against him. He was charged with the "introduction of new demonic beings" (καινὰ δαιμόνια).

We shall not turn to psychopathology to inquire into the nature of this daimonion, nor join Schopenhauer in his attempt to assign it a place among dreams, seeing ghosts, and other occult phenomena.[2] It would be still more inappropriate to try to explain this extraordinary phenomenon rationally by calling it the "inner voice of individual tact," an "expression of spiritual freedom," or a "sure measure of one's own subjectivity," thus confining it to our rational and social world of experience.[3] Indeed, we are already closing off a possible approach by calling it "the daimonion," as if it were an object, instead of using the neutral Greek expression "the demonic," which, on the one hand, expresses an element of uncertainty—"but you do not know whence it comes and whither it goes"—and, on the other, indicates that this force is not within and at the disposal of a person, but is received from a larger sphere external to him, and acknowledged with reverence and awe. On yet another level, there is the "divine." Plato, in the speech of defense, even makes Socrates connect the two and call the phenomenon "a divine and demonic element" (θεῖόν τι καὶ δαιμόνιον γίγνεται, *Apology* 31D), and even "the sign of the god" (τὸ τοῦ θεοῦ σημεῖον, 40B).

In Xenophon's presentation, Socrates states that this power counseled or instructed him beforehand what to do or not to do.[4] The only instance in which a clear effect may be observed is when Socrates is about to prepare his defense: then the power opposes him (ἠναντιώθη, *Memorabilia* IV 8 5). The element of resistance and inhibition is particularly emphasized by Plato. There is no reason to give more credit to Xenophon's rather general description than to Plato's careful delineation, even though Plato may have accentuated and systematized. At least, it is plausible that Socrates was most keenly aware of these active powers when he was faced with obstacles. Goethe, too— if we may call on him as a witness—was at times inclined, though he also held different views, to respect forces of resistance turning to one's advantage as demonic elements, which one worships without presuming to explain them.[5] That the voice never counsels positive action (προτρέπει οὐδέποτε) is expressed in the *Apology* (31D) and, in the same words, in the *Theages* (128D). In a later passage of the *Theages*, it is said that the demonic power "lends support" or "co-operates" (συλλάβηται, 129E), which does not indicate that the dialogue is not of Platonic origin. The author must have thought the two conceptions compatible with each other. In the silence of the demonic, Socrates might also have felt and recognized an element of positive co-operation.

Plato first introduced the daimonion into his portrait of Socrates as a trait just as characteristic of this strange man as his turned-up nose and protruding eyes. Socrates himself says in his speech of defense that it appeared frequently and opposed him even in trifles (*Apology* 40A). Thus, we are not surprised—without forgetting that we are reading the report of Socrates, a master of irony—when we are told in the *Euthydemus* (272E) that the "sign of the demon" prevents him from rising, thus causing his encounter with the quarrelsome fencing masters. We are even less surprised when, in the *Phaedrus*, the sign does not permit him to leave before he has made amends to *Eros* with another and more truthful speech (242c).[6] The *Theages* proves the genuine effect of the voice by relating a number of incidents in which the warning came true: when Charmides was training for the Nemean Games, at the time of the murderous designs of one Timarchos, and at the disastrous departure of the fleet for Sicily. It is very significant, however, that these events are not considered ends in themselves. The *Theages* certainly does not intend to make a sort of miracle man out of Socrates. Socrates himself states the purpose of telling these stories: "because this demonic power is all-important for communion with those who seek my company (129E). For there are many whom it resists. They cannot benefit from intercourse with me, and I am not capable of such intercourse. In many cases, it presents no obstacle to companionship, but the persons concerned derive no aid from it. But if the demonic power participates helpfully in the relationship, the companions immediately find themselves on the path of progress."

Similarly in the *Alcibiades*. Since it is concerned with a first encounter, long delayed and rich in consequence, we are again reminded of Goethe's words to Eckermann (March 24, 1829): "The higher a man is, the more he is under the influence of the demons, and he must constantly take heed lest his guiding will chance upon a wrong path. There was altogether something demonic in my acquaintance with Schiller; we might have been brought together earlier or later; but that we met just at the time when I had the Italian journey behind me, and Schiller began to be weary of philosophical speculations—this was important and highly beneficial for us both." [7] Again, the situation in the *Alcibiades Major* is quite similar: master and disciple could have been brought together sooner or later. Socrates has long kept himself away from the youth because of the resistance of the demon. Meanwhile he has observed him. And now the voice is silent, and he addresses the youth. In the language of the *Theages*, the demonic "co-operates." Or, as the *Alcibiades* (106A) puts it, since the active force is to be more clearly defined: the god who hitherto held me back has now sent me to you. It would be pedantic to ask whether the daimonion and God are one and the same in this context. They are—and they are not. We are dealing with active powers, not with names. [8] Since education, the most important enterprise, is at stake, the demonic is particularly significant. Both elements are combined in the *Theaetetus*. Socrates speaks of his skill as a midwife (150B), and of different effects of this skill: how some men leave him prematurely, to the detriment of what they have borne or still carry unborn within them. As a typical example he names Aristeides, the son of Lysimachos, who also occurs in the related context of the *Theages*, and whom his father, in the *Laches*, presents to Socrates. In the *Theaetetus* it is then said: "If they return, desiring my company and behaving very strangely, the demon which comes to me prevents me from joining some of them; it lets me be with others, and these again make progress" (151A). Thus it becomes clear why

Plato considered this characteristic a more important part of Socrates than his turned-up nose and protruding eyes. In Xenophon, we tend to think of a special little oracle, that gives rather random counsel to its owner and those in his company, such as to do one thing and not to do another (*Memorabilia* I 1 4). In Plato, the demonic in Socrates determines primarily his educational mission. It is not merely a remarkable peculiarity of a single individual, but an integral part of the nature of a great teacher. As an extralogical influence, it protects education progressing within the realm of the *Logos* from becoming a purely rational pursuit, and secures a connection with that element of mystery which is lacking in the Sophists' instruction. Thus Plato must have regarded it as part of the normal, not as something abnormal. He obviously felt such a power within himself—and must not something of it perhaps be felt by all who are called, and not merely appointed, to educate human beings?

The Platonists of later periods often discussed the nature of the Socratic daimonion. We have treatises on the subject by Plutarch, Apuleius, Maximus, and Proklos.[9] All of them try to explain this particular phenomenon by taking it out of its isolated position, that is, by establishing a connection with other "demons," particularly with that demon which, according to widespread belief, accompanies a man through life and, according to the Platonic "doctrine," remains with the human soul even beyond its earthly existence. Perhaps even today it is not absurd to talk about such things. For it is not ghosts and specters, or theurgic and magic rites, that we are concerned with, but real powers, even though in Iamblichos, Proklos, and elsewhere the boundary lines are often blurred.[10] Before we dismiss this subject as superstition, we should at least think of Dante's hierarchy of angels, which ascends through many ranks to the throne of the Supreme Being, or recognize, in the light of the last book of *Dichtung und Wahrheit*, the *Gespräche mit Eckermann*, and the *Urworte: Orphisch*, how much the demonic or the demon meant to Goethe, who was always striving to achieve clarity.[11]

In Plutarch's dialogue *About the Daimonion of Socrates*, a childishly crude confusion of the Socratic daimonion with such phenomena as sneezing or as soothsaying "voices," used for the purposes of popular divination, is replaced by a more profound view probably originating in Poseidonios: [12] as human speech affects the ear, so the *Logoi* (to retain this equivocal term) of the demons directly affect the human soul. What ordinary people experience only in the relaxation of sleep is given to human beings with a pure, serene soul—whom we then call holy or demonic—in their waking lives. Such a human being, free from disharmony and turmoil, was Socrates. A Platonizing myth then seems to reveal what Plutarch means by demons. Timarchos hidden in the cave of Trophonios learns through the voice of an oracle that the demons are the stars he sees floating above the darkness, that is, the purest part of the reason (νοῦς) in especially favored individuals, the part that is excluded from the mingling of soul and body. As the corks float above the net, so the demonic star floats above the human being, and his soul is fastened to it, whether willingly or reluctantly. It is a Stoic doctrine—though with Platonic overtones—this notion of the *Logos*, perceived without senses, penetrating all, and uniting macrocosm with microcosm. The actual demonology slightly changes the Platonic element, though even the Platonic form of the myth is used. According to the *Timaeus*, the god gives to everybody a demon as part of his soul. Its seat is the head, which is akin to heaven and, therefore, raised toward it. And this divine element (τὸ θεῖον) must be cultivated so that man keep the demon in an orderly habitat, and become "eudae-monic." What, from a logical and psychological point of view, is called reason is here reverently related to the highest form of existence.[13] With this "doctrine" of the *Timaeus*, Plutarch appears to have combined what Plato wrote about the demon in the myths of the soul. In the *Phaedo*, the demon who was given to man in this life leads him to the last tribunal after death, and to Hades after judgment has been passed. Another demon then guides him upward again. In the myth of the *Republic*, the situation is reversed. It is the soul which, restricted but not determined by the accident of the lot, prior to its incarnation freely chooses its way of life and thus its demon as the "fulfillment of the choice" (ἀποπληρωτὴς τῶν αἱρεθέντων). These are not different doctrines of Plato's. Plato does not state dogmatic doctrines, least of all about demons. Rather, in order to present imaginatively something of his own experience so that it may be grasped by others, he combines at one place the popular belief in a demon accompanying man through life with his own insight into the human soul and, at another place, with "Orphic" images of the beyond. "Demon" first means something like the innate human form—today it might be called "existence"— the element that remains constant throughout all the accidents and flux of life, that which makes any action of mine *my* action. Herakleitos already had revised the popular belief in this ghostlike companion in his saying, "Man's character is his demon." But Plato thought he saw more and could express more in a myth. This character is not confined to man's earthly life. It follows him across the boundary of the beyond, stands with him before the tribunal, and leads him to the place of punishment. For judgment and atonement are strictly related to the way of life adopted on earth. Again, that way of life is not imposed from the outside. Man has brought it with him, across the threshold of birth, from a previous existence. The myth of the *Republic*, by proclaiming the freedom of individual choice, and by referring to the words of Moira that "guilt lies with the chooser," establishes metaphysical responsibility, and thus seems to be a direct correction of the *Phaedo*, which permits a fatalistic interpretation, dangerous to moral action: "The demon will not cast a lot for you; but you will choose the demon." Thus the demon is, in Plato's world, a symbol not only for that which Goethe respected as a special power, "*So musst du sein*" (*Urworte*, ΔΑΙΜΩΝ), but also for the mysterious and inexorable bond between human life and the beyond. The choice of the demon, given to us in the myth of the *Republic*, symbolizes the "transcendental freedom" (Kant), that "freedom within necessity" (Jaspers) which is peculiar to human existence: "It is as if I had chosen beforehand the being that I now am" (Jaspers).[14] At the same time, the correspondence between demon and *Nous* shows how Plato, despite his insight into the darker elements, reserves the ruling place for the active intellect.

In his later years, Plato liked to indicate the order and objectives of the political life of man by measuring it against a mythical world of perfection. The myth of the *Statesman* (269c *et seq.*) presents such a perfect world cycle during which the highest god cared for the cosmos; a mythically glowing passage in the *Laws* (713B *et seq.*) presents it as the Golden Age of Kronos. In both instances, this state of perfection is communicated to human beings living in society through the mediation of divine demons that have divided all living beings into species and herds (*Statesman* 271), so that peace and lawfulness, i.e., "eudaemonia," should reign among their subjects (*Laws* 713E). In the *Laws*, the conclusion is drawn that only the dominion of God, and not that of a mortal being, can protect the human states from disaster, and that we must strive, by means of the immortal element within us, to regain the perfection of the Golden Age. In the *Statesman*, the myth is continued as follows: if the Supreme Power withdraws his hand from the helm, permitting the world to reverse its course according to its inherent law, "and primal disorder recurs" (καὶ δυναστεύει τὸ τῆς παλαιᾶς ἀναρμοστίας πάθος), then the other deities also leave those parts of the world of which they are guardians, and we humans are deprived of the care of the demon who governs us. Here the demon does not belong to the individual but to the community, acting as an intermediary between it and the cosmic or divine, i.e., the highest form of existence. It is easy to see how this demon of the community can be reconciled with the demon of the individual, especially when we think of the correspondence between *Nous* and demon in the *Timaeus*. But we are not concerned here with combining the elements found in different contexts into conceptual unity. We merely wish to recognize what is common to these mythical symbols.

The last examples also show how close a connection exists between the words "demon" and "god," so that only human imperfection, as it were, makes a distinction necessary. The *Statesman* (272A) calls the Supreme Power the "greatest demon," and those subject to him are called "deities sharing his rule." Certainly we cannot distinguish the "divine demons" from the "ruling gods" (271D), the former evidently being named with Hesiod's man-protecting demons in mind. Consequently, the famous argument of the *Symposium*, according to which *Eros* is not a god but a great demon, must not blind us to the fact that, while god and demon may mean different things in Plato, they are also very close to one another and may even merge into one. The subtle and rigid distinctions of later interpreters remind us of Goethe's remark that "the original teachers are still conscious of the insoluble core of their project, and attempt to approach it in a naïve and flexible manner. The successors are inclined to become didactic, and their dogmatism, gradually, reaches the level of intolerance." [15] Plato, on the contrary, still shows how the same things may be seen and named differently. Reason, cognizant of itself and its own elements, is referred to as *Nous*, pure thought (φρονεῖν), understanding (ἐπιστήμη). Piety, worshiping the same thing as radiance from perfection or "the good," calls it the divine, just as in the *Alcibiades Major*, "knowledge and thought" are called the "most divine parts of the soul," and "God and thought" (θεὸς καὶ φρόνησις), in close juxtaposition, together form "all the divine" (πᾶν τὸ θεῖον).[16] And the very same thing, vaguely felt and named by the awe that senses these incomprehensible and inescapable powers, is called the demon. God and demon are so close in Plato that the dividing line finally disappears altogether, except where, as in the *Symposium*, they are expressly distinguished for a special purpose. We must also bear in mind that he always rejected as unworthy an excessive rigidity in the choice of terms (τὸ σπουδάζειν ἐπὶ τοῖς ὀνόμασι) and the "quarrel about names when matters of such importance are at stake" (*Republic* 533D).[17]

The Platonists of a later period, however, were all too inclined to give way to word worship and dogmatism.[18] Even at the end of Plato's own lifetime, the living myth began to wither before the schematism of a demonology, entering, as in Philippos of Opus, into a strange union with the physical doctrine of the five elements, or, as in Plato's successor, Xenokrates, with the geometry of triangular forms. Later thinkers, similar in general approach though differing in detail, began to incorporate Socrates' daimonion as a special case into a whole order of demons, or into a hierarchy of cosmic forces and cosmic beings. Maximus of Tyre (XIV 8) assigns numerous tasks to the thirty thousand demons that he takes over from Hesiod: ". . . and the one chose this body, and the next another, one Socrates, another Plato, still another Pythagoras." For Proklos, Socrates' daimonion belongs to the highest rank of demons, the divine demons. Plato does not think in terms of such schemata. But as he certainly referred to objective facts, and not to words only—"*ei dice cose e voi dite parole*"—so he must have seen "demon" and "the demonic" as belonging together like "divinity" and "the divine." And nobody can say how much of the ideas and speculations of his own school he would have rejected, in annoyance or with a smile, as attempting to grasp the incomprehensible in too rigid a formula, and how much he would have accepted with friendly indulgence.

These demonologies, from Philippos and Xenokrates to Iamblichos and Proklos, retained throughout the centuries a common view, which, in fact, stems from Plato and must have been of the utmost significance to him. It is the idea or view of "the demonic" as a realm "intermediate" between the human level and the divine, a realm that, because of its intermediate position, "unites the cosmos with itself." Diotima mentions this realm at the beginning of her myth about *Eros*, and makes it the scene of all intercourse between gods and men and, therefore, of mantic and priestly art, ritual, and magic. These customs and rites Plato, however little he may have used them himself, still accepted as a symbol for a hidden realm of higher existence, and therefore, also, as an intermediate or mediating world. Co-ordinate with this realm is the "demonic man"; below it is the "banausic" man; above it, implied though not explicitly stated, is the man endowed with divine wisdom.

Only the *Symposium* develops the intermediate realm of the demonic in the concrete form of a myth. As a prelude to it we may take the myth of the soul in the *Phaedo*, where the demon, "whose function it is to lead thence," accompanies the soul first to the tribunal, and then to Hades, whence another guide leads it back on its return. We are also reminded of the myth of the soul in the *Republic*, where judgment is passed at a "demonic" place "between" heaven and earth (X 614c); and of the faint echo in the *Timaeus* (90A), where the demon, the controlling element in the soul, "lifts us from earth to kinship in heaven." In the *Statesman* (309c), the souls themselves are a "demonic species," receiving "divine" knowledge of the beautiful, the just, and the good. It is always the *metaxy*, or intermediate, which is the symbol for the demon or the demonic. And this is seen in still clearer outlines in the myth of Diotima.

It is a myth, to be sure, and the Platonists were quite wrong to make a dogma out of it. On the other hand, to say that it is "nothing but" a myth is equally wrong, and evades the question of what the point of the myth is, a question that must be asked even though there is no final answer. Plato would not have chosen the form of a myth if he had been able to find a perfect expression in the form of a logical concept.

It is easy to show the genesis of this idea. Homer and Hesiod created the Greek gods; that is, they lifted Olympus and the heaven of the gods out of the realm of demons. Even though Plato still uses the words gods and demons interchangeably, he adopted and systematized this idea of two distinct ranks, placing the demonic as a sort of proportional mean between the human level and the divine. More difficult and important, however, than this background is the question of the purpose for which Plato needed and used this conceptual structure.

Among the very different approaches to a *Weltanschauung* in the European tradition, which was essentially influenced by the thought of classical antiquity, we may distinguish two basic views—seen perhaps in particularly sharp contrast to one another when we compare a landscape by Dürer with one by Rubens.[19] Just as the former leads in distinct, separate sections or layers from the foreground to the back, so the latter leads in continuous, homogeneous movement into the depth of the picture; and this difference in form expresses a contrast in the view of the world. For it makes a basic difference whether the world is viewed as a limited and leveled structure or as a homogeneous spatial continuum. This dual view also appears in antiquity, though it is obvious that the idea of structure belongs much more to the classical view than the idea of a continuum. Thus, in Plato, we may compare the threefold structure of his concept of the soul with the modern concept of the soul as infinite energy; or his state, built upon three classes, with that abundance of mutually supporting or conflicting forces that we usually have in mind when we use the word "state." Structure requires that its elements hold together. "That two things of themselves form a good union is impossible," says the doctrine of the elements in the *Timaeus* (31B). "For there must be a bond (δεσμός) between them, holding them together. The best bond is one that makes itself and the elements it connects into a complete unity. To achieve this most perfectly is the nature of proportion." Thus, the fourfold nature of the elements is constructed by "continued geometrical proportion . . . and from these four elements, the body of the world was created in harmony with itself by means of the law of proportion; and it won 'friendship' (φιλίαν) so that coming into unity with itself it became indissoluble by any other save him who bound it together" (32c). This is the structure of nature in so far as it is governed by the laws of physics. And the more sharply Plato's world was divided into idea and appearance, the stronger must be the bond forcing this separation into a unity. Thus, the human soul is seen as intermediate (μεταξύ) between idea and appearance, the *Doxa* in the three levels of knowledge as intermediate between knowing and not-knowing, becoming as intermediate between being and not-being, or as a path leading from one to the other. *Dianoia*, the world of particular sciences, lies between pure knowledge, or the world of ideas, and mere opinion, or the world of fleeting appearances.[20] Without the proportion of the elements, without the harmonious system of the forms of being and knowledge, without the *metaxy* of the soul, without the realm of the "demonic," heaven and earth would break asunder.

Always one thing or another stands between men and him.
And step by step
The heavenly one descends. (Hölderlin.) [21]

The Socratic "daimonion" must have been for Plato a part of "the demonic," as the name indicates. He does not say so explicitly, for the myth of Diotima is concerned with *Eros*. And yet, daimonion and *Eros*, the inhibiting and the driving force, cannot but appear as fundamentally akin.[22] In Plato it is a natural kinship, not a matter of functioning parts in an intellectual system. We must be careful not to go beyond his own statements more than is necessary. We must, however, call attention to Proklos, for even though this latest disciple tends to force the master's spontaneous images into logical categories, and lives in an entirely different intellectual atmosphere, his absorption in Plato's thoughts, images, and words is still incomparable. Of Socrates, Proklos not only says, "Socrates is at once an erotic and a demonic person" (ὁ γὰρ αὐτός ἐστιν ἐρωτικός τε καὶ δαιμόνιος ἀνήρ); but adds, "The demon is to him altogether responsible for love" (τοῦ ἔρωτος αὐτῷ πάντως ὁ δαίμων αἴτιος).[23] Even if this statement throws too sharp a light upon a subject that Plato chose to leave somewhat obscure, it still expresses a real insight, which Plato himself would hardly have denied. And perhaps we may again find a confirmation in Goethe, speaking from an entirely different world, yet expressing a profound affinity: "Not merely *we* are the love," he said to Eckermann on March 5, 1830, "but also the beloved object that charms us. And then—what we must not forget—we have as a powerful third element the Daemonic, which accompanies every passion, and which finds its proper element in love."[24]

Returning to Socrates, he lived—as we have seen—in every respect the life of Athens. It was the life of a city-state, which, not unlike the Italian city-republics of the later Middle Ages, had inherited a declining aristocratic culture and absorbed much of its knightly customs. Founded on the customs of Doric warriors, the παιδικὸς ἔρως is also "political," as it were, and this society, the most productive the world has ever seen, is completely filled with male love on every level and in all its manifestations, from the most passionate devotion to casual play, from loftiest adoration to crudest sensuality, rising to the heights of creative power, as it survives in Greek art, and reverberating in the halls of state, as it causes the fall of the house of the Peisistratidai through physical desire and jealousy. No doubt, *Eros* was for Socrates an original and living experience. There is, for example, the story about Zopyros, the founder of the science of physiognomy, who saw sensuality and lust for women expressed in Socrates' features. The story is well substantiated; it probably appeared in a dialogue composed in Socrates' own circle.[25] This fact alone demonstrates, more than anything else, the original nature of his erotic drive. How powerfully it was expressed, by inclination and custom especially directed toward boys and young men, is fully confirmed by all the statements from the circle of Socrates. Plato's dialogues are full of this. Even if we make allowance for Plato's effect upon his companions, it is unthinkable that the real Socrates was an unerotic (because completely rational) character whom Plato, in a paradoxical reversal, by the force of his own, entirely different nature, transformed into the type of the loving educator.[26] In the *Alcibiades* of Aischines, Socrates compares his love for Alkibiades with the divine ecstasy of Bacchic maenads. As they draw milk and honey from dried wells, so he hopes to improve the beloved friend by his mere presence.[27] Nor is this element lacking in Xenophon. The *Memorabilia*, to be sure, say little about it; their apologetic and moralistic attitude was probably disturbed by this dangerous power, and wherever it occurs, it is changed or diverted. But the statement "he often said he loved someone" is probably closer to the truth of the matter, all the more so as it is presently given a bourgeois-moral interpretation: "It was clear, however, that his desire was moved not by youth, excelling in physical beauty, but by those favored with excellence of the soul [virtue]" (VI 1 2). In a long conversation with Kritobulos on how to win friends, Socrates interrupts rather suddenly: "Perhaps I can assist you in your pursuit of the beautiful and good because I am a lover myself (διὰ τὸ ἐρωτικὸς εἶναι). For when I desire someone, I give the whole strength of my being to be loved by him in return for my love, to arouse longing in return for my longing, and to see my desire for companionship reciprocated by his desire" (II 6 28). This is just a brief interlude, quickly to disappear again in the patter of moralistic exhortations. Xenophon's

Banquet, lighter, livelier, and more dramatic than the *Memorabilia,* conveys by its free invention a greater sense of life and even of reality. Thus one of his drinking companions suspects Socrates of the vain conceit that the youths of the company desire his kisses (IV 20); or Charmides says teasingly that, in writing school, Socrates had sat down beside the beautiful Kritobulos, reading from the same book, only to bring his head close to the other's and to touch Kritobulos' bare shoulder with his own (IV 27).[28] Socrates' speech in praise of *Eros* begins by calling all companions "fellow revelers of the god," and by saying of himself: "I could not name a time when I was not in love with someone." All this, to be sure, is still little enough as compared with the abundance in Plato. But is this not the most realistic and simple explanation: that Xenophon only described, but did not experience what he wrote, while Plato was bound to depict Socrates as an entirely erotic character because he had experienced the god or the demon in contact with the master? Friendship and love are always mutual in their fulfillment, though they may originate only in one person: this Plato shows, primarily in the *Lysis,* the *Alcibiades,* and then in the great dialogues on love. Convinced of this, could Plato transform Socrates into an erotic character and have him teach the mutuality of all friendship and love if, in the passion of his own youth, he had met in him a man devoid of love?

In Plato's *Theages* (128B), Socrates counters the professional teachers of wisdom with the ironic reply: "I know nothing about these lofty matters—how I wish that I did!—but, as I am always saying, I am quite ignorant in general save for one small subject: the nature of love." Similarly, in a passage from the *Symposium* (177D), Socrates refers to himself, "I say of myself that I am ignorant about all things except the nature of love." The more limited statement in the *Lysis* (204B) also belongs in this context: "Ignorant as I am in all other things, God gave me the power to recognize one who loves and who is loved." If we consider these statements, which strikingly combine the Socratic *Eros,* Socratic ignorance, and Socratic irony, we must conclude that Plato recorded a fixed figure of speech, a "habitual saying," of the historical Socrates. And even if we reject this conclusion—and it is, of course, impossible to prove because Plato's Socrates almost hides the historical figure—the nature of the Platonic Socrates is completely revealed in these words. Thus the following discussion must now turn upon the "great lover" as revealed in Plato's dialogues.

In the *Charmides*, Socrates has just returned, the previous night, from the military campaign. His first walk leads him "to the accustomed meeting places," to the palaestra. After giving a report on the campaign, his first question is directed at what he considers more important than anything else: what is the present state of "philosophy" at home; have young boys grown up excelling in intelligence or beauty? When Charmides enters, admired and pursued by all, Socrates admits that, for measuring beautiful youths, he is like a white line (on a white surface); he cannot (as a red line does) distinguish among them; all youths appear beautiful to him. Charmides, to be sure, appears particularly admirable in stature and beauty. And in the manner of the *Lysis*, where he seems to pride himself on his expert knowledge, he continues: the general amazement of the grown-up men was not surprising; but even the boys saw only him, and looked at him as if he were a divine statue.

We must not overlook the irony of this passage—Socrates pretending he cannot make distinctions—but what shines forth unmistakably through the ironic concealment is a passionate love of beauty. Later Plato will say that the beautiful body evokes a memory of the original vision of beauty through the eye of the soul. The boys, the men, Socrates himself, are all "confused and as struck by lightning." No one has a right to weaken these strong words or to say that Socrates is only playing a part. His feeling for physical beauty was as strong as in others. What distinguishes him from the others is that they are satisfied with physical beauty as an end, while Socrates requires an additional "small point," namely, that Charmides also have a noble soul. When Socrates misses a "small point," it is always the decisive thing. Nobility of mind does not detract from physical beauty; together they produce the perfect nature. The same tension and movement recur presently. Charmides sits down beside Socrates and looks at him expectantly. "Then I saw what was inside his garments, and I was aflame and beside myself. And I thought how well Kydias understood the nature of love, when, in speaking of a fair youth, he warns someone not to come as a fawn in the sight of the lion to fetch his share of the meat." All this may be taken quite literally—as is shown by the glance at veiled nakedness—even though we may also detect a hint of gentle self-mockery in these strong poetic words. As soon as the conversation develops, however, it becomes clear that both good and evil for the body and, indeed, for man as a whole, proceed from the soul. The subsequent discussion remains on the level of the soul, dealing with *sophrosyne*, the moderation and discipline of the beautiful soul.

In the opening passages of the *Protagoras*, the companion remarks teasingly that Socrates has probably come from the chase after Alkibiades' youthful beauty. Socrates enters into the mood and proves well versed in matters of love. But something strange has happened: "Although he [i.e., Alkibiades] was present, I paid no heed to him. Indeed, I often forgot him completely." And what caused him to forget was that there was someone more beautiful—Protagoras; for wisdom is beautiful. This is jest, of course, jest throughout. That does not mean, however, that love, even the physical love for Alkibiades, is but a mask. It is quite genuine, a step toward the practice of philosophy, just as, in the *Charmides*, the physical beauty of the youth was a step toward nobility of soul, in himself and in general. Thus the ascent (ὥσπερ ἐπαναβαθμοῖς χρώμενον, *Symposium* 211c) of love as well as wisdom, described by Diotima, takes its point of departure from physical beauty, later to rise toward beauty of the soul where, to be sure, "even a small flower of the body suffices" (210b). This is Platonic and Greek in feeling, in contrast to Nietzsche's words that "the fairest body is but a veil, modestly donned by things more beautiful," where the little word "but" sounds an echo from an entirely different world.

The *Alcibiades*, more than any other dialogue, demonstrates the contrast between Socrates' love and that of other men. The many lovers who had pursued the young man left him when the

flower of his youth began to fade. Socrates, who had long observed him, now approaches him for the first time. This curious
difference forms the starting point of the discussion, and the
solution is found at the end: the others loved only the body, not
Alkibiades himself. Socrates loving the soul of Alkibiades is the
only lover. This is the way in which the argument is presented
in conceptual form; but this isolation of the love of the soul
emerges only in the contrast to the common sensual love.
Socrates' love is truly an all-human phenomenon. Perhaps we
feel affection of the senses is not lacking when Socrates, in the
beginning, refers to the "beauty and stature" of the youth; at
any rate, what is hinted at here could certainly be supplemented
by the *Protagoras* and the *Symposium*. Moreover, the sensual
element is not merely mask or veil. It is a steppingstone to a
higher level, but a necessary steppingstone whose absence would
make that higher level inaccessible.

Still another insight is conveyed by this encounter more
clearly than in any other work. Alkibiades has felt the silent
observation by Socrates as "annoying." It is a strong word;
and we sense the annoyance, but also the curiosity with which
he almost anticipated the approach by Socrates. In the end, however, after the first pedagogic conversation has run its course,
the relationship between the two has changed; and from the
words of enthusiastic attachment Socrates concludes rightly
that his love for the disciple has, "after the manner of storks,
hatched the winged fruit of love, and must now, in turn, be
cared for by the other's love." Where passion encounters the
right object, it must necessarily engender passion. And, whether
more strongly or weakly, Socrates always has this magnetic
power. When he enters the palaestra, the boys soon surround
him; they sit on his bench; they blush when he addresses them.
In the poignant words of the youth in the *Theages*: "My greatest
progress by far came when I sat next to you and touched you." [29]

For the first time, the lover addresses the youth whose sight
has long moved him. Are they talking about the "I" and the
"thou," and the force that brought them together? No, instead,
their conversation is concerned with learning and self-improve-
ment, with the state and effective action in the state. Instead

of being praised by his lover, the haughty youth feels tested, humbled, educated. This is the Socratic conversation about love, the genuine "dialogue" as against the false talk by others. In the *Lysis*, after giving a similar example, Socrates says: "That is the way, my dear Hippothales, in which we should talk to the beloved, humbling and lowering him, and not as you do, puffing him up and pampering him." Testing of the soul and guidance toward *Arete* and *Polis* are the proper subjects between lovers for both Socrates and Plato, probably more profoundly akin and less distinguishable on this point than on any other. And the Platonic Socrates expresses a general principle often confirmed by other great sayings: by Hölderlin's "Mortal man gives his best when he loves," by Goethe's "We learn only from those we love," by Nietzsche's "The deepest insights spring from love alone." These sayings, collected by Ernst Bertram in his book on Nietzsche, complement each other: Hölderlin was thinking of the teacher, Goethe of the disciple, and Nietzsche of the product of this union.[30] All three elements are found in Plato; let us now turn to the third.

Eros brings two people together. If these two are Socrates and Alkibiades, they will philosophize. This others saw; Plato saw more. He saw the power of the great demon extend to a new dimension: not only does the lover teach and the beloved learn; it is their love from which "the deepest insights spring." Thus *Eros* becomes the guide to the *Idea*; this is the truly Platonic turn. It remains, by necessity, an interpretation of the Socratic existence.

This Platonic turn first appears in the *Lysis*, where Plato, in the form and on the level of an early work, discusses those questions which the *Symposium* later transfers to a higher level. The subject of the conversation is "friendship" (φιλία). But behind this word, it is clear, as will be briefly sketched, hides the more powerful *Eros*.[31] The atmosphere pervading the conversation is erotic. Moreover, Socrates confesses that the quick recognition of lover and beloved is his only gift (204в). Indeed, Socrates may say of himself that, from the time of his youth, his erotic passion has been devoted to acquiring friends (πρὸς τὴν τῶν φίλων κτῆσιν πάνυ ἐρωτικῶς ἔχω). There is hardly any terminological distinction between love and friendship, so that, first, desire is said to wish that of which it is in want, and then that the congenial be the object of "love, friendship, and desire" (τοῦ οἰκείου ὅ τε ἔρως καὶ ἡ φιλία καὶ ἡ ἐπιθυμία τυγχάνει οὖσα, 221E).

The dialogue deals with the nature of friendship, that is, at first with questions such as whether affection may be one-sided or must be mutual, whether friendship unites like with like or unlike with unlike; in short, the conversation stays on the dimension between the "I" and the "thou." Only toward the end, after a long dialectical and apparently fruitless exchange, Socrates calls attention to a most important point. Affection exists for the sake of an object; its "intentional nature" (to use modern terminology) becomes visible; and this object is something "dear," or a "good." Moreover, since every good may be superseded by a higher good, the search is an ascent to the highest object of love" (πρῶτον φίλον), or to that which is good in itself and not for the sake of another (τὸ τῷ ὄντι φίλον). Thus, proceeding from the "I-thou" dimension, a new dimension has been reached; the *Eidos* is in sight.

Socrates' speech in the *Symposium* points to this "intentional nature" of love right from the very beginning: love aims at something. This relationship apparently is necessary in order to grasp the demonic element, beyond the hymnic festival, the myth, and the music of words, in its philosophical or conceptual meaning. This formal element has a content because the beautiful and the good are recognized as the object of the intentional act. Thus the objective dimension is grasped from the beginning. And as if conceptual clarity had thus received its due, Socrates now resumes his tale in the solemn language of prophecy by the priestess Diotima. Love longs for procreation in beauty, whether physical or spiritual; and this desire for procreation is a longing for immortality, as love desires that it may "forever" partake of the good. Begetting of one soul in another occurs when the lover comes upon a beautiful soul in a fair body. What he begets is "virtue," which he nourishes in the soul. We see how the "I," the "thou," and the "object" are concentrated in this act of procreation; and how the two dimensions we recognized are clearly outlined. The same basic relationship is repeated on a higher level. The dual movement toward the beloved and, with him, toward virtue becomes a gradual ascent leading to the intuition of *Ideas:* at first, we desire physical beauty; from here, we progress, in stages of which none may be omitted, until we finally reach that which is "beautiful in itself, of single form and eternal" (ἀεὶ καθ' αὑτὸ μεθ' αὑτοῦ μονοειδὲς ἀεὶ ὄν). Love has found its highest fulfillment; the deepest insights have sprung from love; but even the view of the highest idea of beauty still reflects its origin from the encounter between the "I" and the "thou." Beginning and end are both under the aspect of the same great demon.

A still clearer view of the necessary connection between the two dimensions, the unity of the erotic experience and the vision of *Ideas,* is presented in the *Phaedrus.* The moment at which the vision of beauty awakens love is like a double ray falling from the realm of *Ideas* into our world of becoming and passing away. For he who sees the beautiful remembers the pure beauty, which every human being—as part of being human—has seen in the realm beyond the heavens before he was born. He sees beauty in the other because he perceives features molded in God's image, or a body resembling the original image of beauty (ὅταν θεοειδὲς πρόσωπον ἴδῃ κάλλος εὖ μεμιμημένον ἤ τινα σώματος ἰδέαν, 251A). The awe he feels and his divine adoration of the beloved are like a gleam of silver in which memory and image awaken each other; and the path is cleared to the realm of *Ideas.* But this is only the beginning. Different kinds of human nature, bequeathed to the souls from their following of a god in the heavenly realm—or, in non-mythical terminology, the creative law of the individual now pursues different paths, seeking in others what is akin to himself. Thus love makes the soul conscious of its innate divine element, the highest type of soul, a follower of Zeus, conscious of its destiny for philosophy and ruling. Love compels it to look toward Zeus and shape itself according to his image. Zeus means the highest form of divine existence in the view of the eternal forms; for the divine has its own hierarchy as in Dante's *Paradiso.* This hierarchical structure determines the hierarchy of man on earth, and of all human community in love. The love of philosophers for each other and for the *Idea* is a function of Zeus' contemplation of the *Ideas*. Only the world beyond helps us to comprehend how the highest form of love may lead directly to philosophy, or philosophical education of the congenial partner, just as genuine love, coming from the highest god, is true education toward the highest god. The loving encounter of two human beings belonging to Zeus, that is, two philosophers and rulers, at once includes the new dimension, the movement toward the *Idea*.

Loving desire is part of the philo-sopher's name. Now, while a sexual element is—at least potentially—always present in *Eros*, even the quest for truth and the penetration to truth may for a moment, as in a passage of the *Republic* (490AB), be felt as an act of begetting. Just as the begetter must be of the same nature (συγγενής) as the object of his love, so the lover of truth must approach true being and touch it with that part of the soul (almost, with that organ) which is akin to true being. The true nature or being of the soul combines, in an act of creative union, with true being or form, akin to the nature of the soul. And just as true sexual union not only begets but creates, so the knowing self, too, must create—what? Mind and truth. The child bears the features of both parents. But, unlike a natural birth, the product of this union is not external to its parents; but the lover of wisdom himself, after this kind of procreation and birth, is as one "who has now attained insight and now truly lives and grows united with it." Insight and knowledge thus grow as part of one's own existence, not separate from it. It is "existential" insight, an indissoluble union of insight and life. "And then pain will have an end," Socrates concludes, once more evoking the basis of the simile of procreation and birth.

Why is *Eros* not called a god, but a great demon? What is the common element of demon, daimonion, *Eros?* They do not designate complete being, but rather aspects, movements, and powers leading toward such being. *Eros*, too, is part of the world of *metaxy*, transition to a beyond of the soul in a double sense, first uniting the "I" and the "thou" in dialogue, and then raising them both to the level of the *Eidos*.

In the power he called *Eros*, Plato saw the dual (yet united) movement toward the beautiful person and the idea of beauty. Erotic experience and knowledge of *Ideas* are indissolubly united. This is not a matter of conceptual thought, but the formulation of direct, personal experience. Confirmed by a long life, it is still implied in Plato's words when he was an old man. In the *Seventh Letter*, Plato talks about the things to which he is committed most wholeheartedly (περὶ ὧν σπουδάζω, 341c). They are not communicable in language as other objects of knowledge, ". . . but, after a long communion and common effort on behalf of the matter, a fire is suddenly kindled in the soul, as if lit by a flying spark, and henceforth can nourish itself." This, to be sure, does not convey the idea—or no longer does so—that the philosopher gains the path to knowledge through the experience of love. Here we hear only about communication, not discovery, of the highest truths. But where is the line of distinction? Even for the old man, every communication is an act of creation; and from the inexpressible nature of the highest truths, it would seem to follow that the "doctrine" is not rigid, but an unending quest.

We mentioned before that Plato—from inner necessity rather than theoretical construction—saw a "systematic" connection between *Eidos* and *Polis*, as well as between *Eros* and *Eidos*. This means that *Eros* and *Polis* are also inextricably united. Plato thought of Socrates as the only true statesman because he was a teacher inspired by love; Plato himself, the discoverer of the realm of *Ideas* and the founder of the Academy—owing to the historical situation—recognized the primacy of the political life: these facts alone show unmistakably that the Platonic *Eros* and his guidance toward the *Idea* do not merely satisfy individual inclinations and needs, isolating the individual from the life of the community. There is no *Arete* and *Paideia* without a "political" meaning. We cannot overlook the political overtones in Diotima's statement that love inspires the teacher with ready speech on "what the perfect man (ἀγαθὸς ἀνήρ) ought to be, and what he ought to do," which becomes still more explicit when, beside the poetic works of Homer and Hesiod, the laws of Lykurgos and Solon are mentioned as the finest examples of intellectual creation. The *Republic*, finally, teaches that *Eros* and *Eidos* are effective only within the *Polis*, just as the *Polis*, in turn, is founded on *Eros* and *Eidos*. For it is founded around the *Agathón*, and *Eros* is the union of its rulers in their striving toward this center.

Man and *Polis* are part of the cosmic order. Without *Eros*, heaven and earth would break asunder. Thus the function of *Eros* is fulfilled only within the widest possible context. The demonic realm, says Diotima, "unites the All with itself." This is merely a hint; for in this passage, Socrates, speaking through Diotima, is referring to man. But Phaidros has conjured up the cosmogonic *Eros* of the ancient poets at the outset of the speeches on *Eros*. Eryximachos has shown *Eros* to be active not only in men's souls, but in the bodies of all living beings and in vegetation, or quite generally in all forms of existence, as the power reconciling hostile opposites such as cold and warm, bitter and sweet, dry and wet, ruling in harmony and reaching into the cosmic order. Aristophanes, finally, expresses the hope that *Eros*, in the future, will lead the divided fragments of men, descended from the heavenly bodies, back to the former state, that is, will restore us to the state of original perfection resembling that of our creators. This is poetic play, to be sure; but what is the point of the play? That things strive toward and desire the *Eidos*, so that *Eros* is the bond between them, is stated with a higher "seriousness," though still in half-mythical form, in the *Phaedo*.[32] The *Phaedrus*, again, speaks the language of myth: the vision of the eternal forms is the highest aim of divine and human souls; the "desire for the beyond" is the motivating power; the wings, borrowed from the god of love, are symbolic of this striving which pervades and unifies the world. Other mythical themes predominate in the myth of the creation in the *Timaeus*, which probably explains the absence of the cosmic and cosmogonic *Eros* in this dialogue.

If we wish to grasp the full depth and meaning of Plato's *Eros*, it is helpful not only to consider the level beyond which Plato rose, the Socratic level, but also the sublimation and desensualization of the Platonic world as we find it in Plotinos and later Platonists. On the "Socratic" level—as we may say with a full realization of the ultimate doubt of what we mean by Socrates—*Eros* is effective within a single dimension, between "loving" and "philosophizing" men, an active force driving them in an unending quest, or "existential communication," to use Jaspers' words. Plato adds to this Socratic force an objective element, if not a system, at least a striving toward an objective system. This will help to make clear how Plotinos failed to retain this force and content. For him *Eros* only means movement upward to the highest One. A man of whom his pupil Porphyry says, in the first words of his biography, "Plotinos, the philosopher of our time, was like one ashamed to be in the flesh," could not regard the union of physical love as the creative point of departure for philosophical activity.

The distance between Plato and Plotinos is most evident when the latter apparently follows the master most closely. Plotinos attempts to show the path leading home from aimless wandering, that is, to the place of trust, belonging to the soul, to the Good and the One (V 9 2). It can be reached by a "man endowed by nature with love, and of a true and original philosophical inclination. Such a man suffers a painful struggle for the sake of beauty; but, not being able to endure physical beauty, he flees from it, upward to the beauty of the soul, the virtues, knowledge, actions, and universal principles, thence upward to the cause of spiritual beauty of the soul, until he reaches that which is still higher, the One, beauty in itself. Only then will he be free from painful struggle." This is almost the same ascent that Diotima describes in the *Symposium*, with one great exception: in Plato, everyone taking the right path must first love one beautiful body and "generate in it beautiful words"; then recognize the one beauty in all beautiful bodies, becoming a lover of all. No one may omit these preliminary stages, beyond which leads the soul's path to beauty and upward. Plotinos no longer recognizes these stages. To him the ascent actually begins when man turns away from physical beauty that his soul "does not endure." The soul of Plotinos is alienated from this world, and his concept of disembodied spirituality is far separated from the abundance of Plato's spirit.

Pausanias' speech in the *Symposium*—long before Socrates

takes the floor and reduces all previous speeches to insignificance—divides the apparent unity of Aphrodite and Eros: there are Aphrodite Urania and Aphrodite Pandemos, each with her son Eros. This dualism has never died since, and is also implicit in Plotinos. But the latter again draws a distinction between the two realms quite different from that of Pausanias; and this difference again shows up the distance between Plato and Plotinos. For Pausanias, the division runs through this world, separating nobility and vulgarity in the love between human beings. This is not Socrates speaking, to be sure, and the separation is not final in Plato's sense. Yet he would never have drawn the line where Plotinos drew it. For the latter, love is the necessary drive of the soul for union with God, from whom it has come and is separated (VI 9 9). Like a virgin, it bears noble love for a noble father. Upon reaching its goal, the soul possesses divine *Eros* and itself becomes heavenly Aphrodite. If it becomes immersed in the world of becoming, however, accepting mortal love, separated from the father, it becomes Pandemos itself and adopts, as it were, a hetaira's life (ἐνταῦθα γίνεται πάνδημος οἷον ἑταιρὶς οὖσα).

Earthly life and earthly love are a fall; the soul must hate this outrage, and cleanse itself from this life to return to the father. Thus it is consistent to conclude that "love" is actually meaningless within the world of phenomena. Love is born when the undivided soul creates a nonsensible prototype (οὐκ αἰσθητὸν τύπον, VI 7 33). Thus love between human beings is no longer, as in Plato, a necessary stage, but merely a mark of weak-minded souls. "He who does not know the state of true love, the union with the godhead, may realize from the experience of earthly love what it means to attain that for which we most long" (VI 9 9). The earthly lovers' desire for physical union is but a feeble copy, an "imitation" of much greater experiences (VI 7 34). The prototype, however, true love, is the union of the soul with the highest god. In this the soul then sheds its own form. For as long as it is still in its own state, it can neither see the highest being nor merge into harmonious unity with him. Only when it has shed these obstacles, prepared itself for the encounter, and become like the highest being is there a sudden perception within. "There is nothing in between. They are no longer two, but have merged into one. As long as he is present, we cannot distinguish one from the other." Thus *unio mystica* not only leads to a contempt of the delightful instrument of the body; it also extinguishes all spiritual form. This is *Eros* according to Plotinos, far removed from Plato's.

CHAPTER THREE

Beyond Being

EROS is a great demon, mediator between God and man. He lifts the human soul from the world of becoming to the sphere above the heavens, home of the gods and the eternal forms. In these mythical realms, Plato, as a philosopher-poet, saw the nature of the world. One is reluctant to express his vision in purely conceptual terms; yet one may attempt to follow him to the threshold of the highest sphere.

Nothing is known about how Plato became conscious of this mystery; but we do know that he met Socrates. Despite all his peculiarities, Socrates shared the life of his fellow citizens in the market place and at the symposium, in the people's assembly, and in battle. His life, however, extended beyond this sphere, reaching the plane of wisdom and losing itself in the "ineffable," in "transcendence." He himself would have been unable to explain the difference between what he asked and what he taught others to ask, on the one hand, and what he demonstrated by his way of living and dying, on the other. Did he experience this mysterious transcendence other than in the fullness of his life, in the sense of a divine calling, and in the prayer to the god who had summoned him? Others perhaps perceived it when the tireless speaker and questioner suddenly stopped and grew silent, standing for a long while near the home to which he had been invited, or when in camp he stood from early morning throughout the day, and all night long until the hour of sunrise. "Then he went away after offering prayers to Helios." To one who saw below the surface, the mystery penetrated every one of his sayings.

59

Plato transformed what Socrates asked into questions and answers, what Socrates lived into life and doctrine. Socrates asks: What is justice? He makes the others see that they do not know. He seeks the answer through a concept, but ultimately gives it through his life and death. Plato gives artistic expression to this life and death, but he also reaches the answer in philosophical terms: through the figure of Socrates he sees the *Idea.* The "just" envisaged as an eternal form, a prototype— that is his answer to the Socratic question, the answer perceived through the existence of Socrates.

Having studied the writings of modern thinkers on "Plato's Doctrine of *Ideas,*" and then returning to Plato's own dialogues, one might well be surprised at how little the latter contain of this principal element of Plato's philosophy. In the early dialogues, even in the *Gorgias,* there are only hints to the effect that there are such things as "the good," "that which is eminently loved or dear" (πρῶτον φίλον), or "the truly beautiful." The *Phaedo* constructs, or rather seems to do so, proofs of immortality that presuppose the existence of *Ideas.* The *Symposium* describes the path to the eternal forms; the *Republic* sets forth the ascent through the sciences and, in a great allegory, gives a symbolic representation of this path to the world of *Ideas,* and their nature and function; the *Phaedrus* weaves a myth through the realm of *Ideas;* the *Parmenides* deals with the logical difficulties; other late works are concerned with the logical presuppositions and implications of the theory of *Ideas.* Yet nowhere do we find a "doctrine" as such, or a system comprising the order of these forms, communicating their knowledge, or clarifying their relationship to the world of appearance.

Why this is so may be seen from the *Seventh Letter,* to whose most important passages we must so often return. There exists no written work of Plato's—there can and will be none— concerning that part of knowledge which is to him most significant "because it is in no way expressible like other subjects of teaching." Doubtless this refers to the realm of *Ideas.* Why can it not be written about or expressed? First, because it is not intended for everyone. Only the "well-constituted" (man) may hope to grasp the "well-constituted" (object). In addition to the intellectual capacities of learning and memory, an "affinity" is required: a special receptiveness of the soul to *Ideas*. Even though, according to the *Phaedo*, the human soul itself belongs to the realm of *Ideas*, the myth in the *Phaedrus* shows a hierarchical order among the souls, depending on whether they raised themselves, for a shorter or longer period, to the heavenly sphere, and whether they followed Zeus or some other god. This explains what, in the less enthusiastic language of the *Letter*, is meant by "affinity": only a few rare individuals possess it. It is necessary, too, that "master and disciple live together for a long time in common effort on behalf of the matter itself." For there is a path to knowledge leading upward through predetermined stages: from the name or the word (ὄνομα) to the statement (speech, definition, λόγος), and thence through image, view, and perception (εἴδωλον, 342D; ὄψεις τε καὶ αἰσθήσεις, 344B) to the higher and highest forms of knowledge. Ascent and descent must be repeated often, the forms of understanding on the various levels must be "rubbed against one another" (τριβόμενα πρὸς ἄλληλα, 344B); until finally, after toil and and labor (μόγις), rational insight suddenly lights up, or, as it is said earlier, "the spark is transmitted to and the fire kindled in the companion's soul" (341C). Here it may suffice to observe that the stages of the path to knowledge are partly of a conceptual or linguistic nature, like word and sentence, and partly of a visual nature, like image. "Knowledge of the Fifth" (ἐπιστήμη τοῦ πέμπτου, 342), that is, of true being, must therefore partake of both kinds of intellectual activity. The goal is an intellectual vision of the highest reality. The path leading to it may be outlined, as in the *Letter*. But it is one thing to point it out, another to follow it. And in the end it leads to something that cannot be said in words. This may almost suggest a mystical realm and a path of personal salvation, provided we do not think of mysticism in terms of wild ecstasy, and of salvation in doctrinal terms.

Plato alone could be undogmatic concerning the path and the goal; every interpretation of Plato is almost necessarily exposed to the danger of dogmatism. One should at least be aware of this danger. In the *Seventh Letter*, Plato does not set up any order within the realm of what he calls "the Fifth," that is, true being. He does not elevate the good, for example, into a position of superior rank, but leaves it, beside the straight and the round, the beautiful and the just, without that mark of distinction which Socrates, much to the astonishment of his listeners, assigns to it in the *Republic*. In the *Letter* the entire realm of being is, as it were, stamped with the seal of ineffability. We must, therefore, be careful not to be dogmatic about what Plato himself—apart from the myth in the *Timaeus*—presented only once and still in half-mythical form, though with unforgettable power, at the very heart of the *Republic*. In the center of this work, and after the completion of its essential structure, the question arises about the highest object of teaching (μέγιστον μάθημα, 504D). The conversation has long bypassed it, has "hidden away" from it (503A). And even now Socrates is reluctant, letting the participants urge him on (506B). We are persuaded that something of utmost importance is imminent; we are now entering upon the "longer path," which is to lead to a "precise" formulation of what has been previously said, in a preliminary way, about the virtues (434D, 504B). What has only been a "sketched outline" is now to receive "finished form" (504D). The state will be arranged in perfect harmony if its ruler possesses this knowledge (506A). The completion of the whole plan is anticipated. But this expectation is disappointed. Again Socrates appears as one who does not know (506C). We shall not be told the real thing, but will have to be content if the discussion remains quite as tentative and provisional as it was in the case of justice and the other virtues. Thus, far from completing the previous conversation, what we now learn will be just as incomplete as what we heard before. The knowledge we are seeking would be ours if we knew "the nature of the good." But about the good itself —about the "father"—Socrates will be silent. We shall hear about its offspring only (ἔκγονος τοῦ ἀγαθοῦ); and we shall only be able to view the reality from a distance in the form of a simile.

As the sun bestows light upon the objects of the world of becoming and perception so that they may be seen, and power of vision upon the eye so that it may perceive, so the highest good, in the world of being, endows the object of knowledge with "truth" (ἀλήθεια) and the mind with the power of perceiving true knowledge. The simile then turns from epistemology to ontology. As the sun bestows development and growth, as well as the law of growth, upon the objects of the world of becoming, so the *Idea* of the Good gives being and order to the objects of the world of being. Thus the true circle, like true justice, owes its perfection to that ultimate perfection. At last, still another dimension becomes visible above the level of being. As the cause of becoming is not itself becoming, so the source of being is not itself being. Then we encounter the highest paradox: not itself being, but beyond being. While there is still knowledge about being, though not purely conceptual knowledge, there can be no knowledge about what is "beyond" being. "After you have pronounced the good, do not add anything; you will only detract from it by adding," says Plotinos (III 8 11), apparently still quite in the sense of Plato.[1] Socrates cannot say anything about the good; he has to be ignorant because something ineffable has here come into view. There is a paradoxical tension in this antithesis: on the one hand, the *Logoi*, and only the *Logoi*, are the keys to the world of being—"It appeared to me as if one ought to seek refuge in the *Logoi*, and perceive through them the true nature of being" (*Phaedo* 99E)—on the other hand, above this world of being towers that which is beyond everything and, therefore, cannot be grasped even by the *Logoi*.[2]

The highest goal thus fades into mystery—yet, unlike Plotinos', not a mystery that is already profaned by contact with words. "That the *Idea* of the Good is the highest subject of teaching you have often heard" (505A), says Socrates. Thus speech has often aimed at it before as the origin and goal of philosophical discourse. Yet it was not known, not even discussed; for, while we may be able to name it, we cannot describe it, and therefore it need not be artificially restricted, like an "esoteric doctrine," by injunctions and symbolism, because its own being, or rather its existence "beyond all being," protects it from being profaned.

"It makes a great deal of difference," Goethe writes,

"whether I strive from light into darkness or from darkness into the light; whether, when clarity does not appeal to me, I seek to surround myself with a certain twilight or, in the conviction that clarity rests in depths difficult to explore, I attempt to bring to the surface as much as is possible from these depths, hard as they are to express." [3] We cannot doubt that Plato passionately strove from darkness into the light. All of his work is but an ever-renewed attempt to bring to light as much as possible from "the depths" spoken of in these words by Goethe. In what has been said, to suspect an intentional mystification on Plato's part would be a misunderstanding. Plato is not a Neoplatonist.[4] But he—perhaps more than anyone else—understood both the *Logoi* and the *Arrheton*, and knew both that to approach the latter one must pass through the former, as far as this is humanly possible, and that the *Logoi* invariably lead to the *Arrheton* as their goal.

To lead to a vision of the *Idea* and a hint of the highest good is Plato's task. Is this perhaps also the true meaning of his decision to write dialogues? However that may be, the dialogues point in different ways to the final goal. While the *Seventh Letter* suggests briefly a progression (διαγωγή) through four definite stages toward "knowledge of the Fifth," i.e., the highest being, the main works delineate three definite paths. The principal path is described in the *Republic*, first in the famous image of man originally enchained, then liberated and rising toward the light; later in the interpretation of the simile expressly worked out as the "dialectical path." In the *Symposium*, the prophetess Diotima reveals the true lover's ascent to eternal beauty, and in the same category belongs the myth of the soul in the *Phaedrus*, the myth of the winged soul's flight to the realm above the heavens. Finally, the *Phaedo* praises the separation of the soul from the body, presenting the philosopher's life as a pilgrimage to this goal, and his death as the completion of a life so oriented. These three paths may be called the path of knowledge, the path of love, and the path of death. Yet they are ultimately one and the same. For love and death lead to knowledge, and knowledge, in turn, is nothing without love and death, which complete it. Thus the three paths may and must be seen as one.

The most general aspect characteristic of this experience is that it is always seen through the simile of a road or way.[5] The *Republic* refers to a "dialectical journey" (διαλεκτικὴ πορεία, 532B). Expressions of walking, striding, and leading abound. "Method," in the sense of a "path leading toward something," still faintly reveals its origin in the context of this image (*Republic* 533C, *Phaedo* 79E). The path takes a certain direction: it leads upward. In the *Phaedrus*, the power of wings lifts the soul to the gods' abode (246D), and thence upward; for the gods are shown driving their chariots upward and along the dome of heaven on their journey to the feast and enjoyment of the eternal forms (247A). "Rising upward from here through the true love of boys" is what Diotima teaches in the *Symposium* (211B). The allegory of the cave in the *Republic* is based on the same view; its symbolism is felt so little that "the ascent and vision of what is above" (ἡ ἄνω ἀνάβασις) recurs in the interpretation as the ascent of the soul to the intelligible place" (εἰς τὸν νοητὸν τόπον τῆς ψυχῆς ἄνοδος, 517B). The image of the "above" stands for an ageless view of man. Where the light shines, in the "above" toward which our heads are raised, we place God, truth, and purity; even though we know—as did Plato—that the mind's eye is not literally oriented toward the starry sky above any more than downward (*Republic* 529B).

Next, the ascent is made in stages. The *Seventh Letter* names four stages to be run through repeatedly and without omission both upward and downward (ἄνω καὶ κάτω μεταβαίνουσα ἐφ᾽ ἕκαστον). Diotima describes the gradual ascent of love, demands that its steps be taken "in the right order and succession" (ἐφεξῆς τε καὶ ὀρθῶς, 210E), and, at the end, again emphasizes the importance of the proper sequence (211C). The "dialectical journey" becomes apparent in the allegory of the cave in the *Republic*, subsequently interpreted as the upward progression, in a precise sequence and order, through the sciences to dialectics, and through dialectics to the final goal.

The point of departure is not always explicitly stated. When it is, it is not always expressed by the same image. But it cannot be seen in any way other than as a contrast to the brightness of the goal above. Thus the most general, the most powerful image is that of darkness: from darkness to light,

from light to darkness, eyes full of darkness (*Republic* 518A;
516E, 517D). An allusion is made to the Orphic symbol of the
mud in which the mind's eye is buried (533D). The imagination
is caught in images of hollowness and cave. In the geophysical
myth at the end of the *Phaedo*, man is presented as inhabiting
one of the hollows (ἔγκοιλα, 111c) carved in the sphere of the
earth. Added to this is the idea of prison. The cave in the
Republic is a prison holding its inmates enchained at the neck
and legs—a symbol, as we presently learn, for the world of the
senses perceived by the eye (517B). In the *Phaedo*, again with
Orphic undertones, the physical body is the soul's prison
(ἐκλυομένην ὥσπερ δεσμῶν ἐκ τοῦ σώματος, 67D); and in the concluding myth of the same dialogue, the pious of this earth
"are liberated, as from prisons, so that they may rise to a pure
habitation above the true earth" (114B *et seq.*). Is it perhaps
possible to say that the experience of the prison in which
Socrates was confined—his legs in chains (*Phaedo* 60c), and
from which his soul was liberated to its true home, the light—
that this experience, fusing with Orphic images, assumed the
status of a myth for Plato?

Liberation necessarily complements the prison image: "to be
as free as possible from the body, and to remain pure until God
comes to release us" (*Phaedo* 67A). The dialectical journey in
the *Republic* begins with this liberation. Connected with it, yet
set apart as a new element, is the turning back, the turning
around, the reversal or "conversion" (περιαγωγή, μεταστροφή),
of the man facing the wall of shadows (514B, 518E, 532B, and
elsewhere). In the image, this turning around is an act involving the entire body; in meaning, the whole soul (518c).
Powerful language conveys the decisive importance of the
moment.

While the image of "turning around" occurs only in the
simile of the *Republic*, the ascent that follows, the "upward"
movement, is, with slight variations, a common characteristic
of all other paths as well: the path of love in the *Symposium* and
the *Phaedrus*, the path of death in the *Phaedo*, and the path of
knowledge in the *Seventh Letter*. Everywhere, toil and labor
accompany this striving. "The way upward and downward,

through all its stages, produces knowledge through effort and toil" (μόγις), says the *Letter* (343E). The prisoner in the cave of the *Republic* rises, turns his neck, takes the first steps, and looks up into the light. Each of these steps is accompanied by pain (πάντα δὲ ταῦτα ποιῶν ἀλγοῖ, 515C). When liberated he is in a state of confusion (ἀπορεῖν ἄν, 515D), his eyes hurt as they look into the light, and he wants to turn to run away (515E); and as he, freed from his chains, is drawn upward by force (βίᾳ ἑλκόμενον), he feels anguish and resistance (ὀδυνᾶσθαι καὶ ἀγανακτεῖν). In the *Symposium*, upon reaching the heights, he views "that for the sake of which he has endured all the toil" (πόνοι, 210E). In the myth of the *Phaedrus*, the chariots are driven upward, those of the gods pulling evenly and easily, those of men with trouble (μόγις, 247B), because the wicked steed of the soul is pulling downward to the earth, causing great pain and conflict in the soul (πόνος καὶ ἀγών, 247B). Even in the regions above, the soul is still confused by the steeds (θορυβουμένη) and can perceive the eternal forms again only with strain (μόγις, 248A). In the *Phaedo*, it is aimless wandering (πλάνος, πλάνη, 79D, 81A) from which the soul is liberated when it enters the realm of purity and eternal being. And Socrates expresses the hope that at the end of the journey he will acquire that "for the sake of which all the toil (πραγματεία) has been endured" (67B), in language quite similar to that used by Diotima in connection with the path of love.

This troublesome journey always requires guidance, even compulsion. "Guidance up and down all these steps," says the *Seventh Letter* (ἡ διὰ πάντων αὐτῶν διαγωγή, 343E). In the simile of the *Republic*, the prisoner in the cave is freed from his chains and "compelled" to rise and turn around. The liberator "compels" him to look into the light; he pulls him out of the darkness "by force"; "he does not let go of him before he has dragged him out" (515E). With regard to the stages of knowledge, "it is our, the founders', task to compel the best souls to attain the highest knowledge" (519C). Those who remain after the process of selection has been completed must, at the age of fifty, be led to the goal and compelled to look upon the source of all light (540A). In the *Symposium*, the prophetess constantly alludes to a guide or guidance: "to approach the nature of love correctly, or to be led to it by another" (211B), "if the guide guides correctly" (210A). Diotima envisages the way of love as guidance of young boys, as an act of education (ὃς ἂν παιδαγωγηθῇ, 210E). The pupil must be compelled to view the beautiful under the aspect of an ever-increasing spiritual content (210C). The same basic image, perhaps, in a highly accentuated form, may also be discerned in the myth of the *Phaedrus*, where Zeus is shown as the great leader in heaven, followed by the host of gods, demons, and souls (246E), the individual hosts, in turn, following the god who is their "ruler" (274A, 248A, 253B). It is important that the soul does not seek salvation in lonely introspection and search. Plato himself guided his pupils, and was keenly aware of the firm hand required for such guidance—all the firmer the more willful and strong the pupil, and the farther above the level of mediocrity least likely to achieve anything of value. He had himself experienced, in his relationship with Socrates, the firm hand of a guide, the liberation from chains, the painful "conversion," and the compulsion pulling him upward. That Socrates himself is ultimately the liberator from the cave is apparent from the words that "if they could lay hands on and destroy him who attempts to break their chains and to lead them upward, they would kill him."

Plato experienced this guidance and compulsion as the compulsion of love. There is no contradiction in showing that the path that just appeared as full of troubles is the path of Eros in the *Symposium*. If Eros is a mediator between gods and men, this defines his function as guide upward to divine beauty. At the end of the path it is expressly stated that Eros is man's best helper in attaining the highest form of being, beloved by the gods and immortal, in so far as this state is possible for human beings (212AB). In the *Phaedrus*, it is "divine madness" of Eros which guides the lover to the beautiful object of his love (249D). Again, the notion of a "path" is suggested or implied: it is the education of the beloved by the lover in the image of the god to whom both of them belong in their existence beyond time (252E). The lover forms the beloved. To this end, he must himself concentrate his view upon the god, form his own being and his actions according to the latter, and mold the disciple in his own and the god's image. The goal is man's participation in God to the best of human power (καθ' ὅσον δυνατὸν θεοῦ ἀνθρώπῳ μετασχεῖν, 253A) and a state of beautiful blessedness (τελετὴ καλή τε καὶ εὐδαιμονική, 253C).

After the joy and labor of the ascent, after compulsion, love, and anguish, something "suddenly" happens. Suddenly (ἐξαίφνης), Plato says in the *Seventh Letter* (341C), through long common endeavor for the cause, a fire is kindled in the soul as by a spark. The path of love shown by Diotima terminates in a sudden (ἐξαίφνης) vision of marvelous beauty (210E).[6]

Conceivable as it may be that our imagination might express the ultimate value envisaged by the human soul in a symbolism from the world of sound, the Greeks preferred one from the world of vision. This is particularly true of Plato, who, corresponding to "the keenest of all physical senses," as vision is called in the *Phaedrus* (250D), even endows the mind with an eye capable of grasping the highest reality. Then the goal of the dialectical path is represented with spatial and visual plasticity. It is a realm filled with purest brightness. Just as the noblest of the senses, in our world of becoming, remains inactive and ineffectual in darkness, so, in the world of being, light must pervade the realm surrounding the highest good. Moreover, an innate resistance to deformity and repulsive ugliness will also make us perceive this bright realm as the home of greatest purity. The image of light predominates in the allegory of the *Republic*. It is interpreted as the soul's ascent to the intelligible realm (τὴν εἰς τὸν νοητὸν τόπον τῆς ψυχῆς ἄνοδον, 517B). The soul longs for a permanent abode in purity (οἰκεῖν ἐν τῷ καθαρῷ, 520D). In the *Phaedrus* it is a view of the "realm above the heavens" or "the external realm" (τὰ ἔξω τοῦ οὐρανοῦ, 247C; ὁ ἔξω τόπος, 248A), where the perfect soul dwells in pure brightness (ἐν αὐγῇ καθαρᾷ), clean and unpolluted by the body (καθαροὶ ὄντες καὶ ἀσήμαντοι, 250C). And the same view is expressed in the *Phaedo* when the invisible soul arrives at a noble, pure, invisible place, which, in an etymological interpretation, is given the popular name of Hades (τόπον ἀιδῆ, εἰς "Αιδου, 80D).

As the ascent was accompanied by great toil, so, having

reached the goal, the eye cannot immediately perceive the highest reality. For vision is confused by the transition from light to dark, as well as from darkness to light (*Republic* 518A). Now the eyes are at first so blinded by the dazzling light that they cannot perceive what is truly real (516A). Only then follows the perfect "view of what is above" (θέα τῶν ἄνω, 517B). The soul, growing accustomed to the brightness, finally endures even the brightest vision in the world of being, the *Idea* of the Good (518C). In the myth of the *Phaedrus*, it is the souls of the gods enjoying this vision undisturbed. Wondrous things are beheld by the race of gods in their journey through the heavens (247D). Of human souls, only the best succeeds—and then only as far as the charioteer's head—in raising itself to the external realm and participating in the journey of the gods. Even so, the soul is still disturbed and can view the forms only with difficulty (μόγις καθορῶσα τὰ ὄντα, 248A); likewise the *Sophist* (254A) says that, in the case of most people, the eyes of the soul are incapable of persistently viewing the divine (καρτερεῖν πρὸς τὸ θεῖον ἀφορῶντα ἀδύνατα). Nevertheless, it is the nature of the soul to have beheld the forms; else it would not have become incorporated in a human body (πᾶσα ψυχὴ φύσει τεθέαται τὰ ὄντα, ἢ οὐκ ἂν ἦλθεν εἰς τόδε τὸ ζῷον, *Phaedrus* 249E). Therefore, it is its task, during its earthly existence, through *Eros*, "to partake of God, so far as this is humanly possible" (253A). In the *Phaedo*, the soul—by way of the right philosophy and by way of truly practicing to be dead to the world—enters the realm akin to it, the invisible, divine, immortal, and wise, where it is destined to become "eudaemonic" (81A). In the mythical cosmology at the end, "the true earth" opens up, in all its splendor, the pure dwelling place of the pious (114C) as "a vision to blessed beholders" (θέαμα εὐδαιμόνων θεατῶν, 111A).

This vision is always accompanied by eudaemonia—a term for which our bliss or blessedness is an approximate translation, if we include the notions of perfection and fulfillment. The world of being that is beheld in the vision itself exists in a state of blessed perfection (τὸ εὐδαιμονέστατον τοῦ ὄντος, *Republic* 526E). He who attains to it delights in being "eudaemonic" (516C), believing himself on the Isle of the Blessed (519C). To him who beholds beauty itself, Diotima assigns a life worth living (*Symposium* 211D), and him who begets and cultivates true virtue she calls "Beloved by God" (212A). In the *Phaedrus*, the race of blessed gods beholds the forms on its journey (247A)—praiseworthy the vision, and blessed the chorus partaking in it (ὅτε σὺν εὐδαίμονι χορῷ μακαρίαν τὴν ὄψιν τε καὶ θέαν εἶδον, 250B). The mind of the philosopher dwells, to the best of his powers, on that which is the god's domain, and by virtue of which he is a divine being (πρὸς οἷσπερ θεὸς ὢν θεῖός ἐστιν, 249C).

A path from darkness to light; a path in stages not without numerous labors and not accessible to everybody; a path at the end of which the eye beholds, in dazzling light, something divine; the highest goal shrouded in mystery not arbitrarily posited, and not exposed to profanation by words, because words cannot express it—if we look at these characteristics of Plato's speculation, we cannot fail to see an affinity with the elements of the mysteries, especially the Eleusinian.[7] Plato, aware of these affinities, adopted some of their elements for his own language. The *Phaedo* alludes to this area of mystery cults through the concept of "purification," signifying the soul's separation from the body (67C); for cathartic rites are characteristic of mystic initiation. To Plato, however, "purification" is knowledge or pure thought (φρόνησις). The secret rites and their revelations are seen as allusions (κινδυνεύουσιν αἰνίττεσθαι) to a process of spiritual purification. The contrast between the uninitiated who dwell in the mud of Hades and the purified and enlightened who dwell with the gods represents a contrast between those who seek the truth in the right manner and those who do not. The Orphic verse, "Many are the thyrsus bearers but few are the initiates," points to this notion of contrasting stages. When the soul has arrived at the invisible realm akin to itself, as a later passage says, it is "eudaemonic," and "as is said of the initiated, it dwells for the rest of its life with the gods" (ὥσπερ δὲ λέγεται κατὰ τῶν μεμυημένων, ὡς ἀληθῶς τὸν λοιπὸν χρόνον μετὰ θεῶν διάγουσα, 81A). Thus we may even recognize, in the "wandering, the folly, the horrors, the violent passions of love, and the rest of human suffering," elements of the states of initiation through all kinds of darkness and horror, which are part of the tradition about the mysteries.⁸ In the *Symposium* (209ε) Diotima distinguishes between the lower and the higher rites. The proclamation of *Eros* as the striving for immortality is the preliminary mystery (κἂν σὺ μυηθείης). The gradual ascent to the vision of the eternal forms is the completion of the rite, the elevation to the state of initiate (τὰ τέλεα καὶ ἐποπτικά). The *Phaedrus*, finally, envisages the cosmic destiny of the soul as a mystery rite. Prior to our earthly existence, we rejoiced "in the company of the blessed chorus, in the divine vision and spectacle, and were initiated into a mystery that may be truly called most blessed, celebrated by us in our state of innocence, before we had any experience of the evils to come, and when we were admitted to visions innocent, simple, calm, and blessed, which we beheld in the highest rite in purest light" (φάσματα μυούμενοί τε καὶ ἐποπτεύοντες ἐν αὐγῇ καθαρᾷ, 250c). He who has experienced this lives, during his earthly existence, as far as possible, in these memories and thus "initiated into perfect mystery he becomes truly perfect" (τελέους ἀεὶ τελετὰς τελούμενος, τέλεος ὄντως μόνος γίγνεται, 249c). Here Plato's words reflect the illumination in which the faithful rejoiced in the telesterion of Eleusis, and the firm hope of immortality they received from these mysteries. Viewed from this perspective— though only from it—Plato's theory of the eternal forms appears not as an individual experience, but as a sublimation in truly Hellenic spirit of the noblest form of piety of a people.⁹

Painful progressing in stages, from darkness to the beholding of the divine light—if we reconsider this picture imbued with the awe of the Eleusinian mysteries, must we not, to see Plato clearly, ask the question: Is Plato a mystic? The question is the more justified because, while all mysticism expresses a timeless striving of the human soul, the historical forms in which this eternal dimension has manifested itself in Christian, Islamic, and cabalistic mysticism were primarily influenced by Plotinos and thus, at least to a high degree, by Plato.¹⁰

Plato's "dialectical journey," his rise from the darkness of the cave to the light of the sun, the ascent of the soul's chariot to the realm beyond the heavens—all these elements have their equivalents in any form of mysticism. Dante's pilgrimage through the three realms is the highest poetic expression of this theme. But the same thing is envisaged in the *Itinerarium mentis ad Deum* of St. Bonaventura, which outlines "the ascent from the lowest to the highest, from the external to the inner-most, from the temporal to the eternal"; and in the "ladder to heaven" and the "stairway to perfection" found in the writings of mystic monks. Mystical pilgrimages are made in Protestant England as well as in the Islamic Orient. The Sufi is a voyager upon a road; he must pass through seven valleys or climb seven steps, from "remorse" to "union," each station bringing him closer to God. In India, the Buddha taught the "noble eightfold path." Beginning with right faith and ending with right con-templation, it leads to release from suffering. The religion of Vishnu also knows the "path of knowledge" and the "path of divine love" whose common goal is union with the godhead.[11]

Darkness and light, prison and freedom. To the Indian worshiper of Shiva, man is an animal enchained in matter. Only by breaking these chains can the soul get to Shiva.[12] For the Sufi the soul is imprisoned, separated by seventy thousand veils from the godhead from which it has sprung. "The body, you know, is a prison," says Goethe in the *Westöstlicher Diwan*, in the Sufi spirit. Above all, there is the broad stream of the "metaphysics of illumination" flowing through late antiquity and the Middle Ages; originating in a deep human impulse, it has several historical sources beside Plato's *Republic*, primarily the Fourth Gospel ("and the light shineth in darkness"), and the circle of Hellenistic mystery worship to which this "mys-tical" gospel belongs. Platonic elements are present in the Hermetic writings and in Philo, though Oriental sources must not be overlooked.[13] Running through Plotinos, Dionysius the Areopagite, and St. Augustine, this stream continues into the Middle Ages. Henry Suso "stares into the glorious reflected light"; Mechthild of Magdeburg sees the "flowing light of the godhead." Dante's point of departure is the "dark forest," his goal is "To fix upon the eternal light my gaze," and his union with the highest reality he describes thus: "That what I speak of is one simple flame." [14]

Like Plato's dialectical way, the path of the mystic begins

with a release and reversal, severance of the bonds with the sensual world, and turning of the soul to God. Again, the intellectual structure—though not the historical movement itself—comes from Plato. Following Plato, the Neoplatonists envisaged the soul's destiny as a "descent" from (πρόοδος), and an "ascent" to (ἄνοδος) God, adding the act of "turning" (ἐπιστροφή) between these two movements. Augustine combined the latter with the call of the new teaching, "change your minds," and with the turning around (ἐπιστροφή), which, in the New Testament, meant the "conversion" of the pagan to the true God, and which, as such, became part of the permanent structure of Western life and thought.[15] But even this experience is much more general; there is no mystical way of life whose beginning is not marked by such a radical turn. Often it is experienced as a sudden act: "As lightning flashes in the dark of night, so it comes to pass that by the grace of the Buddha man's thought of a sudden turns to the good." [16]

The Platonic path is accompanied by anguish. So is the path of the mystics, whether they chastise their bodies, struggle with their inner selves, or suffer because they relapse into remoteness from God. The tortures that Henry Suso inflicted upon his poor body belong in the same category as the greatest horrors depicted in Gothic sculpture. But the sufferings of the soul are even worse; and the struggle against the passions, which is the path to enlightenment, is described by the Persian al-Ghazali in words very similar to those used by the Silesian Jakob Böhme.[17] In India, finally, Yoga has been taught in books and practiced as a technique for thousands of years. Anguish is most moving when expressed almost silently. "*Mon Dieu, me quitterez-vous?*" writes Pascal when the light of his soul begins to fade. The *exilium cordis*, the dark night of the soul, spiritual dearth, are sufferings that invariably are part of the mystic's experience. The distinction that the methodology of mysticism has introduced between the suffering along the path and that at the goal is hardly essential; for the way is infinite, and there is another way—and hence more anguish—behind every goal.

After many troubles along the way the soul "suddenly" attains the desired goal. This part of Plato's exposition, again, has often been repeated elsewhere. "We must believe we have beheld [the truth] when the soul is suddenly seized by illumination," says Plotinos (V 3 17).[18] Ecstasy and illumination "often comes like a strong, swift impulse, before your thought can forewarn you of it," says St. Teresa in describing her experience.[19] "*En Dio stando rapido*," Thomas of Celano says in praise of his own. According to Shankara, the realization of one's own existence as Brahman comes with striking suddenness when he grasps the great words *tat tvam asi*. Only for him who is deprived of this experience is repeated thinking on and through the texts of the Veda the right path. Removed from all earthly things, the Sufi transports himself into a state in which the highest revelation strikes him like a flash of lightning.[20] A report about an ecstatic vision in modern days suggests a common human element in these experiences: "Suddenly, without any previous sign, I found myself wrapped in a fiery cloud."[21]

Mysticism is rarely without the primacy of the love of God. We encounter "love" in the most various forms, whether it is at the beginning of the *Confessions* of St. Augustine, in the last words of the *Paradiso*, or in the language of courtly love in Suso, Tauler, and Mechthild.[22] Spinoza's intellectual love of God—comprising the mind's love of God, God's love of man, and God's love of himself—is also mystical.[23] Outside the Western world, we find the love-drunken Sufis, who, in the "secret double script" of their love songs, in the allegories of nightingale and rose, butterfly and candle, at once veil and reveal the soul's desire for the highest reality. India, too, has the singer drunk with *bhakti*, the love of God, praising his deity as a "deceiver, thief, and great seducer. Like a magician he came and penetrated my heart and life."[24] The *Bhagavad-Gita* (XVIII, 55) sings:

The highest spirit is attained through love that seeks but Him;
Through love He knows me truly, who and how I am.

The highest good to which love elevates the seeker is, according to Plato, "not being, but beyond being." This paradoxical form of expression is another trait characteristic of mysticism in general. The Neoplatonists are constantly engaged in asserting that the highest One is beyond all form of predication, sometimes by echoing and enlarging upon the Platonic concept of the "beyond," [25] sometimes by heaping contradictory predicates upon the same One. To mention only one such statement: "The One has no being and all being—no being because being comes later; all being because it comes from the One" (Plotinos VI 7 32). The Christian Neoplatonist Dionysius the Areopagite, in an effort "to name the many names of the godhead, nameless and unreachable," expressed the same idea in an almost theoretical formulation: "With regard to God, we must assert and affirm all forms of being; for He is the cause of all—and, at the same time, negate the predications, for He is beyond all being. And we must not think that the negations contradict the affirmations; rather, that He is beyond negations—He from whom nothing can be taken away, or to whom nothing can be added." [26] This apophatic theology re-echoes in Eckhart's "It is His nature to be without nature," in Scotus Erigena's *Deus propter excellentiam non immerito nihil vocatur*," in Suso's "not-being," in Angelus Silesius' "God is a pure Nothingness," and likewise in the cabala's names for the unlimited.[27] But aside from this development Indian thinkers have, on their own, said strikingly similar things. In the *Upanishads* we find the same contradictory assertions: "The One moves and does not move; it is remote and near; it is within and beyond all things." We find the same abundance of negations: "The imperishable is neither crude nor fine, neither short nor long; it is without taste or smell, vision or hearing, speech or reason, without life or breath, without mouth or measure, without inside or outside. Consumed by nothing, it consumes nothing." And we know that it is the double negation, the "not-not," which, to many of the old Indian sages, most truly characterizes the nature of the Brahman.[28]

The structure of mystical consciousness, and especially of mystic thought, shows a great similarity with the structure of Plato's view of the world. This is due to the fact of Plato's historical influence upon many systems of mysticism on the one hand, and of common roots in both owing to a basic human

orientation on the other. We have now reached the point, however, where we must say that Plato, after all, is not a mystic,
and show how he differs from genuine mysticism.

Plato's highest idea does not extinguish being, but is, as it
were, within the chain of being; only it is so far above everything else that paradoxically it may be called *beyond* being,
though still beyond *being*. It is reached, not through lonely
introspection, violent leaps, and submergence in darkness, but
through a path by which knowledge grasps the nature of being.
Without arithmetic, geometry, astronomy, musical theory,
without the discipline of philosophical dialectics, the goal cannot
be approached—although, once in view, words and concepts are
no longer adequate. Mysticism, on the other hand, even when
it is most concerned with knowledge, remains within the realm
of theology, conscious, moreover, that the object of its quest
cannot be discovered through ratio, but only through a descent
"to a depth that is unfathomable." Usually it is even more
emphatic in its rejection of knowledge. The "gnosis" prevailing
in the Hermetic writings, to be sure, uses Platonic patches to
weave a glittering garb for its ecstasies; but we must not be
deceived. "To make oneself like God," "to become eternity"
(αἰὼν γενοῦ), "to consider oneself as immortal and capable of
knowing everything, all art, all science, the nature of all living
beings, to be everywhere and everything, to know everything
simultaneously, times, places, objects, qualities, quantities"—
this excited collection is symptomatic of a new spirit.[29] The same
spirit is apparent when, instead of the knowledge of everything,
the silence of knowledge is proclaimed. Thus, according to
Philo, to cite but one voice among many, the divine light dawns
only when human reason has perished and darkness, surrounding
man, produces ecstasy and God-inspired madness.[30] Nothing
could be more foreign to Plato than such ecstatic exaggeration,
using Platonic phrases, yet denying man's highest power. If
a step further is taken, the life of the mystic is subject to
the compulsion of magic: the Christian mystic's castigations; the
wild dance of the dervishes and the endless repetition of the
name Allah in Islam; and, in India, regulation of the breath,
rigid contemplation of the tip of the nose, the magic of the

sacred syllable *om*. There is a world of difference between these ritualistic acts and Plato's severe scientific attitude and discipline. Plato not only avoided any form of magic; from the point of view of mysticism, he must even be regarded as a rationalist. To him, no God made folly of this world's wisdom. He would not understand the contradiction so moving in Pascal's exclamation: *"Dieu d'Abraham, Dieu d'Isaac, Dieu de Jacob, non des philosophes et des savants!"* In Plato, both divine inspiration and mathematical science lead man upward—geometry leads to God. His world is one, unbroken in its dynamic tension.

Plato, comprehending all aspects of the intellectual world, also accepted all human powers: love of the senses, precise thinking, highest aspiration. To the mystic, whether in the Christian world, in Islam, or in India, the senses are to be destroyed. Only surreptitiously, as it were, borne upon the wings of the Song of Songs, or Sufi poetry, sensuality, often in distorted form, finds its way back into mysticism. Plato's work, to be sure, contains elements hostile to the senses. According to the *Phaedo*, to live is learning to die; pleasure and pain fasten the soul to the body; in order that one may become a true philosopher, the soul must free itself from the body. But the *Symposium* and the *Phaedrus* sound a different note. Bitter as may be the struggle with the beast of wild desire, there is no suggestion of an anxious choice between pleasure of the senses and peace of mind. Love of the senses and love of God are not in hostile opposition; rather, love of a beautiful body is a necessary stage in the ascent toward the highest form of being. Even if we grant that Plato left the contradiction between the *Phaedo* and the dialogues on love as it stands, and that his work already shows the thin crack that in later thinkers widens into a deep break, we must also recognize that Plato's world still holds all human powers together in a vast arc.

The mystical soul is lonely. Plotinos (I 6 7, VI 9 11) calls the soul's way to God "the flight of the One to the One," just as the Neopythagoreans had spoken of the community of the One with the One.[31] The same idea appears everywhere in mysticism. Seclusion is the greatest good for Eckhart; it is that by which we "come to know God"; that which "isolates the creature and unites it with God." While mysticism has known great spiritual leaders, and while, especially in Islam and in India, but also among the Greek monks, it has acknowledged discipleship with a wise man as a means of salvation, the act of mystic union must probably always be thought of as Plotinos described it.[32] But in this respect Plotinos is not a Platonist. According to Plato, "a fire is kindled in the soul, transmitted from one to the other as by a flying spark, after long-continued communion in joint pursuit of the object they are seeking to apprehend"; and while it would be presumptuous to say anything about how the soul achieves the *epekeina*, it is perfectly clear that affectionate communion with others engaged in the same quest is an indispensable condition for the dialectical path.

The dialectical path leads to the realm of pure forms or *Ideas*—and to that which is beyond all being. If it is called "the good," this term suggests the aspect of productive beauty, efficient order, and creative perfection. It is reached by passing even beyond the highest forms. As the highest principle in the realm of forms, and only as such, it is beyond all being. It is form so high that it may be said to be beyond all form. This is quite different from Eckhart's formless godhead, or from the colorless sea of the divine in Angelus Silesius, or, especially, from the utterly shapeless Brahman of the *Upanishads*. It is not easy to make the difference quite clear. We must note the different paths the soul takes in one system and the other as well as the form it attains in each. One of the *Upanishads* says: "Just as the flowing rivers disappear in the ocean casting off name and shape, even so the knower, freed from name and shape, attains to the divine person, higher than the high." [33] According to Jalal-ud-din Rumi: "O let me never be; for never-being proclaims with the voice of an organ: we come home to Him." [34] According to Eckhart: "All our perfection and blessedness consist in this—that man pass through and beyond all creatureliness, temporality, and essence and descend to a depth that is unfathomable." [35] European adherence to the principle of form and the Greek heritage have generally saved Western man from a complete obliteration of the self for which Eastern mystics have always longed. The Christian mystic has usually

retained his nature as man, though in a different form.³⁶ Still
for Eckhart and other mystics release (*Entwerden*), isolation,
and self-negation characterize the path of the soul to its fulfillment: eternal peace in God our Lord. Thus the mystic knows
only one movement: release from the here and now, in which
the man of classical antiquity finds his fulfillment. Although,
from a historical point of view, Plato initiated this escape
through his orientation toward the *epekeina*, and thus became
the source for many mystical systems, he still belongs so much
to the classical type of man that he must ultimately be seen in
contrast to mysticism. In conclusion, we may clarify this contrast
by comparing the final visions of Platonic and Plotinian speculation just as we previously contrasted the meaning of *Eros* in
Plato and Plotinos.

He who follows Diotima's guidance and "touches the goal"
(σχεδόν ἄν τι ἅπτοιτο τοῦ τέλους, *Symposium* 211B) beholds the
prototype of beauty (κατόψεται, 210E). The words "seeing"
and "viewing" are often repeated. The prototype is called an
object of learning (μάθημα, 211c). He who beholds the beautiful
finds his own life worth living (211D). He must then "produce
and nourish true virtue, and thus become beloved of the gods
and immortal in so far as this is possible to man" (212A). In
the *Phaedrus*, the perfect gods view the eternal forms in
invisible space; human souls, striving after them, attain the
same vision only with difficulty. This vision provides nourishment for the noblest part of the soul (ἡ προσήκουσα ψυχῆς
τῷ ἀρίστῳ νομή, 248B) and causes its wings to grow. The fate
of the soul depends on whether or not it catches a vision of the
truth (249D). The philosopher, in so far as it is in his power,
dwells upon these memories. He steps outside (ἐξιστάμενος)
human activities; and as he is in communion with the divine,
the mass of people, ignorant of his ecstasy (ἐνθουσιάζων, 249D),
considers him mad.

Throughout, there is a strict counterposing of soul and
eternal form. Enthusiasm and divine madness do not mean a
merging of the soul with something entirely different, but
simply an aloofness or withdrawal from what people ordinarily
call serious activities (ἀνθρώπινα σπουδάσματα). Plotinos puts

quite different experiences into the same systematic context. In his treatise *On Intelligible Beauty*, he repeats the image of the *Phaedrus*, describing the movement of the gods and souls toward a view of the eternal forms. But here the positing of beholder against object of vision begins to dissolve. "For everything bursts forth in a glow, filling those who have arrived so that they, too, grow beautiful, as oftentimes people who ascend great heights, steeped in the gleaming yellow color of the earth, grow to look like the soil upon which they stand." Here the radiation, the power emanating from the vision, is more strongly felt and expressed. The activity of the beholder ceases; he finds himself enveloped by that power. Moreover, he becomes "intoxicated and completely filled with the nectar." Separate existence has ceased. "For it is no longer the case that one person is outside and the other object outside. The beholder now has the vision within himself; but although he has it, he is usually not aware of it, looking upon it as if it were something external." "Everything seen as a visible object is seen as something external. But one must now absorb it within himself, seeing it as One and seeing it as himself; like a man who, seized by one of the gods, by Phoebus or by one of the Muses, could evoke the vision of God within himself, if he had the strength to see God within himself." Plotinos employs still another mode of expression to emphasize the unity of vision and beholder. "But when one of us, at first incapable of seeing himself, seized by the gods, gets hold of an object of vision, he beholds himself—a more beautiful image of himself. Then he lets go of the image, beautiful as it is, and becomes one within himself and no longer split; he is one and, at the same time, united with the God, who is silently present, and he is with Him as long as he can and will." The union or the cessation of separate existences is expressed in numerous variations. "Turning toward the inside, he has everything; and by renouncing perception of the past, for fear of being somebody else, he is one within himself." "One must give himself to what is within, and thus, instead of a beholder, become object of vision for somebody else." The activity of the beholder has thus become a state in which he, devoid of will, surrenders to the emanation, letting it seize and transform him. "As long as he sees it as something other, he is not yet within the beautiful; but when he becomes the beautiful, he is completely within it." Now that we have seen the strength of this union, let us turn back to Plato, who maintains the separation of the "I" and the "object" in strict counterposition to each other.

What Plotinos experienced in the presence of "the beautiful" is repeated, on the highest level, when he reaches "the good or the One" (VI 9). Repeatedly he asserts that the soul merges with a formless element (εἰς ἀνείδειον, §3); that the latter is even without the form accessible only to pure thought (ἄμορφον δ᾽ἐκεῖνο καὶ μορφῆς νοητῆς, §3); that it is formless in the sense of being prior to all form (ἀνείδεον πρὸ εἴδους ἅπαντος). Thus man also needs a special way of comprehending this special notion. "It is not grasped by knowledge or pure thought as are the other intelligible forms, but in a presence or immediacy that is beyond all knowledge." For this reason, the soul, too, must be of a special kind, akin to what it comprehends, that is, itself without form and shape. "As it is said of matter that it must be free of all concrete determination in order to receive impressions of everything, so—and even more so—must the soul be formless in order to be filled and illuminated, without hindrance, by the highest essence." Reaching this goal, the soul "beholds the other and itself according to the principle: illuminated, filled with the intelligible light, or rather itself pure light, weightless and light, it has become or is divine." The act of union—which can no longer be called an act of intuition—is consummated (ὡς ἂν μὴ ἑωραμένον ἀλλ᾽ ἡνωμένον, §11) when the soul has become as formless as the "One." Beholder and vision are no longer separate, but one. "Then the beholder neither sees nor distinguishes, nor does he imagine two beings; but he becomes another, and is not himself, not master of himself, but having become the property of the other, he is now One, uniting center with center, as it were." [37] And the process is called, "not intuition, but another way of seeing, an ecstasy, a simplification and surrender of oneself, a desire for contact, a standstill, and a turning toward union." [38]

In calling this highest One "the good," Plotinos follows Plato, whose interpreter he wants to be (VI 8). And the beyond, attributed by Socrates, in the *Republic*, to this highest good, is frequently re-echoed by Plotinos. "Beyond all being does not assert any definite predicate; for it does not posit or name anything, but merely expresses that it is not 'this' or 'that.'" Nevertheless, the difference between him and Plato is equally striking. The old form has been imbued with a different content. That the Highest must be without form or shape, that the soul must become formless in order to comprehend it—there is nothing like this in Plato. Socrates is silent on these points. But it is likely that Plato would have considered these statements as a weakening of his own thought, and that it would be more in keeping with his spirit to expand the paradoxical phrase "beyond all being" into something like "still beyond all form and shape." It never did or could enter the mind of Plato, a citizen of so form-conscious a world, to let the soul be dissolved in formlessness. Similarly, the ecstatic union of the soul with the Highest is not known to him either. To be sure, he is silent on this point, and Plotinos could interpret this silence in his own way. But just as Plato thought that the soul would form itself in imitation of one it loved and admired—in other words, just as the view of what is "well ordered and permanent in its being" must necessarily make the soul similar to the object of its vision, the *Idea* (*Republic* 500c)—so the soul must have a similar experience, only more intense, approaching that which is beyond all being. "To become God" is Plotinos' longing: "Our striving is not to be without flaw, but to be God" (I 2 6). Plato's object is to grow in the image of God, beloved of God, and, as far as possible, similar to God.[39] This is not merely a difference of words; on the contrary, Plato's dialectical path and Plotinos' *scala mystica*—wrongly taking its name from the former—sharply divide at this point. Plotinos says more about the goal than Plato; but he does not speak in Plato's name. Plato's path to the mystery leads through the realm of the eternal forms. How well structured the soul must be to retain its identity while intuiting the eternal forms to which it is akin! Since this is the path to the *Arrheton*, the highest stage cannot be reached through self-surrender. Face to face with it, the soul must not dissolve but still, though mysteriously, remain intact.[40] Thus we may hope to have clarified, by contrast with Plotinos, what is essential to Plato's thought—presumptuous as it may be to put into words what he himself left unsaid.

The Academy

WHETHER or not to found a school was not exactly a free decision on Plato's part. In Socrates he had met a personal force whose life combined thinking and teaching in so inseparable a unity that it would be meaningless to speak of a Socratic philosophy apart from the teaching of Socrates. Plato is a theoretical thinker quite different from his teacher. Instead of moments of deep absorption, the mysterious phenomenon in the life of Socrates, as Plato presents it, Plato himself must have experienced long periods of lonely thinking, research, contemplation, and writing. Yet he also absorbed the basic element of the Socratic life so completely that philosophy and teaching were again but two aspects of the same power emanating from a single center. Finally, if it was indeed his ultimate goal to renew the foundations of the state, how else could this be achieved except by teaching? Thus he has Socrates—both model and spokesman—say in the *Meno* (100A) that he alone is a truly political man, who can make another into such a political man. In a famous passage of the *Gorgias* (521D), Socrates paradoxically claims to be the only one who puts his hand to true statecraft; the only one, among the people of his time, who is active in the affairs of the state. This is spoken by the same Socrates who, in the *Apology*, defends his aloofness from the state by saying that "He who will truly fight for justice, if he would live even for a little while, must be a private, not a public, person" (32A). Education has become the true political function.

Socrates walks through the city and talks to people. By the

special nature of his conversation, he teaches all those willing to be taught. That he is eventually surrounded by a circle of disciples happens almost as if by a natural law. Plato founded his institution at a specific locality, provided for its external maintenance, and designated a temple of the Muses as its sacral center. Excavations in the area of the Academy during the last few decades have unearthed—besides the columned halls to be expected—an unexpected inscription dating back to the fifth century (i.e., older than Plato's foundation), containing names that recur in Socrates' circle and in Plato's family. The question, "What was Plato's Academy?" cannot be answered by any excavation.[1]

Whatever may have been the way in which the first followers gathered around Plato, a school of this type requires the conscious selection of qualified students. This is confirmed by the *Seventh Letter*, in which Plato speaks for himself and, accordingly, with reference to the Academy. After discussing the stages of knowledge upward to the eternal forms, he continues as follows (343E): "Guidance through these stages, all of which must be run through upward and downward, only after great toil produces knowledge of the well-constituted [object] in the well-constituted [individual]. People of poor constitution, however, and—partly by origin, partly by corruption—most people's souls are ill-suited for learning and that which we call character—people of such nature cannot be made to see the light even by a Lynkeus. In a word, the one who has no affinity with the subject cannot acquire it either by easy comprehension or by the power of memory; for the subject does not even take root in alien soil. Thus those not akin to nor belonging to justice or the other virtues, however talented in this or that field and however good their memory; or those who are akin to the subject but not talented, or wanting in memory—none of these can come to know the truth about the good (in so far as it can be known at all) or about evil." Easy comprehension, keen attention, combined with an "inclination" to "virtue" and an aversion to "lust and luxury"—these are also the things which Plato, in another passage of the same letter (327A *et seq.*), praises in the young Dion, an impression of the first journey to Sicily, made shortly before the founding of the Academy. Similar intellectual and moral criteria determine the choice of those qualified to become philosopher-kings in the utopia of the *Republic*. "One must first learn their nature" (485A).[2] And how must they be constituted? Gifted with good memory and a talent for knowledge, high-minded, harmonious, and graceful (ἔμμετρος καὶ εὔχαρις), congenial and akin to truth, justice, valor, and temperance (487A). These criteria, stated in the words of Socrates, coincide with those set forth by Plato himself in the *Letter*. Thus it is likely that much of what is said in the *Republic* about the progressive stages of education was at least initiated, if not fully accomplished, in the Academy.

Does this mean that the dialogues reflect life in the Academy? They are not meant to do so; for they portray the world of Socrates. In particular, the school itself can hardly have afforded an example of the collision between Socrates and the intellectual forces hostile to him, which is presented in the dialogues. Yet, again, it is hardly likely that there should be no functional relationship between Plato's literary activity and his teaching, and this perhaps in a threefold sense: his dialogues reflected life in the Academy; they, in turn, penetrated this life with their light; and finally, the Academy was the place where Plato's works were "published" and preserved.[3]

The attempts to penetrate from these general considerations to something more concrete have resulted in altogether different interpretations. Those who were inspired by the *Symposium* saw the Academy as a festive society governed by divine madness and singing hymns to Eros or discussing the nature of love. It was in this spirit that the Florentines attempted to resurrect it. But suppose we look at the *Phaedo*: the Academy becomes a religious sect of salvation around the figure of the executed savior. Professors are apt to confuse it with a university seminar, and members of "academic" societies involuntarily think of it in terms of the organized sciences of today. The most noteworthy recent attempt at interpretation sees it in an altogether different light: as a school almost exclusively concerned with mathematics, Plato affiliated with it and engaged in writing philosophical dialogues. One thing is clear from these contradictory interpretations: we do not grasp the whole if we generalize from a partial view. And another thing is clear: it is necessary to distinguish, more sharply than is often done, between the Academy as an institution and as a sphere of intellectual endeavor; the former is much less important than the latter, and, fortunately, we know more about the latter than about the former.[4]

To begin with, we may ascribe to Plato's Academy only the elements common to all his writings: first, ceaseless critical conversation and inquiry with a view to knowledge and the "good life"; next, something that, like an invisible magnet, gives a definite direction to all the dialogues: they are constructed around the *Idea;* they aim at the *Idea.* One may still doubt whether Plato had already reached this goal when he wrote his early dialogues. And yet, all of them, ever more distinctly, point to that center around which the works of his mature period revolve at a greater or smaller distance. As the *Idea,* by implication or explicitly, is the center of gravity in all of Plato's works, so it is, in every sense of the word, the center of Plato's *Republic. Idea* and state are inseparable; the state surrounds the *Idea* as the protective skin covers core and seed. Thus we get a general impression of the basic structure of Plato's written work to use as a clue to the Academy. The Academy, too, was a community animated by dialogical movement. The Academy, too, revolved around the *Eidos.* Whether little or much was said about the *Eidos,* everything said or written derived its ultimate meaning from it. Finally, in a way more fully discussed below, the Academy was oriented toward the state, although, or precisely because, it was removed from contemporary Athenian politics. This could not be otherwise, if we keep in mind that the realm of *Ideas* was discovered by Plato in his quest of the true state, and that he founded the Academy when he felt he was compelled to renounce participation in the political affairs of his time.

Consider the *Symposium* and the *Phaedo:* it is again their basic theme rather than their "atmosphere"—and the modern reader is inclined to see even the atmosphere in too sharp a contrast—that we should apply to the Academy. The *Phaedo*

celebrates the memory of the dying Socrates. This must have
been celebrated by the Academy, too. But, more important, the
Phaedo teaches that living is learning how to die. This does not
mean a surrender to death from a yearning for salvation; rather,
it means a way of life with the *Idea* in view, and in such a way
that the knowledge of death becomes a law for one's life; and
that in spite of this, or because of it, physical death has no significance for this life—let alone putting an end to it. The
Symposium speaks of love and feasting. And, just as hardly anything was taken more seriously in the city of Athens than
festive play, so the feast was part of the fullness of life in the
Academy. Even Aristotle's school still invoked, for its own
banquets, the tradition of "Plato and Speusippos." [5] Still more
important is the inner movement, the "ascent" from sensual to
eternal beauty, to the *Idea*. All else contained in the two works
with regard to the conflict and tension between affirmation and
negation of life must be projected into the Academy.[6] For no
certainly as the "beyond" is the soul's home, and the ascent its
appropriate movement, so—as the *Timaeus* shows—is this
world, in its order, proof of the creator's goodness, and full of
the copies of pure being. Thus only the full cycle—ascent and
descent in an eternal chain—describes the whole of reality. Or,
according to the *Republic*, he who has passed through the highest
stages of instruction is compelled to return to this world in
order to be active in it (539E). The strong emphasis placed on
the word "compulsion" indicates how difficult, but also how
indispensable, it was to achieve this balance. In order to do
justice to the fullness of life comprised by the Academy, therefore, both forces of the Platonic cosmos—affirmative and
negative—must be envisaged in a state of equilibrium.

The dialogues may prompt us to ask whether the life of the
Academy centered more around the living master or around the
image of Socrates. But this question need not be decided definitely, since it will be shown how completely Plato had absorbed
the living force of Socrates.[7] "Let me tell you that none of you
knows Socrates; but I shall reveal him to you." These are the
words of Plato's Alkibiades (*Symposium* 216C); [8] but, in like
manner, the Academy saw Socrates only through Plato, who

constantly reinterpreted him and thus kept him alive. That the
Academy was a community of teachers and disciples united by
Eros is apparent throughout all the dialogues, from the earliest
to the *Phaedrus*. For while one must be careful in ascribing
details of the dialogues to the Academy, it is inconceivable that
it was devoid of the moving power of the great demon. Indeed,
the Academy is a historically unique embodiment of *Eros*.

By transforming the creative powers experienced in his life
with Socrates, Plato produced an institution that, while Socratic
in origin, rather resembled the Pythagorean order. In southern
Italy, Plato came in contact with a community bearing Pythagoras' name. In the *Republic* (600AB), he praises Pythagoras as
the "leader of education" (ἡγεμὼν παιδείας), the beloved and
admired head of a host of disciples, and the founder of what later
followers called the Pythagorean way of life (Πυθαγόρειος τρόπος
τοῦ βίου). Comparing the Pythagorean and the Platonic schools,
we see the master as the center of each, surrounded by a circle of
disciples who regard him with a veneration approaching apoth-
eosis. In both institutions, the object of communal teaching and
learning is an intellectual unity comprising religion and knowledge, ethics and politics. Both institutions are completely
different from the schools of the Sophists. They are organic
creations, not technical organizations. In them the spirit, which
the Sophists sell as a commodity, is the master's free gift, and
the material needs of the community are supplied by voluntary
contributions. Unlike the courses of the itinerant teachers, who
pitch their tents now here now there, they are permanent in
time and fixed in a definite location.

The Platonic community, nevertheless, differs from the Pythagorean—which it resembled most closely—in that it was
permeated by the spirit of Socrates. As Plutarch nicely put it—
paraphrasing a self-characterization of the Platonic Socrates—
"Socrates, by his simplicity and lack of pretense, did most to
humanize philosophy." [9] For those who followed him, mysterious symbols and customs, or asceticism in dress and food,
could be but bonds with darkness and the realm of superstition,
unrelated to true being. The Pythagorean mysteries appear
deliberate and enforced by prohibitions of silence; whereas

Plato's mystery necessarily results from the view that the highest knowledge "cannot be expressed like other sciences, but, out of long communion in joint pursuit of the object, just as light flashes forth when a fire is kindled, this knowledge is suddenly born in the soul and henceforth nourishes itself" (*Letter VII* 341c). But the most basic difference, perhaps, is this: for the Pythagoreans, it is always an *ipse dixit* that decides every question; the Socratic heritage in the Platonic school, on the other hand, is the birth of philosophy in conversation between teacher and disciple, as both of them, engaged in a common quest, ascend, through the path of dialectics, to the *Ideas* and to what is "beyond."

So much for the general features, which must have remained constant. In detail, much, if not everything, must have changed in the four decades that Plato was the head of the Academy. The young men who first gathered around the beloved master grew into manhood. Those who leave the school, such as Euphraios going to Macedonia, and Koriskos and Erastos to Assos, take a part of the Academy with them, thus spreading Plato's influence afar. Others remain permanent dwellers in the grove of Academe, and become teachers of other disciples in a system perhaps not unlike, though less rigid than, the hierarchy of "youths" (νεανίσκοι), "elders" (πρεσβύτεροι), and "the ruler" (ἄρχων) among the Peripatetics.[10] Aristotle was for twenty years a member of the Academy. Can one possibly imagine him silently listening in secret opposition and writing Platonizing dialogues? Herakleides Pontikos, the well-known astronomer, statesman, and versatile writer, is known as a disciple of Plato and Speusippos.[11] A princely figure such as Dion associates himself with the Academy in Athens; an astronomer of the stature of Helikon joins it, or a number of mathematicians, including disciples of Eudoxos; Eudoxos himself is referred to as a companion of the Platonic circle—the original relation between master and disciple has lost its simple form, and a complex system of human and intellectual relationships has taken its place. This change, perhaps, is also reflected in the dialogues. When Timaios presents his philosophy of nature, or Hermokrates wants to talk about politics, or Kritias begins to tell his fable of the state, or the "stranger from Elea" engages in long dialectical exercises with the young people introduced to him, Socrates, though present, participates only occasionally. To be sure, he is present, and everything that is said has its ultimate meaning in relation to the Socratic existence and the *Idea*. Similarly, Plato may often have been silent when (let us suppose) Eudoxos lectured on the theory of irrational numbers or on the orbits of the planets. Yet, though silent, he still influenced the lecture that perhaps received its ultimate meaning through the fact that it was delivered, not at the planetarium at Kyzikos, but at the Academy in Athens.

If any details of the dialogues may be assigned to the Academy, it is the instruction of the guardians in the *Republic*. To be sure, this instruction in arithmetic, geometry, stereometry, astronomy, and harmony is set forth as a requirement for the ideal state; and the mere fact that stereometry, which did not yet exist, was included in the plan shows that, again, we must not generalize too much. Nevertheless, the education of the guardians cannot differ significantly from that of the students at the Academy, especially if the Academy, as was said before and will be made more explicit below, had political significance. At least, geometry is always mentioned whenever academic instruction is discussed—even if we may safely disregard the story of the inscription on the Academy's gate, which allegedly barred entrance to all those "not trained in geometry." [12] The first demand Plato made on the young Dionysios was that he occupy himself with geometry, and soon after Plato's arrival—as a satirical report goes—the same rooms in the king's palace that had but recently resounded with the joyous noise of feasting were covered with dust in which geometrical figures were drawn. The members of the opposition party jeered: a single Sophist had so completely prevailed over Dionysios as to make him surrender all of his sovereign power in order "to seek the hidden good in the circle of the Academy, and to attain perfection by way of geometry" (ἐν Ἀκαδημείᾳ τὸ σιωπώμενον ἀγαθὸν ζητεῖν καὶ διὰ γεωμετρίας εὐδαίμονα γενέσθαι).[12a] In much the same manner Plato's disciple Euphraios transplanted the study of geometry to the court of Perdikkas III of Macedon and, according to a report hostile to Plato, "regulated court society in such bad taste that only those who knew geometry or philosophy were admitted to the king's table."

The *Republic* has sometimes been read as if Plato, in the mathematical sciences, was concerned only with number speculation, that is, with the a priori knowledge of absolute relations and congruences between numbers.[13] This view is certainly correct in so far as he was unwilling to confine himself to the astronomy and harmony of the "so-called Pythagoreans" because they seemed to him to be limited to the realm of empirical facts (*Republic* 531c). A general tendency is perhaps indicated by his curious playing with numbers—play and seriousness are twins—such as the calculations of the "wedding number" and the "computation of pleasure and pain" in the *Republic*, by the construction of the world soul according to the principles of harmony in the *Timaeus*, or by the efforts of Speusippos and Philippos of Opus, disciples of his old age.[14] On the other hand, one must not forget that his disciple Theaitetos discovered the stereometry Plato had asked for; and that the founder of mathematical astronomy, the great Eudoxos, with his system of homocentric spheres, provided an answer to the question Plato had put to the astronomers: What homogeneous movements must be assumed to "save the phenomena," that is, the apparent motion of the planets? [15] The contradiction is resolved when it is taken into account that, for the Greeks, number and geometrical figure probably always retained an element of beauty and magic that elevated them above colorless abstraction. Moreover, while Plato always pursued, and encouraged others to pursue, mathematical sciences with the greatest energy, it is equally important to recognize that for him their meaning transcended the nature of an individual scientific discipline and led to the *Idea*. Otherwise, his teaching would have been just another collection of learning; for Hippias, the Sophist, had already given instruction in "rhetoric, astronomy, geometry, and music." [16] Instead, the element peculiar to Plato is this: the sciences elevate the soul to truth, are directed toward knowledge of eternal being (527B), purify the instrument of the soul (527D), and serve the quest for the beautiful and the good (531c). From this point of view, the sciences cannot develop into independent special disciplines as they do in our age. Inquiry into a single science for its own sake and pushed too far is always "ridiculous" (531A). The opposite view, however, that the Academy was occupied only with abstruse speculations, is also contrary to the facts. A much more correct approach to an understanding of the hierarchical structure of research and teaching in the Academy is to visualize the pursuit of mathematics, astronomy, and harmony with a passion motivated, as well as controlled, not by the impetus of the individual problems and their systems, but rather by the ultimate goal transcending them.

Even the Platonic dialogues, though not designed to reflect research and teaching in the Academy, reveal nonetheless how Plato gradually extended his domain to regions that he had not considered in the beginning. Again and again, the same questions arise concerning the structure and meaning of this intellectual cosmos. Well known is the delightful scene from a comedy by Epikrates: Plato's disciples, engrossed in deep study classifying animals, trees, and lettuces, and attempting to define the genus of the pumpkin. Plato is present; and without permitting an unseemly interruption to disturb his majestic calm, he exhorts them to renew their efforts at classification: "And so they continued to classify." According to Usener, the historical fact visible behind the slight distortion by the poet was a preparation for Aristotelian empiricism; seeing biology as combined with the other sciences, especially mathematics, he referred to an "organization of scientific disciplines" in the Academy. Epikrates, however, seems to suggest that instead of a broad and liberal empiricism, the goal was rather conceptual "definition" and "classification," perhaps recalling the *furor dichotomicus* of the late dialogues, on the one hand, and Speusippos' work *Resemblances* ('Ομοιότητες, ῎Ομοια), on the other. Moreover, the rather obscene comment made by a visiting physician from Sicily in response to the "chatter" of these boys seems also to be in a certain contrast to the pursuit of empirical research. Thus one is rather inclined today to credit Plato with "little interest in empirical natural science," and to reject Usener's interpretation as confusing the Academy with contemporary "academic societies," or as confusing Plato with Aristotle.[17] On the other hand, there is no doubt, according to Jaeger, "that a wide range of material was investigated and discussed in the school of the old Plato, and that Aristotle could acquire, in this environment, an appreciation for the significance of particular facts subsequently so essential to his method of research." While the "classification of plants" was, perhaps, "undertaken without the thought of a positive science of botany in mind," the latter came about, as it were, incidentally; for in order to classify, "animals, trees, and lettuces" had to be carefully studied in the Academy. Indeed, even the few meager but characteristic fragments of Speusippos suggest that a good deal of the systematic classification of animals and plants accepted since had its origin in the Academy.[18] The term "species" in biology—the Latin version of the Greek *Eidos*—suggests in symbolic form, first, that we owe to Plato the principle of classification still prevailing, and second, that this principle of classification was discovered not out of passion for the abundance of particular facts, but because its creator envisaged the eternal forms and their structure high above physical reality.

Unlike Demokritos and Aristotle, Plato included the principles of physics in the mathematical sciences. To be sure, the fact that the *Timaeus* describes the strictly stereometrically-formed bodies of the four elements, their structure, destruction, and reconstruction, would not prove anything for the Academy, considering the half-mythical poetic quality of the book. But there is additional evidence on this point. Aristotle quotes a work, which he calls *Plato's Classifications*, in connection with a theory of three elements. Xenokrates, who must have known, ascribed to Plato a theory of five elements, just as he, Philippos of Opus, Speusippos, and Aristotle agreed upon five elements. Plato was probably reluctant to be dogmatic concerning these basic physical principles. But the various sources suggest that lively discussions about the foundations of physics and cosmology took place in his circle.[19]

Still another field should be mentioned here in order to complete the basic plan of research in the Academy and to clarify its internal structure: spherical geography.[20] The myth in the *Phaedo* presents, as the scene for the mystical events, what may be called an exact model of a spherical earth, just as the myth of the *Republic* provides an exactly constructed model of the cosmos. The sphere of the earth is very large as compared with the inhabited world. For the latter occupies so small a space upon the large sphere that we dwell around the central sea "like frogs or ants around a puddle." Our inhabited world is not situated upon the surface of the sphere, but in one of the many hollows cut in that surface. Ours, however, is the only one we know, and the only one we can know; for only the hollows are filled with the kind of air in which we breathe, whereas the actual surface of the sphere reaches into the pure ether. This constitutes an early, probably the first, attempt to transpose on to the Pythagorean sphere the picture of our world as drawn by Anaximander and subsequently—in an almost paradigmatic alternation of construction and experience—by a number of scientists, e.g., Hekataios, Herodotos, and Demokritos. Not only are where and how we live depicted graphically, but a system of subterranean passages and chambers serves to demonstrate a highly detailed theory of geophysical processes. One may assume that it was in the circle of Archytas that Plato encountered such views.

Perhaps these views were still not very significant to the work of the Academy—although we should recall that in Aristophanes' *Clouds* (200 *et seq.*) the study of the Sophist Socrates is already shown as equipped with a globe of the heavens and a map of the earth, and that the testament of Theophrastus (Diogenes Laërtius V 51) refers to the "boards with the maps" in a hall of the Lyceum.[21] But there is a second description of the earth in Plato's works, at the beginning of the *Timaeus*, tracing the spatial dimensions for the legend of Atlantis in the *Critias*. Again, our world forms an immeasurably small part of the huge sphere. The hollows, however, no longer exist, and the walls that formerly separated our living space from numerous other indentations are thus eliminated. Our inhabited world is now one of several islands, of which the submerged Atlantis was another. All are surrounded by the "true ocean," which, in turn, is ringed by the "true continent." If there were no empirical difficulties to prevent us from advancing from our world-island to others or to the true continent, there would be no insuperable physical or, one might almost say, metaphysical barriers to the journey. Now the surface of the spherical earth has become a unit, open to exploration.

Plato's work, thus, does not present two separate, unconnected myths, but two strictly scientific constructions of the earth in historical continuity. We do not know whether Plato himself or somebody else made the transition from the first to the second version; but even if both originated outside the Academy, they would still confirm Plato's keen interest, over a period of decades, in the problems of spherical geography.

In this case, too, it is evident that, at least at the beginning, Plato was not motivated by observation of physical reality for its own sake. In the myth of the *Phaedo*, the picture of the earth with its indentations, particularly the hollow of our own *oikoumene*, is merely an appropriate place for the destiny of the human soul. The metaphysical dualism between the realm of *Ideas* and the world of appearances is brought down to earth and mirrored in the different values assigned to the "true earth," the actual surface of the globe, gleaming in the brightest colors and composed of the most precious materials, and our own *oikoumene*, which, set deeply into this plane, is a reflection of the splendor above. We human beings dwell below without suspecting that what we see above us is not the true sky, but that we view the ether only through the opaque medium of our atmosphere. Eventually, the supreme judge will decide whether our soul must spend its future in the interior of the earth or may ascend to its true surface in the pure ether.

In this manner, Plato combined his work in the natural sciences with his mythical-metaphysical constructions. Even decades later, the second construction of the spherical earth preserved, in the distinction between "true ocean" and "true continent" as against "our" ocean and "our" continent, the old—though attenuated—contrast between *Idea* and appearance. This is characteristic of Plato's shifting from philosophical speculation to work in the special sciences, on the one hand, and his subordination of the special sciences to metaphysics, on the other. Only if we appreciate the interaction of these two factors will we be able to see Plato's work in the proper perspective.

Thus we may here and there lay hold of a fragment of the research carried on in the Academy without grasping the whole, least of all in its historic change. This would be most unsatisfactory, were it not for the fact that every fragment suggests the structure of the whole. But although we must forgo an accurate description of the Academy's complete system of research, this element of uncertainty is perhaps not too important in the end. The significant thing is not the Academy as an institution, but as a way of life. As such, *one* task was paramount and unchanging: regardless of the methods or order of instruction, all the separate subjects and special sciences had to be "brought together, in a comprehensive view, in their connections with one another and with the nature of true being. For this is the only kind of knowledge that takes firm root in the mind; and the capacity for it is the most valid criterion of a talent for dialectics, which is the same thing as the ability to see the connection of things" (*Republic* 537c).

Plato did not appeal to the intellect alone, however much he insisted upon its training. He was concerned with man as a whole—though distinguishing more clearly than was customary in his age between what was eternal and what was transitory, and thus determining the proper rank of "body" and "soul." We no longer see the generation he trained and, therefore, fail to see the most immediate effects produced by the Academy. And yet, just as in Xenophon's *Memorabilia* the Socratic turning toward the life within is reflected in conversations with the painter Parrhasios and a sculptor named Kleiton, whom Socrates teaches how to express emotions in the human figure, so the Platonic penetration of mania and dialectic, of pathos and irony, the new tension between this world and the world beyond, must have found expression in the works of the plastic arts. And perhaps this question is justified: What is the Platonic element in an Apollo, Eros, or Hermes by Skopas or Praxiteles? [22]

In the surface reactions, as it were, or in the gossip of citizens as caught by contemporary comedy, one gets a picture of the disciples of Plato.[23] They dressed and carried themselves better than the crowd; they talked and moved with a certain solemnity. At the same time, it could not be denied that they were precise in expression (εὔστοχος) and capable of well-reasoned thought (οὐκ ἄσκεπτα δυνάμενος λέγειν). If someone attracted attention by

> *A cloak of white, the grace of line, gray garments elegant and fine,*
> *Soft cap and shapely cane,*

"they thought they beheld the whole Academy." Or "one of those from the Academy, a disciple of Plato's," rose in the people's assembly:

> *He wore his hair trimmed by the knife—so fine*
> *And did not tamper with the fullness of his beard—so fine*
> *His foot enclosed by shoes whose laces—so fine—*
> *He'd tied most evenly around his legs,*
> *And by the richness of his cloak well-fortified,*
> *His stately figure leaning on a cane,*
> *Not in the home town's manner, but in foreign style*
> *He began to speak: Oh men of the Athenian land.*

The majority of the citizens, of course, perceived only these outward characteristics. They saw Plato's posture, a slight stoop, which some of his disciples liked to imitate, or that he paced the floor in meditation, and a comedy character exclaimed:

> *Oh, Plato, all you know is how to frown*
> *And solemnly raise your eyebrows like a snail.*

Just as the people did not suspect what took place behind this forehead, so they could not know that the man they saw walking in a finer cloak and in shoes more gracefully laced was, perhaps, a new type of man, educated in Plato's *Arete*.

This presentation of Plato's doctrine and the Platonic way of life is still open to a final misunderstanding. For it may still be thought that the Academy presented an escape from reality, a cult of the *Idea* accompanied by a rejection of life, a purely "theoretical" attitude, and that Plato's disciples were educated for no purpose other than self-centered perfection. This, however, cannot be true if there is any validity in what was said before: namely, that the Academy had a practical meaning, that its objective was the state, not the world of the *Ideas* only.

Plato discovered the realm of *Ideas* in search of the true state. For him *Eidos* and *Polis*, the highest theoretical and practical goal, were inextricably linked. So it appears from the community of philosophers in the *Republic*, which, despite all poetic license, is still the most faithful reflection of the Academy. This inmost circle, the ruling center of the entire structure of the state, has been led upward to the view of the *Idea*. But however firmly the philosopher is oriented toward the *Idea*, he must be compelled to turn downward again so that his vision may be incorporated in the state. The Academy, the empirical model—or, in Platonic terms, the copy—of this ideal circle, pursues the same type of instruction, that is, the dialectical path, the same orientation in the view upward to the *Idea*; but it lacks a real state for its completion. Thus the return to the area of practical action can only be found in its incipient states, as it were, not in its fulfillment. If the relationship between the Academy and the guardians has been correctly interpreted, it was necessity rather than intention which caused the Academy to remain aloof from Athenian politics, the same necessity which had convinced its master, according to his own report, that it was impossible to participate in political action. But just as Plato "always waited for the right moment for action," until he finally realized that only a philosophical ruler or a ruling philosopher could provide the solution,[24] so the Academy, too, we must conclude, was oriented in a political sense and waited, as it were, for the moment when it could become the center of an ideal state that had become a reality.

Plato's written work confirms this hypothesis; for although the relationship between his works and the structure of the Academy may have been loose and very general, the predominant place occupied by the *Republic*, the *Statesman*, and the *Laws* within Plato's written work makes it impossible to think of the Academy as a place of seclusion from politics like the Garden of Epicurus. Since the day when the concept of the philosopher-king appeared to him as an intellectual vision, Plato, ever oriented toward the world of being, never lost sight of the ideal state. In his major work, he constructs it in detail, showing alternative systems of government as varying degrees of failure. In the *Statesman*, it is placed even further within the realm of the transcendental, in contrast to all other forms of state, as the unique prototype, of which the empirical historical constitutions are nothing but more or less (mostly less) perfect imitations (μιμήματα). In the *Laws*, finally, it still appears as a vision on the distant horizon, appropriate "for gods and the sons of gods," while a state of a lesser order is constructed before our eyes. If the Academy was a necessary emanation from Plato's central idea, it, too, must have kept the state in view at all times. This is confirmed by Aristotle; in the earliest parts of his *Politics*, where he still speaks as a member of the Academy, his view, too, aims at the "best state." [25]

At the same time, Plato did not miss any opportunity to gather experience in Athens and a knowledge of the other states of his time. This is revealed by his autobiographical sketch in the *Seventh Letter*, and confirmed by his works on politics, especially by the *Laws*, which contain detailed studies of the constitutions of Crete and Sparta, more from the synoptic view of philosophy, however, than from that of constitutional law. Forms of education are studied along with forms of communal life and government. A history of Doric constitutions—prepared in order to contrast forms of government that survived with those that perished and to study the causes of perishing—is followed by an analysis of the constitution of Sparta, whose stability is ascribed to the beneficial mixture of its elements (691D *et seq.*), an analysis that influenced Polybios and Cicero. When we learn elsewhere in the *Laws* that in Tarentum the entire town got drunk during the feast of Dionysos (637B), that the Locrians, who had had the best laws among the states of southern Italy, nevertheless were conquered by the Syracusans (638B), such remarks strike us as derived from observations made during Plato's journey to Sicily. Egypt is praised as exemplary because for a period of "thousands of years" its plastic art and music did not change, and the words "if you look, you shall find" again suggest that these were travel observations (656DE). The decline of Persia's hegemony is described and explained (695A *et seq.*); but occasionally Plato also gives us a glimpse of the customs of primitive peoples: the drinking customs of the Scythians, Carthaginians, Celts, Iberians, and Thracians (637DE), the position of women among the Thracians and Sarmatians (805D, 806B). Homer is called upon as a witness for the early stages of human civilization (680B, 681E). Not to mention explicitly the extensive knowledge of Athenian legislation required for a construction of the state in the *Laws*— including such details as regulations concerning private gardens and the use of public waters—it is perfectly evident what a wealth of experience served as the basis of Plato's theories.[26] To be sure, this was not the kind of empiricism which motivated Aristotle to collect, in his great work, the *Constitutions*, all available constitutional material of the ancient world; but there can be no doubt about the lively attention to empirical facts, always subordinated, however, to the view of the "best state." It is inconceivable that both of these elements should not have been present in the Academy.

While all these observations and reflections might still be considered "theoretical," the historical evidence leaves no doubt that Plato and his Academy were definitely regarded as a political power and exercised political influence.[27] The Cyrenaeans called Plato to serve as their legislator, but he declined. Nor did he accept the call to Megalopolis, but sent Aristonymos instead; and to Elis he dispatched his "companion" Phormion, who modified the extreme oligarchical constitution of its legislative council. In the middle of the sixties, King Perdikkas of Macedon asked Plato for a counselor. Plato sent Euphraios, who exhorted the court society to "study geometry and philosophize," and prevailed upon Perdikkas to place a special section of the country under the administration of the young Philip. After Philip had risen to power, Speusippos reminded him that he owed the origin of his rule to Plato.[28] We are even better informed about Koriskos and Erastos, disciples of Plato's who moved to Assos in Aeolia (Asia Minor), establishing close connections with Hermias, ruler of Atarneus. There is a letter revealing Plato's role as the adviser of this union; and we know that, influenced by Plato and his disciples, Hermias changed the tyranny into a milder and more lawful form of government.[29] This development, as well as the reform of Phormion, are instances in which Plato's concepts of rulership found concrete expression in contemporary states; and the political success of Hermias suggests that there is little justification for the patronizing air of those who, interpreting "political" in the modern, narrow sense of the word, regard Plato as an "ivory-tower ideologist."

Some of the rebels against tyranny, such as Chion of Herakleia or the assassins of Kotys, tyrant of the Odrysai, were known as members of the Academy. But contemporary hostile criticism also held Plato responsible for totalitarian revolutions in democratically governed cities because he was the teacher of Euaion of Lampsakos, Timolaos of Kyzikos, and Chairon of Pallene. The maliciously distorted account according to which Chairon committed his atrocities, "with the aid of the beautiful *Republic* and the unlawful *Laws* (ὠφεληθεὶς ἐκ τῆς καλῆς Πολιτείας καὶ τῶν παρανόμων Νόμων, Athenaeus XI 509β), shows more clearly than anything else what was credited to the Academy. The Academy also produced the Athenian statesman Phokion; and while we may doubt that he owed to it his sober estimate of Athenian capabilities for power and his faith in Macedonia's rising star, we know that he concealed his pusillanimity in his dealings with Cassander behind misinterpretation of the doctrine stated in Plato's first great ethico-political dialogue: that it is better to suffer than to commit injustice [30] (*Gorgias* 469c, 473a).

The most substantial argument may be presented last: the Academy's support of Dion in his military campaign against Dionysios. Plutarch's account of this event certainly does not convey the impression that a society of scholars, hitherto completely engrossed in their studies, suddenly awoke to activities of an entirely different nature; but rather, that their thinking and planning concerning the state found its legitimate fulfillment in this campaign. It is obvious how impossible such an undertaking would have been for the Garden of Epicurus.

Thus, the present survey must finally deal with Plato's own activity in the practical politics of Sicily, inasmuch as it throws the most revealing light upon the Academy. The actors in this moving drama, besides Plato, are the younger Dionysios, a gifted but vain and unstable ruler; Dion, united with Plato by the bonds of a passionate friendship, aspiring to the highest goal without being quite equal to it, and suffering guilt and defeat because he became involved in the evils of this world; his antagonist, the treacherous demagogue Herakleides, now acquiescent, now rebellious, depending upon the changing fortunes of Dion; Kallippos, the Judas of the circle; and other characters, more distant and less sharply outlined—the drama itself may be considered as known from Plato's own letters as well as from the detailed accounts by historians.[31] The judgment of these events is still almost unanimous: this is the great historical example of destructive and irresponsible transgression by a man of theory into the world of action.[32]

Now we know that Plato was anything but a "theoretical man" in Aristotle's sense, let alone in the modern sense of the word. His participation in political affairs, therefore, cannot be a trespassing into an entirely alien field. Rather, he finally perceived that opportunity for which he had never ceased to look, as he himself says in the *Seventh Letter*. Thus, considering Plato's life as a whole, the enterprise appears as the consequence of an innate and, for a scion of Solon's family, most legitimate impulse toward political action.

What Plato experienced was by no means the tragic defeat of his boldest plans. He had had great misgivings about his second journey to Sicily, still greater about his third. Why should one doubt his own testimony? He describes in detail how Dion urged him to come to Syracuse after the accession to power of the younger Dionysios: the young ruler and his youthful relatives might be easily won over to the Platonic ideal; now the hope of a union of philosophy and rulership in one man might be fulfilled. "My mind, however," Plato continues (*Letter VII* 328b), "was assailed by fear when I thought of these young people and what would become of them; for the impulses of such young men are quick and often contradictory. Dion's character, on the other hand—and this I knew—had natural stability; besides, he was more mature in years. As I

was deliberating whether I should undertake the journey, or
what, the final decision, after all, was this: if ever an attempt
were to be made to put into practice one's ideas about laws and
constitutions, this would be the time to do it. For if I were to
win over one man alone, I would have set everything to rights.
In this spirit, and aware of the risk, I left home—not as some
people thought, but because the most important thing was a
sense of shame lest I might, some day, look upon myself as
a man of words only who would never voluntarily put his hand
to action; and that I would find myself in the precarious situation
of betraying the hospitality of and my bond with Dion, who was
really in considerable danger." And now that his inner tension
has become strongest, he is led to a form of thought and expression that we have known since the *Crito*. The consequences
become alive in all their details. He sees Dion coming to him as
an exile, reproaching him with betrayal, not only of Dion himself, but of philosophy: "Philosophy, whose praises you have al
ways sung and who, in your opinion, has remained without honor
from others, was she not now betrayed together with myself as
far as was in your power?" Thus Plato had no choice. He did not
go with a light heart. "I abandoned my daily occupation, which
was by no means discreditable, and placed myself under a
tyranny obviously ill-suited to my principles and to me." "By
going, however," he summarizes his motives in conclusion,
"I discharged an obligation toward Zeus, the protector of
hospitality; and I acted with integrity toward philosophy, who
would have become the object of mockery and abuse had I
proved soft and cowardly and behaved disgracefully." These
are the words of a man who has enough knowledge of human
nature not to indulge in any illusions about the prospects of his
undertaking, and enough sense of responsibility toward friend
and cause to make him take the risk despite these doubts. And
what about the third journey? First, he declines the urgent
request of Dionysios, as well as of Dion. Then the ruler becomes
even more pressing. He sends a ship to facilitate the journey,
and along with it he dispatches men who had been closest to
Plato during his previous sojourn in Syracuse. They report that
Dionysios has shown the most lively interest in philosophy. A

letter from the ruler's own hand makes Dion's fate entirely dependent upon Plato's acceptance of the invitation. Other letters, from Archytas and the circle of Tarentum, confirm the account of the messengers from Syracuse as to the philosophical inclinations on the part of Dionysios, and explain that another visit would be of the highest importance to their political position vis-à-vis the tyrant. Again, every possible pressure is employed to make him decide in favor of the journey. "And so I set forth, weighing all these considerations in my mind, although I had many misgivings and foresaw that not much good would come of it" (340A). These are not the words of a man without a sense of reality. Plato knew human nature, and when, now in his late sixties, he again crossed the seas, he was convinced that he had to go without deceiving himself.

The Academy actively participated in the armed expedition against Syracuse, which had become unavoidable as a result of the failure of Plato's last journey. Its concern with the state thus seemed to find its fulfillment, though in the absence of a real leader it was unequal to the task. For the master himself kept aloof, partly because of his age, and partly because Dionysios was sacred to him as a former host. No one will doubt that he wished the undertaking success once Dion had decided upon it. But he did not recommend it, and he did not urge but permitted his disciples to participate in it. Once more he intervened with political advice at a time when Dion's companions, after the assassination of their leader, approached the master who had shared the latter's plans. Plato's two long communications throw a clear light upon the political ideology falsely attributed to him. The truth of the matter is that no one saw more clearly than he that the situation in Sicily was dominated by power politics. He well knew that it had been the great achievement of the elder Dionysios "to save the Hellenes from the barbarians so that, in fact, it has now become.possible to discuss a constitution" (*Letter VIII* 355D); and his counsel has the ring of urgency when he points out the danger threatening the life of the state from the Carthaginians and Oscans (353E). This counsel proposes a constitutional monarchy reconciling the rivalry of the pretenders and granting the security of law and order to the governed. Ought he to have said what the political historians of our day seem to demand of him; namely, that only a tyrant of the type of the first Dionysios could save the situation? Plato's wisdom and political sagacity prevented such counsel. Moreover, what he advised Dion's followers to do had been successfully carried out by Hermias in Asia, so that it could not be considered unrealistic planning in the West. Finally, what is the basis for the objections to Plato's proposals? Perhaps the miserable failure of the action taken contrary to his advice? No one knew better than he that "such counsel was like a wishful prayer" (352E), whose fulfillment was on the knees of the gods.

Plato's failure, then, cannot have dispelled illusions that, to begin with, were entirely alien to him. Dion's death, to be sure, must have moved him deeply. The epitaph he composed for him bears witness to his grief,[33] and the same emotion may be felt at the end of the great *Letter:* "Thus, he lies prostrate, having brought infinite sorrow to Sicily" (351E). That it was a member of the Academy who committed the vile murder of Dion must have shaken him deeply, although he must have known something of the nature of Kallippos, since he wrote: "That those who finally caused his [Dion's] downfall were of evil nature, in this he was not deceived; only the height their folly was to reach, and their wickedness and greed in general—about this he was indeed deceived." How could these events fail to make Plato gloomy? His name was tossed back and forth in the contest of conflicting factions; and, in the great manifesto of the *Letter*, he defends himself against the attacks made upon him. But if we can surmise anything about him, the depths of his soul remained unscathed. He had certainly seen too much of human malice, since the days of his youth, to learn anything new from this experience in his old age. Moreover, the fact that to build the *Idea* into human existence necessarily involved a loss of true reality and a traffic with evil was a principal basis of his teaching. His soul did not really live in the world in which these things occurred, for its eyes remained fixed upon the eternal forms and the true state.

CHAPTER FIVE

The Written Work

CERTAIN peoples lose themselves in their thoughts; but for us Greeks all things are forms. We retain only their relations; and enclosed as it were in the limpid day, Orpheuslike we build, by means of the word, temples of wisdom and science that may suffice for all reasonable creatures. This great art requires of us an admirably exact language. The very word that signifies language is also the name, with us, for reason and calculation; a single word says these three things." These are the words of Socrates in the dialogue *Eupalinos, or The Architect*, by Paul Valéry.[1]

After the Greeks discovered what we know as philosophy and realized that the *Logos* was the key to the nature of things, this *Logos* acquired an almost overpowering status. When Herakleitos speaks of *"this Logos,"* he means his own words as well as the eternal law of the cosmos, which his words are trying to approximate.[2] In a famous passage of the *Phaedo*—where Socrates apparently gives an autobiographical account of his own philosophical development, but where in reality philosophy gains self-consciousness—the crucial moment occurs when Socrates escapes from the "things" to the *Logoi*, or withdraws from speculation in natural philosophy to the instrument that alone makes philosophical thinking possible (99E). Thus *Logos* with Plato becomes a living thing, pre-existing, as it were, before particular verbal expressions and to be realized by the speaker. It makes demands; at times it leads us to the goal by apparently wrong ways; it runs away; it must not be deserted; it accuses us like a human being and laughs at us; it tramples upon us and treats us as it pleases; wherever it is carried like a breath of wind, one must follow.[3]

Originally *Logos* is oral speech, and with the Greeks the oral *Logos* always retained a status of priority over the written word. No god gave to mankind the art of writing as Apollo discovered verse or playing on the lyre. Writing was brought by a Phoenician and, before the influx of the Oriental world during the age of Alexander, it was hardly ever thought of as possessing a sacred or magic power. The Greeks did not use "hieroglyphics"; they did not know the sacred book of the Eastern religions, or rather they knew it only in Orphic circles, that is, at the limits of what is genuinely Hellenic.[4]

The written language for centuries was an auxiliary, not a substitute, for the spoken word. The Homeric epic is only written down in order to be sung. The written version of a poem by Pindar means preparation and memory; it comes alive only at the high moment of the festival, when it is sung to the honor of the victor, his family, and his city. And the same goes for all forms of dramatic play. Only with the discovery of solitary thinking must have come the impulse to share one's thoughts silently with others far away. It is hard to imagine that Herakleitos' pronouncements were still public speech in the same way that Hesiod's didactic poems certainly were. Thus the written word gains its independence from the spoken. And a remarkable growth takes place, during the fifth and fourth centuries, in both domains, not unrelated, yet freely parallel to each other as compared with their former connection or unity. Plato's philosophical dramas, unlike the plays of Sophocles or Aristophanes, did not have a certain time or hour when— and only when—they came to "real" life. They were meant just as much for reading by the individual as for being read aloud within a circle. And Plato's contemporary Isokrates wrote treatises and manifestoes for the purpose of political action and rhetorical training as if they were to be publicly delivered before the people of Athens or Greece. Thus it was only natural that the relationship between the spoken and the written *Logos* became a subject for thought.

While philosophizing and teaching, Plato could consider himself an instrument of the power *Socrates*, which he had deeply absorbed. In addition, however, he also wrote books throughout his long life, whereas Socrates lived so completely in the medium of conversation that one cannot even imagine him writing. Thus was not Plato farthest removed from Socrates precisely where he depicted him most intimately? Indeed, we encounter here, in symbolic form, an original difference between him and his teacher. Socrates received in oft-recurring dreams, with deep astonishment, the command, *Practice music art!* and believed, to the end of his days, that he had obeyed through his way of philosophizing. Plato's writing, on the other hand, or his need to write, indicates how irresistibly he was drawn toward creative form, that is, toward something for which Socrates felt no impulse. But did Plato, at the beginning of his new life, burn his tragedies only to begin the same game all over again and write about precisely this new life which had nothing in common with any writing or art? What was the point of his writing, to which he was compelled by an inner necessity, and which seemed to be irreconcilable with the basic attitude of Socrates? What value did writing have in general?

In connection with questions of this kind, Plato must have come into contact with the lively discussions that engaged the rhetoricians of the age with regard to the relationship between the spoken and written word—little as they were able to reach the depth at which he viewed these problems.

Oratory—though practiced for a long time and for decades also taught as a theory—remained a verbal art even after letters began to be used as "auxiliaries of the word." Lysias, in order to make money, became a "writer of speeches" for others. But the written *Logos* (still "speech," though written down) conquered the spoken word, the ideal of artistic "precision" (ἀκρίβεια) overcame that of extemporaneous speech, only in Isokrates, the greatest rhetorical talent among Plato's contemporaries.[5] He made a doctrine out of a necessity; and just as he worked out his political "speeches," actually brochures and manifestoes, in the quiet of his study, so he taught his pupils to do likewise. Then opposition arose from the ranks of other members of the craft, who defended the purely oral art of their master Gorgias against these innovators. Documents concerning this controversy, at times rather bitterly fought, are available in the speeches of two leading representatives, Isokrates and Alkidamas. They date from the eighties of the fourth century.[6] Plato had these discussions at his disposal when he composed the *Phaedrus*, the dialogue that begins with the current discussions among rhetoricians and then returns to them in a completely changed attitude after it has risen, with an incredible impulse, through the mania of Eros to the heights of philosophy.

Alkidamas, in his (written) speech "Against the Authors of Written Speeches," looks upon himself as a powerful rhetorician (ῥήτωρ δεινός, 34) who gives his extemporaneous speeches (αὐτοσχεδιαστικοὶ λόγοι) without much preparation (εἰκῆ, 29). Opposed to him he sees the "manufacturer of speeches or "poet ⌜maker⌝ of words" (ποιητὴς λόγων), a phrase referring to Isokrates, who used it of himself. This is the kind of man who prepares his speeches well and carefully (σχολή, μετὰ παρασκευῆς). In Plato, Socrates, with ironic self-denigration, contrasts himself, as an unskilled extemporaneous speaker (ἰδιώτης αὐτοσχεδιάζων, 236D), with the skilled artisan (ποιητής, 236D, 278E) Lysias, who has worked out his oration on love over a long period of time and with leisure and care (ἐν πολλῷ χρόνῳ κατὰ σχολήν, 228A; ἐν χρόνῳ, 278D). According to Alkidamas, only the word arising spontaneously out of thought is possessed of soul and life (ἔμψυχός ἐστι καὶ ζῆ, 28). A written speech is not a genuine "speech" at all, but only a copy, form, or imitation (εἴδωλα καὶ σχήματα καὶ μιμήματα λόγων, εἰκὼν λόγου). It cannot be likened to a real body, but only to a plastic or painted figure (χαλκῶν ἀνδριάντων καὶ λιθίνων ἀγαλμάτων καὶ γεγραμμένων ζῴων), and it is unmoving (ἀκίνητος) and useless like the latter. Socrates in the *Phaedrus* also calls the spoken word "living and possessed of soul" (λόγον ζῶντα καὶ ἔμψυχον, 276A), and the written word a mere copy (εἴδωλον). He, too, places written language side by side with painting (ὅμοιον ζωγραφίᾳ, 275D). Its offspring stand as if alive (ἕστηκεν ὡς ζῶντα), but they are unmoving, and they only say the same things over again.[7] Adding that written speech "always requires its father as a helper" (δεῖται βοηθοῦ), "for it is incapable of defending or helping itself" (οὔτ᾽ ἀμύνασθαι οὔτε βοηθῆσαι δυνατὸς αὐτῷ), he now draws support from Isokrates, who used the occasion of a letter to Dionysios of Syracuse as an opportunity to emphasize for once the disadvantages of the written word as against conversation: "When the writer is absent, the written word is deprived of its helper" (ἔρημα τοῦ βοηθήσαντός ἐστι, § 3).[8] Nevertheless, strong as the opposition to the written word was in Alkidamas as well as in Plato, they could not, since both of them wrote, repudiate it entirely. For Alkidamas (29–31), it serves to extend our renown, gives testimony, and preserves, for our own memory and as a monument for others, what we have said. For Plato's Socrates, the written word serves as memory for ourselves and as a marker along the way for others who follow us (275D, 276D). Ultimately, it is a form of play (παιδιά, 35) for Alkidamas, and Plato, too, considers it justified only as play (παιδιᾶς χάριν, παίζειν, 276D).

It is quite apparent how lively current controversies furnished a mine of material, which could be exploited by Plato. Thus the beginning of the *Phaedrus* and, apparently, the end too have much in common with the representatives of the strictly verbal tradition of oratory. But the problems that engaged Plato as the result of his encounter with Socrates reach much deeper. Rhetoric is the point of departure; but after the concept of love has been disentangled from the talk of the rhetoricians and grasped in its essential nature as guide to the *Idea*; after philosophy has been shown to be the only true form of oratory, and what is commonly called oratory only babble—what, then, is left of the current controversy among the schools as to the respective merits of extemporaneous speech or written preparation? It is no longer Alkidamas for whom, nor Isokrates against whom, Plato decides. The value of writing in general has become problematic to him. Are not the letters far removed from being "auxiliaries of the word," as his uncle Kritias had said (γράμματ᾽ ἀλεξίλογα, frag. 2 li. 10); far removed from being a medicinal herb for memory and wisdom, as Thoth, the Egyptian discoverer of the written character, imagines they are in the fable told by Plato's Socrates? Are they not, rather, conducive to forgetfulness in the soul whose power of memory remains without exercise? And will there not arise a contradiction between the apparent possession of that which is written down in black and white and the real possession of that which is inscribed in the soul? "You produce the illusion of wisdom among the disciples, not truth," says Ammon about Thoth's discovery.

But even this would still be little more than sophisticated play, if the words appearance, truth, wisdom did not point to the ultimate depth, if "philosophy" was not the focus for this discussion on talking and writing. Even if from the viewpoint of oratory it is the same whether one talks or writes (λέγει ἢ γράφει, 277B), from the point of view of justice, beauty, and truth, where ignorance is disgraceful, there can be no question that the written *Logos* necessarily contains much play and is not completely serious (277DE). It is foolish to think that one can leave one's written knowledge behind as a doctrine (τέχνη, 275c) to be learned. The written word is rigid. Beyond its natural limits it cannot give an answer to the questioner or protect itself against attacks. Thus it contradicts the basic Socratic-Platonic principle: philosophy is possible only as an exchange between two people; it is an infinite conversation renewing itself constantly out of a personal question. For this reason, genuine philosophical discourse must decide whom it is addressed to and whom not—a principle that must have determined Plato's teaching in contrast to Sophistic instruction. The written word, on the other hand, is addressed to each and everyone.

So much was Plato in doubt as to the value of writing after he had written books throughout his life. Nor did these doubts arise gradually or late; [9] they accompanied him throughout his life's work, as is evident from a passage in the early dialogue *Protagoras* (329A), where Socrates contrasts this way of dialogic conversation with the long speeches of the Sophists and politicians: "When one has a question to ask of any of them, like books they can neither answer nor ask; and if anyone challenges the least particular of their speech, they go ringing on like brazen pots, which when struck continue to sound unless someone puts his hand on them. Thus with the speakers: if one puts a small question to them, they go into a long harangue." This does not yet show the awareness of all of the problems as Plato saw them in his later years. But it is perfectly apparent how this doubt about the value of the written word came to him through Socrates, who never wrote a book, and became a conviction that he never abandoned.

His letters confirm what Socrates says in the dialogues.[10] "Beware," he tells Dionysios in the *Second Letter* (between 360 and 357), "lest these doctrines fall among the ignorant. For there is hardly anything, I believe, that sounds more absurd to the vulgar or, on the other hand, more admirable and inspired to men of fine disposition" (314A). Well, Plato himself was cautious. Diplomat that he was, he communicated his doctrines to the prince, whom he did not wish to offend, in "enigmatic words," hardly for the reason that "if anything should happen to the writing in the folds of the land or sea, nobody reading it would be able to understand it," but rather that it remain a riddle to the person addressed. Dionysios, vain and ambitious, composed a "treatise" on the Platonic philosophy, as Plato informs the friends of Dion in the *Seventh Letter*. Thus the following statement in the *Second Letter* is addressed to the tyrant himself. "Take care lest one day you should repent of what has now been divulged improperly. The greatest safeguard is to avoid all writing and to learn by heart only; for it is impossible that what is written down should not be divulged. For this reason I myself have never yet written anything on these subjects, and no treatise by Plato exists or will exist. Those which now bear his name [he concludes by concealing himself mysteriously, or, if one likes, with a profound jest] belong to a Socrates become young and fair." [11] In the *Seventh Letter*, he scorns Dionysios, who claimed to have composed a treatise out of what he had learned from Plato himself, from intermediaries about Plato's teachings, and from all others writing about such subjects. "This much I can certainly declare concerning all these writers or prospective writers, who claim to know the subjects that I seriously study, whether they claim to have heard it from me or from others, or discovered it them-

selves: it is impossible, in my opinion, that they should understand anything at all about the subject. There does not exist,
nor will there ever exist, any treatise of mine dealing with this
subject. For it does not admit of verbal expression like other
studies; but, as a result of continued application to and communion with the subject, it is suddenly brought to birth in the soul
as a light is kindled by a leaping spark and thereafter nourishes
itself." And then again, after a few sentences have sketched his
method: "Whenever one sees a man's written compositions—
whether they be the laws of a legislator or anything else in any
other form—these are not his most serious pursuits, if the writer
himself be serious; rather, those pursuits abide in the fairest
region he possesses.[12] If, however, these are really his serious
efforts, it is not (as Homer says) the gods, but mortal men 'who
have utterly ruined his senses' " (344CD).

There is evidence that the relationship between the spoken
and written word had a symbolic meaning for Plato. For this
problematic situation is repeated in another context. Why does
Plato, in the passage from the letter just cited, mention the
written laws as illustrating that writing does not express the
true seriousness of a truly serious person? Is it not likely that
he is thinking of himself who was engaged in the writing of
laws for many years, first for Syracuse, then for his Utopia on
Crete, and who, in this last great dialogue, makes the Athenian
say (858E) that, of everything ever written, the laws of the
state are the most beautiful and best and the measure for everything written by the poets? Thus was not even this enterprise
pursued with complete seriousness? We may remember how,
in this last great work, that which is pursued so studiously, the
construction of the laws of the state, is designated as jest and
play (παιδιά). "This we must now inquire into," says the
Athenian (685A), "this being our old man's sober game of
play, whereby we beguile the way." And similarly in other
passages. But the deeper meaning of these words is revealed
only in the course of a very important discussion in the *Statesman* (293 *et seq.*).[13]

The true monarch, it is said, is distinguished from all other
rulers by the fact that "wisdom and justice" are guides of his

actions (293D) or, as it is said in another passage (297B), that "by distributing justice to the citizens with intelligence and skill, he is able to preserve them and, as far as possible, make them better." [14] Thus he cannot ultimately be bound by any laws, but must always decide freely. For laws are rigid and impose limits upon the fullness and complexity of life. "It is impossible that a simple principle be applied to a state of affairs which is never simple." [15] To be sure, in order to make his task easier, the wise ruler will also use laws. But they must not limit him, and as he has laid them down, so he will disregard them according to his own judgment. Yet Plato is the last person to give a free rein to arbitrary caprice. The judgment of the ruler can only be based upon true wisdom speaking through him; and as long as there is no such true statesman, that is, in all the empirical states, the laws must be observed all the more strictly. For whoever disregards the laws would throw matters only into a worse state than that which the written laws seem to have brought about. After all, laws are the precipitation of much experience, and good counselors urged the people to write them down. Laws are "copies of the truth" (μιμήματα τῆς ἀληθείας, 300c). Strictest observance of the laws is the "second-best journey" (δεύτερος πλοῦς), when the best is impossible. If ignorant people presume to live without a law, this would truly be a bad copy of that pure wisdom which, in the ideal state, makes written laws superfluous. Here the contrast between the two greatest Platonic writings on the state becomes apparent: the *Republic* constructs the kind of state in which true wisdom prevails and which, therefore, does not need laws; the *Laws*, proceeding along a "second way," since the first, the way "for gods and sons of gods," cannot be realized, is designed to preserve the structure of this second-best state through the strictest rules.

What depths of Platonic thinking and being are reached in this connection is shown by a few passages in the *Statesman* not yet discussed (298 *et seq.*). It is unreasonable to limit the wise ruler through laws or constitutional provisions. To make this as clear as possible, Plato, in ironic play, uses the analogy of the physician and pilot, that is, craftsmen expert in their own fields, being bound by the same regulations—laws, majority decisions, public accounting of their work—as the statesman. This analogy then is developed into a grotesque caricature. A hypothetical law is enacted: anybody in the fields of navigation or medicine who makes inquiries into what is beyond or contrary to the written rules and has ingenious ideas about such matters (ζητῶν παρὰ τὰ γράμματα καὶ σοφιζόμενος ὁτιοῦν περὶ τὰ τοιαῦτα) is not to be called an expert in medicine or navigation, but a stargazer (μετεωρολόγος) and prating Sophist. Next, he is to be indicted in court on the grounds that he is a corrupter of youth, who would persuade them to use the science of medicine or navigation in an unlawful manner; and if he is found to have influenced anyone, young or old, contrary to the written laws, he is to be punished most severely. For no one should presume to be wiser than the laws. And just as medicine, health, or the art of navigation are known to all, so anybody who wishes can learn what the written laws and the customs of the forefathers are.

It is not hard to see that these sarcastic words are aimed at the fate of Socrates. And suddenly it is clear what Plato meant. The wise man is above the law, not in the sense of arbitrary caprice, but as the higher norm is above the lower. Where this is not recognized, the worst form of judicial murder may take place; and, beyond the fate of the individual, "all arts must perish altogether" and "life, which is hard enough as it is, will in the future no longer be worth living." [16] This is the view of the old Plato who is generally supposed to have coerced life into unbearably rigid forms. But no one knew better than he that what is appropriate for one is not so for all. The rule without laws by the wise prince represents the extreme opposite of the capricious lawlessness of the tyrant. The middle position is occupied by the state, in which laws are necessary, though they never attain perfection (οὐκ ὀρθότατον ὁ νόμος, 294D). Compared with Plato's levels of being and knowledge, the philosopher-king represents the level of pure being and knowledge, the tyrant that of not-being and ignorance, and to the middle realm of becoming belong, in various gradations, the lawful states. This also explains the true value of the laws. As all value in the world of becoming depends on participation in the

Eidos, so the laws are "imitations of true being" (μιμήματα τῆς ἀληθείας, 300c). The main question is not even whether they are written down or not; thus the written laws are frequently mentioned on the same level of being and value as the "unwritten," to wit, the firm, inflexible traditions of the ancestors.[17] The written language is only the clearest symbol for rigidity, or for the admixture of matter, as it were, to pure form.

Returning now from the writing of laws to the writing of dialogues, several points can be seen more clearly. There is no doubt that Plato, in his early and even in his later years, was conscious of the problematic nature of all writing and that he did not believe he had said the most serious things in his written work, that is, in what has come down to us and what we are often inclined to regard as his greatest creation, and perhaps the greatest achievement of the Greek genius. He was truly serious in his philosophy and his teaching, that is, ultimately, in his knowledge of God and in the guidance of his disciples to this knowledge. But the composing of dialogues was a game that he pursued "as others indulge in other games, banqueting and the like," as Socrates says in the *Phaedrus* (276D). To be sure, Phaidros replies: "To be able to play with words and to tell tales about justice and the like is as noble a game as the others are ignoble," and Socrates assents.[18]

The place that play (παιδιά) occupies in the Platonic world is still to be defined more precisely. Let us consider the concluding part of the *Republic*. The structure stands completed to the top, the "degenerate" constitutions have been portrayed, and, later, the discussion has turned from the structure of the state to the soul of the individual. Then a seal has been placed upon the whole discussion by a few words about the location of the ideal state—"in heaven as a prototype for those who can see and wish to model themselves accordingly." Now, shortly before the great concluding myth, there follows, like a forced intrusion, the episode of the "imitating" poet and the opposition of Plato's state to the latter. Why is this topic so important to Plato that he assigns it such an unexpected place? Had he not previously treated this subject while discussing the musical education of the guardians (394 *et seq.*)? Why, then, return to something that apparently has already been disposed of?[19] There would be no point in this if Plato did not have in mind the writing of his own dialogues and did not wish to secure for them an appropriate place in the new state.

At the beginning of this section (595c), Plato presents a theory of "imitation," which cannot be evaluated properly as long as it is viewed as a generally valid philosophy of art (the construction of which Plato never envisaged)[20] instead of as a weapon with which he intended to defeat the artists, and especially the poets, of his time. The painter, it is said, is like a person carrying a mirror and making therewith all sorts of objects, not producing a bed, but only rendering a deceitful copy of it, and thus inferior to the carpenter. Is this not being frankly malicious; and is it not apparent that Plato did not mean Polygnotos—the "good artist who paints a model of what might be the most beautiful human being" (472D)?[21] What he had in mind was the younger generation of painters, who in their manners as well as in their products are rightly compared to the "Sophists": Apollodoros, for example, the inventor of the illusionistic "paintings with shadows" (σκιαγραφία) rejected by Plato as deceitful; Zeuxis, who in Aristotle's judgment lacked the "ethos" of Polygnotos, and who took delight in the portrayal of the individual, concrete object, painting grapes with such an illusion of reality that birds came to peck at them; or Parrhasios and Pauson.[22]

In the field of poetry, the art of Euripides in his later years and that of his successors was, in many respects, comparable to this type of mimetic painting. Seeing Euripides as the poet who destroyed high tragedy and prepared the way for the bourgeois drama; who did not, like Aeschylus, form the Athenian people; who did not, like Sophocles, set up the inexorableness of tragedy in contrast to the social decline, but who admitted these social movements to his own poetry[23]—seeing him from this perspective, it is perhaps clear that the masses could not and Plato would not see anything else in him but imitation of nature, and not even beautiful nature. And since the prevailing art is usually the measure for the art of former ages, this point of view, then, also determined the way of responding to Aeschylus, Sophocles, or Homer, the ancestor of tragic poetry. This explains why Plato could not exempt the great old masters—by whom he was "often charmed"—from his judgment. Imitation, then, was nothing but the ruling tendency in art, expressed as a concept and justifying the verdict. Imitation is one step farther removed from true being than the world of objects produced by the demiurge with a view to the prototypes. It occupies "the third place as seen from the king and truth" (τρίτος τις ἀπὸ βασιλέως καὶ τῆς ἀληθείας, 597E), and whoever practices it has no knowledge, not even right opinion, of the thing. Nobody, therefore, who understands both—how to produce a work after the model of the eternal *Eidos* and, at the same time, a copy of this work—will apply himself seriously to such imitating activity, and regard it as the chief business of his life. Rather, he will put much more seriousness into the works themselves and try to leave behind many beautiful works. Does not the same Socrates, in the *Phaedrus* (276c *et seq.*), suggest a similar contrast between the "play" of writing books and the "seriousness" of cultivating wisdom in the soul? Why, then, should not the reader notice that the words in the *Republic* are meant for someone who is conscious of producing both the works themselves and the copies, and who is fully informed as to the respective merit of these two activities?

It is an incredible exaggeration, therefore, Socrates continues (599c *et seq.*), to make Homer into an educator of a political community, as Lykurgos truly was; into an educator of the individual human being, like Pythagoras, who had become a "leader of education" for many; or even like Prodikos and Protagoras, the Sophists, who had persuaded many to accept them as teachers. Indeed, the *Ion* shows that people held such an opinion of Homer, which may have made sense in some former age, but which now only deflected from the essential task. Is it not strange that Lykurgos as the founder of a state or Pythagoras and the Sophists as educators are contrasted with the poets? But has not Plato, through Socrates, just completed the construction of the state as an organ of education, and integrated Pythagorean education in it as part of a more inclusive structure? Does this not explain who really claims to take the place of Homer? [24] And now the art of the latter is judged according to its proper rank: as mere imitation it is play and not seriousness (εἶναι παιδιάν τινα καὶ οὐ σπουδὴν τὴν μίμησιν, 602β). If we recall once more that Plato, in the *Phaedrus*, referred to his own dialogues as "play," and if we ask how he could have possibly characterized them except as an imitation of the Socratic life, it is perfectly clear that he is here speaking of himself, not only as the founder of a state and teacher but also as a mimetic artist.

The next question, then, is: What place did he claim for himself within the field of mimetic art? Subject matter of poetry, it is said, is men in action (πράττοντας μιμεῖται, 603c), men passionately active, thrown into violent emotions and conflicts within, heroes giving free rein to their sufferings, comic figures behaving disgracefully. But our own soul is full of all these things and, therefore, should not be shown what, by setting a bad example, must damage it in the struggle for balance, but only what would help it to establish the order of the "inner state," the victory of mind. Now, to be sure, a reasonable and quiet human type of stable character (τὸ φρόνιμόν τε καὶ ἡσύχιον ἦθος παραπλήσιον ὂν ἀεὶ αὐτὸ αὐτῷ, 604ε) is not easily represented by the poet; it is difficult to grasp and, hence, unpopular with the audience. But did not Plato represent, always and everywhere, precisely this type of man in Socrates? In the *Phaedo*, when Socrates sends away the women dissolved in sorrow and admonishes and cheers the weeping friends? In the *Symposium*, when the *Logos* defeats the danger of comic disorder and humiliation? And when it is said that the mimetic poet "produces an evil political order in the soul of the individual" (κακὴν πολιτείαν ἰδίᾳ ἑκάστου τῇ ψυχῇ ἐμποιεῖν, *Republic* 605β) by pleasing the irrational part of the soul, we may recall that Plato has just completed the work of ordering the state of the citizens as well as that of the individual and securing the sovereignty of reason in both. Thus it is even more clear than before that he claimed for himself the very place he asked the tragic poets to vacate.

Finally, the conclusion: in our state there is no place for any mimetic art and its ancestor Homer. We accept only hymns to the gods and panegyrics to the noble souls (ὕμνους θεοῖς καὶ ἐγκώμια τοῖς ἀγαθοῖς, 607A). This, to begin with, must be taken quite literally; but then we must also recall that the *Symposium* and the *Phaedrus* are full of hymns to the gods, and that the *Symposium* culminates in Alkibiades' encomium of the noble Socrates. And what are all Platonic dialogues ultimately but encomiums to Socrates and the *Agathón?*

The contest is once more resumed in the late work, the *Laws* (817 *et seq.*). The creator (ποιητής) of tragedy claims to be recognized in our state. But, says the Athenian, we are creators (ποιηταί) ourselves. For if tragedy be an imitation of life, the founding of our state as an "imitation of the most beautiful and best life"—envisaged as an *Idea* and to be realized by us—is the most beautiful and best tragedy. Thus we are rival poets and competitors for the prize awarded the most beautiful drama (ἀντίτεχνοί τε καὶ ἀνταγωνισταὶ τοῦ καλλίστου δράματος), and it would not make sense to concede to the others a place in our state without careful scrutiny. On the contrary, they have to put their songs up against ours so that the ruler of the state can compare them. Again, the allusion is veiled, while the notion of a contest is made quite explicit and integrated into the dialogue. Thus dialogue as a form of art could not be put against tragedy as a form of art without destroying the illusion or the total structure, but there is no doubt that at least part of the meaning is the contest between tragedy and philosophical dialogue. Did not Plato, who originally wanted to become a poet of tragedies, first fight this struggle through within himself?

There is an ancient quarrel, Plato says in the *Republic*, between philosophy and poetry (607B). He engages in a contest with the mimetic poetry that dominated the previous ages, breaks its primacy, and brings philosophy to the fore—and at the same time a new mimetic art. The latter, to be sure, is not the kind of imitation that aims at pleasure. It aims at truth and, therefore, it will not only be pleasant as the old art was but also useful (οὐ μόνον ἡδεῖα ἀλλὰ καὶ ὠφελίμη, 607D) for the state and the life of man. But it is still mimesis, occupying "the third place as seen from the king and truth." However much it approaches seriousness, it is still play.

Once more we must return to the high, though not highest, value that Plato, who knew the law of levels as few did, assigned to jest and play. "Swear," he writes in a letter to the disciples in Assos with the subtle concealment now characteristic of him, "with a seriousness that is not out of tune combined with the playfulness that is the sister of seriousness" (ἐπομνύντας σπουδῇ τε ἅμα μὴ ἀμούσῳ καὶ τῇ τῆς σπουδῆς ἀδελφῇ παιδιᾷ, *Letter VI* 323D). In the *Timaeus*, mythical (that is, the only possible) discourse about the world of becoming is referred to as a "pleasure not to be regretted" and a "measured and reasonable play" (μετρία καὶ φρόνιμος παιδιά, 59D). For high above these discourses—however much power of thought they may have consumed—are the "discourses about being" (λόγοι περὶ τῶν ὄντων) as the object of our true seriousness (ἐκεῖνα ἐφ' οἷς σπουδάζομεν).[25] Play, legend, and dreams Plato calls, in the *Laws*, the work of legislation to which he devoted so many years of strenuous labors. And the relationship between the two sisters, play and seriousness, is perhaps most pregnantly expressed in the following passage of this late work (803B)—an almost literal transcription of an earlier passage in the *Republic* (604B): "The life of man is not worth great seriousness." He continues: "God is the worthy object of our most serious and blessed endeavors; man, on the other hand, is only a plaything in the hand of God, and this, truly considered, is the best of him." [26] Thus only he should talk who "fastens his view upon God" (804B). Yet the fact that man is still—and perhaps from this perspective—"worthy of some serious consideration" (804B), and "education is for us the most serious pursuit" (803D), is also affirmed within the same context. Thus may we say that even the writing of books is playfulness—play compared with the seriousness of Plato's philosophizing and teaching, and yet serious play—precisely because it is related, under the aspect of imitation, to genuine seriousness? Because it is also, in some way, a form of education—thus not only a mimesis of something already created, but rather a demiurgic creation with a view to the prototypes?

Seen in this light, Plato's struggle against mimesis has still another aspect. Plato wages his struggle against Homer as the founder of all imitative art, although Plato himself is praised, in the most significant Greek work of aesthetic criticism (*De Sublimitate* ch. 13), as the "most Homeric" of all authors. And this judgment seems justified; for do not the Platonic dialogues contain a stream of artistic presentation, that is, of "Homeric" elements, far beyond anything created by earlier forms of mimetic art: Socrates taking a walk with Phaidros, Socrates at the banquet, in the gymnasium, in prison? Thus this struggle with mimesis is, after all and primarily, also a struggle of Plato with himself, struggle of the philosopher against the poet, and therefore a form of watchfulness constantly exercised against himself and others. Again and again Plato's written work is mimesis; but it struggles against being nothing but mimesis. And where it seems to represent most strongly a pure work of art, it must not ultimately be read as such, but as an "existential" document, that is, with the constant reminder *tua res agitur*.

The Platonic school had already inquired into the problem with which we have been concerned.[27] A Neoplatonic treatise refers to the aporetic dilemma presented by the fact that while the master in the *Phaedrus* spoke so disparagingly about writing, he still considered his own works as worthy of being written down. As a solution, it is proposed that he also tried to follow the deity in this respect. Just as the deity created both the invisible and what is visible to our senses, so he, too, wrote down many things and transmitted others unwritten. Even though this line of thought reflects the rigid dogmatism of Neoplatonic doctrine, something at least of the relationship between Plato's poetic writing, on the one hand, and his philosophizing, on the other, seems to have been correctly seen.[28]

Human life a play, man a plaything—yet what ethical strength did the old Plato, who said this, expend upon this life and with what a sense of responsibility did he always look upon it as a task! Legislation a play—but is not the picture of the old man unforgettable, writing laws despite the failure of all his political aspirations, laws for the founding of yet another Utopia, this time called Crete? Literature, the new form of art, the whole set of dramatic philosophical dialogues a play—what aesthetic passion and seriousness went into this play for half a century. Thus we are perhaps not entirely untrue to his spirit if we interpret, in a preliminary way, the meaning of his written work according to the model of the world of appearances, which, to be sure, is only a *copy* of the eternal forms, but a copy of *eternal forms*, though afflicted with all the limitations of transitory existence, yet, to the eye which has learned to see, pointing toward eternal being and toward what is beyond being.

CHAPTER SIX

Socrates in Plato

HESIOD OF ASKRA is the first person in the history of
the Western mind to appear as an individual—all the
more audaciously inasmuch as he puts his own self side by side
with the self of the highest deity. "Judge, O Zeus, according to
unbending law; I, for my part, will tell Perses the truth." The
traditional epic form makes it still more apparent that the
integument, behind which the self of the poet had previously
hidden, is here broken through, and suggests something of the
strong inner tension resulting from the collision of one's own
sense of justice, or rather one's faith in the all-prevailing justice
of Zeus, with the distortion of the law by secular judges. This
liberated self subsequently manifests itself in many ways,
speaking of strife and love, sorrow and festive joy, in the elegiac
and iambic poetry and in the songs of Sappho and Alkaios. And
when thought is born, the personal "I" is used by thinkers,
poets, and writers proudly distinguishing themselves from each
other and from the many.[1] The victors in wrestling and running,
says Xenophanes, are "not so worthy of the prize as I am; for
better is our wisdom than the victorious strength of horses and
men." Parmenides composes a poem about *his* ascent to the
Goddess Truth. "I wander about, honored as an immortal god,
no longer a mortal man : : ." thus Empedokles appears before
his friends of Agrigentum. Those who practice the new art of
prose are no less inclined to use the "I." Herakleitos sharply
contrasts the "words and works as I proclaim them" with the
"speeches of ignorant men"; and the same "I" still echoes
proudly even when he bids us listen, "not to me, but to the

Logos," in order to grasp the principle of the unity of all being. For the *Logos* becomes audible in him. Few of the philosophers or philosophizing physicians of the fifth century came before their readers without a phrase such as "It seems to me," "I say," or "I shall plainly say." [2] The new writing of history differs from chronicles by virtue of the "I" of Hekataios, Herodotos, and Thucydides. The Sophists use the same "I" rather more than less, and the Socratic literature did not, by any means, push it into the background. Xenophon writes the *Memorabilia,* his memoirs, he is personally present at the *Banquet,* and he opens and closes the *Apology of Socrates* with reflections of his own; in short, the "I" of personal memoirs accompanies everything he has to say about Socrates.

These things must be called to mind when we look at Plato. Plato wrote over a period of fifty years for his contemporaries and for posterity. But, with the exception of a few letters addressed to a smaller circle and written for a special purpose, he never speaks in his own person. [3] Consider what this means: Plato did not wish that we should hear him. His name, which must have meant something in the Socratic circles, appears in the dialogues only rarely and, as it were, marginally. In the *Apology,* Socrates himself twice mentions Plato as present among his closest friends and, like them, interested in working for the acquittal of the accused. And, as a contrast to this episode, the *Phaedo* justifies, almost incidentally, Plato's absence at the death of Socrates: "but Plato, I believe, was ill." One reads behind these words a justification similar—only less solemn—to that which Dante uses where he once mentions his own name in the *Divine Comedy*: "which of necessity is written here."

No less surprising than the silence of Plato's "I" is something else that necessarily corresponds to this silence, namely, the incomparable status of Socrates in Plato's works. Where else do we find anything similar to this phenomenon: that a philosopher, for decades, designates the most important things he has to say by the name—or conceals them behind the name—of someone else, his teacher? Aside from the *Laws,* there is no written work of Plato's in which Socrates is not present. For the most part, he says the decisive things; at the least, they are said in his presence. If we ask what the predominance of this figure means in Plato's written work, the answer can only be given from the work itself. On the level of Plato's life, however, the answer must first be that Plato had a fateful encounter in comparison with which everything else—his intercourse with other people, even Dion; travels into distant lands, even to the Pythagorean sages or the Egyptian priests; political action, even his interference in Sicilian affairs—was merely episodic. For all this left more or less definite traces in his works, but only traces. The greatness of the one fateful encounter comes out by contrast with these episodes. The fateful encounter was Socrates.

The spirit of a declining age in which Plato grew into manhood is perhaps nowhere better revealed than by the masters of political comedy. In his *Demes*, the great Eupolis, after the collapse of the Sicilian expedition, orders the old statesmen to be fetched from Hades because the small politicians of the age have led Athens to destruction. A year before the city is conquered by Lysander, Aristophanes, in the *Frogs*, also conjures the great tragic poets up from the underworld, "because you cannot any longer find, as much as you may seek, a creative poet who could sound an authentic phrase." The comic poet could not guess that he was also singing the swan song of his own art, the great ancient comedy. In the plastic arts, too, a period of exhaustion seems to set in, lasting for decades after Pheidias and the generation of his disciples.[4] The brilliant protagonists of the Sophist movement are either dead like Protagoras or, like Gorgias, old and far away from Athens. The disintegration of the political and social structure, indicated rather than caused by the theoretical undermining of absolute norms, is revealed to the anxious onlooker in the lack of leadership, in the failure of foreign enterprises, in the domestic revolutions, and in the infamous deeds of those in power. Plato saw the disintegration of the old order all the more clearly because he felt entitled, by birth and by inclination, to take part in the life of his state and "intended, like many others, after coming of age, to go into public affairs." In this process of disintegration, he saw one firm foundation: Socrates.

In the invaluable autobiographical letter, Plato proposes to give an account only of his own intellectual growth. He shows how he came to understand the general collapse and the growing decay; how Socrates was the only one to stand up against his age in the two great tests, once when he refused to join the aristocratic revolt of the Thirty, and again when the democratic restoration got rid of him as an unbearable warning voice. Plato's account does not claim to be complete. He does not mention a third incident, although, as the *Apology* shows, it must have made a deep impression upon him. This is the opposition shown by Socrates to the tumultuous proceedings at the trial of the generals after the battle of Arginusai. Moreover, Plato only suggests that Socrates became for him the measure of what was meant by "justice" or "piety," and does not even say that he owed the "true philosophy" into which he withdrew to this experience of justice and piety in Socrates. But he does not have to say what everybody would know.

Finally, he does not have to speak about the human relationship existing between him and Socrates. This is toned down and made distant in the words of the old Plato: "Socrates, an older friend of mine" (φίλον ἄνδρα ἐμοὶ πρεσβύτερον Σωκράτη), and "our companion Socrates" (τὸν ἑταῖρον ἡμῶν Σωκράτη). If this were all Socrates meant to him, the predominance of Socrates in Plato's writings would remain an enigma. Thus Plato's biography is in a sense quite right in depicting the encounter of these two as a fable. Socrates, dreaming, sees a fledgling swan sitting on his knees, which soon grows wings and flies away with sweet song. In front of the theater of Dionysos, Plato burns the tragedy that he is about to have performed—after he has heard Socrates. Socrates must have known that he had found his greatest disciple, Plato that he had encountered a power that was to be decisive for his life. Of course, we shall never know just how this encounter occurred. But we shall not be wrong if we put Plato in the group of young men like Charmides, Lysis, or Menexenos who listen attentively when they hear the name of Socrates, who ask their fathers that they may become his disciples, and who enter the dressing room of the Gymnasium where he is sitting down as if unaware of them, and then blush when he addresses them. And what the young man Aristeides says to Socrates in the *Theages* also sounds as if spoken from experience: "I made progress when I was with you, if only in the same house, not even in the same room; but more progress when I was with you in the same room; and still more, so it seemed to me, when I was in the same room and looked at you (rather than elsewhere) while you were talking; but most of all when I sat beside you, quite close, and touched you." No wonder that people today, lacking the experience, call this sort of thing un-Platonic and mistake it for "occult phenomena." Finally, as far as Alkibiades' description of Socrates in the *Symposium* is concerned, could Plato have written anything like this without having experienced it in his own encounter with Socrates? "When your words are heard, even at second hand, and however imperfectly repeated, we are shaken and possessed, whether man, woman, or child. . . . When I hear him, my heart leaps within me more than that of any Corybantian reveler, and tears stream from my eyes; and I have seen many others affected in the same manner. . . . This Marsyas has often brought me to such a pass that the life I am leading does not seem worth living" (215c). Must one add still more reasons to prove that this encounter, so decisive in Plato's life, could not have been without the power of the great demon? Would Plato again and again have shown Socrates as the erotic man in his writings if this element had not been present in their lives? Finally, would Plato have assigned to this force which he called *Eros* such a place in his cosmos if the encounter determining his own life had not been affected by it?

The strength of this love and the transforming power of this unique personality combined to throw the young Plato out of the course for which he seemed to be destined. But there are times when even the greatest must lose himself in order to find himself.[5] What would have become of Plato if he had not met the older man of so different a composition? A political leader in the party struggle of Athens, a successor of Kritias in a period of political disintegration, when even for the best such struggle was no longer worth the trouble. In addition, an author of tragedies, following Euripides and Agathon, as the historic epoch of Athenian tragedy drew to a close. Thus he had to be a Socratic for many years in order to become himself. He was not permitted to develop his political and poetic impulses freely if he was destined to attain knowledge, to construct the ideal state, and to become the poet of philosophical dramas and myths. He knew this himself. He thanked Socrates for changing the course of his life as no mortal ever thanked another. He elevated him for all time out of the mass of Sophist teachers (where he might otherwise have been lost to posterity) and projected the image of the man who died for truth against the heavens as the only guide to philosophy.[6]

From the *Seventh Letter* alone it would never be possible to estimate what Socrates meant to Plato. In addition, one must read the dialogues; and here one must again recognize the unique phenomenon that Plato in his written work never spoke without concealment and, over a period of forty years, always used Socrates as the speaker or, at least, as a silent auditor. This fact is brought out by Plato (and again concealed in the strangely arabesque style of his old age) in the *Second Letter*, where he says (314c) that he has never written anything about the principles of philosophy; that there is no work by Plato and never will be; and that what is now called by his name belonged to "a Socrates made young and fair"—in short, to "a rejuvenated Socrates." Even if there are still many people today who do not believe that these words were written by Plato, the statement would still be the most striking expression of what is even to us the unique phenomenon about Plato's written work. How are we to understand this phenomenon?

It is quite right to see in it a mark of gratitude of the disciple toward his teacher such as is not found again in man's entire intellectual history. Aristotle spent twenty years as a student in Plato's Academy. Until mature age, if not always, he remains a Platonist in the total structure of his mind. But in his later years, at least, he finds himself in constant opposition to his master; at times it seems as if he could only find his own thought by means of this opposition. Perhaps this was his form of gratitude. Plato, on the other hand, never placed himself in opposition to Socrates; for decades he spoke through the mouth of Socrates.

Thus it is quite right—yet not enough—to say that the written works of the pupil are a monument of gratitude to the teacher.

"In every noble heart burns a perpetual thirst for a nobler, in the fair, for a fairer; it wishes to behold its ideal out of itself, in bodily presence, with glorified or adopted form, in order the more easily to attain to it, because the lofty man can ripen only by a lofty one, as diamonds are made brilliant only by diamonds." These words, from Jean Paul's *Titan*, Plato had experienced.[7] In the Academy, his pupils came to maturity through him. Addressing others through his written work, words alone—even the clearest and most glowing words—would have seemed to him ineffective without the living embodiment, although the "discourse" itself meant everything, the "speaker" nothing, precisely because "one can easily contradict Socrates, but not the truth" (*Symposium* 201c). Thus he must have made Socrates the most powerful force in his written work because he could not in any other way determine unequivocally the necessary relationship between "speaker" and "discourse"; because it seemed to him that only in this way could education and struggle, research and construction, festival and death—in short, "philosophy"—become audible. By placing Socrates in the center of his philosophical dramas, he thus erected, for all time, not only a monument of gratitude, but the highest one of formative power. This, to be sure, might still be misunderstood as an artistic device or a choice. Obviously, to Plato it was a necessity.

What does Plato's Socrates represent? He inquires into the "teachability of virtue," into the nature of the "virtues," into the nature of other vital forces such as friendship and knowledge. He represents the unimpeachable dignity of justice and the other "virtues." He constructs the ideal state. From his mouth flows the praise of *Eros*, resound the myths of immortality, judgment of the dead, and elevation of the soul to the invisible realm. Finally, he represents what is shown about the *Ideas* and about the ascent, through the realm of *Ideas*, to the *Arrheton*. He does not, however, represent everything that Plato communicates to his readers. Not that anything carried in opposition to Socrates is ever meant to be definitely valid or that Plato was even surreptitiously fighting against Socrates, except in so far as he was fighting against the Socrates within himself, against himself.[8] But it is the Pythagorean Timaios, an astronomer and scientist of nature, who constructs a mythico-scientific cosmology; it is Kritias, heir to ancient Athenian nobility, who tells the legendary tale of the warfare between Atlantis and earliest Athens. In these cases, Socrates lets himself "be entertained by speeches." He is likewise satisfied with listening in the second part of the *Parmenides*, and in the dialogues about the *Sophist* and the *Statesman*, where he only instigates the dialectical exercises without taking a leading part. And he does not even listen to the great mass of practical legislation presented in the *Laws*.[9]

To be sure, the natural science of the *Timaeus* was of the highest importance for Plato—just as it came to be the central Platonic view of the world for centuries. To be sure, the dialectical exercises, in the course of which the "Sophist" and the "Statesman" are defined, and the paradoxes of the One and the Many are devised, are preparatory—since the process of analysis and synthesis characterizes the dialectician—to reaching the highest levels. To be sure, the great work of the *Laws* contains the labors of many years; in its origins it goes back to the attempts to shape practical politics in Sicily; and how deeply these labors are rooted in his nature may be seen from the passage of the *Letter* in which he expressed his early judgment of all contemporary states: "that they are altogether in bad condition; for the state of their laws is such as to be almost incurable—unless some marvelous action should combine with good luck."

But now let us also look at the other side. In the *Laws*, the Athenian stranger acknowledges explicitly that the type of state embodying the principle of the community of possessions, women, and children occupies the first place, though it may be suitable only for gods or the sons of gods, while the constitution outlined in this dialogue only approximates immortality and occupies the second place—the latter, however, unchallenged (739c *et seq.*). The earlier construction of the state is not, as it might seem, given up; on the contrary, "it is inevitably to be kept in view as a model." Thus it may be assumed that it was not Socrates who was displaced from the center of Plato's perspective, but rather that he continued to be recognized as the central power, and that only the state outlined in the *Laws* was, despite the labors that went into it, so far removed from the center that it could no longer be subsumed under his great name.

Dialectics practiced in the *Parmenides*, *Sophist*, and *Statesman* is, to be sure, preparation for the highest philosophical tasks— but still preparation. And Socrates has by no means become less important.[10] He represents unshakably the existence of the philosopher; he symbolizes true being, which those inquiries, as in a game with blindfolded eyes, now seize on unexpectedly, now lose again. Thus these late dialogues still seem to indicate that even those most important analytic exercises do not ultimately have a value of their own, but are subservient to something higher. In Plato, the Eleatic is focused upon the Socratic center, and so is the Pythagorean scientist in him. For while Plato devoted many years of strenuous labor to the construction of a scientific cosmology, the results of this labor could never achieve the certainty of dialectics, must always remain "probable discourse";[11] and for this reason Socrates, the guide on the dialectical path, could not represent them. But he must still be present listening, because natural science for Plato makes sense only in so far as it aims at the "science of *Ideas*"; because nature is an actualization or—to use a Platonizing paradox— a "deactualization" of the *Eidos* in space. And is it now still necessary to point out why nobody could expect to hear the political legend of the *Critias* from the mouth of Socrates? It lay so far outside the Platonic sphere that the forces at the center could no longer hold on to it, as it were, and form it into a completed work.

Thus the very dialogues in which Socrates apparently is displaced or disappears altogether reveal all the more clearly what he does—and does not—represent in Plato. It would obviously be quite false to say that the figure of his teacher gradually paled as Plato grew older; for this would be incompatible with the significance of Socrates in the *Philebus*—not to mention the *Phaedrus*, which presents him in the liveliest colors. And that he is not simply retained from habit and thus reduced to the role of a supernumerary in the *Sophist*, the *Statesman*, or the second part of the *Parmenides* becomes clear as soon as we think of him as absent: presently, the meaning changes, the depth is lost, if the discussion takes place without him. Similarly, the manner in which Plato used the figure of his teacher in the dialogues is no clue to any judgment about the historical Socrates. For what did history matter to Plato? And the historical Socrates, confronted with the proofs of immortality in the *Phaedo*, the speech in praise of *Eros* in the *Symposium*, or the construction of the state and the intuition of *Ideas* in the *Republic*, could only have said, shaking his head, something like what he is reported to have exclaimed after listening to a recital of the *Lysis:* "By Herakles, how much this young man has invented about me!" Still less does Plato play the role of a director in his dialogues in the manner of Cicero, who hesitates to the very end to whom he should give the various parts in the *Academica* or in the *De re publica;* obviously, profound necessity decided for Plato what Socrates is to say and where he is to be a listener. This necessity, therefore, must be looked into and the question must be asked how the Platonic (let us say) creation called "Socrates" is related to the historic Socrates.

Socrates as he appears in Plato's dialogues bears the characteristic traits of the real Socrates: bulging eyes, flat nose, walking barefoot; habits of ceaselessly asking and probing, affable sociability, and losing himself in imperturbably deep thought; hardness toward himself and prudent courage. Nevertheless, striking as is the similarity, so is the difference as soon as we look more deeply into the area where philosophical controversy takes place. From the very beginning, there are no "Socratic" dialogues that might be distinguished from purely Platonic dialogues of a later period. Although the distance between the two men may have become wider through the years, there is only more or less of this distance. The *Protagoras, Laches,* and *Charmides* already show a convergence upon a goal, not only suggested but almost explicit, which is a Platonic goal and which, in its theoretical elaboration, was foreign to the son of Sophroniskos. Still, the Platonic Socrates grows out of the historic Socrates. How this growth took place becomes apparent from the picture of Socrates in Plato's later work. The doctrine of order in the individual soul and in the large structure of the state is the conceptual form of what Plato saw in Socrates, and the widening application to the nature of the state, upon which the questions and thoughts of the historic Socrates were also focused. The Platonic "theory of love" is a translation into thought, words, and images of what Socrates embodied in his life and what Plato experienced in and with him. The Platonic "theory of *Ideas*" is the answer to the question of Socrates, the ὃ ἔστι the answer to the question τί ἔστι, the vision of true justice the answer to the question what justice really is. And it would not be correct to say that Plato gave the answer after Socrates had posed the question. The question—seen as a demand for clarity and a turning of the Socratic existence toward the object itself (and turning, at the same time, the disciple toward the same object)—already contained the answer in a very definite sense. Moreover, Socrates through his life was the answer that Plato gave in philosophical form. The Platonic Socrates proclaims what the historic Socrates was, confirming Heidegger's insight that "any answer is valid only as long as the question pertaining to it remains alive."

Whether Socrates talks, whether he listens, whether he is altogether absent—these differences must symbolize levels within the Platonic realm. Socrates could only represent the central sphere of Plato's thoughts, those areas which are Plato's interpretation of the living Socrates. The answer grew out of the question, interpretation out of experience, the poetic-philosophical figure out of the living human being engaged in philosophy, in a necessary growth of which Plato certainly was not conscious in the rational-historical perspective in which we, living in a historically minded age, grasp phenomena of this kind; but which he nevertheless expressed, in clear and, at the same time, veiled language, as was his way in old age, in the symbolic words of the "rejuvenated Socrates."

CHAPTER SEVEN

Irony

HE WHO would explain to us when men like Plato spoke in earnest, when in jest or half-jest, what they wrote from conviction and what merely for the sake of the argument, would certainly render us an extraordinary service and contribute greatly to our education." [1] These words of Goethe do not seem to have been taken with sufficient seriousness even as an ideal postulate. It is quite certain, however, that one cannot approach Plato without taking into account what irony is and what it means in his work.

If irony were nothing but "a mere swapping of a Yes for a No"—to put it into the jocularly polemical definition of Jean Paul—then we would be at the end of our discussion even before we had started it. It is only recently that we have begun again to learn something about the problem of irony, "incomparably the most profound and alluring problem in the world"—and from whom more than from Thomas Mann, the great ironist.[2] Otherwise our knowledge of the subject has been declining for the last hundred years. The Romanticists, however, especially Friedrich Schlegel and Solger, and later Kierkegaard as their successor, knew about the metaphysical significance of irony and deepened their insight by looking upon Socrates, Plato's Socrates, as their model. "Plato's irony," says Jean Paul, "could, if there is such a thing as world humor, be called world irony, singing and hovering playfully not only over human errors (as humor hovers not only over human folly), but over all human knowledge, free as a flame that devours, delights, moves with ease, yet aspires only toward heaven." [3]

Even though our printers still lack an "irony mark"—which the same Jean Paul, ironically, proposed in addition to the question mark and the exclamation mark—we do not need it in order to know that, besides being a man of sublimity, Plato is a master of irony, and often both at the same moment. But we cannot doubt that the Platonic Socrates did not get his irony from Plato alone, that Socrates was much more exclusively ironical than his more many-sided disciple, and that many people felt or said in conversation with Socrates what Plato puts into the scornful words of the Sophist Thrasymachos: "There we have the usual irony of Socrates" (*Republic* 337A). When a rhetorician talks about the concept of irony and wants to show that it not only has a definite place in the technique of oratory, but that "a whole life may be filled with irony," he calls on the life of Socrates as an example (Quintilian IX 2 46). There is no reason in this case to distinguish sharply between the historical and the Platonic Socrates. We see the former only through the latter, but we cannot doubt that we do see the real Socrates. The question is: What is the place of irony in the Socratic and Platonic way of life?

According to Theophrastus' *Characters*, the ironic man is a person who disparages himself in word and deed, who hides his views and intentions, his actions and energies.[4] The "moral botanist" does not evaluate irony, even though his entire work is based on the ethical system of his master Aristotle, according to whom irony is a deviation from the path of truth. Thus the concept may waver between mean dissimulation, hated or despised, playful hide and seek (a common idiom of the intellectually brilliant and critically suspicious society of democratic Athens), and dangerous concealment, feared or admired. Indeed, friends as well as enemies could talk about Socrates' irony with very different meanings. For in him such a contrast between external conduct and appearance, on the one hand, and inner character, on the other, was particularly striking. Nobody expresses this more pregnantly than Alkibiades in the *Symposium*, who uses as a simile the figures of Silenus that contain images of gods inside. Externally ugly, internally divine; thus Socrates appears more lowly than other beings who are nothing but beautiful, and he *is* so, as long as beauty is taken at its face value. But as soon as we have realized that there is a deeper and more hidden beauty, that "inner beauty" for which Plato makes Socrates pray to Pan and the nymphs at the end of the *Phaedrus* (δοίητέ μοι καλῷ γενέσθαι τἀνδοθεν, 279β), then the two levels change place, just as foreground and background may shift in a perspective drawing. He who hitherto seemed more lowly is suddenly seen as superior, and in the end there is the great wonder at the unexpected that has come into sight.

Plato's Alkibiades describes the master primarily in his contact with youth: "Know you that beauty, wealth, and honor, at which the many wonder, are of no account to him, and are utterly despised by him. He regards all this and us as worth nothing. And all his life he spends ironically and playfully mocking people" (*Symposium* 216D *et seq.*). Is even his *Eros* just a mask? To be sure, those who know only Eros Pandemos will see nothing but dissimulation in Socrates' character. In Alkibiades this feeling is very strong; at least he acts as if it were. He hears the flute-playing of Socrates-Marsyas. He sees Socrates following him and in a naïve manner he wants to exploit this, for he feels that Socrates would be his strongest supporter in his desire to excel (συλλήπτορα οὐδένα κυριώτερον εἶναι σοῦ, 218D). But he does not see that Socrates could not fulfill this role in a deeper sense if he were possessed by the lower *Eros*. Therefore Socrates, perceptive as he is, says "in the ironical manner so characteristic of him": "If this were so, then indeed my beauty would be much superior to that which I see in you. Then you would really exchange gold for brass. But this is not so." The essential reality becomes manifest in the disguise of this unreal condition. Yes and No are peculiarly intertwined in the words of the ironic man. Repulsion struggles with attraction in the soul of Alkibiades, and attraction finally wins out and retains its opposite only as a goading sting. Socrates, however, shows not by words but by his self-control that he truly possesses the higher beauty.

A great deal in the erotic nature of Socrates is but a mask. He pretends to be subject to the erotic drive, "in thrall to beautiful youths" (ἥττων τῶν καλῶν, *Meno* 76c), and he appears to participate in the erotic play in the same way as the others do; he even seems to surpass them in the degree of erotic, sensuous passion. But Socrates is a magician. Encountering the desired object of his love, he shows immediately that he is the master, not the slave, of his instincts. The conversation with Charmides, as well as that with Alkibiades in the dialogue bearing his name, after the very first words leaves all eroticism behind. And the Alkibiades of the *Symposium* receives a lesson that is more penetrating than the strictest catechism: "I rose from the couch, after I had spent the night with Socrates, as if I had slept with my father or an elder brother" (219D). This, of course, has a tremendous effect: "I wondered at his self-restraint and endurance, as I never imagined I would meet with a man such as he is in wisdom and temperance." Socrates never descends to the level of the others in his dealings with young men, but he sets an example of what they should be like: "Thus, my dear Hippothales, one must converse with a beloved friend in such a way as will bring down his pride and humble him, but not make him more blown up and conceited" (*Lysis* 210E). It is not his *Eros* that is a mask; if anything is a mask, it is the form he adopts, his adaptation to the social forms of his age. The *Eros* of Socrates differs from any other *Eros* just as his notion of ignorance differs. As the latter conceals a profound wisdom, so is his *Eros* an all-encompassing power—equal in weight with the *Logos*. For him who experienced this as something new, a depth opened up, which he had never imagined.

And now irony is carried into the discussion itself, into the pedagogic dialogue. The form this ironic discourse takes is that Socrates places himself side by side and on the same level with the young men, though, according to common opinion and the actual practice of the Sophists, he, as teacher, should hold them at a distance. The *Charmides* begins the inquiry: "Jointly we must inquire and test" (κοινῇ ἂν εἴη σκεπτέον, 158D). The *Alcibiades Major* makes the same point even more strikingly: "Let us jointly consult how we can acquire as much excellence as possible. For I am far from believing that you must be educated while I have no need of education" (124C). Later, when Alkibiades asks what he should do, the reply is: "Answer questions. That is the way which will bring improvement to both of us, to you as well as to me." Or in *Meno:* "We, my dear Menon, seem to be men who are not good for anything; and Gorgias does not seem to have sufficiently educated you, nor Prodikos me. It is, therefore, more important than anything else to be concerned with ourselves and to search for anyone who might improve us in any way" (96D). Or, in *Laches*, Socrates addresses the fathers who want him to be the teacher of their sons: "I maintain, my friends, that every one of us should seek out the best teacher he can find, first for ourselves, who are greatly in need of one, and then for the youths. . . . But I cannot advise that we remain as we are. . . . Let us, then, jointly take care of ourselves and of the youths" (201 AB). Again, there is no point in calling this a mask. Socrates can, indeed, seek only in the process of a common conversation; and this search is a perennial task, never completed for anybody, including himself. Yet does not Charmides, still in the process of developing, look to Socrates as to a man who has already attained perfection? Does not Socrates, though never standing still in his quest for knowledge, indeed represent perfection in every moment of his existence? And does not Socrates need Charmides? Indeed, is not even Charmides, as a youth, perfect in his own natural growth? Thus the peculiar seduction lies precisely in this gentle and concealed dialectical tension: irony is the net of the great educator.

Irony is particularly prominent at the conclusion of the aporetic dialogues. To admit ignorance—this experience, this confession, forced upon us by logical reasoning, brings about a humbling of the self. Yet Socrates always includes himself: "I too am ignorant." Thus the partner is received into a human community that almost transforms defeat into its opposite. The participants, in taking leave, realize that they have not discovered what courage is, or temperance. But they also feel that not everything is said with this confession of ignorance. Charmides says (176A): "How can I know whether I have a thing of which even you and Kritias are, as you say, unable to discover the nature—not that I believe you entirely (ὡς φῆς σύ · ἐγὼ μέντοι οὐ πάνυ σοι πείθομαι). And furthermore I am sure, Socrates, that I do need the charm [the ironic reference to the charm goes through the whole dialogue], and as far as I am concerned I shall be willing to be charmed by you daily until you say that I have had enough." The disciple has observed that Socrates knows more than just nothing, especially that he *is* more than he has expressed, perhaps more than he is able to express. And this superiority, concealed not intentionally but necessarily, and marvelously bound up with love, is the seduction felt by all the disciples. Again, it is Alkibiades who expresses this in almost extreme terms in the *Symposium:* "How badly he deceived me. And he has done this not only to me but also to Charmides and Euthydemos and to many others. He pretends to be their lover and then turns out to be the beloved rather than the lover" (222B). This very transformation takes place in the *Alcibiades.* In the beginning Socrates appears as the pursuer and Alkibiades as reluctant; in the end Alkibiades says: "Our roles will seem to be reversed. . . . From this day, it shall be I who shall wait upon you, and you who will be waited upon by me" (135D). Thus eroticism, not as a mask, but permeated with irony, and the probing dialogue manifest themselves as the highest expression of Socratic nature: he transforms, he educates in the sense of leading upward.

Irony means attraction and repulsion at the same time.[5] In the Alkibiades of the *Symposium*, these two opposing forces struggle with each other most painfully. The more susceptible Alkibiades is to Socrates' education, the more does attraction tend to include its opposite as a sting. The repulsive element in irony becomes dominant at a point where there is no more education because the other has become completely rigid in his ways. This is especially evident in Socrates' contact with professional teachers of wisdom, such as Thrasymachos; with tyrannical natures, such as Kallikles; with bigoted natures, such as Euthyphron. In the *Apology* (21B *et seq.*), Socrates describes how he was summoned by the god to examine the various professions. He goes to the politicians, the poets, the artisans, and examines their "knowledge." It turns out that the higher their claim to knowledge, the less it is confirmed, or can be confirmed, since knowledge is not something that is given to man and since these people even lack insight into their own ignorance. The clash is sharpest with the professional teachers of wisdom who are not mentioned in the *Apology*. For according to the *Meno* (93A *et seq.*), even politicians may accomplish good results though guided only by instinct. But he who claims to possess wisdom and to act according to its teachings cannot know or accomplish anything.

The conversation about "justice," from which the structure of the *Republic* emerges, has reached a point of admitted ignorance. Here Thrasymachos interrupts as the prototype of the Sophist, the exact counterpart of the genuine philosopher. This, he says, is pure babble. Socrates should not only ask but answer questions. And let him beware of phrasing his answers with reference to this, that, or another thing. This, of course, is an impossible request because it demands one, and only one, already determined answer from a man for whom there is, as an answer, only continuous search. Socrates would be a dogmatist and a Sophist, not a lover of wisdom, if he yielded to this point. Thrasymachos, on the other hand, fails to understand why it is impossible. He regards it as arbitrary dissimulation, as "irony" in the ordinary sense of the word. "I knew you would not answer, but play hide and seek" (εἰρωνεύσοιο, 337A). He would have to grow beyond his own nature if he were to understand that this irony is not willful, but necessary.

To be sure, there is play in Socrates' attitude—for example, when he depicts his horror at the interruption by Thrasymachos, or when he asks to be pitied rather than scolded. But precisely that which appears as hypocrisy to Thrasymachos, "we cannot" (336E), is completely genuine, or at least contains an element that is completely genuine. To say "you are the stronger" (ὑπὸ ὑμῶν τῶν δεινῶν) is, of course, wrong in Plato's sense. But, from the common point of view, the learned Thrasymachos is superior to the ignorant Socrates. This, however, is only the beginning of the peculiar game that might be called ironic self-entanglement. The learned man "thinks he has a beautiful answer" (ἡγούμενος ἔχειν ἀπόκρισιν παγκάλην, 338A), which he wants to display. But this lack of self-knowledge, at the same time a lack of irony, is precisely what fells the "strong" man. For as soon as the answer is out, it is easy for Socrates to show that it is nothing. Just as

Socrates' ugliness concealed a beauty of a higher order, the erotic play a more genuine love, so does a profound knowledge become visible behind his ignorance. As soon as this new aspect appears, the knowledge of the Sophist and the ignorance of the philosopher are reversed in rank, and the participants in the discussion experience that strange "reversal" and the inner astonishment awakened by it.

Hegel regarded Socratic irony as one side of the Socratic "method" (maieutics is the other): "What Socrates wanted was to let others express themselves and set forth their principles." [6] This is undoubtedly an essential element. But the phenomenon of irony will always be misunderstood if what can be truly educating only as an inner necessity is held to be an intentional pedagogic rule. Genuine irony contains an element of tension: on the one hand deceptively concealing, on the other uncompromisingly revealing, the truth. Socrates could control the interplay between the outward appearance of a Silenus and his inner beauty as little as he could capriciously conceal knowledge behind ignorance. Both are connected in a continuous circular or pendulous motion. Obviously he did have knowledge. For he led the others; and those who thought they knew were soon exposed in their ignorance. But in particular, as he often said, he knew that he did not know anything. Thus knowledge turns into its opposite. Indeed, he could not express what justice is, and his never-ceasing testing and questioning were determined by this ignorance. But now ignorance turns back to an ultimate stage of wisdom. For the ignorance revealed in the dialectical process was grounded in the living experience of the unknown. And where is a deeper knowledge than that found in a man representing in his life and death what he never ceases to explore in words?

Goethe's aphorism that "Kant limited himself intentionally to a certain field and ironically pointed beyond it" [7] would, if "intentionally" is not pressed too much, apply to Socrates as we have so far seen him in the creative mirror of Plato's art. It applies no less, or even more, to Plato himself, in whose creation Socrates is the central force. Just as, in Emerson's words, "Socrates and Plato are the double star which the most powerful instruments will not entirely separate," [8] so it is impossible to draw a sharp line of demarcation between Socratic and Platonic irony. Even those features of Socrates which we have so far seen—however much they were part of the life of the son of Sophroniskos—required Plato's hand in order to become as visible as they are. But gradually we ascend to forms of irony for which Plato, the artist and thinker, alone is responsible.

How Plato the artist joins and fuses different kinds of irony in a variety of ways—this polyphonic structure of irony—is best illustrated on a narrow scale in the *Euthydemus*. The dialogue consists for the most part of a Punch and Judy show performed by the two Sophistic fencing masters and clowns, with fireworks of amazing eristic acrobatics, fallacies, and equivocations. Here open opposition would be entirely futile and so much below the dignity of Socrates that only the most biting ironic rejection is an appropriate countermeasure. For possessing the true science he deems both of them much happier than the Great King for possessing his power (274A). "You are much better in the art of the philosophical discourse (κάλλιον ἐπίστασαι διαλέγεσθαι, 295E) than I, who have only the art of the common man at my disposal," says the master of the dialogue and dialectics to one of the counterfeiters. Then he encourages them to be serious at the end, since they have only been jesting up to this point (278c). If they should finally turn to a serious discussion, it would undoubtedly result in something very beautiful (288c), in the kind of knowledge that would teach us to spend our future life rightly (293A). Like a cheap comedian, he pretends to be a slave to their wisdom. Interwoven with these Punch and Judy scenes are pieces of a serious educational conversation that Socrates conducts with Kleinias. While he handles the former scenes with a caustic, bitter, or, as it were, repulsive irony, the tone of a gentle, attractive irony may be heard softly and infrequently during the other conversation—for example, when he addresses the disciple as "most beautiful and wisest Kleinias" (290c), or when, in his customary manner, he puts himself on the same level with his pupil: "We have almost made ourselves ridiculous before these strangers, you and I, son of Axiochos" (279c). Both forms of irony give us the "double irony" that Friedrich Schlegel defined as "two lines of irony running parallel, without disturbing one another, one for the pit, the other for the stalls." [9]

These two scenic developments of the dialogues are constantly interacting with each other in ironic tension. To be sure, Socrates shows the two Sophists, with an exemplary conversation, how it should be done. But it is biting irony when he pretends to presuppose that they would follow his example and that the outcome would then be something particularly beautiful (278D, 288c). Seen from the other side, the effect is still more radical. To pretend that both Kleinias and he had made themselves ridiculous, not only in general, but before the strangers (279c), is putting on quite an act. This turns almost into a farce when, reaching a point where he is stuck, he appeals to the Sophists for help: "When I was thrown into this difficulty, I cried out with all my voice, asking the strangers, as one calls upon the Dioscuri, to save us, the boy and myself, from these overwhelming waves of the *Logos*" (ἐκ τῆς τρικυμίας τοῦ λόγου, 293A). He expects them "to reveal the knowledge we must have in order to lead a beautiful life."

But this parallelism of ironies and ironic tensions is not yet the whole story. Now these conversations, full of ironies, are told by Socrates to his disciple Kriton and, of course, told ironically—for how else could Socrates tell a story? Considering the way in which the whole work is once more permeated with irony, we might speak with Schlegel of an "irony of ironies," if at this point we did not reach a still higher dimension. We breathe this air everywhere without always being aware of it. But at a certain place it makes the whole story suddenly transparent. Socrates makes Kleinias say so many intelligent things that Kriton, the listener, becomes suspicious and interrupts (290E). Kriton: "What do you mean, Socrates; did this young fellow say things like that?" Socrates: "Don't you believe me, Kriton?" Kriton: "By Zeus, not at all. For if he said that, he would not need Euthydemos or anybody else for his education." Socrates: "But, my noble Kriton, might it perhaps be that some higher being [i.e., a god] was present and said that?" Kriton: "By Zeus, yes, Socrates, so it seems to me indeed, some higher

being, much higher." The conviction that Socrates is giving an
accurate account is shaken; the illusion of the inner dialogue is
broken through as in a romantic comedy. But we are not in a
romantic world; it is inconceivable that this romantic dissolution
would also affect the framework of the dialogue. The iridescent
motion does not vanish away; and the sharpest ironic rays of
light remain fastened upon the figure of Socrates, both knowing
and ignorant.

According to Friedrich Schlegel, "Irony contains and excites
a feeling of insoluble opposition between the unconditional and
the conditional, between the impossibility and the necessity of a
complete communication." [10] The words show how irony points
straight to a metaphysical dimension, to the ultimate height to
which it is raised by Plato, the ironic metaphysician. The Platonic Socrates manifests the Socratic secret and the Socratic
irony, which expresses and bridges the tension between the
ignorance of his words and the knowledge of his existence, but
he also manifests, as he grows in and with Plato, the Platonic
secret and the Platonic irony. Is it not astonishing how Plato
veils with irony the highest truth he wants to show? When, in
the *Phaedo*, he is approaching the archetypes, he says, "If there
is such a thing as we constantly babble about, the beautiful,
the good, and all the forms of this kind;" and elsewhere he
speaks of them as the things "much prated about," as if he
intentionally chose derogatory terms.[11] The discussion in the
central part of the *Republic* goes still farther. It was shown
earlier [12] how long the discussion evaded the last and highest
form, and how insistently these deviations are pointed to as the
"highest fulfillment" (τελεωτάτη ἀπεργασία, 504D) is approached. But despite tense expectations this highest perfection
is not reached. Socrates appears as one who does not know.
"How would it be right to speak of that about which we have no
knowledge as if we did have knowledge?" (506C). When his
listeners declare themselves content with this conditional
account of the good, he adds ironically: "So am I, more than
content. I am afraid it is beyond my power and, with the best
will in the world, I should only make myself ridiculous" (506D).
This is the ineffability of the highest Platonic vision, symbolized

by the irony of Socratic ignorance. At last "the good" appears as something "beyond being and essence, exceeding in dignity and power" (509B). At this point Glaukon interrupts with some amusement: "By Apollo, what a demonic hyperbole" (or: "What an extravagant exaggeration," δαιμονίας ὑπερβολῆς, 509C). And Socrates replies: "It is your fault; you forced me to say what I think." This reveals most clearly, to come back to Schlegel, the impossibility and necessity of a complete communication. The ironic tension is expressed not only through the customary Socratic irony, the Socratic ignorance, but also through the device of putting a coarse jest side by side with the most solemn expression. Thus Socrates is not the only representative of irony; irony is also carried by the interlocutor to the "object" of the discussion; and this shows that we are dealing not only with Socratic irony, but with a matter of a more complex order.

When, in the *Symposium*, after many preliminaries, the speech of Socrates is to open up the road to the realm of eternal forms, a strange thing happens. It is not, strictly speaking, Socrates who leads the way; but he shows how the prophetess Diotima led the way for him. There is little doubt that the essential features of Diotima are a creation of the Platonic Socrates—the highest embodiment, as it were, of the more or less vague "somebody" whom he frequently posits playfully in conversation or debate as another person in order to conceal himself ironically. But there is much disagreement on the meaning or purpose of this creation. Socrates, it is said, is presenting ideas that were not part of the teachings of the historical Socrates. But Plato has put in the mouth of Socrates an enormous amount of material that the son of Sophroniskos never thought of. Or it is said to be an act of courtesy toward Agathon to show that he is not defeated by Socrates himself. But while the spirit of liberal courtesy characteristic of a secure social order runs through the language and form of the Platonic dialogues, it seems impossible to derive this highest creation of Plato's entirely from the sphere of social conventions. Or it is said that Socrates, as a dialectician, was not permitted to make a long speech, so that Plato, in order to preserve the unity of the

Socratic picture, had to break the speech up into the form of a dialogue. But Socrates makes long speeches in the *Phaedrus*; thus this technical consideration is no more satisfactory as a final answer than the social explanation. It is more correct to say that Socrates as the "ignorant" man cannot be the guide to the complete fulfillment of the philosophical quest; [13] but the whole structure of the work requires a deeper analysis.

When Socrates, after his numerous predecessors, begins to speak, it is immediately apparent that a new level of discussion has been reached. "Then I realized how foolish I had been, consenting to take my turn with you in praising *Eros*, and saying that I was a master in this art, when I really have no understanding as to how anything ought to be praised. For in my simplicity I imagined that the truth should be told" (198c). With this last phrase all the former speeches are devaluated; they must be justified before the new, surprisingly simple idea of—truth. "It is the truth, beloved Agathon, that you cannot refute; for Socrates is easily refuted" (201c). This distance of the new level from the old is suggested by the well-known forms of irony. "I did not know the nature of praise and, without knowing it, I consented to take my turn in making a speech of praise. Thus the lips have given a promise, but not the mind. Farewell then to such a promise. For I do not praise in that way; no, indeed, I could not. But if you like to hear the truth, I am ready to speak in my own manner, but not in rivalry with your speeches, lest I make myself ridiculous" (199AB). Thus irony points to (at the same time as it conceals) the road leading from the many to Socrates.

Socrates has hardly begun to speak when he is no longer the highest figure himself. A still higher figure looms above him. Diotima catechizes him as he usually does others. She plays with him ironically and jestingly (202B). The answer to one of his questions, she says, "would be clear even to a child" (204B). But most illuminating are her words pointing out the path of highest fulfillment: "These are the lesser mysteries of love, into which even you, Socrates, may enter; but to the deepest mysteries of the complete vision, to which the former, if you take the right path, will lead, I know not whether you will be able to attain" (209E). The single power by which Socrates opposes the flowery speeches and half-truths of the others thus undergoes an *ironic division*, as it were, into Socrates, representing the principle of truth but otherwise ignorant, and the priestess leading to the highest secrets. The ironic tensions between him and the others are superseded, at the crucial point, by an ironic tension between the seeker for truth and a power that, though shining through him, is also above him. It is uncertain whether Socrates was ever "initiated," and still more so whether we are chosen to be participants of the mystery. Thus the ladder of ironic tensions raises the reader to the divination of a higher being and leaves behind the impulse of unceasing search for what he has divined. It excites, to speak with Friedrich Schlegel, a feeling of the insoluble opposition between the unconditional and the conditional.[14]

Another kind of irony, which serves a similar purpose, is what may be called *ironic shift of balance* in a work of art. The *Symposium* is a dialogue about the nature of *Eros*, and all the speeches aim at this clearly defined goal. The speeches about love in the *Phaedrus* are quite different. This dialogue proceeds from a discussion of the art of rhetoric and the passionate admiration that Phaidros has for it and Socrates pretends to have. Lysias' speech, delivered by Phaidros, is an example of an abstruse rhetorical exercise proving the proposition that it is better to favor the nonlover than the lover. Love for the rhetorician is without any deeper meaning; and Socrates is quite right in saying that, for the lover and nonlover, we might as well substitute the rich man and the poor man, the young man and the old man, or anything else (227c). Socrates' first speech is only supposed to show that something else and something better may be said about the same topic. Only later does Socrates seem to come back to the subject matter itself. Lysias and he have offended *Eros*. He now wants "to wash the brine out of my ears with water from the spring." But apparently we are still on the level of a debating contest; for Socrates now counsels Lysias to write, as soon as possible, another discourse proving the opposite thesis (i.e., that it is better to favor the lover than the nonlover) (243D).

After the third speech about love, Socrates' second, has risen under the impact of mania (madness) into the heaven of forms, the discussion comes abruptly back to earth. It seems as if these sublime topics had not been under discussion at all; what follows deals with the technique of debating, the training of the orator, the relations between the written and the spoken word. If we take the dialogue literally, it is concerned with rhetoric; and the speeches about love are rhetorical illustrations to show the correct or false structure of an oration, or the difference between an improvised and a prepared, written-out speech. But even one's first impression shows that this is not so; and if we were to characterize the content of the dialogue in this way, we would be misled by Plato's ironic art. Just as there are pictures in which the pictorial center remains vacant, and the center of attention is transferred by the arrangement of lines, colors, and light effect to one of the corners, so the dialogue, if seen as a whole, confers essential meaning on that which appeared only as a means; and this meaning, in turn, illuminates and deepens even that which, as long as we did not recognize this ironic shift, appeared to be its primary purpose.

This artistic irony is worked out still more consciously in two late dialogues, the *Sophist* and the *Statesman*. These dialogues show a peculiar mixture: on the one hand, they are long, formal dialectical exercises to reach a definition by the method of division; on the other, they search for those realities designated by the names of Sophist, Statesman, and Philosopher. If we listen to what is said, the inquiry into the subject matter appears only as a formal exercise: "the inquiry about the statesman is only undertaken so that we may become more dialectical in all things" (*Statesman* 285D). "For the immaterial things, the most beautiful and greatest, are shown only through the *Logos*, and in no other way, and all that we are now saying is said for the sake of them" (286A). And yet it is difficult to listen with a straight face to the classification of the Sophist as an angler, and to many other things of this kind. If we really took seriously the grouping of men and birds as bipeds in contrast to the quadrupeds (266E), Diogenes the Cynic would be quite right with his plucked cock as a satire upon this Platonic classification.

But the comic side of these divisions is explicitly touched upon in the dialogue itself (266BC). Ironic tensions are employed between correct and false classifications, on the one hand, in order to arouse critical thinking; between intention and execution, on the other, in order to indicate that these exercises are preparatory—and only preparatory—for the most important task.

While these ironic tensions are concerned with formal elements, another tension permeates the subject matter itself. The nature of the Sophist is the goal of the inquiry; yet, as in a blindfold game, we come up against the Philosopher. And the question arises whether we are not paying too much honor to the Sophist with this definition (231A). But is it not the Philosopher whom we are really looking for, who looms behind the inquiry and whose definition must be given after we have determined the nature of the Sophist and the Statesman? Thus the ironic tension here exists between that which is the immediate subject of definition and that which is ultimately looked for; and this tension is reinforced by coming very close, accidentally as it seems, and for a moment, to the ultimate goal of the inquiry.

The dialectical exercise and the subject matter itself are therefore not combined so arbitrarily as it would at times appear. It is highly unlikely that the definition of the Statesman would seriously serve only the purpose of a dialectical exercise, as the dialogue itself claims it does. In this way the true order of rank and value seems to be rather veiled by irony. For the dialectical exercise is supposed to prepare us ultimately for the goal of the vision of the forms; and this goal is the goal of the Philosopher, whose nature must therefore be distinguished from that of the Sophist and the Statesman. Thus, ultimately, material and formal elements coincide. Even the ironic tensions of the two lines are not accidentally placed beside each other. In each case they designate the conditional and point suggestively to the depth of the unconditional.

Consequently, both dialogues lead to the last manifestation of ironic play: *wordless irony* consisting in the fact that Socrates, by virtue of his silent presence, represents ironic tensions— unspoken yet felt. Behind the two definitions of the Sophist and the Statesman remains the task of discovering the nature of the Philosopher. This is mentioned frequently and is so much in the center of expectation that it has generally been assumed that there should have been a third dialogue called "Philosophos"; some have either found this dialogue in one of the others which are extant or concluded that the two dialogues are fragments of an uncompleted trilogy.[15] But suppose this only made us victims of Platonic irony? An ironic tension connects Socrates, silently listening, with the Eleatic stranger and his youthful partners in the conversation. The goal is the path to the highest form. Socrates stands by as silent representative of this path. The same ironic dialectic that leads back and forth from the definitions of the two dialogues to the hidden definition of the Philosopher reverberates, in the veiled manner of Plato's late works, between the representatives of the dialectical exercises and the Philosopher, who, like a Homeric god, stands by "hidden in air."

Socratic irony, at its center, expresses the tension between ignorance—that is, the impossibility ultimately to put into words "what justice is"—and the direct experience of the unknown, the existence of the just man, whom justice raises to the level of the divine. For Plato the Socratic question becomes answerable "in words" (ἐν λόγοις). But this answer is only complete in the vision of the eternal forms and in the dawning realization of something that is beyond being. Here once more the same basic relationship, the same opposition between the conditional and the unconditional, is repeated. And thus Platonic irony, incorporating the whole teaching and magic of the figure of Socrates, is revealed as veiling and protecting the Platonic secret. However, as in a Greek statue the garment not only serves as a veil but at the same time reveals that which it veils, so is Plato's irony also a guide on the path to the eternal forms and to that which is beyond being.

CHAPTER EIGHT

Dialogue

JUST as there are no adequate equivalents in any modern language for concepts like *Logos* and *Eidos*, so such words as "inwardness" (*Innerlichkeit*) or "landscape" could not be translated into Greek. Even when a Greek flees from the world, his loneliness is accident or necessity, not happiness or a path toward human perfection. And if the loneliness of the tragic hero in the works of Sophocles is indispensable to his fulfilling himself, it is also responsible for his destruction. For the nature of a Greek man is inseparable from the community. To be seen and to be heard is an indispensable condition for Greek life and Greek form.[1]

Epideictic or declamatory speech is a recognized category of ancient oratory. But an epideictic element is in every Greek speech, and it might be possible to order all forms of oratory on a scale according to the degree to which the declamatory element predominates. Speeches for a practical purpose contain less of it than general oratory, dialogue less than speech by an individual. And the Socratic conversation would be the farthest removed from all *epideixis*. For never before did the Greek world find words so entirely focused upon real being as the words of Socrates, and those he elicited from others. What distinguished him above all was that he simply *was* and did not display himself. Perhaps this part of his nature, which everybody must feel, comes out even more clearly when we compare him with Diogenes the Cynic, who claimed to walk in the footsteps of Socrates. In the case of Diogenes, the absence of display is so conscious that it again turns into a self-display.

It is a constantly recurring characteristic of the Platonic dialogues that Socrates contrasts the kind of conversation he conducts with the lectures of the Sophists. The dialogue *Protagoras* is entirely built around this contrast, re-echoed in the *Gorgias*. Socrates is incapable of delivering speeches like the Sophists; he cannot even listen to them owing to his "faulty memory." If they insist upon their procedure and refuse to enter into a "dialogical" conversation, he cannot be an active participant. The orator is intoxicated with the sound of his own words: "They go on ringing in a long harangue, like brazen vessels, which when struck continue to sound" (*Protagoras* 329A). Socrates, however, is only interested in bringing the truth to light, not in winning an argument (*Gorgias* 457E). To be sure, even the dialogue may become deceptive and an instrument for self-display. The Sophist know-alls had to prove themselves in oratorical debates as well, and in Plato they expressly include this point in their program (*Protagoras* 329B, *Gorgias* 447C). And the acrobatic pair in Plato's *Euthydemus*, entertaining with their dialectical capers, give a regular performance of an oratorical debate. "Show yourselves," Socrates says; "and all present asked them jointly to display their ability in the art" (274D). Even Plato's Socrates often resorts intentionally to eristic arguments when he wants to overwhelm or frighten his listeners, or stun them into awareness of the worst stupidities, or when he wants to show the right goal by following a wrong path. Judging it from the outside, a piece of a Socratic conversation might often sound as if it were nothing but a fragment of Sophistic eristics. What radically separated him from this procedure was the final goal he aimed at: even when Socrates adopted Sophistic ways, when—as in the *Hippias Minor*—he was "knowingly deceptive," he still aimed at the truth of the matter.

For this was the task which the god imposed upon him as he described it in the *Apology:* "Going about in the world, obedient to the god, I seek and make inquiry into the wisdom of citizens and strangers, whether any one of them appears wise. And when he is not wise, then in vindication of the oracle I show him that he is not wise" (23B). His age—like ours—was filled with

all kinds of intellectual counterfeiting. Socrates felt called upon
by the god to make inquiry and to make distinctions, and to test
the "pots" for their soundness. He inquired into any assertion
by "bringing the whole discourse back to its basic foundations"
(Xenophon, *Memorabilia* IV 6 13). And it usually turned out
that his opponent could not give an adequate account of "what
is": "I am one of those who are willing to be refuted if I say
anything that is not true, and willing to refute anyone else who
says what is not true, and quite as ready to be refuted as to
refute" (*Gorgias* 458A). The Socratic *elenchos* can only become
effective in conversation. It is a step on the way to *paideia*. To
educate means to evoke knowledge. But knowledge is not something which, as in communicating pipes, "runs from the full to
the empty" (*Symposium* 175D). It is the wrong kind of educators
who believe "they can put into the soul knowledge that was
not there before, like sight into blind eyes" (*Republic* 518B).
This belief, as is well known, is in sharp contrast to the Socratic
and perennial principle of education dedicated only to what the
individual can discover for himself. "A person will say the right
things if one can only put the right questions to him" [2]—this is
the standard approach of Plato's Socrates. And what is called
the "theory of recollection" in the *Meno* is a half-mythical way
of leading to the pre-existing *Eidos*, a way that was undoubtedly
part of this original Socratic conviction. The loving teacher,
the "midwife," produces his own formal approach, the dialogue,
through which the pupil finds the way to truth in a process of
continuous, critical affirmation and negation.

Xenophon portrays Socrates as also making hortatory,
educational, and sermonizing speeches. He says something
about Socrates' method of speaking, when not engaged in
conversation, but "when pursuing something in a discourse of
his own. Then he would take a position on which there was most
general agreement, believing that this would produce the
greatest certainty in the discussion" (*Memorabilia* IV 6 15).
This is in contrast to the Platonic Socrates, especially in respect
to what the latter himself says about his attitude toward speech
and dialogue. It is not improbable that Xenophon's description
is derived from what he correctly remembered about the

protreptic Socrates. Even so, Plato's account would still give us the greater truth because it brings out explicitly what distinguished Socrates and what made him unique. "Socrates asked questions, but he did not answer; for he professed not to know" (Σωκράτης ἠρώτα, ἀλλ' οὐκ ἀπεκρίνατο· ὡμολόγει γὰρ οὐκ εἰδέναι)—thus Aristotle (*De sophisticis elenchis* 183ᵇ 7), in the briefest of formulations, derives the Socratic method from the center of Socrates' intellectual attitude. In Plato, Socrates even transforms prolonged speeches that he is called upon to make—whether due to the law of the state or to the rules of the banquet—into a dialogical structure. There are exceptions, but they are usually mentioned as exceptions: e.g., in the *Protagoras, Menexenus, Phaedrus*. In the great myths we undoubtedly reach the point where the speech of the Platonic Socrates grows farthest beyond that of the historical Socrates.

With Socrates a "dialogical" movement enters Greek thought—and the intellectual life of the Western world—a movement that did not exist previously. This is apparent when we consider how differently earlier Greek thinkers expressed themselves.[3] And what we know about conversations and controversies of the fifth century written in dialogue form is not much, compared with the Socratic impetus, which only spent itself gradually, never completely.[4] All his disciples, in so far as they wrote anything, produced dialogues. But none of them dedicated the creative power of a long lifetime so exclusively to this form of exposition as did Plato. Thus only for him was the creation of "Socratic dialogues" an inescapable necessity. The other Socratics who have left extensive writings, Aristippos, Antisthenes, and Xenophon, did not restrict themselves to the form of the dialogue, and not all their dialogues were Socratic conversations. The few dialogues produced by Eukleides, Phaidon, and Aischines cannot be compared, either in scope or merit, with those written by Plato. Thus, even though the Socratic conversations may have left their imprint upon literature before him, Plato may still rightly be called the creator of the philosophical dialogue as a genuine work of art, comparable to the tragedy and comedy of the preceding age.

The conversations of the historic Socrates are lost to us, and

this necessarily so. For it was characteristic of his conversation
that it was only oral. Moreover, it dealt with many more
subjects than we know from Plato. It is undoubtedly a historical
fact that Xenophon asked advice of Socrates as to whether he
should participate in the campaign of Cyrus (*Anabasis* III 1 5).
In Plato's *Apology*, Socrates himself says that he tested politicians, poets, and artisans. Not all these professions—and there
must have been more—are represented in Plato's dialogues, so
that we must consult Xenophon in order to appreciate the rich
variety of occasions and participants in the Socratic conversations. Yet Xenophon's conversations lack the energy, the
liberating and purifying power, that our imagination necessarily
attributes to the most "Socratic" among the talks of Socrates.
For these were not simply, in Xenophon's sense, didactic and
"useful for everybody." They must have left a much sharper
sting, since Socratic "ignorance" must have impressed upon
them the much more powerful imprint of the aporetic conclusion.

The Platonic dialogue mirrors Socratic conversation; but it
necessarily differs from the latter in the final analysis.[5] The two
are related to each other as art is to nature. A work of art is
detached from the context of nature; it is a whole that must make
up, by its completeness and richness, for not permitting any
arbitrary addition. This is also true of the Platonic dialogue,
however tentative it may be to designate it as a work of art.
Socrates' dialogue originates most often in an occasional
encounter, "as talk developing out of a living, accidental contact, in the manner of a free conversation conducted with an art
of spontaneity and the gift of dealing with men" (Karl Justi).
Plato could not tolerate any accidental elements in his work.
He was compelled to select the participants and to integrate
them into the work according to aesthetic requirements, to
attune the surroundings to the inner content, to strip the
natural setting of accidental factors so that it could become an
effective agent in the total work.

"Art has reached perfection when it gives the appearance of
being nature" (or history). Thus it is Plato's artistic triumph
that we take what he invented as historical reality. Perhaps

Socrates did meet, in some public place, a visiting Sophist accompanied by his pupil and his Athenian host. But that these are combined to form, as if accidentally, an order of rank in clarity and honesty of self-interpretation, that the pupil discards the ethical ambiguities of his master for the sake of greater logical consistency, that the host, finally, represents a position of irresponsible immoralism, which, in turn, appears only as the logical consequence of the rhetorical position of the Sophist—all this is Plato's invention in the *Gorgias*. Socrates certainly used to meet with boys and young men at different places, in the streets, in homes, or in the gymnasia. But that Plato invariably places these encounters (in so far as a location is given at all) in the gymnasia, or even in the apodyterion, as in the *Euthydemus* and the major part of the *Lysis*—that must have been his invention to provide an appropriate setting for the mental gymnastics and a concrete image of the intellectual undressing with which he liked to play," or possibly to represent his own educational ideal through a parallelism of physical and intellectual discipline. In the *Protagoras*, the Sophists are all brought together in one house, as they may never have met. Again, in the beginning, they are in different rooms; and it is not accidental that the most superior of them, Socrates' real opponent, is walking up and down in the outer hall as Socrates liked to do, while Hippias is sitting in the background "on a chair of state" and Prodikos is still lying in bed in a dark room apart. It is Socrates entering among them who brings all these different men together into a unified group of "Sophists." How the element of time co-operates with the spatial element in the development of the dramatic—and philosophical—themes may be seen from the introductory conversation in the same dialogue. Young Hippokrates finds Socrates lying in bed, and the two exchange the first words in the darkness of the bedroom. Then they step outside into the court, that is, into the open, and begin to walk up and down. At the same time, the conversation turns from discussion of personalities to the subject matter itself. And as they had agreed to delay their departure "until it is light," the day actually begins to dawn just when Socrates is posing the crucial question—undoubtedly so that one can see the young man blushing; but his blushing again is only a sign that "day had also begun to dawn" in a different sense.[7]

The spatial setting in the *Euthydemus*, after a brief introductory flurry, is as follows: The young Kleinias is sitting down on the bench beside Socrates; and both are flanked, right and left, by the pair of Sophists. Ktesippos, the lover of Kleinias, originally the fifth man on the bench, has risen and now stands facing the others. The circle is completed by the other friends of Kleinias and by the followers of the Sophists. Socrates sits on a bench beside a youth; the same picture occurs in the *Lysis* and *Charmides*. It is the picture of the "fisher of men" who has drawn the young boy toward him, the "ironic man" sitting side by side with his pupil, not opposite and superior to him. In the *Euthydemus* this group of two is flanked by the two Sophistic debaters. Thus the spatial arrangement expresses, as it were, the double theme of the work, interweaving variations of the educational dialogue—in the manner of the *Lysis*—with those of the debating dialogue—in the manner of the *Protagoras*. The contrast introduced by making Ktesippos stand up facing the others while Socrates is sitting on the same bench with them also has symbolic significance. Ktesippos later leaps into the fray on behalf of his young friend against the eristic Sophists and carries the fight against them with considerable violence, though not always with equal success. Socrates, on the other hand, never surrenders the ironic attitude by which he professes to be a disciple (together with Kleinias) of Euthydemos and Dionysodoros. Ktesippos, therefore, is seen in contrast to Socrates; and this contrast is symbolized, from the very beginning, by the spatial arrangement of the figures in the dialogue.

In the *Symposium* by Xenophon, Socrates is present from the outset and participates in the conversation throughout. In this way Xenophon forgoes precisely that suspenseful element that creates such a strong dual tension in the space-time construction of Plato's *Symposium*: Socrates entering only after the others have sat down to the banquet, and beginning his speech in praise of *Eros* only after all the others have spoken. Thus we are compelled twice, and with increasing seriousness, to wait for him and to bring everything that is being said into relation with him. But why does Aristophanes suffer an attack of hiccups when it is his turn to speak, so that his neighbor, the physician Eryximachos, must take his place? Why did not Plato assign to the two men an order at the table that would have corresponded to the order in which he was to let them speak? What, in short, is the point of this reversal? Was it in order to give the imagination a brief rest in delightful social play and at the same time show the people involved in their appropriate roles: the comic poet in a ridiculous situation, the physician with the slight pedantry of the expert? Or was it to interrupt the monotony of a clockwise order of speeches by its opposite? The last question leads even further: What does the clockwise order mean but to refer to Socrates? We know that he will speak in the end—if the others leave anything for him to say! The interruption of the orderly procedure, therefore, throws the order itself into sharp relief—the order pointing to him. What we have half forgotten in the midst of the long eulogies is suddenly brought back to us concretely, as the countermovement makes visible the essential movement toward the goal and toward Socrates as the last appeal for adjudicating what the others have said—and, indeed, what they are.

Thus, for an understanding of the dialogues, it may be necessary to inquire more deeply than is usually done into the symbolic meaning of the spatial setting and the physical happenings. Not that they should be treated as allegories in the manner of the Neoplatonists—among whom, incidentally, Proklos comments wisely that the introductory action not only fulfills an aesthetic and historical function, but has a genuinely philosophical significance.[8] What the philosophical analyst of Plato prefers to leave to the literary and historical interpreter must be seen within its existential context. For the frame action is not constructed accidentally, especially since Plato's works do not belong to a naturalistic, but to a classical form of art.

Similar questions arise in connection with the relation of the dialogues to each other. In Plato, Socrates often refers to the continuation, at some future time, of the discussion now interrupted. And we can read in Xenophon how Socrates had to work on Euthydemos three times before he could cure him of his arrogance (*Memorabilia* IV 2). Thus the conversations of the historic Socrates must often have been connected with one another. On the other hand, there were numerous encounters, more or less accidental, with a variety of people, whereas the work of a great artist is governed by necessity. It has been mentioned reproachfully that Plato did not—as Phaidon of Elis did in dialogues lost to us—bring his master together with artisans.[9] Perhaps it would be more correct to say that Plato only selected such participants and situations as promised to be fruitful. Now peasants, shoemakers, carpenters, flute players, and other craftsmen are always representative examples for someone who has learned the art he practices and thus truly knows what he claims to know under his professional name. But behind the artisan there was no intellectual world that had to be combated, no intellectual power worthy of being developed. And somebody who was probing the depth of essential problems could not be concerned with the question whether the picture he outlined was complete from the point of view of empirical reality. Thus, on the one hand, there was selection of the material; on the other, integration of the selected material. When a great artist throughout a long life produces a number of works, it cannot be said that he does so according to a master plan projected in the beginning and only executed later; but even less can it be said that each individual work is nothing but an accidental product of a given mood or situation. Indeed, a first glance brings a number of dialogues together into groups: the works of the first period by virtue of their aporetic form and orientation toward a goal not yet revealed; then the *Republic, Timaeus*, and *Critias* on the one hand, and the *Theaetetus, Sophist*, and *Statesman* on the other, either group characterized by the same participants and by a unified action. And certain references are equally obvious, from the *Phaedo* to the *Meno*, or from the *Laws* to the *Republic*. All this can be seen at first glance, but it may be assumed that much cannot thus be seen. Perhaps it is an insoluble task—but it must be attempted—"to envisage the works of Plato as a planetary system in which no source of light or energy may be omitted."[10]

We interrupt here to recall that there exists—probably without historical connection with the Platonic dialogues—another great literature of philosophical conversations in the entirely different world of India. They, too, mirror a life marked by the dialogue; and despite their internal differences, as well as their difference from the Greek form, they may be compared to the Socratic dialogues in that they, too, are constructed as literary works in contrast to natural conversation. This, however, would seem to be the only element they have in common. The reality depicted in the two dialogical art forms is totally different. With the Greeks, it is Socrates, both knowing and ignorant, inquiring, testing, and educating. In the *Upanishads*, it is the many wise men competing with each other and proclaiming the dogma from the depth of their wisdom. Even if one of them raises himself above the others, as when Yajnavalkya is victorious in the debating contest over all other Brahmins, he has a different nature from Socrates. The person matters so little that in other *Upanishads* the ascetic Aruni or even the god Prajapati may be spokesmen of the same proclamation of wisdom.[11]

Closer to the Socratic dialogues, perhaps, seem to be the educational conversations and competitive debates that we find in the sermons of Gautama the Buddha.[12] Here it is indeed primarily the enlightened one, partly preaching to the monks and partly communicating to them in conversation the dogma of suffering, the origin of suffering, the elimination of suffering, and the right path, partly converting keenly debating opponents to this doctrine. Indeed, in situation as well as form of conversation, there are similarities with the Socratic dialogues. But not to mention the incomparableness of the two worlds depicted and the fact that Gautama has a doctrine unshakably formulated down to the very words; that he claims "insight, self-immersion, and wisdom" for himself; that his opponent Saccaka, refusing to answer, is confronted by a lightning-carrying spirit that threatens to smash his head into seven parts—nowhere among the Indian scriptures is there a single creative mind who captures the image of the master. Thus the many conversations of the enlightened one as well as the many *Upanishads* lack that higher organic unity achieved by Plato's total work. But even this point is not yet the most decisive, and only leads to the crucial issue raised by this comparison.

In India the author of the dialogue or sermon teaches nothing but what he says (or believes he says) after his master. At any rate, there is no element of tension between his own thought processes and those which he is describing. The Platonic world, however, stands apart from the Socratic with a center and periphery of its own.

Thus what distinguishes, finally and perhaps above all, the Platonic dialogue from the Socratic is the fact that, in addition to a mirroring of the Socratic life, it is also—to put it tentatively—a presentation of Plato's philosophy. Two altogether different purposes, it would seem; and it remains to be asked whether these are compatible with each other. It has been said that they are not, that the ironic man, always inquiring, searching, and professing ignorance, as he had to be represented from a sense of hero worship, is in constant struggle with the dogmatist in Plato, whose full expression is curbed by a voluntary submission to the former image.[13] This would mean that Plato had chosen a form, and retained it until his old age, which was to bring him into constant conflict within himself. And he would never have shed this burden—except in the *Laws*, where Socrates, to be sure, is no longer present, but where the last of Plato's teachings are also more concealed from than revealed to the world. After what we have said previously, this interpretation cannot be accepted, because Socrates lives in Plato and speaks out of Plato's works. It is, therefore, imperative to find out whether the two purposes apparently leading into opposite directions do not, in the final analysis, meet and become one.

What, then, does the dialogue—especially the Socratic dialogue—mean in Plato? Sometimes a view is held (more frequently it is tacitly assumed) that Plato, having once begun to write Socratic dialogues, retained this form even in his late period when he should have discarded it in favor of writing treatises, the form developed by the Ionian physicians and later used by Aristotle.[14] But if this view is true, would it not apply just as much to Plato's *Republic*, the central work of his creative powers? What a monster, indeed: a conversation related by

Socrates without an interruption, of such a length that later editors divided it into ten books, which nobody could listen to uninterruptedly. Besides, it is a conversation that, over long stretches, contains (or seems to contain) nothing but straight communication or teaching by Socrates, restricting the partner in the dialogue to comments like "Yes" or "No" or "What do you mean?" But would one of the greatest artists have erred on so essential a point and left his error to be discovered by posterity when, in fact, to quote Schleiermacher, "the cause of the feeling is falsely diagnosed; instead of seeing it in the judge, it is projected into the thing or person judged." That he went against common practice nobody knew better than Plato. If necessary, the beginning of the *Theaetetus* would be sufficient evidence that he was perfectly clear, even in theory, about the basic principles of the dialogue as an art form. Just as he makes the reporter say he is repeating the conversation in its dramatic simplicity in order to avoid the cumbersome interlocutory remarks, so he would not have hesitated to cut out interruptions by the participants altogether. But the inner need compelling him to write dialogues must have been so great that it conquered all possible objections and prevailed throughout his life. This need must be explained.

Socrates was so completely committed to oral discourse that he never thought of writing down any philosophical ideas, and the question is whether he ever gave a thought to the value or worthlessness of writing. He does so in Plato, already in the *Protagoras* and still in the *Phaedrus*, because Plato did so himself. For that which was a simple characteristic of Socrates' nature manifested itself in Plato in the form of doubts as to the value of the written word and a conviction as to its hazards, even its worthlessness; and these sentiments are expressed by Socrates in the dialogues and by Plato himself in his letters.[15] Yet the impulse of the creative artist was ever alive in him with a tremendous power. He had burned his tragedies; yet the new experience—no longer Oedipus or Philoktetes, but Socrates only—demanded creative expression. If he was successful in this, if he found the means to raise the Socratic conversation itself to the heights of a new dramatic art, this way of writing would at

least obviate the objection made against written books that they
are rigid and do not know how to answer, but only sound one
tone like a brazen pot. For the written dialogue transmits its
dialogical and dialectical dynamics to the reader. To him is addressed every question raised by Socrates; every aye of Glaukon
or Lysis is his aye—or his nay—and this dialogical dynamics
continues to echo within him beyond the conclusion. The dialogue is the only form of book that seems to suspend the book
form itself.

Plato also inherited the insight from Socrates that there is no
ready-made knowledge simply transferable from one person to
another, but only philosophy as an activity, the level of which is
invariably determined by one's partner. Every philosophical
conversation conducted by Socrates is new and different according to the partner—this is the Socratic principle of education. Or
as Nietzsche remarks, thinking still more of his ideal Socrates
than of himself: "An educator never says what he himself thinks;
but only that which he thinks it is good for those whom he is
educating to hear upon any subject." [16] Plato gives wisdom and
doctrine; but the Socratic principle is still so commanding
within him that for him, too, knowledge would be "deceit" if it
purported to be the same for everybody and everywhere. Philosophy is conducted from a constantly changing perspective
that reveals different heights and breadths, different aspects of
the total horizon. Nor is human knowledge of such a kind that it
remains in a quiescent state, as it were, after it has once been
acquired. Just as Socrates found his opponents by his mere existence, so they were called forth by Plato's new vision; when
none were available, he had to create them himself. Philosophy
is the making of a cosmos out of chaos. What is formed and
ordered is constantly threatened and must be protected against
the threatening powers. To be sure, the good is far from existing at the mercy of its opposite; but light cannot be seen or
named without darkness. Moreover, human order would petrify
and atrophy if it did not have to prove itself in the struggle with
rebellious forces. Thus the assertion made in the *Lysis*—and
then refuted—is undoubtedly valid, to a certain extent, at least
within the world of man, to wit, that the good is sought "be-

cause of the presence of the bad." Socrates is not effective without Kallikles. Nor is victory alone the heart of the matter—is Kallikles, after all, "conquered" in the end?—more important than victory is the struggle itself, which here, too, is the father of all things. *"Rien ne nous plaît que le combat, mais non pas la victoire,"* writes Pascal; *"nous ne cherchons jamais les choses, mais la recherche des choses."* [17] Thus Plato was compelled to express his knowledge in the dialectical tension of such a struggle in which it became alive.

Seen from another angle, this intellectual form becomes a dramatic form. For to be a dramatist means to experience the world directly as a struggle of authentic forces, personalized forces.[18] Thus the dialogue of love and struggle is the only art form for Plato, the kind of dialogue that does not simply conquer and discard the opposing elements, but gives concrete expression to the struggle and conquest itself in the work of art. As Goethe is in Tasso *and* Antonio, so Plato is not only in Socrates—or in the disciples Charmides, Theaitetos, Alkibiades—but also, to a certain degree and manner, in the opponents of Socrates. This relationship is seen quite wrongly if we only emphasize the element of resistance to foreign thought and attack. Polemic is struggle against the self—the pointed formulation by Novalis also holds for Plato. It is doubtful whether the historical Socrates was willing to objectify his opponents as Plato did; for Plato was of an entirely different nature. He was delighted by resounding speeches; otherwise he would not have put Agathon and Protagoras upon the stage. He enjoyed the tricks and wily cunning of verbal fencing as they are portrayed—and caricatured—in the *Euthydemus.* If there had not been something of Kallikles—the "Strong Man"—in himself, he would hardly have been able to portray the former with such overwhelming power that there will always be individuals, especially young people, who are more fascinated by the man Socrates opposed and conquered than by Socrates himself.[19] Did not Plato also have, as part of his nature and as a possible danger, something of the versatility of his Sophists, even something of the clerical "piety" of his Euthyphron? "There is much of a mystery priest in Plato," was the judgment of so fine a critic as Demetrios of

Phaleron after an analysis of Plato's style.[20] And is not the struggle against the poets in the *Republic*, and especially against their prototype Homer, admittedly a struggle against a power that had charmed him (607c), a struggle born undoubtedly of the genuinely Greek desire for contest and victory, but just as much out of the old magic that poetry had for him—in other words, a struggle against himself? Plato, endowed with overabundant powers, probably had more to conquer within his nature than is generally assumed. But he also had Socrates within him, and the decisive struggles and victories that he made public were won within himself.

One of the basic principles of the Socratic conversation was to destroy in the pupil his belief that he had knowledge or to awaken him to the realization that he had none—not, by any means, in order to conclude with a skeptical position, but in order to stimulate a continuous mutual quest for the truth. In Plato, this simple method manifests itself as a tension: falsehood must first be rooted out, the opposing forces must first be destroyed, before the truth can be shown and the new realm can be founded. This conquest can only be successful if it is a joint labor, and the struggle must be shown in all its dialectical inexorability. The dialogues of the early period have (or seem to have) only this one purpose, although they also prepare us for what is to come. The *Alcibiades*, the *Gorgias*, and, on the largest scale, the *Republic* first tear down and then embark upon a reconstruction. This process of rebuilding also is a matter of philosophizing together. For since, according to the *Seventh Letter*, the spark is kindled only "after a long joint life on behalf of the matter itself," and since the "path must go up and down through all the grades of knowledge," it follows that each step must be taken by the pupil himself and according to a definite order. In the realm of the philosophical life this hierarchical path of knowledge is the "dialectical path"; its reflection in the realm of philosophical literature is the dialogue.

At this point, however, we have touched upon a contrast between the Socratic and the Platonic way of philosophy. Plato does not conclude, as Socrates did, with an assertion of not-knowing. He discovered a metaphysical world, and it was his task to make others see it through his own eyes. How, then, in the light of this contrast, could the form of the Socratic conversation be adequate to express the entirely new vision? Further, why was it the only form in which the new vision could be expressed?

The solution to this question is not difficult. Plato discovered what Socrates was "merely" seeking or taught to seek. But it is well known what the right kind of search means and is worth. "With the question is given the answer, the feeling that something may be thought or surmised about a given point," said Goethe.[21] In accepting the Socratic dialectics, Plato gained access to the eternal forms. Through and in Socrates he envisaged the form of justice. Thus, on the new level that he had reached, he was compelled to carry the Socratic discourse beyond itself, not to a skeptically negative conclusion, but to an answer to the questions posed by it and, if possible, to a knowledge of the world of being. Only the "dialectical path" could carry this knowledge beyond a merely subjective and irresponsible vision. Only in this way could Plato become more than a mere "teller of fables," as the old physiologists appeared to him (*Sophist* 242c). Only in this Socratic, and more than Socratic, way could he "give an account" of his new vision and "fasten it by causal reasoning" (*Meno* 98a). Only in this way could he ascend on the hierarchical ladder of conditional hypotheses to the unconditional (ἀνυπό-θετον, *Republic* 510B, 511B).

There is still a final perspective that enables us to see the form of the dialogue as necessary for Plato, because seen from this perspective the structure of Plato's world view seems to repeat, on a larger scale, the Socratic structure. For Socrates the answer to his quest vanished in an admission of not-knowing. For Plato the dialectical path leads to that which is "beyond being." The "beyond" (*epekeina*) is not knowable; hence, not communicable. Only the way to it can be prepared. The dialogue, therefore, is such a way, leading, step by step, to a goal that, beyond the Socratic admission of ignorance and beyond the inexpressible of the highest Platonic vision, is ultimately vouched for as real by the living person of the master. And just as it is characteristic of the Socratic conversation to conclude with an admission of ignorance, so it is characteristic of Plato's dialogues to fall short of expressing the final truth; instead, it is brought into view as from a distance. This is apparent even in the structure of the *Republic*, all the more so in the other works.

To what we said above [22]—that the figure of Socrates signifies the central plane in Plato's world view—we must now add that this figure also conceals the final goal envisaged by Plato. That is the dual function of the ironic man in Plato's work, just as we had previously seen it to be the dual function of irony.[23] There is no struggle between Plato, the metaphysician, and Socrates, the ironic inquirer: Plato himself has always seen in Socrates a symbol both of the reality and the inexpressibility of that which he—quite simply—called "the good."

CHAPTER NINE

Myth

IN THE history of the Greek myth, running like a fateful thread through the life of the Greek people, the fifth century is the decisive age. Myth reaches its climax in tragedy at a time when it has also been exposed, for several generations, to critical forces preparing its disintegration. Plato's youth coincides with the last decades of Euripides, who—both creator and destroyer of myth—extended the processes of dissolution to its very roots. It is well to remember that Kritias was Plato's uncle and admired example, and that it was the same Kritias who, following Euripides, showed on the stage of Athens the traditional world of the gods as the purposeful invention of a clever human being.

How the world of the myth was looked upon in the circle in which Plato grew up may be seen from a few statements in the dialogues. Hippothales puts into verse, in honor of the beautiful Lysis, the well-known racing victories of his ancestors; and, in addition, something else that goes back to "an even more distant past" (κρονικώτερα, *Lysis* 205c): how the founder of the family, himself a link in a mythical genealogy, once was host to Herakles as a relative. To the maker of the verses—who perhaps aspires to follow in the tradition of Pindar—this is good enough as an embellishment for his passion; to the sober judge, it is nothing but "old wives' tales" (ἅπερ αἱ γραῖαι ᾄδουσιν). In the *Phaedrus* (229b *et seq.*), the landscape of the Ilissos recalls the tale of Oreithyia's rape by Boreas, and Phaidros asks, as if it were the central question, whether Socrates believes this fairy tale to have any truth. Thus, in the minds of the younger generation depicted by Plato, the mythical tradition has become something of an old wives' tale or an opportunity for critical jest.

Socrates—at least Plato's Socrates—in contrast to the Sophists, does not participate in the process of dissolving the myth. He rejects his companion's curious question because it is more important for him to use even this phenomenon in the service of his single goal—self-knowledge—than to destroy it. But it remains a fact that Socrates—it is perhaps the closest approximation to the historical Socrates as we find him in his own words at the beginning of the *Phaedo*—is not a "mythologist," not a teller of stories. His basic attitude, critical and inquiring, is opposed to that taken by a poet with regard to the world and man.

When Plato accepted Socrates' quest as his own, he burned his tragedies. But he could not root out the poet within himself, even though he became a "Socratic" man. He had to be both, in order to perceive the eternal forms as well as to create the new form of philosophical drama. One might possibly say today that, instead of re-forming the old myths of his people, he created the myth of Socrates. Plato himself would not have used such an expression with regard to the life story he created.[1] For him *Mythos* is opposed to *Logos*,[2] a "story" in contrast to conceptual analysis, primarily an ancient tale, ancestral tradition, folklore, fable, children's story, old wives' tale; myth bears the seal of *pseudos*, though not altogether without a substance of truth.[3] The term usually has a somewhat derogatory connotation, as it often has in ordinary language today. The air of solemnity sometimes attached to it say by Aristotle or in contemporary speculation and research does not accompany Plato's use of the word, even though the subject matter for which he called upon myths often has a sense of the solemn. At any rate, "fable" in the widest sense of the word is a form of speech subject to certain conditions. In the *Phaedo* (61B), Socrates mentions what seems to be a general opinion; namely, that the poet, if he wishes to be a true poet, must create "stories," not "speeches." Since Aristotle holds the same view as to the priority of the "fable" over all other forms of poetic creation, it is likely that it was also binding on Plato. Above all, he still clung to the mythical tradition of his people, which even Euripides and Kritias could not devaluate completely, and was the last to penetrate to its very depth before the myth froze into verbal puzzles or dissolved into fanciful play. These myths were "numerous and ancient" (*Laws* 927A) and seemed, for this reason alone, to have a substance of truth and a connection with the origin of things (*Republic* 271A). At the same time, they presented a serious danger by virtue of the dubious picture they painted of the gods, which was to be met by criticism as well as by the *agon* of the poet against the poets.[4] As an interpreter of the world, Plato saw in these legends pieces of an ancient interpretation of the world—"the lover of myth is in a sense a lover of wisdom" (Aristotle, *Metaphysics* I 982ᵇ 18)— fragments of a great myth half-extinguished and fallen apart through the course of time, which he set out to purify, connect, and create anew.

The fact that Plato was a creator of myths and Socrates apparently far removed from all mythology reveals a contrast similar to that between Plato's vision of the *Ideas* and the unending quest of Socrates, between Plato's written works and the purely oral discourse of Socrates. But just as we have previously seen that, however different, Plato's work invariably had its roots in Socrates, so we may now ask whether the new myth, however much it seems to contradict the Socratic way of speech, did not grow in Plato out of the image of the Socratic existence.

Does the approximation of Socrates to a mythical figure perhaps begin with the genuine Greek pleasure derived from inventing similes or analogies (εἰκάζειν)? Socrates, so Alkibiades claims (*Symposium* 215A *et seq.*), does not resemble anybody, so much "out of or without a place" (ἄτοπος) is he in a world in which everybody and everything has a definite place. But he resembles the Sileni and satyrs, even in his facial features. In addition, he charms his hearers by his words, as does the Silenuslike demon Marsyas with his flute playing. So closely does this Socrates approach the dimension of mythical existence. In the *Phaedrus* (230A), where in spite of all skepticism the atmosphere of the Attic landscape is still full of myth, he looks upon himself as a mythically mixed creature, "even more twisted than Typhon"; in the *Republic* (588B), he "forms a picture of the soul in words," comparing it to a many-headed monster in the series of hybrids. The human soul, therefore, an incomprehensible entity, and Socrates, incomprehensible to himself and others, are closest to these mythical creatures. One step further, and he who was just compared to Marsyas becomes "this Marsyas" himself (*Symposium* 215E): the analogy is raised to the status of myth.

In the *Symposium*, Diotima reveals a strange *Eros:* "he is anything but tender and beautiful, as the many imagine him," and as Agathon has just depicted him, but "rough, unkempt, unshod, and without a house, and he lies on the bare earth, sleeps at the doorsteps, and in the streets under the open sky" (203CD). It has often been pointed out [6] that at least the words "unkempt and unshod" (αὐχμηρὸς καὶ ἀνυπόδητος) must refer to Socrates, especially since, at the beginning of the dialogue, Socrates goes to the banquet "freshly bathed and with soft sandals," which is most unusual for him. That he is the prototype for Diotima's *Eros* is apparent from several other references. Eros "pursues the beautiful and the good, a mighty huntsman" (just as Socrates, at the beginning of the *Protagoras*, is said to come back from "a chase after the youthful beauty of Alkibiades"). Eros is "bold, impulsive, intense" (in *Laches*, Socrates is the man of courage), "always weaving some intrigue or other" (the seducer, the ironic spirit!); but, above all, "desirous of reason and knowing the path, seeking wisdom (φιλοσοφῶν) throughout his life, a great enchanter, sorcerer, and teacher of wisdom." This is nobody but Socrates, even though the picture is ironically exaggerated. No doubt Plato experienced his teacher not only as an erotic man, not only as a demonic man; there also came a moment when the human master grew into the mythical figure of the great demon Eros himself.

The "Orphic" mythology of a transcendent world makes its first appearance in Plato's works in the *Apology* and the *Gorgias*. Toward the end of the *Apology*, Socrates, "freed from those who claim to be judges here," expects "to find the true judges of

whom it is said that they sit in judgment in the world beyond."
And the same "beyond" is suggested still more explicitly in the
Gorgias. It is the trial of Socrates which is the veiled (and at
times open) background of this dialogue. To prepare himself,
with the resources of rhetoric, for the threatening danger of
such a trial is Kallikles' recommendation to Socrates; but the
latter refuses, unafraid, though he clearly anticipates the possibility of his conviction. But now he also looks toward a world
beyond and to the judges in the beyond. While the *Phaedo*
emphasizes reward and punishment, and the *Republic* the choice
of the lots of life, the *Gorgias* puts the emphasis upon the court
of law. Socrates sees himself before such a court of law—for
who else but himself is "the philosopher who has minded his
own work and has not trespassed upon that of others" (526c)?—
and he sees Kallikles threatened precisely by what the latter
had predicted for Socrates in the courts of this world: "You will
gape and your head will spin dizzily" (527a; cf. 486b). In this
way, both *Apology* and *Gorgias* bring out how Plato's mind was
attracted to the myth of judgment of the dead in a world beyond
by the defeat of Socrates before the Athenian court. In contrast
to the judges of this world, passing sentence with a confused
mind, there are the judges in the world below, "beholding,
only with their souls, the soul itself"; in contrast to the convicted Socrates and the victorious, tyrannical politician of
democracy, there is the vision of the tyrant convicted and the
philosopher acquitted. Here, too, Socrates, apparently remote
from anything resembling the mythical world, becomes the
awakener of the Platonic myth.

First Level

In Plato's works the earliest myth is that told in the *Protagoras*:
about the creation and capabilities of living beings, and how the
art of politics came to mankind. Not Socrates but the Sophist
is the speaker, but this in itself does not indicate whether anything of what is being said goes back to a written work by
Protagoras.[7] As a Sophistic product—not synonymous with an
altogether trivial product—Plato put this legend in its appro-

priate place. When Protagoras is given a choice of whether to strengthen his thesis by a myth or by *Logos*, and he first chooses the myth as the more convenient form of exposition, yet later follows it up with a theoretical discussion—this indicates the arbitrariness of the procedure. When Socrates employs a myth in the later dialogues, this means that he cannot express himself in any other form. And here we see a reason why the Socratic myths are found in the middle or at the end of the dialogue, but not at a place where the dialectical method has not yet begun.

Yet it would be wrong to think that the myth in the *Protagoras* introduces a wholly un-Platonic element. How much of the story is Plato's own invention must be left undecided; there are, nevertheless, several themes that establish a clear connection with his later myths. The divine artificers of the "mortal races" recur in the *Timaeus* as the lower gods to whom the demiurge delegates the creation of the "mortal bodies." The material stuff out of which the latter are created is called "earth and fire and the mixture of earth and fire" in the *Protagoras*. This ancient—ultimately, Parmenidean [8]—physics is only given a new mathematical structure in the *Timaeus*. For the body of the world—of which the mortal beings are "borrowed parts"— is also fashioned out of fire and earth, between which the other elements serve as "bonds" according to the laws of proportion. As Epimetheus "contrives" or "devises" (ἐμηχανᾶτο, 320E, 321A), so does the demiurge in the *Timaeus* (37E, 70C, 73C); the former as well as the latter devises the "preservation" (σωτηρία) of the created beings; and as the former has "used up" the capabilities to be distributed, thus the latter has "used up" the mixture of soul stuff (καταναλώσας, *Protagoras* 321C; κατανηλώκει, *Timaeus* 36B). The connectives "in order that" or "in order not" occur in the *Protagoras* and dominate, over long stretches, the sentence structure of the *Timaeus* as an expression of teleological thinking. Other elements again correspond to the myth of the *Statesman*, where origin of the world and origin of the state are likewise connected. "When the time came"; "there were no states"; human beings in the primitive age are naked and lying on the bare earth, a prey to wild animals; Zeus or God devises that creation does not perish; Prometheus, Hephaistos, and Athena transmit to mankind fire and the mechanical arts—it is easy to see how closely the two descriptions resemble each other down to details.[9] The hierarchy of natural powers (δυνάμεις) bestowed by Epimetheus, of the mechanical arts bestowed by Prometheus, and, finally, of virtues bestowed by Zeus can be found again in the *Republic:* the state grows out of nature; the mutual complementarity of human capabilities determines the earliest form of communal life, which *Arete* converts into a state. A great many of the ideas and images that later became important for Plato are already anticipated in the myth of Protagoras. Just as the general position of the Sophists is not only opposed to Socrates as something to be fought and overcome, but is, at the same time, a first approximation to the problems discussed, so the myth of the Sophist is a first hint—though not more than that—not altogether estranged from Plato's thoughts, but something that continues to grow within him throughout the years.[10]

The situation is similar in the case of the earliest myth of the beyond, to be found in the dialogue "Thrasymachus" (*Republic* I). The conversation between Socrates and the old Kephalos deals with the acquisition of money and its use. Kephalos takes a certain middle position concerning possession and the inclination to make money. Socrates then asks what might be the "greatest advantage" accruing therefrom. And the old man recalls vaguely "stories told about the world beyond." The contrast between the just and the unjust life comes to the fore, and fear of punishment and hope for reward are seen as functions of the conception of a life beyond. The name of Pindar suggests here, as well as later, the source for the myth; the vision is sealed with the name of the great poet.

It is to be noted that it is Kephalos who gives the conversation the turn toward the beyond. Whether this is due to the weakness of old age or to his closeness to death, the sentiments expressed about justice and injustice are those of a nonphilosophical man. Socrates only takes hold of the concept of justice, as if there had been no talk about a world beyond, and the

conversation comes to a close on a conceptual and nonmytho-
logical level. The tradition shows us the "Thrasymachus" only
as an integral part of the larger structure of the *Republic*, but
this final version cannot conceal the original composition. For
on the level of the aporetic dialogues Plato does not use a closing
myth, and only after the "Thrasymachus" was enlarged into the
Republic did he construct such a myth at the end of the whole
work in counterposition to the myth at the beginning.

Just as Aristotle thought of the myth as a preliminary stage
to philosophy (*Metaphysics* I 2 982ᵇ 18), so it is not altogether
useless here either. But Socrates goes beyond it in his conceptual analysis and does not return to it. As long as Plato
concluded his dialogues on an aporetic note, he could not—as
he did subsequently, beginning with the *Gorgias*—conclude
them with a Socratic myth. He could only use a myth in the
beginning as a preliminary, non-Socratic form of expression,
a form in which the Sophist or even the ordinary man might
recognize the connection with the eternal. In general, it is
apparent that mythology, from the very beginning, occupies a
place, though still marginal, in Plato's construction of the world.
Only upon a second stage does the myth penetrate more deeply
into the work and become a form of expression used by Plato's
Socrates himself after he has first traveled the dialectical path.

Second Level

The two mythical levels, the pre-Socratic and the Socratic, may
be found beside and above each other in the *Symposium*. The
first five speeches in praise of *Eros* represent the pre-Socratic
stage. The mythical element is weakest in the middle speech of
the natural scientist. The first and fifth speeches, by Phaidros
and Agathon respectively, render the two mythical aspects
represented by tradition: the cosmogonic *Eros* and Eros as the
youthful god of love. The speech of Pausanias, injecting into
the single nature of *Eros* the contrast between Uranios and
Pandemos, is likewise rooted in poetic and popular tradition.
The most original and creative step at this stage is reserved for

Aristophanes. His fantastic story belongs to the type of creation myths already anticipated in the *Protagoras*. In both we behold the gods acting and speaking, Zeus in a state of embarrassment and worry, finally transforming, with the help of Apollo (in the *Protagoras*, it is Hermes), the threatened creation. Otherwise, however, everything is quite original. The spherical human beings, similar in shape and movement to the heavenly bodies, from which they came, anticipate in a fantastic, haunting image the thought developed in the *Phaedrus*, *Timaeus*, and the *Laws* about the kinship between the human soul and the cosmos, between the movement of the souls and that of heavenly bodies.[11] The imperfection, the "halfness," of our physical existence, *Eros* as the "striving toward totality and completion"—these are images the value of which is immediately apparent, but which receive their true meaning and content only after we have learned from Socrates what is meant by perfection and completion.

All these speeches represent mythology on the first level. This does not mean they are nothing but delightfully meaningless play. Would Plato have written them down if they were? And are there not sufficient hints in them of what is genuinely Platonic? The over-all impression, to be sure, is as if they "mythologized" into the blue, and no distinction is made between what is to be retained and what is to be discarded. When Socrates begins to speak, all the earlier speeches collapse as "illusory." For they preceded conceptual discourse; and such a procedure, according to Socrates, is a poor substitute for *Logos* and truth. In Socrates' speech, the fairy tale about the procreation of Eros by Poros (Plenty) and Penia (Poverty) is, in itself, not so different from the previous tales; yet it is most important to appreciate the changed setting. Socrates first clarified the nature of love in rational, conceptual discourse, defining the most important aspects. Love is love of something, namely, of beauty. Love is a desire and a want. Love wishes to possess what it lacks. This is the "truth," before which all previous speeches with their mythical tales vanish. Altogether different is the Socratic myth, which now follows; it is not a will-o'-the-wisp in empty space—at best, an accidental hint pointing toward the truth; at worst, confusing play—but continues upon the lines just drawn by the *Logos*.

It would be a mistake to take—as one might be tempted to do—the story about Penia and Poros as an allegorical symbol for the rational concept of *metaxy*. As soon as Diotima begins to speak through the "demonic" Socrates, Eros is present as a "great demon," and we are in a mythical realm. And the *metaxy* itself is seen just as much from a mythical as from a rational perspective, referring to the cosmos, which "is bound together with itself" through this demonic realm.

The Socratic myth does not conclude the speech, but leads into the description of the hierarchical ascent toward the vision of beauty itself. Thus the allegorical conception of Eros is not accidentally placed in the middle. Eros himself is a mediator between heaven and earth. Plato sees, in the center of being, a miracle that reason cannot explain, but that preserves the universe—to put it in the words of the old Plato—from "dissolving and disappearing in infinite chaos" (*Statesman* 273D). Thus Eros is the *metaxy* in Socrates' speech as he is the *metaxy* in Plato's world.

We have previously shown how the path of love and the path of death for Plato lead to the same goal.[12] We must now turn to the group of eschatological myths.

In the *Apology*, Socrates still speaks in hypothetical terms about the fate of the soul in the beyond—not so much because Socrates would actually have used such language, but rather because he exercises restraint before an indiscriminate public and, more importantly, the previous discussion did not prepare us for more definite language. As far as the content itself is concerned, the world beyond is depicted either in contrast to or as a continuation of existence in this world. The judges below are true judges in contrast to the false ones here above. Meeting heroes who, like himself, were driven to death unjustly somewhat softens, in an ironic way, the bitterness of Socrates' fate. The most important thing in the beyond is the continuation of a life of inquiry into the human condition, which he had accepted as a god-given task and which, ultimately, brought about his death. In the face of eternity, therefore, this life is affirmed, and death divested of its threat, as if it meant a final breaking off. In the end, mythical immortality and blessedness—"if it be true what is told"—are ironically counterpoised with the sentence of death here on earth.

In the *Gorgias*, we find a passage where the myth of the beyond seems to intrude at the wrong time; then, at the end, the myth is admitted as appropriate. First, the thesis as to the natural superiority of the powerful is shown to be an expression of the pleasure principle, and the real struggle flares up over the validity of this principle. At this point, Socrates tries an approach through allegory or "fairy tales" (μυθολογῶ, 493D). We are dead; the body is the grave of the soul. In the world beyond, the uninitiated (ἀμύητοι)—that is, the ignorant, remote from mind (ἀνόητοι)—must pour water into a vessel full of holes by means of a sieve—that is, their soul.[13] The second image, "which comes from the same school," is a variation of the first in that the opposition between the temperate and intemperate is worked out by analogy with casks that are sound and full and those that are leaky.

This eschatology for which Socrates calls upon the support of the poet Euripides and the teachings of wise men—the Orphics and Pythagoreans—; this punishment in the beyond in strict correlation with the corruption of the soul: they are an entering wedge. Socrates realizes himself that he cannot conquer his opponent even "with the help of many such tales." Here it is only an unsatisfactory preliminary attempt waiting for the place where it receives its true meaning. That occurs at the end of the dialogue in the first great eschatological drama constructed by Plato (524A *et seq.*). Like the entire dialogue, it rests upon the contrast between just and unjust: here this contrast is raised to the plane of transcendence.

The theme of the transmigration of the soul, only expressed in a concealed way in the *Gorgias*, so that it is often overlooked, is brought out clearly in the *Meno* (81A–E); in fact, it is the most important theme of this eschatology. For here the myth represents a transition to a new level where the nature of virtue will become visible after it could not be grasped by means of definition. The myth is called upon to safeguard the possibility of knowledge. It is supported by the wisdom of the priests and the divine poets, and verses of Pindar call up the theme of the soul's migration. In the end, the conclusion applies to the nature of knowledge, which is an act of recollection of something perceived before this life; [14] hence, one must not be caught in the intellectually destructive *Logos* of the eristics, but pursue the truth actively and searchingly.

Thus, by means of the myth, a new philosophical level is reached. This cannot be compared with the futile attempts in the *Gorgias*. In the *Meno* the most powerful element is stated at the beginning; the conclusion is anticipated; the theme to be proved is not simply posited, but elevated into the mythical realm. Only then follows what can be proved, namely, knowledge as something eternal. Thus a connection firmly established for Plato is here briefly sketched—the description differs from the other myths of the beyond by its suggestive briefness—because the only thing that matters is the conclusion drawn about the nature of "memory" and the quest for truth. The passage from Pindar refers with good reason to "the mightiest in wisdom" (σοφία μέγιστοι).

Gorgias and *Meno* yield only partial views. The *Gorgias* aimed at right action; the *Meno*, in its central part, almost completely at right knowledge. How inseparable these two aspects are becomes apparent in the latter dialogue. In the *Phaedo*, finally, action and knowledge are inseparably linked as a single task of the soul in the face of death, of "existence" in the face of "transcendence."

It is no accident that Socrates, soon after the beginning of the dialogue, declares he is no "teller of myths" (61B). This is iridescent, ironic play between yes and no. The dialogue is actually filled with "mythology"; and a first glance of it is already visible at the beginning (62B), when the conversation turns to the doctrine of secret sects according to which human beings are in a state of "guardianship" (ἔν τινι φρουρᾷ). The curtain concealing the fate of the soul is for a moment raised a little. Since the *Phaedo* talks about death, and since only the language of myth can speak about that which is beyond the limit, this is a first suggestion as to the connection between this life and the beyond. Later, when the dialogue is under way, the mythology of the beyond is invoked in order to bring to completion the three phases of the work, each time when the circle of the argument is about to be closed.

Within the first circle (69c), after the life of the philosopher has been shown in its direction toward death, the Orphic stream—already anticipated in the concepts of "separation" and "purification"—stands out clearly. As in the *Gorgias* and the *Meno,* Socrates cites as testimony the mysteries and their doctrine of separation between those who are rewarded and those who are punished. The reinterpretation occurs in the same way: "initiation" means reason in the Platonic sense; the initiated, therefore, are the true philosophers. They will dwell with the gods, while the uninitiated "lie in the mud." The basic principles of this Orphic myth of the beyond are again a continuation of philosophical insights.

Within the second circle, the problem centers explicitly around the "immortality of the soul." Thus at the beginning stands "an old story, which we remember"—that we go there from here and return from there to this world, and that the living are born from the dead. The following discourse then asks whether this is really so and, after several lines of inquiry, again resorts to a myth at the end. The soul, which has rightly practiced philosophy and dying to this world, passes in a purified state to the invisible, which is akin to its own nature (the invisible, Hades, and the intelligible world are interchangeable terms); it is liberated from its wandering course and resides, as it is said of the initiated, for the rest of time with the gods (81a 9; cf. 69c 6). The soul that is not purified drags much physical, earthen, heavy, or visible substance along with it— hence, the shadowy images that, according to popular belief, hover around graves. They wander around, suffering punishment for their former bad training, and they will be reincarnated in various animal forms. Falsehood and lust find their eternal equivalent, as it were, in the world beyond, just as the souls of a different nature do in kinship with the divine and membership in the intelligible, "invisible" world. These are variations of what was shown on the first level. Only the theme of the transmigration of the soul is new as the most striking symbol for its eternity.

The *Phaedo* is completed with the third circle. Thus at the end of the inquiry, at the conclusion of the philosophical conversation itself, we find the great myth of the beyond to which the two earlier versions were preliminary steps.

The *Republic* transforms the simple structure of the *Gorgias*—the contrast between justice and injustice—into a new grand design. The eschatological myth at the end of the *Gorgias* is rebuilt in a new medium: as justice and injustice are built into the structure of the state, so the fate of the soul is built into the universe. Since the new work has also absorbed the older "Thrasymachus," with its myth at the beginning, beginning and end are seen in reciprocal correlation. The perfect construction at the end answers the unsatisfactory attempt at the beginning. Whether both are viewed as aspects of the history of Plato's own growth or within the total structure of the completed *Republic*, they represent two levels of Plato's mythology. On the first level, the myth is preparation for the dialectical path; on the second, it is a view beyond the limits to which dialectics can lead.

Now everything that has been said so far fades into the background before a comparison of the three great eschatologies in the *Gorgias*, the *Phaedo*, and the *Republic*.[15]

The *Gorgias* presented the struggle between justice and injustice. This struggle is continued in the myth; hence, the court of the dead and the punishment in the world beyond are the most significant elements. In order to make the essential nature of this court as clearly visible as possible, a story is told to the effect that the present condition has not always existed, but has grown out of its opposite. The former condition is characterized on the part of the judges by the fact that they passed judgment with the troubled perceptions of human existence; on the part of the judged that they were sentenced before their deaths, still had their bodies and garments, and were accompanied by friends testifying in their behalf. The present condition is such that both judges and judged are dead and naked; hence, the judge can see with his naked soul the naked soul of the judged. The radical nature of this decision and, at the same time, the character of pure knowledge cannot be symbolized more strikingly.

The court is not described so explicitly in the *Phaedo* and the *Republic*. In the *Phaedo*, unlike the *Gorgias*, the central theme is not the contrast between justice and injustice, and in the *Republic* this theme is enlarged, and overshadowed, by many other considerations. Moreover, Plato may also have thought that he had described the court of law in sufficient detail in the *Gorgias*. Thus the court as well as the place where it sits is only briefly, but sharply, outlined in the two other dialogues. Instead, the *Phaedo* adds the journey to the court, during which the difference between the reasonable and the lustful soul becomes immediately apparent. The former is gently led by a demon; the latter finds no companion. It wanders about in error and is finally pulled by necessity to the place of judgment. Thus the existence of the philosopher oriented toward the pure essences and, therefore, toward death, and, in contrast, the erring ways of his opponent, are continued into the journey to the beyond. These different attitudes of the soul are characteristic of the *Phaedo*, while this journey is only hinted at in the *Republic* (614B).

In the *Gorgias*, the theme of the transmigration of the soul [16] is not expressly presented; it is only presupposed when the incurable serve as example (παράδειγμα) in the world beyond, so that others may improve themselves. Palingenesis became an open theme in the mythical sketch of the *Meno*, because here the emphasis lay on the a priori nature of knowledge. The *Phaedo*, in emphasizing the same point, briefly states that each individual is led back again to this earth "after many revolutions of ages" (107E). We must, however, add what was said, on the second level of the dialogue, about the incarnations in various forms of animals and human beings (81D *et seq.*). The *Republic* puts a much stronger emphasis upon the return and the choice of new lots. The experiences of one's former life, to be sure, are important for the choice of a new life; but the choice nonetheless is completely free. The metaphysical responsibility of man for his life, the rejection of any form of fatalism, are expressed most sharply, while in the *Phaedo* it was only "probable" that the incarnation takes place according to the type of being which the soul has developed in its previous life.

The human beings whose fate in the beyond is at stake are always divided in the same way. First they are divided into those who are to be punished for their misdeeds, consisting of two groups: the curable and the incurable (ἀνίατοι, *Gorgias* 526B 8, *Phaedo* 113E 2, *Republic* 615E 3). With regard to the former group, punishment is educational; with regard to the latter, it sets a deterrent example for others. The "incurable" group includes, in the primarily political dialogues, the tyrants, princes, and political rulers, among them Archelaos of Macedonia (in the *Gorgias*) and Ardiaios, tyrant of a city in Pamphylia, whose misery is depicted in images reminiscent of Dante (in the *Republic*). The *Phaedo* only mentions the incurable in Tartaros quite generally, without naming anybody, suggesting even in this way the special orientation of this dialogue which does not deal with a "political" theme. Instead, the individuals capable of improvement are again subdivided here into those guilty of serious crimes and those who have led a life somewhere between good and evil. A third group is recognized in all these dialogues in addition to the curable and incurable, namely, the "pious," among whom the true philosophers again occupy a place of special distinction in the *Gorgias* and *Phaedo*.

The myth in the *Gorgias* is restricted to the court. The two other works add—and this is perhaps the most peculiar and magnificent construction—a carefully worked out cosmology in the midst of the report about the soul's fate: [17] the *Phaedo* the construction of the spherical earth with its caves and connecting canals, the *Republic* the image of the spindle of heaven with its spheres. The cosmological idea is already present in the *Gorgias* (507E), when Socrates invokes the "wise men" in support of the best example, the idea of a world order, with which he opposes the representative of disorder. But cosmology does not penetrate to the myth itself, perhaps because the dialogue is restricted almost entirely to the ethical-political field. The two other dialogues, however, are concerned to a much greater degree with the subject of knowledge; and knowledge of nature occupies a particularly high rank in this field.

In the account that Socrates, in the *Phaedo*, gives of his philosophical growth, he asks for a view of the world that would show the universe as an approximately perfect ordered system. In such an interpretation of the world, the shape of the earth and its position in the universe would have to correspond to the principle of the "best." His disappointment with all the explanations found in Anaxagoras and his decision to restrict himself to the realm of the *Logos* (ἐν λόγοις) do not prevent his admission that he would gladly let himself be taught by some expert about nature (99c). Is it accidental that, in the final myth, "somebody" develops a world view which satisfies essentially what Socrates originally asked for? The earth is a sphere in the center of the heavens. It does not need either air or any other mechanical substratum as support, but keeps itself in a state of equilibrium. In this way, Socrates disposes of those who explain the support of the earth by material causes (97D, 98c). Furthermore, the earth is so constructed that the most important natural phenomena—such as high and low tide, winds, springs, or eruptions of volcanoes—become intelligible in terms of this construction and, at the same time, the symbolic places for the fate of the soul come into existence: the interior, the cavity for man's lifetime in this world, and the "true earth." [18] This harmony of causal and teleological construction fulfills the demand and hope voiced earlier. Even the world construction of the *Timaeus* is still seen under the same dual perspective.

In the *Republic*, the object of discussion is no longer the earth as the center of the universe, but the universe itself with its spheres.[18a] Here the fate of man is shown in terms of necessity—not excluding, but implying, the freedom of the individual. The three goddesses of fate—spinning Klotho, Lachesis casting lots, and the inexorable Atropos—are daughters of Necessity (*Ananke*). The lots are taken from the lap of Lachesis. The soul must pass beneath the throne of *Ananke* in order to receive, from the hands of Klotho and Atropos, confirmation and irrevocability for the new life freely elected. But these same hands of the Fates also move the paths of the heavenly bodies, and on the knees of *Ananke* turns the spindle of the world. So closely linked are cosmic events and human fate; but the connection goes deeper. The construction of the world concludes the *Republic*, the educational state, in which astronomy has been put forth as an important instrument of education. This astronomy, however, is propaedeutic for dialectics (VII 529c *et seq.*): its subject is not the colorful variety of heavenly phenomena, but the true velocities, numbers, forms, to be grasped by pure thought, to which the phenomena visible in the sky are related as copies to their prototypes. Such a construction of the universe and its motions according to strictly mathematical proportions— that is the meaning, disguised as a fairy tale, of the spindle with its whorls. When it is said that upon each whorl is a siren always hymning a single tone so that all eight of them together "form a single harmony," we must again remember how, in Book VII, astronomy is followed by the true science of music, which is concerned only with the consonance of pure numerical proportions. This combination of astronomy with music is a special exemplary case—already recognized by the Pythagoreans and most important for Plato—of the unity and kinship among the individual sciences, the *methodos* of which leads to the final goal. The souls see and hear this cosmos of sidereal revolutions and pure sounds in the world beyond. And thus they are near the highest kind of knowledge. The vision of the highest images themselves is reached in the *Phaedrus*. In the *Republic* it is only suggested in a reference to what the soul of the good man beholds in its journey to heaven: "views of inconceivable beauty" (615A).

The Neoplatonic interpretation of the myth, available to us in its final form by Proklos, moves in this direction: as our own soul must be a well-ordered community and the state repeats the structure of the soul on an enlarged scale, so the cosmos as depicted in the final myth represents once more "the same thought on a still larger scale" (τὰ αὐτὰ μειζόνως, II 99 23). The details of this interpretation may be rejected because they go beyond Plato. But as soon as we look forward to the *Timaeus*, where the structure of the state is sketched before the construction of the universe is undertaken, the "symmetry" between state and cosmos becomes apparent. And when it is said in the *Timaeus* (90cd) that it is man's task to know the harmonies and circular motions of the universe, and to assimilate himself to this knowledge "according to original nature" (κατὰ τὴν ἀρχαίαν φύσιν), the symmetry between individual soul and cosmos is perfectly clear. The structure of the *Republic* rests entirely upon the homology between soul and state. And it must be a reading in Plato's sense when we see the final myth as the fulfillment of the entire construction: human soul, state, and cosmos conceived as three forms symmetrically placed around the same center; yet again not as separate spheres, though similarly constructed. But as man, according to his nature, belongs to the state, so he also seems to belong, according to the same nature, to the cosmos. Just as the sphere of the earth in the *Phaedo*, so the entire universe seems to be constructed in order to assign an appropriate place to the human soul.

The great myths of the soul, at the conclusion of a work, evoke the unknowable beyond, after the theoretical and practical order has first been established with a view toward eternal being. They are variations on the same theme, each variation fitting into the particular dialogue where it occurs. For these genuinely Socratic-Platonic myths are quite different from those characteristic of the first phase in Plato's mythology in that they are not irresponsible, jestful play now and then accidentally revealing an essential point. They presuppose conceptual analysis and carry it beyond the limits set for human existence and human knowledge. Or, still more in Plato's sense, the myth—like the *Logos*—not invented, but discovered, has—again like the *Logos*—its own structure. And mythology makes sense only if it can be shown that the myth carries forward the lines of argument set by the *Logos*.

Finally, Plato does not hesitate, at least not in the *Meno* (86b) and the *Phaedo* (114d), to undermine the truth of the myth in the end; and he never leaves any doubt that the myth is a mixture of truth and poetic fancy. This fading into uncertainty belongs to the very nature of the myth, "so that it does not become encased in rigid armor." In the *Meno*: "I would not stand up for it completely"; in the *Phaedo*: "This or

something of the kind is true." All the more unshakable, however, is the certainty of the demands reinforced by the myth:
"One may be confident about the fate of the soul if, avoiding
the pleasures of this life, he has practiced the art of knowledge
and has adorned his soul with the ornaments properly belonging
to it" (*Phaedo* 114E). "To do injustice is more to be avoided
than to suffer injustice; and one must aim at being virtuous,
not only at the appearance of virtue; when anybody has done a
wrong, he must be punished; and to bring about these things
is the function of rhetoric" (*Gorgias* 527B). "One must believe
that the soul is immortal and one must keep to the heavenly
way, always practicing justice along with reason" (*Republic*
621C). The agreement in these passages is revealing. The real
value and meaning of the myth lies in the *directio voluntatis* (to
use Dante's language). Thus, as its outlines coincided har-
moniously with the results of the conceptual analysis, so they
lead back again to the tasks imposed upon our life, clarified and
justified through the dialogue.

Third Level

With the great myth about the world and the soul in the
Phaedrus, we reach a new level in Plato's mythological construction. But there are three smaller mythical tales in the
dialogue surrounding the great central myth. That is no more
an accident than the fact that the landscape occupies a much more
significant place in the *Phaedrus* than anywhere else in Plato.
Nor is it accidental that the story of Boreas is told while Socrates
and Phaidros are taking a walk along the banks of the Ilissos,
or the story about the metamorphosis of the crickets while both
of them are lying under a plane tree lulled by their chirruping
voices in the midday heat of a southern sky. All these things
belong together. Hour and place, along with the mythical tales,
form the actual and symbolic landscape of the work.

The legend of Boreas and Oreithyia (229B–230A) gives to the
locality a kind of mythical, decorative setting, somewhat as in a
painting by Poussin; and it is quite welcome that the setting
includes other fairylike folk, the centaurs, chimeras, and gor-

gons. But then it is immediately made clear what the meaning of this talk is. Socrates pushes aside the precocious question whether the story is true or false, or how one might interpret it. He does not have the time because he has not yet learned— following the Delphic inscription—who he is himself. But this does not mean he is indifferent to the myth; indeed, he is much less indifferent than the alleged precocious interpreters. He uses the myth as a test of himself, whether he is a more twisted and swollen being than the monster Typhon. In other words, he learns from the myth, which he accepts as given, about his single task in life.

The fairy tale about the crickets (258E–259D), once human beings who forgot food and drink over their passion for the Muses, like the earlier story animates the locality with mythical decorative figures. At the same time, it carries the admonition not to let the crickets put us to shame, but "to converse with one another"; and it makes the Muses sponsors of the philosophical conversation, and the latter itself a work of *mousikē*. And the place of the interlude is significant, too, for it occurs where the discussion begins to become serious.

The tale of Thoth and Thamus (274C–275C) does not have a landscape setting, as the two previous stories do. But like the second tale it is placed at an important break in the dialogue where the final discussion begins. And an equally important objective connection exists between the two stories. As the second calls for the harmonious use of speech, the third warns against the abuse of writing. Both of them posit, in a playful manner, two limiting points in the discussion on the nature of the *Logos*.

Thus the first and the second of the brief myths are linked through the spatial setting; the second and the third, through the objective structure of the *Phaedrus*. Together they form, within the context of a very technical and abstract discussion, the mythical range of hills, as it were, above which rises the peak of the great central myth.

This myth is quite different from those in the *Gorgias*, *Phaedo*, and *Republic*. If, in the *Gorgias*, the world beyond was seen, in continuation of this life, as a tribunal bestowing reward and punishment, and if this view was enlarged to include the earth in the *Phaedo*, and finally the cosmos in the *Republic*, the relationship is now reversed. The frame of reference is the cosmos; and only within this vast space appears, as a small replica of the large, the particular fate of the individual human soul, so that, again, life in this world is seen from the perspective of the great body of the universe. The universe and the human soul, finally, are combined with the *Eros* of the *Symposium* in a great synthesis. And this myth—not unlike that of the *Symposium*, but with a much greater power since it reaches so much farther—is placed in the very center of the whole work. As in the *Symposium*, Socrates first posed the basic question under discussion (237BC), then combined the forms of mania into a fourfold system, and finally, in the last phase, the erotic mania, unfolded myth out of doctrine.

A new element in the *Phaedrus* is that the myth is preceded by a discussion about the nature of the soul as movement. New is the tone of strict rational deduction combined with an air of solemnity. New is the conceptual framework: movement, first principle (ἀρχή), becoming and passing away, uncreated and imperishable—though this is, strictly speaking, not new at all; it is precisely the kind of "causal inquiry into the world of becoming and passing away" that Socrates, in the *Phaedo*, characterized as the first stage in his philosophical development. Thus it is actually quite old, "pre-Socratic." As a matter of fact, in Parmenides, Empedokles, and Herakleitos we find agreement as to terminology and line of argument; in Alkmaion (as has been observed long since), a total conception that is very similar because he, too, deduced the immortality of the soul from its eternal movement and envisaged the eternal movement as analogous to that of the heavenly bodies.[19] In the *Phaedo*, Socrates rejected such an inquiry; now he seems to be deeply lost in it. He sees "that which is self-moving" as the necessary condition for the stability of "the whole heavens and the entire world of becoming." At the same time he sees it as the nature (οὐσία καὶ λόγος) of the soul. Hence, the first principle of world and soul is identical. But we must not think that Plato's Socrates simply reverts to a method of inquiry that

he previously rejected. The central point of the myth is again
the necessary correlation between soul and *Eidos*, just as it is
the focal point of all of Plato's philosophy. The conceptual
framework of natural philosophy is not a substitute for this central vision, but only an approach to it—as is apparent from the
place it occupies in the total structure of the myth—because
Plato now follows lines in the field of natural philosophy that
lead into the realm of the philosophy of *Ideas*.

The next stage in the building of the myth is the picture-con-
struction of the soul, after the task of speaking about its real
nature has had to be given up as a "wholly divine" one. In the
new spiritual vision of the *Phaedrus* two pictorial motifs inter-
penetrate: the horse-drawn chariot and the wings that carry it.
The first motif has a remarkable analogy in the *Katha Upanishad*
of India.[20] There the human body is the chariot. The intellect
(*buddhi*) guides it. The taut reins are the thinking organ
(*manas*). The barely manageable steeds are the senses (*indriya*).
The chariot is the body. The true soul, the self (*atman*), rides in
such a hardly dirigible vehicle. Could this figure have found its
way out of the Far East to Plato? If so, then he adapted it to the
theory of the soul which he makes dominant in the *Republic*.[21]
For as compared with the Indian figure, Plato's is both simpli-
fied and differentiated: the two horses are of different kinds, the
one being Desire (ἐπιθυμία), the other Will, Drive (θυμός).
Either the mind bridles the two into balance, or they drag it
with the charioteer into the abyss.

Supposing the figure of the chariot was derived from a distant
source, Plato fused it with a second pictorial motif: the wings.
Who is winged: steeds, driver, or chariot? This is not made
clear. The wings belong to the whole. Plato was surrounded by
Greek works of art in which he saw winged steeds or winged
charioteers—Eros or Nike or Eos. In fact, both may have wings,
the charioteer and the steeds. Finally, the hub caps may also
have wings: how often in pictures that winged chariot was to be
seen in which Triptolemos drove among the people dispensing
wheat or Dionysos dispensing wine. In the Platonic myth, the
addition of wings is a poetic expression for what had been
previously formulated in natural philosophy by the concept of

self-movement. Plato may have leaned to this pictorial motif because in the process of poetic creation, the winged Eros became the model for the winged Psyche. Plato seems to hint at this when soon afterward he puts in the mouth of Socrates two verses on the winged god of love which he traces back to "secret poems of certain Homerids." [22] This adaptation is not accidental or fanciful; it indicates that the soul is wholly soul when it is a loving one.

But now the soul does what is proper to it: it gives life and animation. If at the outset the whole universe was its field of action, now the soul as an animating, moving principle has specific functions. Two forms of "living creatures" (ζῷα) become visible: the immortal ones, the heavenly bodies, and the mortal ones, the human beings. Seen from the perspective of perfect motion with which the former circle the heavens, the motion of the human soul is already a deterioration. It has already "lost feathers" and fallen when it combines with a human body. The incarnation had already been shown as the fall of the soul, by its own fault, in the *Phaedo* and the *Republic*, and the cosmos as the space for the soul's fate. In the *Phaedrus*, with a change in the general perspective, everything is seen from the perfection of the cosmos, and the world of the heavenly bodies as a more perfect world of beings precedes, and is contrasted with, the human world.[23] Within these new dimensions, the immortal soul once more beholds the eternal forms as it did in the *Meno*, *Phaedo*, and *Republic*. The movement "upward" under the aspect of "guidance" (ἄνω ἀγωγή), of "ascent" (ἄνω ἀνάβασις), or of a "vision of the above" (θέα τῶν ἄνω) had found its fullest expression in the allegory of the cave in the *Republic*. This impulse now becomes an essential attribute of the soul through the image of wingedness, and the dimension of the "above" is stated according to the new cosmic co-ordinates. For the "intelligible place" (τόπος νοητός) in the *Republic* (509D, 517B) now becomes "the place beyond the heavens" (τόπος ὑπερουράνιος); that is, it is now connected with the image of the sky, which, according to Platonic etymology, is always the highest "visible" (οὐρανός = ὁρατόν, *Republic* 509D). And the same cosmic, or, if we like, astronomical, perspective also transforms the vision of the *Ideas* as given in the *Republic*, connecting it with the circular movement of the heavenly bodies or with the divine chariots modeled after them: the immortal beings stand "on the back of the heavens"; the rotation of the sphere carries them along, and they behold that which is beyond the heavens.

The kinship between soul and *Eidos* was the basic insight guiding the "proofs of immortality" in the *Phaedo*. This, too, is now elaborated in the same direction. The view of the eternal forms is the nourishment of the souls. They have access to this meal depending upon the strength of their wings. The incarnation in human form depends, according to the "law of Adrasteia," upon whether they have reached the original view. The periodic sequences governing the fate of the soul were just hinted at, in the *Phaedo* (107E), in the phrase of "many great revolutions of the ages." In the *Republic* (615A), the "thousand-year journey" is a tenfold penalty for a lifetime reckoned at about a hundred years. In the *Phaedrus*, even the thousand-year period is subordinated to a ten times larger one; but the philosophers may leave the circle of becoming after a three-thousand-year period.[24] The *Republic* proceeds from this present world and then orders the rest. The *Phaedrus* first sees the great cosmic order and then determines human existence within this context. Nor is it accidental that the division of souls into three classes, but especially the class of the "incurables," which was retained from the *Gorgias* to the *Republic*, is now given up and we find instead a gradual ordering of nine forms of souls from the philosopher down to the tyrant (248DE).[25] Plato, looking at these matters from the dimension of the cosmos, not from the perspective of human life, and choosing the image of "wingedness" as an essential characteristic of the soul, cannot reject any human soul altogether, because it is part of its nature to have once "beheld the truth" (249B) and it must therefore be potentially capable of doing so again. The court of the dead, the drawing of lots, the choice of the future life, are told with great detail and emphasis in the *Republic*. They are only sketched briefly in the *Phaedrus* (249AB), almost as if they were merely an episode in the great cosmic drama. All the greater is the effect of recollection. As in the *Meno* and the *Phaedo*, recollection is the

connecting ray between *Idea* and soul, except that in the
Phaedrus the journey of the soul and the place beyond the heavens give a much deeper dimension to the simpler setting of the
earlier dialogues. Thus philosophical dialectics itself is actually
called "recollection" (249bc); at the same time, erotic mania is
based upon recollection. Both movements, therefore, leading upward to the *Eidos*, take the path of recollection. This also makes
the picture of the philosopher appear necessary, removed as he
is from the world and almost entranced—the description is
reminiscent of the allegory of the cave in the *Republic* and the
episode in the *Theaetetus* [26]—since the winged soul of him who
has beheld the *Ideas* must seek to dwell in his recollection
"where the god resides in order to be divine" (πρὸς οἷσπερ
ὁ θεὸς ὢν θεῖός ἐστιν).

In the last great part of the long speech in the *Phaedrus*
(249d–256e), the scene changes to human life; and physical
beauty and human community of love, that is, essential parts of
the *Lysis*, the *Alcibiades*, and, above all, the *Symposium*, are now
included and newly penetrated with the mythical dynamics and
imagery of the *Phaedrus*. Beauty, as in the *Symposium*, remains
the goal aimed at by love. But it now appears as a copy of one of
the images beheld by the soul on its journey; not any image,
but that in which, for human eyes, the prototype is most clearly
mirrored.[27] From this point of view, Socrates interprets, in
great detail, the conduct of human lovers in this life. Man seeks
to be near beauty because the soul's wings grow at the sight of
beauty. The pains of love are pains of growth. The complex
mixture of pleasure and pain, characteristic of physical love, and
the strange behavior of physical lovers can be truly explained
only if we know something about the wings of the soul and
about the *Eidos*. But these traits do not ultimately concern Socrates. For him true love is love that educates. The connection
between love and education, however, can only be fully grasped
from the point of view of the beyond. Education means shaping
the beloved after the image of the god, whose followers had
been both lover and beloved; hence, this orientation also
imposes upon the educator the obligation to look up to the
god and to resemble the latter more and more. Even the

highest form of love, Socratic love, is never unimpaired perfection. Love is a perpetual struggle for command between the charioteer and the horses, and this struggle helps to explain all the different forms of behavior that we encounter in the lives of lovers: ecstasy as the effect of recollection on the part of the charioteer, passionate lust as the impetuousness of the irrational horse, respectful awe as an expression of fear on the part of the horse tamed by the bit and halter of the charioteer.

The dialectics of the *Lysis* had brought out the points that the bad man could not be friend of the bad, and the good man must be friend of the good. These statements, too, are now interpreted with reference to a transcendent dimension, since friendship is shown to be based on the joint journey in the following of the god whom the friends resemble and to whom they belong. In this way, the problem of love returned enters into the discussion. To give a concrete image of love, Plato resorted to a concept taken from the world of Empedokles and the atomists. An "effluence" (ἀπορροή) of beauty enters into the lover through the eyes and causes his wings to grow (251B). Some flows out again, but some—reflected as from a solid body—enters into the beloved, passing through the eyes into the soul, where it again causes the wings to grow (255C *et seq.*). The beloved does not know what happens to him, and he is not aware of the fact that the lover is the mirror in which he beholds himself. Thus, being loved is the copy (εἴδωλον) of love. We must recall the relevant passages in the *Alcibiades*, where the contrast of lover and beloved was expressed with an intensity not reached again until the *Symposium*. There, too, was the image of the mirror: "as in a mirror" the beloved beholds himself in the eyes of the lover (132E *et seq.*). And at the end it was shown that the love of Socrates had "hatched winged love" in the youth (135E). It is quite clear how the imagery of the *Phaedrus* draws upon these earlier images; indeed, it is quite obvious that the image of the winged Eros in the *Alcibiades* was transformed into that of the winged soul in the *Phaedrus.*[28]

Finally, even what Alkibiades says in the *Symposium* about being attracted to Socrates is fused with and newly interpreted in the *Phaedrus*. The beloved longs to behold the lover, to touch

and kiss him, to lie in his arms, and when the tumult in the soul
of the lover is depicted—how charioteer and horses struggle for
command in the soul—this description raises the relationship
between Alkibiades and Socrates to a general level and endows
it with a new, powerful imagery. At the end, the different ranks
of purity recognized in the love relationship—the first rank
given to the "lovers of wisdom," in whom the charioteer remains master; the second to the "lovers of honor," in whom the
noble steed, together with the ignoble, wins out temporarily—
these ranks again become significant, from an eschatological
perspective, for the future fate of the soul.[29]

The myth in the *Phaedrus*, like that in the *Symposium*, is
placed in the center of the whole work. This may be explained
in terms of the preliminary plan, according to which the speeches
are paradigms for the theoretical and rhetorical discussion in the
second part of the dialogue. But just as the whole dialogue requires a deeper interpretation, so perhaps does the place occupied by the myth. The *Statesman*, different as it is from the
Phaedrus, follows the latter in this respect. In the *Timaeus*,
finally, the myth fills the entire work.

The creation myth of the *Timaeus*, unique as it is, extends its
roots surprisingly far into Plato's early works. The mythical
theme of creation was already present in the *Protagoras* and,
despite its limitation to the "mortal races," contained traces
indubitably pointing toward the *Timaeus*. Later, the speech by
Aristophanes in the *Symposium* offered similar features. But
even though the fantasy, at first glance, seems to center around
man, it already suggests a noticeable shift in the center of
gravity. The spherical figure of primitive men and their circular
motion, the relationship with their begetters, the heavenly
bodies—these, to be sure, are fairylike, playful images. But they
anticipate the *Timaeus*, where the demiurge plants human souls
in the heavenly bodies (41D), sows them in the earth, the moon,
and the other "instruments of time" (41E), in order that the
lower gods—and again this means, besides the gods of popular
religion, the heavenly bodies—can make human bodies for them,
and where the path of human life consists in restoring, out of
confused motions, the original circular movements (90CD). In

this way Aristophanean fantasy reveals the essential bond of man with an ordered and divine cosmos.

Thus the image of "creation" is present in Plato's thought from the beginning and soon attracts the "world" as its object; similarly, it is apparent how in a second line of development, in Plato's eschatology, this object, "the world"—always in the sense of a divine cosmos ordered according to the *Ideas*—gains more and more importance. While the *Gorgias* still singles out the fate of the human soul, the *Phaedo* provides a spatial setting for this fate by constructing a picture of the earth. And as this spherical earth is already suspended in the center of the universe, the concluding myth of the *Republic* enlarges this picture of the earth into a cosmic construction. In the *Phaedrus*, finally, the fate of the human soul is an integral link of the universe. Thus it becomes apparent how the aspect of "creation" and the aspect of "world" converge toward the myth of the creation of the world.

In this myth Plato's thought, absorbing the richness of the previous philosophies of nature, spreads, in a last and widest circle, as it were, over the vast field of earlier speculations. He thus fulfills a strict inner law.[30] If, as we saw earlier, Parmenides and Herakleitos helped him to designate the nature of being as it presented itself to him after the discovery of the Forms, if Pythagoras taught him to envisage the universe as an orderly, mathematical system and to build the state of man in this cosmos, so he now finds help, in his quest to master the abundance of physical phenomena, from those who had previously written "about nature." We shall later inquire into the degree to which he is indebted, even in the language itself, to the doctrines of Parmenides, Empedokles, Anaxagoras, Leukippos, Demokritos, Diogenes of Apollonia, and, not least, to Alkmaion and the physicians, and how he fused their teachings with his own thinking.

Parmenides and Empedokles had already presented their accounts of nature in the form of cosmogonies, that is, mythical tales according to which divine powers—Aphrodite, or Strife and Love—are charged with the creation of the world. Thus, in this respect too, Plato had predecessors in the Greek world. Whether earlier Oriental stories of creation also influenced him, whether, for instance, Ormuzd was the prototype for his demi-urge, is a legitimate question, but cannot be answered at the present state of our knowledge.[31] At any rate, it is not imitation, but an inner necessity, when he speaks in mythical form about the world stuff and the heavenly bodies, the human body and its connection with the soul. The dialectical path leads to the threshold of eternal being, even to the aura of "the good." But strict rational inquiry (*Logos*) cannot demonstrate how the things in the world of becoming aim at "the good" and thus "become" (we call it: are). Concerning these things, only "probable discourse" is possible (*Timaeus* 59CD), in which we find relaxation after the labors of dialectics, such as when the myth tells the story of how the good god created the world after the model of the eternal forms, or how *Nous* accomplishes its work of persuasion on *Ananke*, and ordered form enters into the chaos of possibility, eternally formless, and eternally the receptacle of form.[32]

In the *Phaedo*, Socrates proclaimed that he would gladly be taught by anybody who would be able to show him that the structure of the world was held together by "the good and fit-ting" (τὸ ἀγαθὸν καὶ δέον). The myth of the *Timaeus* fulfills this deep concern underlying Plato's thinking. It does so because the Pythagorean in Plato subordinated the richness of all earlier natural philosophy to the intellectual theme of mathematical order, and because Socrates in Plato made the ordering and form-giving element of "the good" the central magnet that gives direction to the speculations of natural philosophy. Thus it is Socrates who listens—listens creatively, as it were—while the Pythagorean tells the myth about the perfection of the world shaped according to forms.

Closely connected with the *Timaeus* is the *Critias*, similar also in that the myth fills almost the entire space of the work. One half of the *Critias*, it will be shown, is constructed on the out-lines of the basic plan of the *Menexenus*, though in an entirely different form. The praise of Athens, as it is celebrated, with all possible irony, in the memorial speech of the *Menexenus*, now becomes a myth by virtue of the fact that the original ancestors of Athens grow out of the cosmogony of the *Timaeus*; that the

features of the Platonic state, the state of education, are transformed into a unique mythico-historical existence; and finally
that the Egyptian records, as the memory of mankind, transmit
the ancient tradition to the present generation (*Timaeus* 27AB).
The law of the continuous decline from an original state of
perfection is a necessary auxiliary concept. In the *Timaeus*, it is
expressed as the fate of the souls losing themselves in ever
lower forms of incarnation; in the *Republic*, as the fate of the
degenerate forms of constitutions. In the *Critias*, its geological
counterpart is the degeneration of the Attic soil (112A), the
disappearance of Atlantis, and, hence, the shoaling of the Atlantic Ocean (*Timaeus* 25CD)—all this happening in "one night"
or in "a day and a night." But this story belongs in a wider
context; for at the point where the *Critias* breaks off, we have
just learned how among the people of Atlantis "the divine part
began to fade away and became diluted too much and too often
with the mortal admixture" (*Critias* 121A).

At this point we can dimly see what unifies the different
themes—namely, the *Eidos*. The *Timaeus* realizes the *Idea* of
the Good in creation; the *Republic* presents an order of the human community from the point of view of the Good. Kritias
receives from Timaios man as a natural being, fashioned according to the *Eidos*, but his original purity already tarnished, as is
the case of all forms of creation. He receives from Socrates
"some men who have profited by a special education" (*Timaeus*
27A) and, as such, akin to and aiming at the *Eidos*. Egypt, for
Plato, was an astonishing example of an unchanging cultural
and political existence in contrast to the unceasing changes in
the Greek forms of life; in Plato's systematically graded world,
it became a political unit somewhere between Athens and the
ideal state. The idea of a decline, finally, presented itself when he
saw the twofold relationship—the *Eidos* immanent in the reality
of this world, yet this reality infinitely different from the
Eidos—and when he translated his insight into the mythico-
historical dimension, which, since Hesiod's legend of the ages of
the world, had been a genuinely Greek tradition. This could only
be traced in detail if he had completed the *Critias*, but it is suggested throughout. When the "true ocean" and the "true conti-

nent" (*Timaeus* 24E *et seq.*), surrounding our so-called oceans and continents, are related to the latter, even in name, as *Idea* to appearance, we cannot speculate how this contrast would have been developed further. But though it is not explicitly stated, the relationship is similar to that of the Akropolis, as it originally was, to its remains, i.e., the Lykabettos, the present citadel, and the Pnyx; or that of the one original fountain (κρήνη) within the area of the present Akropolis to the many small wells and streams (νάματα) that still exist in its vicinity (*Critias* 112A *et seq.*). All this may also fit into the period of nine thousand years set by the priest as the time that had elapsed between then and now (*Timaeus* 23E). From the myth in the *Phaedrus*, we learn that ten thousand years are one world period; from the myth in the *Statesman*, that great world periods alternate with each other: now the god seated at the helm of the world, now the world left to itself and the course of necessity. These myths and the *Critias*, to be sure, are independent constructions. If one nevertheless tried to bring them together, he might come to the conclusion that Atlantis and primitive Athens must be placed at the beginning of our world period; that is, when the world "still remembered, so far as possible, the teachings of the demiurge and father" (*Statesman* 273B).

What does the myth of an original Athens ultimately mean? The conventional answer that this is an "idealized" Athens remains as far behind Plato's intentions as the "ideal" behind the *Eidos*. A more correct answer would be that Athens becomes infused with the *Eidos* just as the state does in the *Republic* and the universe in the *Timaeus*. In the case of Athens as a unique historical phenomenon, this could only happen in the form of a historical myth or a utopian novel. By devising this poetic creation; by reciting the myth of the universe at the festival of the Greater Panathenaia; by putting it in the mouth of his ancestor Kritias, the grandfather of the "tyrant" Kritias; [33] by making Socrates, the victim of this city of Athens, a listener to this paean of praise—by doing all this Plato brings about a reconciliation of the hostile forces. The path from the *Menexenus* to the *Critias* is a path that proceeds from a very ironical panegyric in the old style, in praise of the Athens of the eighties of the fourth century, to a description that reveals the *Eidos* of this Athens, its true being and meaning. In the *Critias*, Plato replies to the reproach (raised by his contemporaries certainly as much as by B. G. Niebuhr in the nineteenth century and recently by G. Sarton) that he was a bad citizen.[34] It is his reconciliation with Athens. Perhaps that this reconciliation remained incomplete reflects an inner necessity.

If the mythological Athens is an Athens infused with the *Idea*, then Atlantis represents an ideated Orient.[35] Both are exact counterparts; yet Athens is by no means, as it is generally said, superior from the very beginning. For both states are founded by the gods, even though Atlantis, as the richer and more artificially constructed of the two, contains more dangerous seeds of disintegration and, at the time of the war with the mythological Athens, is already farther removed from the original state of perfection. What is here contrasted are the two basic constitutions, monarchy and democracy, from which, according to the *Laws* (693D *et seq.*), all other constitutions are derived. Persia is the greatest historical example of monarchy, Athens of democracy. Both forms of state must necessarily be combined if freedom and friendship are to rule in conjunction with wisdom. The mythical contrast between the original Athens and Atlantis corresponds to the historical contrast between Athens and Persia.

Atlantis is ruled by a king and nine princes. The palace of the king and the temple of the divine founder of the dynasty are situated exactly in the center of the main city on a circular island surrounded by circular canals. A rigid feudal system exacts definite military services from each of the 60,000 geometrically apportioned lots of land. The princes have absolute control over their regions. Their mutual relations, however, are regulated by a sacred law that is inscribed on a column of orichalch situated at the center of the circular middle island. Thus, in the strict sense of the word, it is the law and not the individual that is ruler of this monarchy. Nothing is more characteristic of its original nature than the fact that its citizens "carry lightly the possession of gold and the burden of property" (120E *et seq.*) and their conviction that "these goods are increased by virtue and friendship with one another" (ἐκ φιλίας τῆς κοινῆς μετ᾽-ἀρετῆς, 121A).

In the case of the Persians, as Plato describes them in the *Laws*, Cyrus is a good statesman who loves his country (φιλόπολις), but lacks education and is not concerned with administration. In the case of Darius, it is even more apparent that he is not thought of as an absolute despot. He has won his empire with six others; he has divided it into seven parts, and traces of this division still survive. He has decreed laws and introduced a certain kind of equality, he has incorporated the "tribute of Cyrus" (τὸν τοῦ Κύρου δασμόν) in the law, and he has spread friendship and partnership (φιλίαν καὶ κοινωνίαν) among all Persians. This order perishes because luxury (τρυφή 695B) gains the upper hand in the state, just as it threatens the community of Atlantis (*Critias* 121A), and because despotism takes over to such a degree that friendship and partnership (τὸ φίλον καὶ τὸ κοινόν, 697C) are destroyed. The lust for more and more causes the state to disintegrate (*Critias* 121A, *Laws* 697D) because it leads to the ruthlessness of destructive wars of conquest. And just as we are shown, from this point of view, the disintegration of the military system of the Persians, so we may assume that the conditions of life in Atlantis are calculated in such precise details because the disintegration of these conditions was to be shown in the war of conquest against Athens.

Thus Atlantis is a monarchy infused with the *Idea*, that is, a centralized absolute state in which the rulers, however, are bound by partnership and law; original Athens, on the other hand, is the ideal democracy (in the sense of Plato's *Laws*), that is, a form of state built upon the community of its citizens in which the principle of command is represented by a feudal order and by a law binding everybody to his specific task. Both states carry seeds of disintegration; the former, built according to numerical laws and geometrical proportions, is more threatened by disintegrative forces. If Plato had completed the work, they would have led to the war of conquest that probably would have become an "ideated" Marathon.[36]

In his later writings, besides the *Critias*, Plato presents in the *Statesman* another political myth (268D *et seq.*). We have already pointed out, in connection with the *Protagoras*, that the *Statesman* contains certain elements very similar to those found in the first stage of Plato's mythological creation, e.g., certain assumptions about human existence in a primitive state, about the origin of civilization, and about the participation of the gods in the fate of man. These elements are now, on the third level, translated into an entirely different form, which may become clear by comparison with the *Timaeus*, on the one hand, and the *Critias*, on the other. There is agreement with the former as to the concept of the demiurge, the goodness of the Creator guaranteeing existence, the creation of the universe as a perfect body, the circular motion as an approximation to perfect motion, the aboriginal chaos. With the *Critias* there is agreement—though with a modification—as to the idea of dividing the world into different places to be allotted to various gods. In the *Critias*, the gods are compared to shepherds; in the *Statesman*, the divine demons, looking after the human race, are called shepherds. In the former, they govern the human soul as if they were at the helm of a ship; in the latter, the divine steersman stands at the helm of the world or withdraws from the helm. In the former, the godlike part in man declines with the admixture of too much mortal stuff, and the physical, human attitude prevails; in the latter, it is the cosmos which gradually loses its perfection because of the admixture of physical stuff, or because it contains too little of the good and too strong an admixture of the opposite.[37] It is evident how differently from the *Protagoras*, and how much more strikingly than in the *Critias*, the human, political way of life is co-ordinated with the cosmos. What was merely suggested in the repetition of the political Utopia at the beginning of the *Timaeus* is now formulated in the *Statesman* with incomparable power: the grounding of the human state in the cosmos.

The *Timaeus* describes the origin of the world as a function of the forms entering into physical stuff. The perfect form is both represented in and tarnished by physical matter. In the whole and in every part, *Nous* and *Ananke* co-operate; the world is a mixture resulting from this combination. The cosmos came into being when *Nous* mastered *Ananke* (47E *et seq.*).

Similarly, the world soul is a mixture of the "same" and the "other," and it is bent apart into the two circles of the same and the other, which, in the sidereal sky, are represented by the fixed stars and by the planets (38c); in the human soul, by truth and knowledge on the one hand, and opinion and belief on the other (36E *et seq.*). This principle of both unity and duality, expressed in the picture of the universe as well as in that of the world soul, is now transferred, in the myth of the *Statesman*, from a simultaneous or concentric perspective, as it were, to a perspective of successive moments by means of the theme of the world periods. Ages during which the god stands at the helm of the world alternate with others during which the steersman has withdrawn, and the cosmos swings into the opposite direction through the necessity of fate (εἱμαρμένη) and through its own inherent desire (σύμφυτος ἐπιθυμία, 272E). The period of divine rule means perfect order, the immediate realization of the *Eidos* in the mortal stuff so far as possible; and the ironic play, even with the picture of the Golden Age, indicates how inadequate every human description of such a perfect condition must necessarily be.[38] The period of the god's withdrawal and distance from the world swings back to the condition of original chaos out of which divine goodness once created the cosmos, and which is responsible for all the evil and injustice in this world. Whatever is left of perfection and order in this world is due to our recollection of the period of divine rule. Even if this idea of periodicity was influenced by the Empedoklean image of the alternation between love and hate, and even if Oriental sources contributed to it,[39] this was only raw material for Plato, and his own contribution, which brings together the world and human-political existence in it under the aspect of the *Eidos*, is the essential part of the myth. Since the relations described are social and historical, the myth is dominated by the temporal element; and this, in turn, could only take the form of periodicity, for it was under this aspect that Plato had previously, in the *Republic* and the *Phaedrus*, envisaged the fate of the soul. Time, too, is seen, in the *Timaeus*, as running a cyclical course, time that is a copy of eternity and thus becomes the origin of all

inquiry into the nature of the universe, or the origin of philosophy itself (*Timaeus* 47AB).

The myth occurs in the middle of the *Statesman*. The Eleatic
stranger seeks relief from the tiring labors of the dialectical
procedure of definition, and hopes that the myth may indeed
further this process (268C *et seq.*). As a matter of fact, it results
in a small change in the definition of the royal art of statesmanship. But Plato gives at once the impression that the gain in
conceptual knowledge does not compensate for the efforts
expended on behalf of the myth: "We have accumulated a
marvelous mass of fable and have been obliged to use more than
was necessary" (277B). Thus it is not so much to advance the
task in the forefront of the dialogue that the dialectical procedure
is interrupted by the mythical "play"; it is rather for the purpose
of leading from the foreground to a deeper perspective. The
state is placed in the cosmos, partaking of its perfection as well
as its necessary imperfection, of the *Eidos* as well as the stuff,
the myth shows the necessary tarnishing of the state by evil,
the necessary belonging of the royal statesman to this world of
imperfection, but also the necessary relation of the state and the
statesman to the world of perfection, the *Eidos*, the God.

*

We have considered three levels in Plato's mythological construction, all three clearly distinguishable, yet one always
pointing to the next and providing a transition. On the first
level, the myth stands at the threshold of the Socratic world.
Apparently inserted quite arbitrarily, it suggests that, in the
case of the human soul or the human political community, there
are points which are not (or not yet) clarified by the strict,
responsible, rational discourse. None of these elements can be
admitted by Socrates until the aporetic attitude has been sharply
outlined. On the second level, Socrates himself takes hold of the
myth. Here it signifies the paths leading to the *Idea*, the path of
Eros leading through human life, the path of death leading the
soul to the limits of human existence, on which Socrates embarks
after he has traveled, as far as possible and as far as was neces-

sary, the path of knowledge. On the third level, Socrates—seized by divine mania—is representative of the myth only in the *Phaedrus*. Otherwise, he is the listener while others tell the mythical fables. At the same time, the myth moves into the center of each work or occupies the total space of the work. These formal changes symbolize changes in content. Now the myth is no longer a symbol for a path at the end of which the *Eidos* becomes visible, but the myth is built into the world, into the state, and into an original Athens. Thus the *Eidos*, secretly and implicitly, is the focal point for the various curves of Plato's myths just as it is the center of Plato's philosophy.

This, too, is the reason why the myth only beckons from afar, as it were, in Plato's *Laws*;[40] for *Eidos*, likewise, becomes visible only at its limits, when, at the conclusion of this huge work, the demand is made that the guardians must be capable "of looking toward the one *Idea*" (965c). At the point where legislation is to begin in earnest, a myth is invoked briefly (IV 713A 6–c 1): about the Golden Age when the god Kronos installed demonic powers as rulers over mankind. But the myth soon gives way to the *Logos* (713E 4): instead of a portrait of the mythical past, a demand is made on us and on any true foundation of the state; and *Nous* and *Nomos* are heard in the mythical name *Kro-nos*. Later we encounter the word "myth" in the great episode of Book X on "the true and false belief in gods." "We have need of myths," it is said (903B), "for the enchantment of the soul." A mythological pattern, too, is briefly suggested: "When the demiurge beheld this, he contrived (ἐμηχανήσατο). . . ." Thus Prometheus "contrived" in the myth of the *Protagoras*; and the same word "contrive" is frequently used in the *Timaeus* in connection with the demiurge. But what, in the *Laws*, is for a moment called "myth" is immediately translated into *Logos*, or, one might say, into theology and into a sermon. The mythological account of the choice of the lots of the soul and of the transmigration of souls in the *Phaedo* is here transformed into the conceptual language of natural science. There follows an accumulation of concepts: change of position or place, movement upward and downward, the better joining the better and the worse the worse (904ff.).

It is as if we were reading Anaxagoras, Empedokles, or Demo-kritos. While, in the *Timaeus*, the mythic vision fills almost the entire realm of the dialogue, in the *Laws* mythological echoes are sounded only for a brief moment, as if they did not properly belong in these Solonian precincts.

Hegel interpreted Plato's myths as representing a necessary stage in the education of the human race, which conceptual knowledge can discard as soon as it has grown up.[41] But to speak of a childhood stage of philosophy, a stage that Aristotle left behind, makes sense only in the very restricted way that Plato's conceptual system was superseded by a more rigorous one. As a creator he is not superseded any more than any other creator by the refinement or elaboration of formal devices. To be sure, to reverse this line of thought and to speak of the myth, in a currently popular exaggeration, as Plato's highest form of expression—because it is concerned with the highest things—would invite opposition from Plato himself. In the unique, unrepeatable, and unsurpassable Platonic world, the myth has its necessary place. Its formal changes tell us something about Plato's growth or, to speak more carefully and correctly, about the growth of Plato's work. But whether they are playfully anticipating, whether they are guides along the path, or, finally, whether they show eternity incorporated in this world of nature and history, the myths invariably have one element in common. Mythology is fiction mixed with truth (*Republic* 377A). This formulation does not mean it is arbitrary, but rather that it is deeply embedded in the nature of being and the human knowledge of this being. Pure truth belongs to God: "For the demonic and divine is absolutely without falsehood" (or deception, ἀψευδές, *Republic* 382E).[42] Thus we gain a final perspective in which the myth appears akin to irony, both revealing and concealing; and we may perhaps surmise why Socrates, the ironic man, may—indeed, must—become the inventor of myths, why myths are infused with irony, and why, in Plato's ironic dialogues, they find a necessary place wherever a ray of transcendence (*epekeina*) and, gradually, the plenitude of *Ideas* penetrate into this life.

In the great letter addressed to Can Grande della Scala,

Dante refers to the ambiguity of his *Commedia:* "the sense of this work is not simple, but on the contrary it may be called polysemous, that is to say, of more senses than one."[43] The simple meaning is the "literal" in contrast to the "allegorical" or "mystical," which in turn assumes various forms. "The subject of the whole work, then, taken in the literal sense only, is 'the state of souls after death, without qualification,' for the whole progress of the work hinges on it and about it. Whereas if the work be taken allegorically the subject is 'man, as by good or ill deserts, in the exercise of the freedom of his choice, he becomes liable to rewarding or punishing justice.' " Plato's myths, too, vaguely akin to Dante's great poem, over and again seem to require to be understood partly *allegorice*, partly *moraliter* or *anagogice*. But Plato always protested against a manner, already popular in his own age, of allegorizing the traditional legends of the gods.[44] Since his myths are never to be understood *literaliter*, they are constantly ready to bring such "mystical" interpretations back to the original concrete image. Thus Plato escapes the danger of a metaphysical dogmatism, just as the artistic form of the dialogue avoids the fixity of the written word, and irony the danger of dogmatic seriousness. The achievement of the myth is that it renders intelligible the mysterious aspects of life, and it does so not only by evoking a vague sentiment. Our intuitive imagination is led along a clear and firm path of ancestral tradition; both the knowledge gained through the dialectical method and the moral obligations immediately felt lead to the myth, and the myth leads back to knowledge and obligation. "For we see many things by the intellect," it is said in Dante's letter, "for which there are no vocal signs, of which Plato gives sufficient hint in his books by having recourse to metaphors; for he saw many things by intellectual light which he could not express in direct speech." (*Quod satis Plato insinuat in suis libris per assumptionem metaphorismorum. Multa enim per lumen intellectuale vidit, quae sermone proprio nequivit exprimere.*) [45]

PART II

CHAPTER TEN

Intuition and Construction

A PATH TO BERGSON AND SCHOPENHAUER

THE TENSION between intuition and construction, *theoria* and theory, mania and dialectic, in Plato exists as a creative tension from the beginning and runs through all of his work. Perhaps it is a stronger and possibly more conscious element in him than in most other philosophers. But the central intuition toward which all conceptual thinking is directed in preparation and exploration, and from which, in turn, all conceptual thinking emanates, is present in every great philosophy. In the case of Plato, this has been shown in the preceding chapters, primarily in the first three. Was my interpretation, from the start, influenced by Bergson and Schopenhauer? Be that as it may, in them it finds its strongest philosophical support.

In the collected volume *La Pensée et le mouvant*, Bergson discusses this subject several times, primarily in his lecture "L'Intuition philosophique" (1911) and his "Introduction à la Métaphysique" (1903).[1] He describes two processes on the basis of the most intense personal experience: first, the origin of a creative philosophy and the manner in which the philosopher attains conceptual mastery of this original element, and second—at a great distance from and yet parallel to it—the way in which the historian of philosophy attempts to grasp a philosophical system by discovering its creative origin and separating it from the constructive elements by which the philosopher holds the intuitive element before himself and makes it communicable to others.

The absolute contemplated from within, as Bergson describes his individual experience in the "Introduction" (p. 205), is

213

something quite simple. From without we can only approach
it by an infinite number of steps. It follows that the absolute
can only be given in an intuition, whereas everything else
depends upon analysis. Intuition is the sympathy by means of
which we project ourselves into an object in order to achieve
identification with that element in which it is unique and which
is inexpressible. Analysis is the operation that reduces the
object to previously known elements, i.e., to those it has in
common with others. The philosopher, according to the
"Intuition philosophique" (p. 153), does not proceed from ideas
existing prior to his own. To say that he arrives at them would
be much closer to the truth. And when he arrives at an idea, and
this idea is absorbed into the movement of his mind, it ceases
to be what it had been outside this movement. It is animated
with a new spirit, like the word that receives its meaning from
the sentence.

To this process, then, corresponds the dual method of the
historian of philosophy. We see, Bergson says (p. 136), the
completed structure of a philosophical system. We attempt to
reconstruct rationally the order within this system. We inquire
into the origin of its materials and find the elements of previous
systems. This continues until we finally arrive at a more or less
original synthesis of the ideas in whose midst the philosopher
lived. What Bergson describes here is roughly the method employed in what we have come to know as the history of philosophy. To return to Plato, we are shown how, in his early works,
the concept of the *Idea* grows slowly out of the Socratic definition, or out of a hypostatization of the ethical concept that
Socrates discovered.[2] Similar formulations are found elsewhere.
"In Plato, a man of hypersensitive sensuality and phantasy, the
magic of the concept became so powerful that he involuntarily
revered and deified the concept as an ideal Form." In this
sentence of Nietzsche's (*The Will to Power*, § 431) only the key
is his own; the melody often appears elsewhere.[3] But this view
that the ontological significance of the *Idea* developed out of
the logical was too limited even for the analytical-genetic approach. Stewart saw in the *Idea* a union of a methodological

and an aesthetic element. Friedemann describes it as a fusion of a logical and a religious element. R. S. Bluck distinguishes four aspects of the Forms: metaphysical, ontological, epistemological, and logical.[4] An ingenious attempt to explain the "Doctrine of the *Ideas*" on the basis of the residual problems of Plato's predecessors was made by Cherniss by means of what he calls "economy of thought":[5] at the end of the fifth century, says Cherniss, the doctrines that had developed in the fields of ethics, epistemology, and ontology were so paradoxical and irreconcilable that Plato thought it necessary to find one single hypothesis in order to solve the problems of the three spheres and thus to unify the separate phases of knowledge. Even Cherniss had his predecessors (who has not?), for example, Windelband: in the Doctrine of the Forms, all the different ideas about the physical, ethical, and logical principles are gathered together. Zeller's detailed presentation had been similar to Windelband's. Finally, this approach goes back to Aristotle, who constructed the Platonic system out of the intersection of three lines, the Herakleitean, the Socratic, and the Pythagorean (*Metaphysics* I 6 987ª 29 *et seq.*, XIII 4 1078ᵇ 9 *et seq.*).

It stands to reason that there should be much that is true in these constructions. Perhaps, after we have acknowledged that all of them fail to recognize the originality of Plato's metaphysics, we might ask how much. Residual problems? Derivations? Economy of thought? It may be that questions of this kind will receive their proper place only when the origin has been found elsewhere, and the task at hand will then be to investigate by what means the original vision is rationalized and incorporated in the existing body of thought. For the relationship of a philosophy (that is, of a great and genuine philosophy) to previous and contemporary philosophies, and here we again return to Bergson (p. 152), is not what a certain interpretation of the history of philosophy would have us believe. The philosopher (that is, the great and genuine philosopher) does not seize upon pre-existing ideas in order to combine them in a superior synthesis or to connect them with a new insight. Perhaps repeated contact with the works of a master may lead us to a point where all his thoughts are concentrated in a central idea, which we approach ever more closely, without, however, completely reaching it. That is the original intuition. So extraordinary is its simplicity that the philosopher has never quite succeeded in expressing it. *Et c'est pourquoi il a parlé toute sa vie* (p. 137).

Besides those attempting to find a purely conceptual derivation of Plato's metaphysics or the so-called Doctrine of the *Ideas*, there were others who tried to do justice to vision and intuition. It was hard to ignore this element completely while listening to Plato's words, regardless of whether it was seen as an original element, or classified as one motif among others, or condemned as an aberration of Plato's thought. To trace the history of the interpretation of Plato or the history of Platonism through the centuries is a great task yet to be accomplished. The present chapter must confine itself to an almost accidental selection of a few points.

As a psychologist, Stewart sees in the Platonic *Idea* a union of the experiences of a man who was both a great scientist and a great artist. Accordingly, the Doctrine of the *Ideas* has two aspects, methodological and aesthetic. In Plato's mind, scientific concepts merged with the artist's ideogram, dream image, or contemplation.

Stewart goes back to Łutoslawski,[6] who, with his "Stylometry," attempted to determine the exact chronology of the dialogues and, on this basis, to prove the alleged development of Plato's philosophy from dialogue to dialogue. According to him, Plato's own philosophy developed from a Socratic stage. The *Cratylus* is considered to be the beginning of Plato's own logic, which, in the *Symposium*, reached its next higher level. Plato became aware of the limitations of the purely ethical science, of which he was so proud in the *Gorgias*, and the artist in him intuited the *Idea* of beauty in a sudden vision.

Dean Inge,[7] proceeding from Plotinos, abandons the hypothesis of development: Plato *saw* his universal *Ideas* as clearly as the Greek sculptors saw their ideal types. Łutoslawski, too, had referred to Pheidias. And we find more than one reference to Greek sculpture in discussions of Plato's *Eidos*. What

Schopenhauer sees is not yet Pheidias but still the Apollo Belvedere—"the head . . . with eyes fixed on the far distance, stands so freely on his shoulders that it seems wholly delivered from the body, and no more subject to its cares"—in the very passage of his principal work (end of § 33) that precedes the "sudden transition . . . from the common knowledge of particular things to the knowledge of the *Idea*" (beginning of § 34).[8]

Among the German historians of philosophy of the last few decades, Hönigswald,[9] with all due regard for the strictly conceptual element, strongly emphasizes the role of intuition in the grasping of the Platonic *Idea*, while dissociating this intuition from all ecstatic-romantic forms. In Platonic thought, the intuitive comprehension of the *Idea* is inseparably linked with the logical motif of a priori certainty in knowledge. The methodological validity of the Platonic *Idea* for him is at the same time its aesthetic validity.

Stenzel tries to explain how, with the Greeks, thought directed toward subjects such as virtue and the good became of necessity a matter of vision.[10] The *Eidos*, according to him, has the same determinate quality as the scientific concept; at the same time, it is also result and organ of an intuition in which not a single feature of concrete reality is stunted or distorted. He tries to distinguish "Plato's concept of illumination," as it occurs in the *Republic* and in the *Seventh Letter*, from all Platonizing, but un-Platonic, mysticism.

Dilthey, in his *Einleitung in die Geisteswissenschaften* (1883) attempts to present a history of European metaphysics.[11] In this history, he says that the "doctrine of the substantial forms" constituted a methodologically necessary advance which took Plato, supported by Socrates, beyond the metaphysics of the pre-Socratics and the skepticism of the Sophists. The science of the future would dissolve this metaphysics. But it is the task of historical consciousness to show the connection between the individual objectives, the increasing depth of the questions, the generalization of the problems, the broadening of the horizon. Thus Dilthey sees the theory of the substantial forms arise as the condition on the basis of which it is possible to construct conceptually being as well as knowledge, the cosmos as well as moral volition. It is born in Plato, fulfills itself in Aristotle, and later disintegrates.

For one strange moment, however, Dilthey pauses and, in a tone to which his factual, searching survey has not accustomed us, exclaims: "In the golden light of Plato's most beautiful passages, who would not feel that, in his rich poetic and morally powerful mind, the *Ideas* existed as something more than conditions of empirical reality?" Thus something has been omitted in this linear interpretation of the history of philosophy, something essential, if not to this interpretation, at least to Plato: "He viewed the *Ideas* in this reality, and did not merely think of them as preconditions of it." Does this change anything in the historical construction? By no means. "Any discussion of the origin of this great doctrine, however, must be avoided here." The origin in this context means the biographical origin, as it were; for, indeed, the factual historical origin has been discussed in detail. "We are concerned," Dilthey concludes, "with the context of his thoughts, in so far as this context appears in the argument and, in this systematic form, determined the further development of European metaphysics." The question arises whether it is in fact possible to divorce the origin of the doctrine from its position and effect within the history of philosophy. Does this limitation leave out what is nowadays called "existence"?

During his first years in Basle, Nietzsche wrote the *Unzeitgemässe Betrachtung* about "Schopenhauer as Educator" (1874), in order to "remember the one teacher and disciplinarian of whom I may boast." But as a professor of philology, lecturing on Plato during the same period, he was critical of Schopenhauer's "false derivation of the Platonic Doctrine of *Ideas*." The element to which he takes exception is this very "intuitive grasp of the universal" in which Schopenhauer had claimed to recognize the origin of the Platonic *Idea*. In his criticism (*Philologica*, III, 271ff) Nietzsche, one may say, is influenced by Zeller. Schopenhauer, according to Nietzsche, proceeded from the aesthetic idea, while Plato arrived at the idea not from what is sensibly given, but from nonsensible concepts such as just, beautiful, equal, good. Dialectic as a path leading to the *Idea* and Plato's disdain for art and predilection for mathematics are cited as additional arguments against the aesthetic genesis. There is, perhaps, an element of truth in this criticism in that it objects to confining the intuitive to the aesthetic, but it is a mistake—a widespread mistake and one incidentally shared by Schopenhauer—to assume that Plato disdained art in general because he criticized the art of his time. The geometrical forms, moreover, were in all likelihood an element that came to the aid of his intuition.

If Nietzsche sharply criticized Schopenhauer because the latter found the origin of the Platonic *Ideas* in intuition, Karl Justi, the future historian of art, had adopted Schopenhauer's interpretation, and had turned it, in his first work, *Die ästhetischen Elemente in der Platonischen Philosophie* (1860), against Plato himself. To be sure, Socrates found his spokesman in Plato, the artist-philosopher (p. 8). The artistic element, however, became detrimental to Plato's dialectic since it mixed the imaginative with the intellectual element (p. 56). "The very element that we miss in Plato's theory of art, i.e., the representation of the ideal or the improvement of nature, here receives its place as the object of philosophy" (p. 62). Justi shares Schopenhauer's and Nietzsche's misunderstanding of Plato's theory of art. Unlike Nietzsche, however, Justi does not turn against Schopenhauer's interpretation of Plato. In fact, he accepts it and thus condemns Plato's metaphysics. "And in a sort of intellectual Fall of Man, the growth of this promising Socratic seed remains stunted for the time being" (p. 67).

Nietzsche and Justi, each in his own manner, lead us back to Schopenhauer's principal work and thus to that modern metaphysics that aims to absorb the Platonic *Idea* completely. "The Platonic Idea: The Object of Art" reads the title of the third book of *The World as Will and Idea*. Nietzsche's view is correct in that Plato's actual *Idea* extends far beyond the realm of art. Apart from this, however, Schopenhauer had a more profound understanding of the intuitive element in the *Idea* than anyone else in recent times, no doubt because what he found in reading Plato coincided with his most personal experience. The World as *Idea* emerges in perfect purity from the World as Will in so far as the cognizant individual—Plato or Schopenhauer—in the process of knowing becomes the pure subject of knowledge and by this very act elevates the contemplated object to the state of the *Idea*. "The transition . . . from the common knowledge of particular things to the knowledge of the *Idea*, takes place suddenly; for knowledge breaks free from the service of the will . . . " (§ 34). "If [a man] gives the whole power of his mind to perception, sinks himself entirely in this, and lets his whole consciousness be filled with quiet contemplation . . . " (§ 34). "Only through the pure contemplation . . . which ends entirely in the object can *Ideas* be comprehended; and the nature of genius consists in pre-eminent capacity for such contemplation" (§ 36).[12]

CHAPTER ELEVEN

Aletheia

A DISCUSSION WITH MARTIN HEIDEGGER[1]

IN *SEIN UND ZEIT* (1927), Heidegger dealt with the concepts of *logos* and *aletheia* (pp. 52ff., 219ff.) and thereby influenced the thinking of a whole generation. He explained explicitly why he went back to an etymological analysis: it is the business of philosophy "to protect the power of the most fundamental words in which reality [*Dasein*] finds expression against the tendency of common sense [ordinary thinking] to level them to incomprehensibility." In his book *Platons Lehre von der Wahrheit* (1947), Heidegger then gave, on this basis, an interpretation of Plato's allegory of the cave. As a philosopher he tries to bring to light what is contained in language; and where is this undertaking more important than in the case of truth? According to Heidegger, the concept of truth has degenerated in the course of the thinking of many generations: the prevailing opinion makes truth a predicate of thought and speech, not of reality. The meaning of truth has changed "from the unhiddenness [*Unverborgenheit*] of being to the correctness of apprehension" (p. 46). It is Heidegger's intention to reverse this process of decay and to penetrate back to the original meaning. For him, the decay begins with Plato, and the change in the meaning of truth takes place in the determination of being as ἰδέα. We shall show what this means. Meanwhile we may adopt Heidegger's own warning as a general rule that in the admission of such (i.e., linguistic) evidence we must guard against unbridled verbal mysticism (cf. *Sein und Zeit*, p. 220).

The etymology of ἀληθής, ἀλήθεια as ἀ-ληθής, ἀ-λήθεια seems to be generally accepted today either as that which is not hidden, concealed, or forgotten, or as he who does not hide, conceal, or

221

forget. Yet this etymological derivation is by no means as unshakable as it appears.[2] In effect, we may not be able to decide whether the interpretation of ἀληθής as ἀ-ληθής is linguistically correct. Much more important is the fact that the Greeks from Homer on associated ἀληθής with λαθ-, ληθ-, λανθ-. This association persisted in poetry and prose without objection. It was heard from the stage, in the courts, from the orators in the marketplace, and it survived until late times. The ancient lexica register it as a matter of fact. Sextus Empiricus, in *Adversus logicos*, based a whole section on a (highly subjective) variation of this etymology, while the Neoplatonist Olympiodoros apparently appealed to the authority of Plutarch in the matter.

Since the 1958 edition of *Plato* 1, I have learned that my opposition to the various etymological interpretations of the word *aletheia* was unfounded. Nevertheless, it remains true (*1*) that ἀληθής and ἀλήθεια were perhaps originally not negatives, and (*2*) that they were never felt to be pure negatives, as, for example, these words:

ἀν-αιδής	ἀν-αίδεια	ἀ-σεβής	ἀ-σέβεια
ἀ-παθής	ἀ-πάθεια	ἀ-σθενής	ἀ-σθένεια
ἀ-πλανής	ἀ-πλάνεια	ἀ-φανής	ἀ-φάνεια
ἀ-σαφής	ἀ-σάφεια		

For none of these words do we have a negative. For ἀληθής a negative—ἀναληθής—does exist. It does not occur before Polybios, however, and is of no importance, to be sure, for the problem put by Heidegger.

From the early Greek period we have as the most striking example of ἀληθής understood as ἀ-ληθής[3] the testimony of Hesiod, in whose theology etymologizing was an essential element. Yet, in this case (*Theogony* 233), although ἀληθής was understood as ἀ-ληθής, it had nothing to do with the hiddenness of being, but rather designated a person who does not forget or neglect, or does not lose something out of sight or mind. It meant, in short, exactly the "correctness of perception" which Heidegger, in his sketch of the history of the words ἀληθής and ἀλήθεια, attributes to a late period of Greek thought, the Platonic period.

The history of these words thus appears in a rather different

light from Heidegger's account.[4] Homer is less simple to interpret than Hesiod. In Homer, ἀληθείη and ἀληθής, with a single
exception, always occur connected with and dependent on verbs
of assertion. It is extremely difficult to find even one or two
passages in which the object of the assertion could be (let alone
must be) the "unhidden." It is usually much more natural to
render it as that which is not-crooked, not-falsified, not-diluted.
But why use negatives when there is no indication that Homer
understood the word as a negative? This ἀληθής is something
highly positive: the genuine, the completely coherent (πᾶσαν
ἀληθείην κατάλεξον), that which is clear, reality as it really is.
The essential contrary is—and always was for the Greeks—
lying, deception, conscious distortion, silence for the purpose of
sparing or deceiving another person, dreaming—in short,
everything that disturbs, distorts, slants, or conceals the true
and real.

Twice, however, the text of the *Iliad* seems to allow an interpretation of ἀληθής as the unhidden. In VI 376, Hector orders
the maids: "Tell what does not miss the mark, the unerring,
what does not go wrong (νημερτέα μυθήσασθε)!" and one of the
servant women answers: "You have ordered us to tell the unhidden, what does not conceal (ἀληθέα μυθήσασθαι)." In the
second passage (XXIII 361), at the funeral games for Patroklos
Achilles assigns Phoenix to stand at the end of the course "in
order that he remember the races (ὡς μεμνέωτο δρόμους) and
tell the unforgotten, the unhidden (καὶ ἀληθείην ἀποείποι)." It
seems as if Homer had wanted to express here not only the
correctness of the assertion, but also the unhiddenness of the
matter. If Homer and Hesiod are taken together, then, it becomes clear that of the two meanings assigned by Heidegger to
two different periods of Greek thought, both can be attributed
to the early period. Only once in the *Iliad* is the word ἀληθής
used in regard to a person; in a simile (XII 433) a spinning
woman is called "honest or reliable." Because this meaning of
the word occurs only in this single passage, it was doubted in
antiquity whether Homer could have said it.[5] Hesiod employs
the same word in the same sense, however, even if his reference
is not to a woman artisan, but to a god.

So much for the ancient epic: present in it are all the essential aspects that will come out more clearly in later literary language. If, with the help of the dictionaries, we inquire into later usage, for instance, in the tragic poets, the historians, or the orators—disregarding, for the moment, the philosophers—we find that despite all differences there are certain common characteristics. Meanings for the words ἀληθής and ἀλήθεια can be grouped chiefly under three headings. They signify (*1*) the correctness of speech and belief that does not conceal but reveals, (*2*) the unhidden reality of being, and (*3*) the unforgetting, undeceiving truthfulness and honesty of the individual or character—"existence" in the present sense, i.e., "the truth which I am myself" (Jaspers). The opposites are (*1*) lying, deception, error, gossip, concealment, on the side of speech and belief; (*2*) on the side of being, that which is unreal, play, dream, imitation, or fake; and (*3*) on the side of human existence, dishonesty, deceitfulness, and unreliability.

A central point in the history of Greek thought, and thus in the history of the concept of *aletheia*, was reached with Parmenides. His radical doctrine of the One ultimately does not permit of a concept of truth that refers to a separately existing world of the real, or of a concept of reality that is grasped by a truth opposite to or separate from it. On the contrary, truth of thinking and reality of being coincide in the One, the very One outside of which there is nothing real, nothing but the unreality and untruth (or half-reality and half-truth) of that which is *only* opinion and *only* appearance.[6] It is significant that Parmenides received this doctrine of the identity of reality and truth from the Goddess of Truthfulness. The three aspects of the Greek concept of *aletheia* are indissolubly united here in one knot.

We would not have to mention Herakleitos in this brief survey if it were not that Heidegger believed that he had found, in Herakleitos' famous opening sentences, an allusion to the "phenomenon of truth in the sense of uncoveredness" or unhiddenness. Rightly so. For Herakleitos, whose language is full of play on words—which he meant very seriously—would not have placed λανθάνει and ἐπιλανθάνονται next to each other had he not intended to evoke *aletheia* as a contrast to these two verbs.[7] It is doubtful, however, that Herakleitos understood

only the unhiddenness of being, as Heidegger thinks. Herakleitos actually begins his speech with "this *logos*" and man's
inability to grasp it. Thus, *aletheia* may be for him both the
uncovering clarity and truth of his *logos* and the clarity and
truth of the being which this *logos* uncovers. Does not Herakleitos put his own name at the beginning as that of the speaker,
and does he not speak even in the first sentences about the
words and works "as I present them"? Here, then, as in Parmenides, the three aspects of the concept of *aletheia* seem to
combine—though in the more enigmatic manner that is typical
of Herakleitos.

Let us now turn to Plato's allegory of the cave.[8] It is characterized by the dual meaning of the hierarchical ascent: the ascent
of being and the ascent of knowledge, both exactly related to
each other, but the former independent of the latter. Beyond
both hierarchical ascents there becomes visible from afar, without ever being reached, that in which the two converge, that
which presents (offers, grants) being to reality and truth to
knowledge: the "*Idea* of the Good," or the "Form of the Perfect," in its nature or essence not describable in words and thus
only approachable by means of simile. In this systematic
structure, Plato presented his philosophical experience—intuition and construction—at the same time giving it the form in
which it has lasted. As witness for these thoughts he chose
Socrates, facing death for the sake of truth and reality. Thus,
the dual meaning of the hierarchical ascent becomes threefold
if it is kept in mind that the allegory of unhidden and revealing
truth is told by the truthful man.

Heidegger's interpretation of the allegory of the cave is
admirable for its energy; it is instructive even where it over-
looks important points (e.g., the three-dimensional figures that
are carried through the cave),[9] where it uses oracular language
(e.g., *Anwesung*, p. 35), or where it falsely relies upon real or
alleged etymology. (*Aletheia* is not "unhiddenness," p. 34; and
the nature of *Idea* or *Eidos* is to be found not only in its *Schein-
und Sichtsamkeit* [pp. 34ff.], i.e., in its nature as appearance and
vision, but primarily in form and structure.) The following
aspect of Heidegger's interpretation is particularly misleading.

When he speaks of "idea" or ἰδέα (pp. 34ff.), he most often means not the *Idea* in general, not the region of "Forms," but the one, unique *Idea*, the "prototype of perfection," which, comparable to the sun, rises "above" the realm of *Ideas*, "beyond being"—in short, "transcendence," to use Heidegger's and Jaspers' term, the historical origin of which lies in the *epekeina*.[10]

But the most astonishing part of the new interpretation of the cave allegory is yet to come. According to Heidegger, an exciting transformation is taking place. Where? In the history of the human mind, or in Plato's thought, which has its place in this history? There is an early suggestion that something is happening: "Instead of 'unhiddenness' another meaning of truth gains precedence" (p. 33). Let us see what is allegedly taking place. "This simile," says Heidegger (p. 40), "contains Plato's doctrine of truth. For it is based upon the implicit pre-eminence of the ἰδέα, by which the ἰδέα becomes master over ἀλήθεια." Heidegger sees a process, the process of gaining mastery. I see a state of being, the state of being master. The ἰδέα is not (still less becomes) master over ἀλήθεια, since ἀλήθεια is both, the being of forms or *Ideas* as well as their being grasped by the mind. It is not the *Idea* or *Eidos* in general that is master, but it is the highest *Idea:* the *Idea* of the Good, the Form of the Perfect.

Here the discussion must go still further into detail. We may consider Heidegger's remarks in *Platons Lehre von der Wahrheit*, pp. 41ff. (my comments are in the right-hand column):

Plato in speaking of the ἰδέα as the mistress that admits the "unhiddenness"	Not simply of the ἰδέα, but of the ἰδέα of the perfect. Not "admits," but "prepares, makes accessible, offers" (παρασχομένη). Not "unhiddenness," but "less one-sided": the revealing truth and the revealed reality.
refers to something that remains unsaid: namely, that henceforth the essence of truth no longer unfolds as the essence of "un-	With the word "henceforth" the faulty historical construction again comes to the fore, as Hei-

hiddenness" from its own essential content, but is transposed to the essence of the ἰδέα.

degger seems to have Plato mysteriously point here to the post-Platonic history of philosophy. Nothing is transposed. Rather: (1) unhidden reality, (2) truth that discovers it, and (3) the spirit—who, ruled by this truth, discovers reality—are all three grounded in something still higher: the good or the perfect.

The essence of truth surrenders its essential trait of "unhiddenness."

If this means that the "ontological" side of *aletheia* is given up in favor of the "epistemological" side, Heidegger is mistaken. Highest perfection (αὐτὸ τὸ ἀγαθόν, ἡ τοῦ ἀγαθοῦ ἰδέα) radiates aletheia as the reality of being, as the truth of knowledge, and as the truthfulness of the spirit—of existence—that through knowledge perceives the reality of being.

From the preference given to ἰδέα or to ἰδεῖν, there emerges a change in the nature of truth.

Again, rather, the highest ἰδέα. ἰδεῖν, in the Platonic sense, can only be meant as a metaphor for intuitive knowledge. This kind of "vision" is given no preference to *aletheia*, but it is the manner in which ἀλήθεια = ἰδέα becomes accessible.

Truth becomes ὀρθότης, i.e., correctness of apprehension and assertion.

Truth, in Plato's system, is always both: reality of being and correctness of apprehension and assertion—and, in addition, the truthfulness of the *Nous* who directs this cognizance upon that reality. Instead of *Nous* one might say: existence.

This change in the nature of truth, at the same time, defines a change in the locus of truth. As "unhiddenness" it is still a basic aspect of reality itself. As correctness of apprehension it comes to signify a human attitude toward reality.

This reference to a change in the nature as well as the locus of truth, and, consequently, the phrases "it still is" and "it comes to" belong to Heidegger's faulty construction.

To a certain extent, however, Plato must still hold fast to the notion of truth as a basic characteristic of reality.

The qualifications "to a certain extent" and "still" do injustice to the equilibrium within the Platonic construction.

At the same time, the inquiry into the "unhidden" is transposed to the field of appearances and thereby . . . to the correctness of apprehension. For this reason there is a necessary ambiguity in Plato's doctrine.

Nothing "is transposed," but the reality of being and the correctness of apprehension are mutually conditioned. One might say "two-sidedness"; "ambiguity" strikes a false note. Plato's doctrine is unambiguous.

The ambiguity appears most clearly by virtue of the fact that in dealing with ἀλήθεια (in the ontological sense), Plato, nonetheless, means ὀρθότης (in the epistemological sense).

Heidegger's false approach here appears most clearly: both aspects have equal status for Plato.

Both statements speak of the preference given to the *Idea* of the Good as the possibility for the correctness of knowledge and the "unhiddenness" of the known. Truth is here still both "unhiddenness" and correctness, although "unhiddenness" already is put under the yoke of the ἰδέα.

Here at last Heidegger returns to the simple truth. But "unhiddenness" again leads him astray. The subordinate clause beginning with "although" introduces the old error; the yoke of conjunction becomes a yoke of subjection. Instead of ἰδέα, Heidegger should have written "the highest ἰδέα."

In the end Heidegger himself states the whole matter simply, clearly, and correctly (p. 48): "The highest in the realm of the transcendent is that *Idea* which, as the *Idea* of all *Ideas*, remains the cause for the permanence and appearance of all being." But what, then, remains of the whole construction that we have followed?

With regard to Aristotle, I will only make one comment: I do not see that, in the final chapter of the ninth book of the *Metaphysics* (IX 10 1051ª 35 *et seq.*), "the unhiddenness is the over-all, predominating basic element of being." Anybody reading these words will anxiously await Heidegger's interpretation of this difficult chapter.[11] What we have so far been able to see in this chapter is that the opposite of ἀλήθεια is always ψεῦδος, and that ἀλήθεια means, as in Plato, both the nature of the real and the nature of a true statement, both conjoined in a manner hard to explicate precisely. The "existential" aspect, however, represented in Plato through the figure of Socrates, has disappeared in Aristotle.

Three facets of the Greek *aletheia* have become clear: the ontological, the epistemological, and the existential. In Plato they are intimately united; in this respect as well as in most others, he is the summit of Greek philosophy.

In my discussion with Martin Heidegger, I have learned that my earlier opposition to the interpretation of *aletheia* as unhiddenness was unjustified. What stands unchanged is my criticism of Heidegger's historical construction. For the result has become even more clear. It was not "first in Plato" that truth became the correctness of perception and assertion. This meaning was present much earlier, i.e., in the old epic. For Plato, there is in ἀληθής and ἀλήθεια an equilibrium between the revealing truth, the unhidden reality, and the truthfulness which measures that reality by this truth. Plato did not corrupt the concept of *aletheia*, as Heidegger claims. Plato sharpened the concept, systematized it, and heightened it.

CHAPTER TWELVE

Dialogue and Existence

A QUESTION ADDRESSED TO KARL JASPERS

EXISTENCE is a concept characteristic of a great deal of contemporary philosophy, though inevitably also a fashionable catchword. In Jaspers' three-volume *Philosophie* (1932), the volume called *Existenzerhellung* is the central and largest part of the entire work, placed between *Philosophische Weltorientierung* and *Metaphysik*. The title is not "Existence" but "Clarification of existence," for Jaspers undertakes a description and analysis of existence by nonexistential means. The philosopher speaks of "shipwreck," but we do not become aware of the course of his boat. He writes about historicity by progressing, in general statements, to the limits of individual, particular experience, and then leaving it up to the reader to make the "leap." He describes "communication," but while doing so he is perhaps sitting by his stove as isolated as Descartes. There are many questions here for everybody, including the interpreter of Plato's work. The latter, however, would not have to address himself directly to Jaspers, were it not for a few noteworthy lines in which the understanding of Plato is at stake (ii, 115).

In this passage, Jaspers asserts that genuine philosophizing is possible only in communion with others. If this is true, how does it affect the form of philosophy? And this leads him to the question whether the dialogue is not the appropriate form of philosophical communication. At first sight, it may appear to be, says Jaspers, but it is not. Like other styles employed in philosophical writing, the dialogue is merely a form of addressing the reader, and requires complementary response and realization through the latter. This is certainly so, we should say; but is the dialogue not a form particularly suited to elicit such a response, provided it is a genuine and original dialogue and is read as such? At this point, Jaspers himself turns to Plato. We should expect some instruction about "existential communication" from Plato, and perhaps some answer to the question of how the reader may achieve this complementary response and realization. But we are disappointed. "The Platonic dialogues do not express the communication of possible existences, but only the dialectical structure of thought or knowledge." Having said this, Jaspers hesitates for a moment: "The *Symposium*, to be sure, reads in part as if it were a revelation of genuine communication." But this concession is made only with regard to the one dialogue, and only with the strictest reservations. The reason Jaspers gives is that "to the high-minded Greek bound by form, it [communication], so it appears, lay beyond the sphere of which he became conscious as being." This is very strange, indeed. Cannot high-minded people become conscious" of communication "as being"? Cannot people in communication with one another be "bound by form," whatever this term may mean? Furthermore, is not *communicatio* the exact translation of ἀνακοίνωσις, and are not κοινοῦσθαι and ἀνακοινοῦσθαι words often repeated by Plato for the very purpose of expressing the human communion in dialogue? Strange indeed that the *Symposium* should be an exception even for Jaspers. But does not Socrates, in the *Phaedo*, keep alive communication with his friends in the face of and up to the very moment of death? Does he not regard it as the worst evil "if the *Logos* should die"? And how about the *Crito*, where Socrates engages the friend who comes to liberate him in conversation to explain why escape would destroy his life's work? Is the *Euthyphro* or even the *Theaetetus* only an expression of the dialectical structure of thought or knowledge? Is the former merely a search for a definition of "piety," and the latter really nothing but a chapter from the early history of epistemology— whereas, in both of them, the dialectic unfolds with regard to the trial of Socrates; in the *Theaetetus*, moreover, with regard to the bravery of the seriously wounded hero of the dialogue? Does this not raise the legitimate question for the reader—an "existential" question, indeed—what have bravery in war and civil courage to do with the problem of knowledge? Nothing at all, most of our contemporaries, including philosophers, would probably say. But was Plato perhaps of a different opinion and his objective precisely this: to found dialectic in existence and to clarify existence through dialectic?

Thus the Platonic dialogues, or at least many of them, serve other purposes besides expressing "only the dialectical structure of thought or knowledge." When I read this "only" in Jaspers' passage, I remembered what Hermann Bonitz wrote three quarters of a century ago in his *Platonische Studien* (1886), a work held in high esteem at the time and even in the days of my youth, that he was confining himself entirely to the presentation of the philosophical doctrine, disregarding everything pertaining to the artistic composition of the dialogue (i.e., the *Phaedo*). Many years ago, I put an exclamation mark beside this sentence, and out of this exclamation mark grew my interpretation of Plato. If Jaspers is right, I was mistaken in my intention of breaking down the barrier between the philosophical content, on the one hand, and what is called the dramatic form, on the other. For that was what I intended to do, and it goes without saying that I was not alone in doing it, and that it was nothing new, but something quite old. The Neoplatonist Proklos, in his commentary on Plato's *Alcibiades*, makes some thoughtful remarks about Plato's introductory scenes: [1] they were invented neither for the sake of dramatic suspense nor for the historical subject, but they help to determine, from the very beginning, the philosophical objective of the dialogue. The objective of the *Alcibiades*, according to Proklos, is to make clear our nature or essence, and to grasp by scientific concepts the universal nature that determines every individual. In the proem scene, therefore, the young man is turned toward himself, and is made to examine his inner, pre-existing convictions (or thoughts, τῶν ἐν ἑαυτῷ προϋποκειμένων διανοημάτων). Turning to himself, he is then led upward to an understanding of Socratic knowledge and, at the same time, to a recognition of the entire life of Socrates (or, as one might say today, of the Socratic "existence").

So much for Proklos. One thing, at least, is certain: in Plato, philosophy does not begin at the first point of dialectical discussion, but has already begun in the preliminary casual conversation or in the playful or serious imagery of the frame. Jaspers, it seems, has always—or nearly always—left the frame to the reader who is susceptible to artistic beauty, or to the historian, or to others, instead of himself responding to its "existential" appeal, as in the *Phaedo,* for example, when Socrates sits down on the bed, rubs his leg, and starts to talk to his friends, or, for that matter, still earlier, beginning with the very first words of the dialogue.[2]

It is strange how often Jaspers' general remarks about "existence" bring to mind a specific moment of life in one of the Platonic dialogues. "A situation becomes a *marginal situation* if it awakens the subject to existence by a radical upheaval of his being" (I, 56)—that is the dialogue *Alcibiades.* "Existential reality is the unconditional at the decisive moment" (II, 17)—that is the central motif of the *Crito.* "A person given to monologues, to overwhelming the partner in one-sided conversation, is also false in his silence" (II, 101)—examples of this may be found in the *Protagoras.* "Irony is the defense against falling into a false glorification of objective truths" (II, 255). "Play: Nothing said or written is to be taken so seriously as an objective fact that it becomes untouchable." "In the solemnity of possessing the truth as an objective statement, play is forgotten." "Only the medium of play makes true earnestness possible" (II, 286f.). What Jaspers has to say about irony and play outlines essential features in Plato's work. The idea of play calls to mind that the exceedingly difficult dialectic of the second part of the *Parmenides* (137B) is called a game, which we have decided to play; and this game is qualified by an attribute (πραγματειώδη παιδιάν), which may signify either the difficulty of the play, or its serious import, or both. We are also reminded of a characteristic statement in the *Sixth Letter* (323D), and of a number of other passages in Plato.[3]

Why did Jaspers, in discussing Plato, turn against him instead of calling on him for support? Strange as it may seem, we cannot help thinking of Jaspers' preface, in which he places the roots of his philosophy in the great tradition. No one has the right to challenge him on this point. But the list of his philosophical ancestry has its astonishing aspects. First he mentions Kant, "the philosopher *par excellence,* unequaled by any other in the nobility of his wise humanity. . . ." May one ask whether what is meant here is the philosopher in the academic sense or the philosopher in the universal sense—a distinction made by Kant himself—and may one call to mind (as indeed one must) that Kant, a man not lacking in courage by any means, still failed at a decisive moment in his life, and thus set an example that, to this day, weakens German philosophy, the German academic community, and perhaps even Germany itself—the "Seven of Göttingen" notwithstanding.

Let us return to Jaspers' intellectual ancestry. Kant's name is followed by that of Plotinos, Bruno, and others. Plato's is not among them. But a curious paradox is worth mentioning in conclusion. The ancestral list, of course, includes the name of Kierkegaard. It was he who transformed the concept of "existence" into its contemporary meaning. What he meant by "existence" he experienced within himself as a lonely Christian, and one in constant struggle with the kind of systematic philosophy culminating in Hegel. Jaspers' philosophy of existence is influenced through and through by Kierkegaard. But for Kierkegaard—in contrast to Jaspers—Socrates, that is, primarily Plato's Socrates, is always present whenever Kierkegaard speaks of existence.[4] It is not only Kierkegaard's earliest work on the *Concept of Irony* that is written *with constant reference to Socrates.* Let us open *A Fragment of Philosophy,* which deals with faith, sin, and God as the teacher.[5] It begins with the Socratic question: How far can truth be taught? And from there on Socrates is present to the very end, when Johannes Climacus speaks of "that master of Irony, admired through the centuries" whom he could only "approach with a quickened heartbeat of enthusiasm." To prove himself before Socrates with his Socratic or non-Socratic questions appears to be Kierkegaard's major concern. Why? Because, as he himself says, the Socratic relationship is the finest and truest between human beings. "The only one who consoles me is Socrates." Or perhaps we may say that Socrates, as presented by Plato, is philosophical existence itself. "Socrates had no philosophy, he was it" (Gilson).[6]

Thus the Platonic dialogue is, after all, "existential" in a more radical sense than Jaspers' admirable "clarification of existence." For what Jaspers accomplishes is a description, analysis, and systematization of human existence, with a phrase now and then evoking authentic existence. The *Phaedo*, the *Symposium*, and other dialogues are dramas in which human existence presents itself. But they achieve this not—or not only—as works of art that we contemplate with admiration; they are philosophical life, appealing to the reader to share its experience, to enter into the conversation of the dialogue, to offer resistance, or to become a follower. They do not philosophize about existence; they are existence, not always, but most of the time. Or, not to use and abuse the same term, they are reality of life while searching for the truth of being.

CHAPTER THIRTEEN

Plato's Letters

DURING the nineteenth century, Plato's letters were generally dismissed as forgery or fiction, despite the efforts of George Grote, the political historian. In the past fifty years, they have again become the object of lively interest and research. Eduard Meyer, the historian of classical antiquity, considered them "documents of inestimable value," thinking primarily of political history. Wilamowitz-Moellendorff caused quite a stir by unexpectedly and passionately defending the authenticity of the *Seventh* and *Eighth Letters*, after he had already declared that the *Sixth Letter* might be genuine. Recently, Richard S. Bluck has provided us with a gratifying survey of the results of research since 1910.[1] This survey gives the impression that the *Seventh* and *Eighth Letters* are now generally recognized as genuine. Yet an attempt was made not so very long ago to interpret the thirteen epistles as a novel in letter form, composed by a member of Plato's Academy around 300 B.C.[2] Again, quite recently, a heavy attack was launched against the philosophical section of the *Seventh Letter*, tearing, at the same time, two large passages out of the center of the *Republic*, which were condemned as interpolations and as written in poor Greek besides.[3] Nor must we forget that to the last Shorey rejected the entire collection of letters as unauthentic and, at the same time, Robin maintained there was no conclusive evidence for their authenticity.[4] Conclusive evidence? No. I repeat August Boeckh's methodological principle that only forgery, not authenticity, can be proved conclusively—in the absence of external evidence, to be sure. But who is now interested in the mass attacks on the authenticity of the Platonic dialogues, which were a fashion in Germany during the first half of the nineteenth century? [5] Perhaps the problem of authenticity will gradually recede into the background in the case of the *Seventh* and *Eighth Letters*, and the documents themselves will appear the more important. Could we expect the same with regard to the *Second* and *Third Letters* at some future time, it would be easy to reproach both the prediction and the future with being uncritical. Yet how many readers of the *Parmenides* know today that there was a time when reputable and intelligent critics (Ueberweg in 1861, Schaarschmidt in 1866, Huit in 1891, Windelband in 1901) assumed that it was not Platonic? Who cares now about this problem when the interpretation of the dialogue is what matters? And who has actually "proved" its authenticity? In this chapter, then, we shall attempt to show that important questions concerning the letters may be posed and, perhaps, answered, even if their authenticity is not decided one way or another; and further, how concentration upon the problem of authenticity often obscures the view and becomes an obstacle to a calm understanding of the documents.

The *Seventh Letter*, a document unique among Greek letters—despite Hercher's 800-page collection, *Epistolographi Graeci*—and, perhaps, unique in the literature of letters in general, is of the utmost significance for an understanding of Plato, his philosophy, and his circle; the political history of Sicily, which means that of the Mediterranean world; the history of autobiography; and many other subjects—even if it were not written or dictated by Plato himself. As every reader of the letter knows, it contains three elements. First, it is a political communication, designed to intervene with practical advice in the highly confused situation prevailing in Sicily at the time. Second, it is an autobiographical and historical survey, which, to a great extent, assumes the form of a defense of the writer and a warning addressed to its recipients. Third, the letter culminates in the basic principle of Plato's political philosophy— the maxim of the philosopher-ruler (326AB, 328A)—and in the strange insertion about Plato's ontology or metaphysics. These three elements are so divergent that the writing repeatedly changes its direction and level in the most peculiar way; yet they are also strictly related to one another. The epistle is a reply, or pretends to be a reply, to a letter from the "friends and followers of Dion," and the words "counsel" and "counseling" are frequently repeated, as in the *Eighth Letter*, a continuation of the *Seventh*.[6] The historical survey and the self-defense are written explicitly "for the sake of advice" (330c, 334c, 337e). Moreover, the third element, which in a letter by any other writer might appear as an inappropriate digression, is anything but a digression for Plato (regardless of whether he or another composed the letter): the section about the basic principles of philosophy is inserted for the specific reason that only by contrast with it can the pseudo-philosophy of Dionysios be evaluated and the true distinguished from the false. The paradoxical principle of the union of philosophical insight and political power is the intellectual attitude (διάνοια) that forms the basis of Plato's past action as well as his present advice.

That the author has a variety of styles for use according to the level on which he is writing would go without saying if it did not invite a discussion with Georg Misch's *History of Autobiography in Antiquity*. In this work, Socrates is given his due place as the decisive force in the development of man's self-consciousness. But we are disappointed if we hope to find a discussion of that extraordinary piece of autobiography in the *Seventh Letter*. It is entirely lacking in the first edition (1907), for at that time Plato's letters had just begun to come back into the field of research. The omission is mentioned in the second edition (1931), but only the revised English edition (1950) devotes many pages to this great autobiographical document. Here a strange thing happens: the discussion does not deal with the position of the letter in the history of Greek autobiography; rather, the philological-historical problem of its authenticity dominates the thinking of the modern scholar to such an extent that the difference in level of writing is constantly employed as an argument against the Platonic origin of the letter, as if this very difference of writing were not a necessity, and as if Plato were obligated to persist, at all times, in the attitude in which Raphael's fresco portrays him walking through the philosopher's dome. At last, Misch presents what he considers the decisive argument against the authenticity of the letter. "I, myself," writes the author of the letter (348A), "looked out (βλέπων ἔξω, "of my prison," is to be added), like a bird (καθάπερ ὄρνις) that longs for a chance to fly away (ποθῶν ἀναπτέσθαι) and yet cannot. Dionysios, however, was devising schemes for scaring me off without making restitution to Dion of anything he owed him." This attractive picture, says Misch, gives the impression of expressing a sincere feeling. In other words, even the critic cannot help admitting that it is appropriate. As a matter of fact, however, the image is borrowed, namely, from the *Phaedrus* (249D): "When man perceives earthly beauty and thus remembers true beauty, his wings grow, he wants to fly aloft (προθυμούμενος ἀναπτέσθαι), but cannot, and like a bird (ὄρνιθος δίκην) he looks upward." But such plagiarism and profanation of philosophy, we are then told, must not be imputed to Plato.

Strange indeed! The two images are similar, but each is appropriate in its place; and we may well ask whether a great author, with a literary output of astonishing scope, could not employ both without making himself suspect. Nor have we decided in favor of the authenticity of the *Seventh Letter*, if we insist that arguments of much greater weight would be required to prove that it is not genuine.

Thus what is still lacking in the history of Greek autobiography cannot be filled in as part of this discussion.[7] Misch shows how Socrates founded a new conception of human personality; and passing to Plato, he points out that the division of the biography into sharply separate periods was a device by which Plato, with Socrates as his spokesman, transformed, in the *Phaedo* (96A *et seq.*), the development of Greek philosophy into a pseudo-autobiographical report. But there are peculiar points of contact between this account by Socrates and Plato's autobiography at the beginning of the *Seventh Letter*. "When I was young, I felt the desire" (ἐγὼ γὰρ νέος ὢν ἐπεθύμησα), Socrates starts out in the *Phaedo*. "When I was young, I had the experience" (νέος ἐγώ ποτε ὢν ἔπαθον), Plato begins his letter. The different stages in the *Phaedo* are as follows: first, enthusiasm for natural philosophy, followed by disappointment; second, acquaintance with the book of Anaxagoras, and again disappointment; third, the escape into the *Logoi* and the discovery of the world of being. The different stages in the *Letter* are, first, Plato's entrance into politics under the government of the Thirty, his keen expectations, and his disappointment; second, a renewed interest in political life under the reconstituted democracy, followed by the condemnation of Socrates and Plato's renunciation of all further political activity; third, his turning to the right philosophy and the escape into the formula of the philosopher-ruler.

The path leading through these stages is described in similar words in the *Letter* and in the *Phaedo:* "I thought, I came to be of the opinion" (ᾤμην, ᾠήθην, ἡγησάμην); "I became dissatisfied, withdrew, gave it up" (ἐδυσχέρανα, ἐμαυτὸν ἐπανήγαγον, ἀπειρήκη). In both accounts, the participle "considering" (σκοπῶν) is characteristic of the speaker's attitude, the word "at last" (τελευτῶν) of the order in stages. The "complete bewilderment" that, in the *Letter*, "at last" (τελευτῶντα ἰλιγγιᾶν) takes hold of Plato corresponds to the fear of going blind in the *Phaedo* (ἔδεισα μὴ τὴν ψυχὴν τυφλωθείην). Both accounts, in fact, reach the same goal, though without exact correspondence in language; for the "true philosophy" of the *Letter* is the turning to the "truth of being" in the *Phaedo*.

The self-portrait of Plato's philosophical growth, as well as the subsequent passages dealing with his journeys to Sicily, would occupy an important place in the history of Greek autobiography, even if this letter was not written by Plato, but by somebody else under Plato's name. If Plato was indeed the author, the letter assumes an extraordinary significance.

We may add one more comment on this point. A great distance separates the autobiographical account of the philospher-statesman, advising others and justifying himself, from the account by Divus Augustus to the Roman world and posterity. All the more curious, therefore, that the opening sentence of both documents shows two points of agreement that appear the more striking if we place the Greek translation of the *Res gestae* beside the *Letter*. "When I was young".

(νέος ἐγώ ποτε ὤν), begins Plato; "When I was nineteen years of age" (ἐτῶν δεκαεννέα ὤν), begins Augustus; and in the second part of the sentence, both refer to "public life" (τὰ κοινὰ τῆς πόλεως—τὰ κοινὰ πράγματα). Again, it goes without saying that there is a sharp contrast between thought in Plato and action in Augustus: "I thought" or "I considered," as against "I prepared," "I liberated." The question may be raised whether the agreement is mere coincidence or reflects a tradition of autobiographical writing. That Plato's Socrates in the *Phaedo* opens the account of his philosophical development with a similar "When I was young" has been mentioned above.

Many critics who grant the authenticity of the *Seventh Letter* consider the *Second Letter* as definitely not genuine.[8] "Silly, childish; the falseness requires no proof," Wilamowitz said about the *Second Letter*. Shorey held that all the letters were false; the second, however, he says, is so false that one could hardly enter into a discussion with anyone who considered it authentic. In this connection, Shorey quotes a passage, bordering on the absurd (at least at first sight), in which the author of the letter speaks "in enigmas about the nature of the first principle," about the "king of all," and about the "second and the third principle," that is, the passage in which early Christian theologians thought to catch a glimpse of the dogma of the Trinity. Genuine or not, has Shorey so much as understood this peculiar piece of writing? Pathetic half-nonsense, fantastic mysticism? But why not first read on? Plato—real or fictitious— reminds the ruler of Syracuse of a meeting "in the garden under the laurel trees." (This garden is frequently mentioned elsewhere in the letters: *III* 319A; *VII* 341B, 348C.) The prince then had spoken about the ultimate secrets of Plato's philosophy; that he had comprehended them and, indeed, had discovered them for himself. (In other words, he did not need Plato.) And Plato had then replied that if such was the case, His Majesty had saved him much trouble. (The writer heaves a sigh of relief.) To be sure, he, Plato, had never met anyone else who had succeeded in this. Dionysios, therefore, had either heard it from some other man (for, really, these things were as much discussed in Syracuse as in Athens) or had perhaps indeed come upon it himself and, if so, undoubtedly through divine providence. (This sounds very solemn; but what a balance there is between these two possibilities!) [9] If this was the case, then he had not tied up the proofs very securely, and they had flown away (light birds, these princely proofs!). But in this respect, Plato continues, you are not alone; that is the way it goes with everybody at the beginning of his education. (In other words, the prince is a beginner and still has everything to learn, provided . . .)

If we now reread that enigmatic passage of the *Second Letter* which aroused so much indignation, we shall begin to feel the sarcasm, rising to the point of slightly veiled contempt, that permeates the pathos and the mystery. The writer must speak in enigmas; for if anything should happen to the letter "in the recesses of the sea or land"—that is, if it fell into the hands of the wrong person—care must be taken that nobody should understand it. (In Dionysios, apparently, it reached the right person.) Later, the warning: beware lest these philosophical secrets fall into the hands of people without adequate preparation! (The person addressed is thus one of those who are adequately prepared—how adequately will soon be revealed in the conversation under the laurel trees and by the subsequent events.) The best form of caution is not to write at all. (Dionysios, by his pseudo-philosophical piece of writing, has already acted contrary to this advice. But in case he is foolish enough to call on Plato as a predecessor in such writing, this is the answer:) There is no written work of Plato's—and there follow the words, already famous in antiquity, about the so-called writings of Plato that belong to "Socrates grown young." [10]

These parentheses may serve as a very provisional attempt to penetrate to the meaning of the letter, that is, actually to interpret it and to show that we probably here have something quite different from "exaggeration and forgery" (Stefanini); that we must probably read the letter in quite a different light from Souilhé, who describes its tone as "occasionally rather angry, but on the whole affectionate and confident," and very differently from Morrow, who thinks Plato "obviously" believed in Dionysios' philosophical abilities and hoped for the tyrant's philosophical support.[11] Shorey sees little common ground between those who recognize "immediately" (!) that Plato could not have written this mystico-theosophical gabble and those who force an edifying interpretation upon the text. We have at least indicated that there may be a third possibility of interpreting it. This letter, too, to which so many take exception, is a mixture of that "seriousness which is not foreign to the muses and its twin sister, playfulness." Seriousness and playfulness in the *Second Letter*, to be sure, have a different complexion—the seriousness is darker, the jest more bitter—from that in the *Sixth Letter*, where this peculiar passage occurs.[12]

In addition to the enigmatic passage just discussed, the *Second Letter* contains another that proves to many that it cannot be genuine: the remarks at the very beginning (310CD) about the events in Olympia. Dionysios has requested that Plato restrain his followers from hostile action as well as evil talk against him. Plato's reply deals separately with the two complaints—for the request implies complaints. As to hostile action, that is taken care of by the exception the prince himself conceded; for he did not request, and could not request, that Plato should be responsible for Dion's actions. However, Plato continues, I have as little power of command over the men of my circle (i.e., the Academy) as I have, he adds sarcastically, over you. If I had such power, things would look different for us all and, more, for all of Greece. This is perfectly clear. Plato does not say he approves of Dion's actions in collaboration with the Academy; but he includes the ruler of Syracuse among those over whom, to his regret, he has no power of command—a clear and bold reply to the tyrant.

After the hostile action, there is the charge of evil talk. I have not heard, says Plato, anyone speak ill or abusively of you at this meeting in Olympia. Pasquali holds that whoever considers this letter genuine makes a Tartuffe out of Plato;[13] for at Olympia, Plato's disciples and Dion went far beyond the limits of evil talk, discussing armed intervention openly and in detail. But here we should, for a moment, continue the thought along clear legal lines. For injury by words is a legal concept. The law of Attica knew several forms of legal proceedings in connection with *kakegoria*.[14] In the *Laws*, Plato himself states the matter in a single legal decree, condensed in three words, and formulated precisely and clearly (*Laws* XI 934E): μηδένα κακηγορείτω μηδείς, "no one shall insult or slander another." [15] But, as a legislator and educator, Plato also provides a substitute for evil speech: when people get into conflict, they shall instruct each other, and permit themselves to be instructed. Thus, a conversation seriously aiming at the truth cuts the ground from under "evil speech." The author of the letter gives precisely the same advice to the ruler; if you hear that anyone of my circle has spoken ill of you, write and inform me of it in a letter, and I shall tell you the truth without hesitation and fear.

We must, of course, have a clear understanding of the meaning of the term "injury by words." If someone said that Dionysios had acted unjustly and violently against Dion, this was not an injury by words at all but the exact truth; and just as Greek law permitted the defendant charged with *kakegoria* to submit evidence for the truth of his statement, so Plato here suggests to the ruler that he engage in conversations designed to bring out the truth, as proposed in the *Laws*, in place of evil talk. Thus the letter does not speak in the spirit of Tartuffe, but in that of a severe regard for law and education. That the ruler will not heed these words and, indeed, will not even want to understand them is a fact about which the bitter and sarcastic tone of Plato's words does not leave the slightest doubt: he includes Dionysios among those over whom he has no power— "the others and you and Dion"—and refers to himself as the only one who follows his own words.

That the *Second Letter* presupposes Plato's third journey to Syracuse—that is, that the Olympic games to which it refers (310D) are those of the year 360—is hardly subject to doubt according to our interpretation.[16] Plato and the tyrant had parted without an open rupture. Plutarch (*Dion* ch. 20) reports an amusing, though certainly fictitious, conversation between them, shortly before Plato went aboard the vessel sent by Archytas. The *Second Letter* was written (or purports to have been written) very shortly after Plato's departure, at a time when there was still a possibility, however feeble, of an under-

standing between him and the ruler. Our interpretation has
attempted to show how slight this possibility appeared to the
author of the letter. In the *Third Letter*, however, Plato (real or
fictitious) has made the break irrevocable.

Only a misunderstanding of the preciseness of the historical
situation could lead to the misinterpretation that the *Second
Letter* was forged—by Dionysios in order to show his relationship with Plato in a favorable light.[17] Disregarding all details,
such an interpretation would credit the tyrant with a literary
enterprise hardly in keeping with his abilities—unless, of
course, he had a secretary *ab epistulis* of the stature of Thornton
Wilder or Walter Savage Landor. Incidentally, what a seductive
train of thought: Dionysios as the forger of a document whose
most suspicious origin completely escapes the collector of
Plato's letters, and which, after more than five hundred years,
with its enigmatic trinitarian metaphysics, leads or misleads
the Neoplatonists Plotinos and Proklos, and makes a deep
impression on the Greek Fathers of the Christian Church, on
Clement, Origen, Justin Martyr, Hippolytos, and Eusebios.
The tyrant of Syracuse—pioneer of Neoplatonism and precursor
of the doctrine of the Trinity!

CHAPTER FOURTEEN

Plato as Physicist

STRUCTURE AND DESTRUCTION OF THE ATOM

ACCORDING TO PLATO'S TIMAEUS[1]

TO BRIDGE the menacing gap between the natural sciences and the humanities, the "widening cleavage between nature and man" (Riezler), "the chasm which is cutting our culture asunder and threatening to destroy it" (Sarton)—to help reconcile those fundamental human qualities which Pascal called *"l'esprit de géométrie"* and *"l'esprit de finesse"*—is one of the urgent tasks of today, in which scientists and humanists are bound to take part.[2] We humanists, in our ignorance of the natural sciences, must provoke the pity of the scientists as often as we resent their simplicity in things historical when we turn to their books. Yet R. G. Collingwood has declared that no one can understand natural science without understanding history, and Auguste Comte's statement that science is the history of science is cited as the motto for a recently published history of the sciences.[3] But if we look, in this or some other recent work on the subject, for the place assigned to the author of the *Timaeus*, the result is astonishing. To mention only a few recent comments: Plato must be counted "a disaster" in the history of physics (Dampier-Whetham, Jeans); the "reign of pseudo-science in Greece" begins with Plato (P. Rousseau); in the Academy Aristotle suffered "the disastrous influence of Plato" (Mieli); "the *Timaeus* demonstrates how knowledge can be degraded even by Plato" (Singer). These evaluations seem to reflect primarily the prevailing antipathy against teleological explanation and mythical construction; but they are judging the man who in his *Republic* makes the study of the mathematical sciences the necessary propaedeutic of philosophy, and who put such a curriculum into practice in the Academy he founded.[4]

To be sure, other voices, though it seems still a minority, may also be heard. The physicist Heisenberg discovers two primary, basic ideas in Greek natural philosophy influencing the course of the exact natural sciences down to the present: first, the belief of the atomists that matter is composed of very small particles; second, the Pythagorean belief in the mathematical structure of the universe. Both views, according to Heisenberg, are combined in Plato's physics.

All positivistic and antiteleological prejudices are alien to the most penetrating and comprehensive history of ancient science written during the last decades, the work of Abel Rey. For Rey, Plato's dialectic is also the basis of natural science. Plato's physics is mythico-mathematical; what it achieves is *"la grande mathématisation du concret et du sensible"* (III, 286) in two fields, cosmology and the physics of the elements.

Together with Heisenberg and Rey goes Whitehead, the mathematician-philosopher, who links the *Timaeus* and the *Scholium* of Newton as "the two great cosmological documents governing Western thought." [5] The *Scholium*, in Whitehead's judgment, is "an immensely able statement of details"; whereas "what the *Timaeus* lacks in superficial detail, it makes up for by its philosophic depth." To be sure, Whitehead goes on to say, the *Timaeus*, as a statement of scientific details, must seem, when compared with Newton, "simply foolish." [6] This may well be true, although Plato's foolishness, or what seems so to us, is more than once intended to fool his reader—a reader who does not realize how pathos and irony are entwined in this, the strangest of Plato's works. The same reader might shake his head at finding that the digestive and appetitive parts of the body and the soul are stationed below the diaphragm "in order to be as remote as possible from the seat of counsel," or that the length and windings of the intestinal canal were provided by the makers of mankind in order to lessen our appetites for food and drink and incline us to philosophy. It is quite likely that Plato, in passages like these, combines at least three different objectives: first, genuine teleology, which is such a thorn in the flesh of modern natural science; second, mockery of the kind of teleology that reduces nature to human measure; and third, a moral imperative, clothed, with the irony of myth, in teleological language.

Why, when talking about nature, does Timaios the Pythagorean tell Socrates a myth? There are many reasons, Plato might have answered. Thus, a modern botanist may be delighted with the beauty of flowers or leaves, but his delight has little or nothing to do with his scientific search. Plato would not have been able or willing to make such a distinction. The cosmos that his scientific mind tried to penetrate was, at the same time, the object of his aesthetic admiration and of his religious awe—a perceptible god, supreme in greatness and excellence, in beauty and perfection. This is one reason—or two, if you wish—why the *Timaeus* was to have the form, not of a scientific treatise, but of a myth. "For the myth," says Aristotle, "consists of things wondrous."

Another reason is deeply rooted in Plato's epistemology and ontology. We cannot speak with exactness about the world of change. We can speak with exactness only about the world of real being, i.e., the world of mathematics and of the eternal forms. About changing nature we can, at the utmost, give "plausible accounts." How, then, is it possible that we are able to construct "in concepts" (ἐν λόγοις) the world of change? If that world were nothing but change, we could not even speak about it; we could only wag our forefinger to symbolize its complete instability, as did Kratylos, the pupil of Herakleitos. But this changing, moving world has, at the same time, a great deal of stability. Nature, consequently, is constituted by two principles that blended: *Nous*, "mind," accounting for law, order, stability, for that which "makes sense"; and *Ananke*, "necessity," blind force or, to use Henry Adams' phrase, "the futile folly of the Infinite." Both are causes, with the reservation that mind is the real cause, necessity only the concomitant or accessory cause. An arbitrary gradation, one might say. But who of us does not share this belief, if not theoretically, at all events pragmatically? We could not so much as live if we were not convinced, unconsciously or consciously, that order gets the better of brute force, at least in nature, to which human life must turn as its model.

It is a short cut to view Plato's cosmology simply as Pythagorean, whether in the strange way of that eminent English scholar, A. E. Taylor, who regarded Plato as a reporter of fifth-century scientific lore, or in a more general sense, as is common. Of course, the "Pythagorean" trend is very strong. But the *Timaeus* must be understood as concentrating the whole of pre-Platonic thought. There is Anaximander in Plato, and Pythagoras, and Empedokles, and Anaxagoras, and Leukippos, and Demokritos, and there is at the same time a struggle against each one of them. Plato blends their fundamental views into his own cosmological myth and outdistances each of their particular systems. He is no -*ist* or -*ean*, not even a Pythagorean—and least of all a Platonist.

Let us confine ourselves to a few basic concepts of Plato's physics, beginning with matter. "The history of the doctrine of matter has yet to be written. It is the history of the influence of Greek philosophy on science" (Whitehead).[7] Our word "matter" is a cipher, a rubber stamp of today's scientific and un-scientific language. It was probably Aristotle, so discriminating about metaphors,[8] who coined the word that meant "wood, timber" into a philosophic term in order to give a name to that from which bodies are formed, upon which form is imprinted. But it was Plato who originated the concept. "They are correct," remarks Plutarch, "who say that Plato discovered the elementary principle underlying qualitative process, that which is now called 'matter' or 'substance' (ὃ νῦν ὕλην καὶ φύσιν καλοῦσιν), and thus freed the philosophers of many difficulties."[9] Aristotle's "wood" corresponds to, though it is not all the same as, Plato's "Receptacle (δεξαμενή, ὑποδοχή) of all becoming," "shaken and shaking like an instrument producing shocks," or "space" (χώρα)—by no means "empty space," still less "space conceived *more geometrico*,"[10] but rather something like space in which something is going on—or "a lumpish something on which and in which impressions are molded" (ἐκμαγεῖον), or "nurse of all becoming," that "Nature which receives all bodies," "to be compared to a mother": a host of metaphorical words and poetical images. But Plato wanted metaphors and images—though he knew well that "one must keep watch over this most slippery tribe" (*Sophist* 231A) [11]—and he needed a host of them: he could not be satisfied with the one, rather rational, Aristotelian metaphor, because the all-embracing, all-producing, all-receiving is inscrutable. It is shapeless, "apprehended only by a sort of bastard reasoning" (λογισμῷ τινι νόθῳ), "partaking of the intelligible in an extremely bewildering way" (μεταλαμβάνον ἀπορώτατά πη τοῦ νοητοῦ),[12] something "we look upon as in a dream," graspable, seizable, only in its "suchnesses" or qualities, as when it becomes stone or air or cloud. By placing it in his system as a third entity beneath the world of real being and the world of becoming, Plato continues the hylozoistic line of the first Greek cosmologists. But his concept is much more radical than the air or the water of the Milesians, more radical than Anaxagoras' initial mixture of infinitesimals, and probably even more so than the view that may be nearest to his own, the Infinite-Indeterminate of the greatest of these cosmologists, Anaximander. Plato's principle is something like "space" and at the same time something like "stuff." Moreover, since it is "filled with powers unevenly balanced" (διὰ τὸ μήτε ὁμοίων δυνάμεων μήτε ἰσορρόπων ἐμπίμπλασθαι), producing a constant "earthquake" (σεισμός) in it, it also resembles what we call energy, process, or activity.

In contrast to the atom of modern physics, the elementary molecules of Plato (to which we shall return presently) lack the element of energy, since the structure of these primary bodies is held together only by a geometrical or numerical bond, not by dynamic forces. But if the stereometric polyhedra lack a source of energy, Plato's total construction of the universe does not. Such a source may be found in two places: first, at the highest place, in the creative energy of the demiurge, or, in language less mythological, in the formative power of the *Idea* of the Good (which survives in Aristotle's "First Mover"); second, in that matrix of many names in which space, matter, and activity dwell in indeterminate shape. If, according to Collingwood,[13] matter in modern physics is inseparable from energy, while, in classical mechanics, motion was added as something external to matter, then Plato—incidentally, just like Leukippos and Demokritos—sides with modern against classical physics. "There are some, like Leukippos and Plato, who take activity (ἐνέργεια) as always existing; for they say there is always movement" (Aristotle, *Metaphysics* XII 1071ᵇ 31).

More daring is another attempt to find an ancient anticipation for a most recent development. Let it be understood that this attempt is undertaken with the reservation which must always be preserved in such a comparison by analogy. Heisenberg has discovered the "principle of indeterminacy" or uncertainty, "*le principe d'incertitude qui chassait le déterminisme de la microphysique*" (Rousseau). In contrast to classical physics, quantum mechanics has led to the conclusion that "the basic laws of nature do not directly control the universe, but only a substratum of which we cannot form a mental picture without introducing incompatibilities" (Dirac).[14] Is it mere play of fantasy if one comprehending these modern theories only vaguely, if at all, finds an anticipation of them in Plato? However strictly the principle of mathematical order is carried through in Plato's physics, in the cosmos of the fixed stars as well as in that of the primary elements, everything is indeterminate in the realm below the order of the elementary atoms. This indeterminate realm becomes an ordered structure in the world of atoms, and thence upward to the starry heavens. What resists strict order in nature is due to the indeterminate and uneven forces in the Receptacle.

Now this indefinite and unintelligible substratum becomes definite and intelligible by entering its bodily shapes, the four *stoicheia*, *elementa*, elements. The "components" of nature, the "letters" of which the words and sentences and finally the book of nature are composed—this is the image or metaphor, already familiar to Plato, which became a scientific term in his Academy and was handed down to posterity by Aristotle.[15] Modern scientists, in the firm possession of their ninety-four or ninety-six elements with atomic numbers and periodic system, may smile at the four elements fire, water, air, and earth, none of

which, as every schoolboy knows today, is a real element. And
yet, what Plato did was of the greatest consequence. He fused
Empedokles' construction of the "four roots of being things"
into his physical system; he gave them their place above the
chaos on the lowest level at which order can be discerned by
reason; and he assigned them the term that, in its Latin transformation, *elementum*, continues as one basic concept of chemistry. He was, incidentally, far from being dogmatic even about
their number. In his *Timaeus* there is some hesitation on this
point, whereas by Aristotle he is credited with a system of three
elements and by Xenokrates with a system of five. A lively discussion on this score must have taken place in the innermost
circle of the Academy.[16] But a system it was. In the *Timaeus* it is
a proportional system (Fire is to Air as Air is to Water as Water
is to Earth), and though, to be sure, it was not a periodic system
in the sense of modern chemistry, Plato, nevertheless, forces his
elements into a preconceived principle of order. Here, as is
usual, speculation precedes empirical research, whose path it
may either obstruct or clear.[17]

From matter we ascended to the elements; let us now follow
Plato's next step. Modern science, since Robert Boyle and John
Dalton, has maintained the radical stability of the elements.
That, after all, is in the line of Empedokles' doctrine. But as
early as 1815, William Prout proposed the theory that the elements are reducible, reducible to hydrogen as a primary substance—a thesis that was abandoned for a long time, only to be
revived decades later in a new form. That the elements are
reducible, each element a "such," not a "this," or, if a "this,"
only in a preliminary way; that the "letters" of nature are not
really letters but rather syllables or even polysyllables (48B)—
this is the doctrine of the *Timaeus*. The view, moreover, that the
elements are reducible rests in modern science upon the theory
of their atomic structure. And so it does in Plato.

In the history of modern physics and chemistry, Dalton receives the credit for having combined the theory of the element
with the theory of the atom: there are only as many atomic forms
as there are elements. Dalton's merit is in no way lessened by
the fact that it was Plato who first fused into unity—to express

it in a very preliminary way—Empedokles' theory of the elements with a theory of corpuscles in the line of Leukippos and Demokritos. In the *Timaeus*, more than two thousand years before Dalton, each element is given a corpuscular structure of its own.

Let us now consider the form of these corpuscles or, as we may provisionally call them, atoms (figs. 1–4). In the atomism of Leukippos and Demokritos, the atoms have an indefinite number of different shapes, more or less irregular, with all sorts of corners, hooks, bulges, and holes. When they are round they need not be spherical; when they have corners they need not have any regular form. There may be spheres or cubes among them, but only by chance. Plato radically transformed this atomism of the Abderites. He took a step of the greatest importance, though it is not mentioned in the standard histories of the natural sciences and is misjudged even by Heiberg, an authoritative historian of ancient thought.[18] In the *Timaeus* there are only four kinds of corpuscles, each element having its particular atomic structure. These four kinds have stereometrical forms: they are regular pyramids, cubes, octahedra, and icosahedra, four of the five regular solids that still bear the name of Platonic polyhedra. The fire corpuscle is a pyramid, the earth corpuscle a cube, the air corpuscle an octahedron, the water corpuscle an icosahedron. This mathematical construction is fantastic, but much less so than the more naturalistic one of classical atomism. For, granted that the details are fantastic, a truly fundamental idea is established by this construction: the order on the lowest recognizable level of nature accounts for the order on its higher and highest levels. Not chance but reason has shaped the building stones of this universe; they have mathematical form.[19]

Plato, consequently, more nearly anticipates modern physics and chemistry than do the atomists. Today the molecule of methane gas, CH_4, is visualized spatially as a regular pyramid with four hydrogen atoms at its four corners and a carbon atom in the center. A tetravalent carbon atom is represented by some chemists in the form of a tetrahedron, with the united atoms placed at its four vertices. The octahedron, too (the "octahedron of Werner"), has its partisans in modern chemistry, and an entire branch of that science, stereochemistry, has long since been compared with Plato's corpuscular theory.[20] The marvelous forms of mineral crystals, when subjected to penetration by X rays, have begun to surrender the secrets of their atomic and molecular structure. Crystallography shows that the simpler mineral forms, say, of iron or aluminum, have four oxygen atoms at the corners of a tetrahedron or six oxygen atoms at the corners of an octahedron, and that the diamond has a tetrahedral arrangement of bonds around a carbon atom—to mention only a few examples.[21] Finally, and quite generally, the modern atom model has a mathematical form, although, needless to say, it is a long step from Plato's polyhedra to the minute planetary systems of Rutherford and Bohr—systems, incidentally, that have again been transformed by recent discoveries of the wave character of matter and that may be questionable in principle, since "any picture of the atom drawn by the imagination is *eo ipso* erroneous." "The number of mathematical structures at the disposal of ancient science was comparatively small. . . . While ancient philosophy co-ordinated the regular solids with the atomic elements, modern science co-ordinates a mathematical equation with the elementary particles. This equation defines the law of nature governing the structure of matter; it describes the temporal sequence of a chemical reaction as much as the regular shapes of crystals or the tones produced by a vibrating string" (Heisenberg). But Plato's Timaios would have acknowledged such physicists as Rutherford and Bohr as his peers, and would certainly have given them the reward he promises for a hypothesis superior to his own.[22]

It has been stated before that Plato's cosmic myth admits only four atomic models constituting the four elements. This statement is correct, but it needs some restriction. All the atoms of any one element have the same stereometric shape. Yet different sizes of each shape must exist, in the opinion of Timaios, in order to account for the different kinds of air, fire, earth, or water (58c *et seq.*). And again, these differences are not due to mere chance, or, as Plato would call it, to *Ananke*, brute force. They can be accounted for.[23] There is a mathematical ratio between the smaller, say, octahedra or icosahedra, and the larger ones. Each of the different sizes of each polyhedron constitutes one of those similar, though not identical, liquids or gases that the Greeks, in very general terms, called "water" or "air," though Plato and others knew very well that there was not merely one kind of water or air, but many kinds. I am not sure whether I am obscuring or clarifying the problem by giving the modern scientific name "isotopes" to those different kinds of the same element. For many elements are thought of today as having different isotopes: the isotopes of one element "are identical as to both the number and the arrangement of the electrons" in each atom; they "are quite indistinguishable from each other except for those properties which depend only on mass." Analogously, Plato's different species, say, of water or, better, of liquid (e.g., wine, oil, honey, acid) differ only in the size of their corpuscles, not in their form, which is always icosahedral.

But—and this is still more important—Plato's corpuscles are not a-toma, unsplittables, in the true sense, and Plato never uses this term. They can be smashed (λύεσθαι, διαλύεσθαι, τέμνεσθαι, διαθραύεσθαι, μερίζεσθαι, κερματίζεσθαι), and in the Receptacle there is a constant "earthquake" of the splitting and reuniting (συντυχόντα, συστάντα, συναρμοσθέντα) of corpuscles. The sharp pyramids of fire cut open the cubic particles of earth. On the other hand, a few particles of fire may be surrounded and consequently overpowered by a large amount of air, or a few particles of air by a large amount of water. Then the fire pyramids are broken down and the triangles of the tetrahedra combine again into octahedra of air. Or the particles of air are bombarded by the particles of water and the triangles constituting the octahedra of air combine again (συνίστασθαι, συμπήγνυσθαι) into icosahedra of water. Such events occur in nature continuously (55c *et seq.*). The occurrence itself, resulting from the "unbalanced energies" (52E) in the Receptacle, is, or seems to be, brute fact. But the particles are shaped, and their splitting and reuniting occur, according to the laws of mathematics.

To go into more detail and to construct one very simple event: one particle of "water," consisting of 20 equilateral = 40 scalene triangles, may disintegrate and combine again into one particle of "fire" and two particles of "air," the fire particle consisting of 4 equilateral = 8 scalene triangles and each air particle consisting of 8 equilateral = 16 scalene triangles. This is a simple case. But other sorts of "air" or "water" with larger particles may combine in other ways: for example, one particle of "water," consisting of 160 scalene triangles, may recombine into five particles of "air" and ten particles of "fire," each "air" particle having 16, and each "fire" particle 8, scelene triangles. Or the same particle of "water," consisting of 160 scalene triangles, may recombine into two particles of another isotope of "water" (2 × 40), plus one particle of "fire" of another isotope than before (1 × 48), plus two particles of "air" (2 × 16), and so on. "The constancy of these numbers plays the same part in Plato's theory that fixed proportions by weight have done in modern chemistry since Dalton," [24] with the one radical difference, of course, that no exact experiment, only general convictions and sweeping observations, justified those numbers.[25]

The Matrix, or Receptacle, is inscrutable to the human intellect because it is the exact opposite of order: it is *factum brutum*. This is what Plato means when he says, in mythical form, that the Receptacle is not made by the demiurge, but existed before he began his work (53A *et seq*.). The real beginning of that work "is known only to God, or perhaps to someone dear to him" (53D). All Timaios can say is that the work of the demiurge, or the state of reason and, therefore, of cognizability, begins with the right triangles, both isosceles and scalene, out of which are shaped the smallest material bodies, the four fundamental polyhedric corpuscles. When indulging in detailed analyses, as in describing the human frame, marrow, seed, blood, or bones, Plato may on occasion speak playfully of the triangles as flat little plates whirling through space, some, as it were, "fresh from the slips" (81B) and others "warped and rough," having lost their original smoothness. But he really means that they are the constitutional or elementary forms that shape nonbeing, chaotic and irrational, into real existence and clear cognizability.[26] And the apparent irregularities of the apparent triangles symbolize the ever-recurring disturbances of mathematical order by the chaotic element in nature—disturbances that, in turn, are a great enrichment of human life. If Aristotle had expressed the Platonic theory in his own terms, instead of weakly

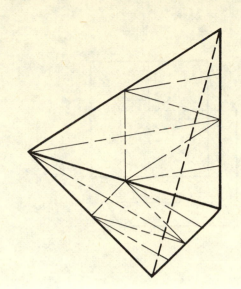
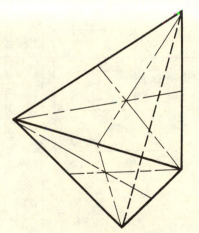
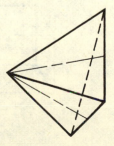

Fig. 1. Regular tetrahedra: corpuscles of fire

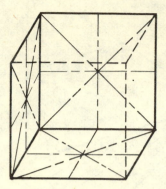

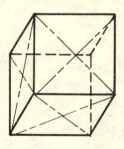

Fig. 2. Regular cubes: corpuscles of earth

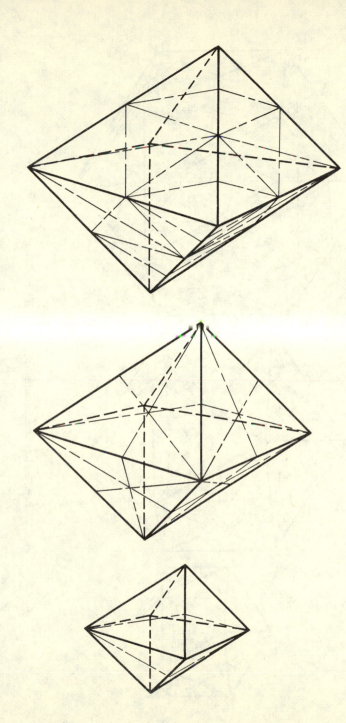

Fig. 3. Regular octahedra: corpuscles of air

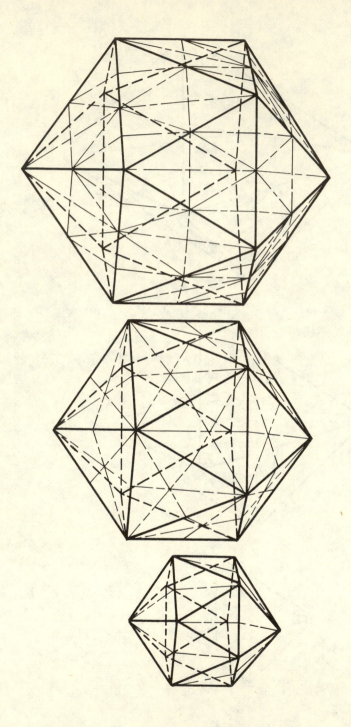

Fig. 4. Regular icosahedra: corpuscles of water

and persistently criticizing it [27] and at the same time reducing it to his theory of the five elements, each of them having its proper motion, he would have said that matter has the potentiality of being actualized in regular stereometrical forms. In order to imagine how this actualization takes place, we must think of a given number of triangles joining in this or that position. And again the polyhedra are split, their triangles disperse, matter returns into potentiality, until at another moment the triangles, i.e., the essential components of form, combine in the actuality of new polyhedra, new systems of order.

Plato's physics of elements being transformed into each other and of regularly divisible atoms was incomprehensible as long as classical mechanics reigned supreme, i.e., from Newton to the recent past. Now these chapters of the *Timaeus* have acquired a new meaning, and perhaps Plato may be looked upon as a predecessor of Rutherford and Bohr in the same sense that Demokritos was a predecessor of Galileo and Newton. The hazard of this procedure is obvious. As a modern historian of science, Sarton, puts it: "One of the most pernicious types of error to which a false or shaky knowledge of living science frequently leads is the reading of modern conceptions into ancient texts." But one must run this risk.[28] For it is senseless, it is even impossible, to study the *Timaeus* with the windows so completely closed that no breath of modern physics is allowed to enter. Today's scientists, in their turn, may enrich their historical background by a critical study of Plato's scientific myth.

Where, finally, does Plato stand on the controversy between law and chance that again has engaged the intellectual world of our own age? In an essay on "The Law of Chance," Erwin Schrödinger contrasts the two predominant points of view in natural philosophy that interpret the status of the causal principle.[29] From the "conservative" point of view, the causal law is an a priori principle, universally valid, but not otherwise explicable; chance, therefore, is only a term indicating our human inability to discover the infinite complexity of all the co-operating causes. From the "revolutionary" point of view, chance is the supreme principle, and what we call causality is ultimately based on chance. For chance may lead to statistically predictable consequences, and natural law, or causal law, is the name we give to these statistical regularities. Thus the "revolutionary" view goes back to Hume's discovery, according to which there is no necessary connection between cause and effect, but only a customary conjunction between events.

Against this view, Plato's Socrates would have argued that Hume's destructive criticism of the causal principle has its place in the simile of the cave in the *Republic*, where human beings fastened to their seats in the deepest and darkest part of the cave only experience the shadowy appearances in terms of earlier, later, and simultaneity; but where the most intelligent among them learn to make predictions on the basis of the frequency of these appearances and the probability of their reappearance. As far as Schrödinger's contrast of the two opposing views in natural philosophy is concerned, Plato might have pointed out that his own mythical interpretation of the universe does not endorse either view, but proceeds from a third position in between or perhaps above the "conservative" and the "revolutionary" one. Nature is both strict mathematical law and chaotic chance: chance dwelling in the realm of the absolutely indeterminate; law supervening, in the form of mathematical order, upon the chaotic disorder without ever being able to control the latter completely. Thus neither law nor chance reigns supreme, but the world as we know it is a product of both.

As often and as critically as Aristotle deals with Plato's physics, he does not ultimately depart from its basic principles, as far as causality and chance are concerned. Aristotle's doctrine of the "four causes" rather systematizes the world view of his master. And would not a genuine interest in these fundamental ideas of the two men be more appropriate than ever for contemporary natural philosophy?

One final question must be raised: Has the physics of the *Timaeus* influenced modern science? Or rather: Where, when, and how far has such an influence taken place? In the current histories of physics and chemistry, this very important chapter seems to be completely overlooked, and I can give little more than the beginnings of an answer.

In the twelfth century,[30] such men as Adelard of Bath, Hugh of St. Victor, and William of Conches were familiar with Plato's theory of matter, elements, and corpuscles. In the thirteenth century, Roger Bacon quotes Averroës when referring to the five regular solids of the *Platonici*, and has a lengthy chapter on the mathematical construction of the five elements that constitute the world. He opposes this theory by using Aristotle's argument, taken again from Averroës, that the result of this stereometrical construction would be empty space and that empty space is impossible. What is perhaps more important, Roger Bacon adds observations on the hexagonal shape of the honey cell in the beehive and hexagonal crystals found in Ireland and India. Here, perhaps, were some rudiments of a new science. It remains to be seen whether future research will discover a current of Plato's mathematical physics in the Ockhamism of the fourteenth century. But, on the whole, the domineering sway of Aristotelian thought, joined with the authority of the Church, seems to have turned the minds of medieval scholars and scientists in another direction.

In the fifteenth century,[31] the great Italian painter Piero della Francesca and his pupil, the Franciscan mathematician Luca Pacioli, renewed the system of the regular polyhedra, Piero in the wake of Euclid, Pacioli with a definite turn to Plato's natural philosophy. Pacioli gave a powerful stimulus both to Leonardo da Vinci, who in his manuscripts shows himself familiar with Plato's theory of the elements, and to the mathematicians of the sixteenth century.

This same stereometrical pattern of thought penetrates the mind, and fills the writings, of Johannes Kepler.[32] He made a strange use of the five regular polyhedra in his cosmography by inserting each of them, in vast dimensions, between every two planetary spheres in order to account for their different distances—a fantastic hypothesis that was immediately attacked by Tycho Brahe and if not given up, at least radically transformed, by its author.[33] Kepler was also familiar with the minute molecules of the *Timaeus*, and was deeply interested in such phenomena as hexagonal ice crystals and the arrangement of leaves around the stalks of plants.

In the seventeenth century, the French mathematician and philosopher Pierre Gassendi renewed the system of Epicurus, that is, the system of classical atomism—an event of the highest importance in the history of physics. It was hardly a progress, but it is worth mentioning that with the Epicurean atoms he combined at least one of the Platonic corpuscles, the regular tetrahedron.[34] In the *Timaeus*, it is the corpuscle of fire; Gassendi makes it the corpuscle of frost. In both, the sensation of prickling is accounted for, rather naïvely, by the vertices of the pyramid.

One cannot help speculating about the path that modern science might have taken if the seventeenth century had revived Plato's mathematical physics instead of, or along with, Demokritean atomism. In going through the bulky volumes of Robert Boyle, the "founder of modern chemistry" in the seventeenth century, I have not found any reference to the *Timaeus*; whereas his contemporary, Ralph Cudworth, the leader of the Cambridge Platonists, is familiar with what he calls "Plato's imitation of the atomical physiology." [35]

The natural philosophy of Emanuel Swedenborg, as set forth in his early scientific treatises, owes many things to many sources.[36] The vortices and the atomic spherules, for example, go back to Bruno and Descartes, the circular movements to the "Pythagoreans." To Bruno he owes the arrangement of his atomic spherules in regular geometric and stereometric systems, such as triangles, squares, hexagons, and pyramids. It would be premature to assert or to deny any hidden undercurrent from the *Timaeus*. Swedenborg's anticipations, on the other hand, of future theories in astronomy, crystallography, chemistry, and physics have often been emphasized.[37]

In 1814, the famous French physicist Ampère published a letter to Count Berthollet in which he constructed twenty-three polyhedra, from the tetrahedron to what he calls the heptaoctahedron, in order to picture mentally the stereometrical position of the atoms within chemical compounds. And a few years earlier, in 1808, William Wollaston, in the Royal Society of London, had given a hint in the same direction.[38] Neither of them seems to have had the slightest notion of a great forerunner. Goethe may have known of Ampère's theory, and he was certainly familiar with the *Timaeus*, when he wrote the remarkable maxim: *"Wäre die Natur in ihren leblosen Anfängen nicht so gründlich stereometrisch, wie wollte sie zuletzt zum unberechenbaren und unermesslichen Leben gelangen?"* [39]

CHAPTER FIFTEEN

Plato as Geographer

THE BEGINNINGS OF SPHERICAL GEOGRAPHY[1]

I

THE MYTH of the fate of the human soul, a comprehensive and intricate construction, comes at the conclusion of the *Phaedo*. It is composed of two lines of thought: one cosmological, physical, geographical; the other mythico-eschatological. No doubt that the eschatology is the ultimate goal, while the physical theory, however much it may have meant to Plato's scientific interests, is only of subsidiary significance. Let us compare the myths of the beyond in the *Gorgias* and the *Republic*. In the *Gorgias*, the cosmos appears as the prototype of the just, i.e., well-ordered, life; [2] but the myth itself still stands as an entirely separate entity: the judgment of the dead on the meadow of the three-forked path, and the two dwelling places for the good and the damned, the Isle of the Blessed and Tartaros—in other words, a purely mythical landscape, without any attempt to support the myth by a scientific picture of the earth or the universe. This attempt is made in the *Phaedo*, and with such detail that the judgment of the dead and the fate of the soul may appear as annexes, if we superficially judge by the distribution of the material. At the end of the *Republic*, Plato first constructs a precisely conceived and calculated picture of the universe in the form of a spindle with eight whorls fitted one into the other and revolving around the axis of the earth. And only after this is completed do the souls appear before the Fates. This comparison tends to suggest that the connection between cosmology and eschatology was achieved by Plato himself. We must, in any case, attempt to separate the various elements contained in the concluding myth of the *Phaedo*.

Neither the size nor the composition of the earth, Socrates begins, corresponds to the view generally held by the experts. The spherical earth stays in the center of the universe owing to its own equilibrium and the uniform shape of the celestial sphere. This is precisely the theory which has been reported as that of Parmenides [3] and, except for the spherical shape of the earth,

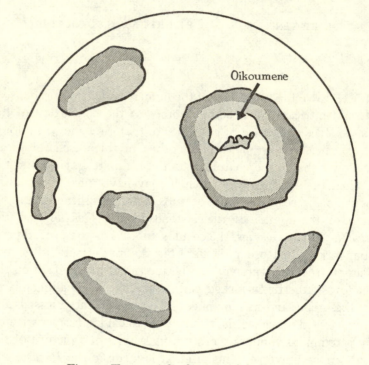

Fig. 5. Terrestrial sphere (with hollows)
according to the *Phaedo*

was already Anaximander's. The sphere of the earth is called "very large," not in relation to the universe—at least, nothing is said about that—but in relation to the space that man occupies on it, "we who dwell in the region extending from the river Phasis to the Pillars of Hercules," from the western to the eastern end of our *oikoumene*. The land mass known to us covers so small an area on the large sphere that we dwell around the central sea "like frogs or ants about a marsh."

Our dwelling place, however, is only one of many distributed around the sphere of the earth as caves or hollows (κοῖλα). Water, mist, and air collect in these hollows, while "the true earth" (αὐτὴ ἡ γῆ), that is, the surface without hollows, reaches into the pure ether. This is described precisely and can be seen easily on the accompanying sketches (figs. 5 and 6). Below, at the bottom of the hollow, water has collected; above it rises the land upon which we live, surrounded by air; and the highest layer is the "true earth," washed by the body of air as our own dwelling place is by the waters of the ocean, and reaching into the ether just as our dwelling place reaches into the denser atmosphere. How plastically all this is seen may be illustrated

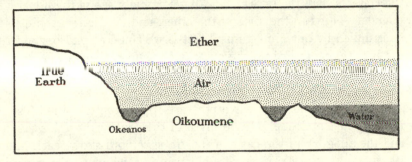

Fig. 6. Cross-section: half of the hollow of the Oikoumene

by a detail: corresponding to the islands of our dwelling place, the "true earth" has its islands, surrounded by air and lying close to the mainland (111A). Fig. 6 shows that they can hardly be envisaged as lying far from land, i.e., as rising from the center of the hollow.

What we have seen so far is physical theory that might have been constructed by any natural scientist. Soon, however, the dazzling description reveals Plato's own very personal hand (110B). If anyone could view the earth from a distance, it would look to him like a colorful ball; for the true surface shines in the purest and most wonderful colors, of which the colors used by painters are only samples, as it were; even the dim hollows, when seen in this larger context, appear as colorful spots. The most beautiful plants and precious stones are found above—of which we know only deposits as precious jewels and gold and silver. There are living beings, even human beings, in this upper world, endowed, to the degree that they dwell in a purer element, with more sensitive organs and clearer minds than ours. Perpetual spring reigns and gives them permanent health and longer life. And the gods dwell among them and hold converse with them. All these features are derived from the image of the Isle of the Blessed or Paradise.[4]

Platonic spirit, however, already colors the earlier passage (109c): Our world at the bottom of the hollow is only a dim reflection of the splendor above. Yet, strangely deceived, we are unaware of our condition, believing that we dwell upon the surface of the earth rather than at the bottom of a deep indentation.[5] We think that what we see above us is the sky and the stars as they really are; but all we actually see is the upper boundary between the air and the ether, and the light reaching us is dulled by our dim atmosphere. If we could ascend beyond the surface of our air into the ether, we would realize our errors and we would have the true sky and the true light above us, being surrounded by the true earth.

It is obvious how close we now are to the center of Plato's imagery and philosophy. The myth of the soul in the *Phaedrus* and the allegory of the cave in the *Republic* both show, each in its own way, the greatest resemblance, extending to the very words;[6] the expressions in the *Phaedo*, like "the earth itself," "the true earth," "the true sky" (αὐτὴ ἡ γῆ, ἡ ὡς ἀληθῶς γῆ, ὁ ἀληθῶς οὐρανός, τὸ ἀληθινὸν φῶς), belong to Plato's central thoughts. The metaphysical contrast between the world of *Ideas* and the world of appearances has here been brought down to earth, and is reflected in the value contrast between the "true earth" and our *oikoumene* at the bottom of the hollow. This value contrast, then, and along with it the entire imaginative description of the "true earth," and the name itself, are peculiarly Platonic creations, and belong to a different sphere from the physical geography with which Socrates begins his discourse.

Abstracting from this aspect of Plato's imaginative world of *Ideas*, we have a self-contained cosmological picture: the earth as a large sphere, resting in the middle of a spherical universe; upon this sphere, numerous hollows, of which our *oikoumene* is one. The distribution of the elements, too, according to which water and air collect in these hollows, while the true shell of the earth rises into the ether, fits into this picture. Now, as mentioned above, the theory of a sphere, together with the earth's suspension in the center, may be traced back to Parmenides. But there is no previous record of the hollows; and we may raise the question whether they were also taken over from somebody else, and Plato merely projected the colors of his own imagination upon them, or whether he invented them as a material basis to point up the mythical contrast. For the time being, however, the question of origin is not the essential point. The main thing is that we realize that the picture of the universe, as we have seen it up to this point, represents two entirely different realms of thought; that the geophysical substructure and the upper stratum of mythico-metaphysical elements are distinct from one another; and that the theory of the hollows belongs to geophysics.

The result so far reached may be confirmed by an analysis of the literary form and expression. Let us note how Plato, at the beginning, repeatedly insists upon the scientific nature of what is to come. First (108c), Socrates' theory of the form and shape of the earth is in contrast to the theories of most experts (οἱ περὶ γῆς εἰωθότες λέγειν). He himself has been "convinced" by somebody (πέπεισμαι). Simmias, too, has heard several views about the nature of the earth. Now he wants to learn the "conviction" of Socrates (ἃ σε πείθει). To describe how things are (ἃ γ᾽ ἔστιν), Socrates replies, is not difficult; to prove that the description is true, however, is a big and tremendously difficult task. But he is willing to describe the shape of the earth according to his "conviction." Then the cosmological-physical discourse begins with the words, "I am convinced." Quite different is the later passage (110B), in which he describes the "true earth," and which, preceded by a remark of the interlocutor, clearly marks a new point of departure. In this passage, he speaks of a "myth" he wants to tell, thus emphasizing the contrast to the geophysical description at the beginning. Recognizing this contrast as a matter of principle, we must, however, admit that these parts are not strictly separated from one another, just as there are no disconnected elements anywhere in Plato's thought. For even before the "myth" sets a line of demarcation, and before the description of the true earth above begins, the contrast between appearance and reality has been brought down to earth, and this contrast can be understood only from the point of view of the *Idea*, and not of physics. Though the transition is somewhat fluid, Plato's own statement that one of the poles of the construction is scientific (in our sense of the word), while the other is mythical, must not be underestimated. And Plato makes it equally clear at what point the myth comes to an end. For after intimations of the bliss enjoyed by the inhabitants of that true earth (καὶ τὴν ἄλλην εὐδαιμονίαν τούτων ἀκόλουθον εἶναι, 111c), he returns, in a clearly recognizable transition, to the point he had previously reached in developing the scientific picture.

Previously (109b) Socrates had merely emphasized that the "places" were numerous and of different shape and size; now he describes these differences. Some of the hollows have greater depth and a larger opening than our *oikoumene;* some are deeper but have a narrower opening; others are shallower and curve downward more gradually. Many other variations are conceivable. Below the surface of the earth, the hollows are connected by a great number of channels filled with water, warm and cold, but also with streams of liquid mud and powerful rivers of fire. The movement in these veins is regulated by the great central reservoir, Tartaros. The latter itself is a hollow, differing from the others by virtue of the fact that it penetrates the entire sphere of the earth. The water content of these subterranean channels depends upon whether the "balance" (αἰώρα) of this mass of water tilts in one direction or another from the center of the earth.[7] The most important of the numerous streams of different kinds running through the earth is Okeanos, and then the following: Acheron, Pyriphlegethon, and Kokytos.

The courses of the subterranean streams need not be traced here in all details. They originate in Tartaros and ultimately return to it, meandering in the earth's interior; both Kokytos and Pyriphlegethon, for example, at one point, come very close to the Acherusian Lake without, however, mingling their water with it. The important thing is that we realize that all these features are invented and described in order to prepare, and make possible, the destiny of the different categories of souls. The Acherusian Lake is intended for the "mediocre," where they receive reward and punishment. The serious, but not incurable, criminals float in Kokytos and Pyriphlegethon. The current leads them to the points where each river comes closest to the lake, and from these points they must attempt to obtain the forgiveness of the victims of their sins, who dwell in the lake, so that they themselves may be released from the stream and transferred to it. We could develop in detail how the description of the subterranean streams does not originate in natural science, but is designed as a topographical basis for the description of the world beyond, which it precedes.

Now the four streams particularly singled out are by no means the only ones of their kind, they are rather the most significant among innumerable streams of the same type. Moreover, these subterranean passages, filled more or less with water, liquid mud, and fire, as fed by the great central reservoir, do not have anything to do with eschatology. In Plato's context, to be sure, they serve the purpose of including the subterranean streams within a larger category of phenomena, lest the former, if isolated, appear incredible and incomprehensible. Their meaning, however, reaches much further. They furnish a theory, developed in great detail, of source and river, ebb and flow, flood and drought, mud and lava eruptions, wind, and other geophysical processes. This is very far removed from theological, eschatological categories of thought; and just as Aristotle in his *Meteorology* (II 2 355^b) considered the theory important enough to refute it, so we, too, must assign it a place with Plato's science of nature.

This geophysical theory, freed from all theology, is closely connected with the theory of the "hollows," discussed above, and presupposes the latter as a prerequisite. For, in the first place, these hollows are connected by the channels; the channels pierce the walls that, as it were, remained between the individual hollows (fig. 7), so that, if we were to omit the hollows, the passageways between them would obviously also lose their meaning. In the second place, Tartaros, i.e., the great regulator, in which all of the channels have their origin and their end, is itself only one of the hollows, though the most powerful and the only one that extends through the entire sphere of the earth, so that if we were to disregard the hollows, we would also have to dispense with Tartaros and the channels.[8]

An analysis of the factual situation, therefore, reveals that the two theories belong together, and this is again confirmed by

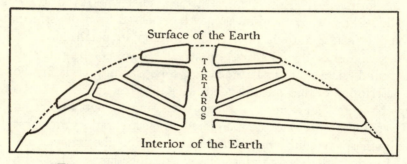

Fig. 7. Cross-section: part of the terrestrial sphere

a consideration of the formal elements. After the imaginary description of the "true earth" (110B–111C), the author (as pointed out above) expressly returns to the "regions in the hollows" situated about the sphere, and describes their different shapes more precisely, while previously (109B) he had merely mentioned the fact that they were different from one another. This description serves as an introduction to the physical theory. Thus the very structure of the work conveys the feeling that the myth of the "true earth" is a self-contained element, while, at the same time, the two areas of natural science fit together as a unity.

The eschatological myth still requires a brief discussion, which we shall begin by a comparison with the corresponding myth in the *Gorgias*. In the latter work, Plato recognizes only two classes of souls, the sinners and the just, and, correspondingly, two dwellings after death, Tartaros and the Isle of the Blessed. In the *Phaedo*, the two classes have been increased to four, and the topography of the world beyond is developed accordingly. But if we look more closely, we can easily see the path leading from the older, simpler view to the more recent and more elaborate image. The Blessed Ones have remained a unit, except that the *Phaedo* assigns a special position to the philosophers. The sinners, however, have been replaced by three groups: the mediocre, the curable criminals, and the incurable. The dwelling place of all three groups is below the earth, which indicates that they belong together in contrast to the good souls who alone lead their lives of bliss upon the true earth above. In order to make this dwelling worthy of them, Plato's poetic imagination adorned the true earth with all the colors provided both by the popular conception of Paradise and by his own rich and plastic world of *Ideas*.

We have previously separated the metaphysical myth from its physical foundation, the theory of hollows, and the eschatology from its physical foundation, the theory of the channels. The physical theories were then seen to combine; and now we realize how myth and eschatology also interlock: how the myth is designed to prepare for the eschatology. We may, therefore, in a rough schema, divide the structure of the total work into four parts. Parts one and three are to be understood as natural science; parts two and four, as myth and eschatology.

II

If we wish to determine the place of Plato's conception of the earth within the history of geography as a science, we must begin by asking ourselves what Plato had in mind when he conceived the peculiar "hollows" in the surface of the earth. This much seems clear: if there are many such hollows, and our inhabited world is one of them—the only one we can know—it must have been the starting point of the theory and the model for the other hollows. For it stands to reason that one could not begin by constructing the unknown, fashioning the relatively well known after what was unknown. Rather, the procedure must have been something like this. Our *oikoumene* was believed to be situated within a relatively small hollow upon the vast sphere of the earth. Since it would have been against all probability that this inhabited space known to us was really the only one in existence, numerous other dwelling places were, by way of analogy, placed upon the surface of the earth and given an appropriate shape; i.e., they were conceived as hollows. To grasp the origin of this strange thought, therefore, we have to start out with our *oikoumene* and ask why it was placed at the bottom of such a hollow; to arrive at an answer will require a brief review of the two lines of thought along which the science of geography had developed up to that time.

In Ionia, Anaximander originated geography as a science by designing the first map of the earth. The records of antiquity that so inform us are correct; for it must be emphasized that this map was not a practical, but essentially a theoretical, accomplishment and that it became, for this very reason, the foundation for a science.[9] Maps for practical use, itineraries and harbor maps, had long been in existence. The colonizing voyages of the Greeks could not have been undertaken without such aids; why should the Ionians have lacked what the Orient possessed, and what the inhabitants of the South Sea islands know how to produce with rods and shells? Anaximander's accomplishment must have been the fact that he created a *whole*—even though it may not have been particularly useful in practice; for when the Milesian oarsman crossed the Dardanelles, he did not have to know about the Peloponnesos or Sicily, and anyone with a definite destination in mind was more likely to be confused than aided by a map of the earth. This map was so theoretical that it included regions not known by any experience, but pure constructions of thought, even areas believed to be inaccessible at any time, such as those shown on the outer edge of the map, Okeanos and its shores.

While Anaximander, then, did something quite different from composing a total picture of the earth out of parts meant for practical use, he did not, perhaps, construct it in a vacuum. We possess a Babylonian map of the earth, from a period no earlier, or not much earlier, than Anaximander, which, in turn, represents a copy of an older original, dated by the experts as from the ninth century. Its construction coincides with Anaximander's in an important formal aspect, for both of them are circular maps: the Babylonian is surrounded by the circular "bitter river," and the Milesian by Okeanos. The design for a total picture is analogous in both of them; and just as Miletus had gotten the sun dial from Babylon, so it is more probable than not that it was also familiar, at the same time, with a Babylonian map of the earth.[10]

Nevertheless, Anaximander's map was still an essentially new creation. On the Babylonian map, the "bitter river" is immediately adjacent to the land traversed by the Euphrates. To the Babylonian, Mesopotamia constituted the entire inhabited world; even Egypt and Asia Minor do not seem to have existed for him. Thus, if Anaximander (as might be expected from a compatriot of Homer's) had a much more open conception of the world, he also had a greater sense of reality, which did not incorporate those seven or eight triangular islands protruding on the Babylonian map from the outer edge of the bitter river—whither? Into a fantastic no man's land, a mythical world beyond, which had no place in Anaximander's scientific mind.[11]

As an empiricist Herodotos protested against the premature construction of things about which there was no assured knowledge. In a sense his objection was justified and not without good results; for nothing helped more to advance this science than the continual alternation between theoretical construction and experience. But the Ionian circular map persisted; and from the point of view of spherical geography and the theory of zones, Aristotle more or less echoed Herodotos' objections when he raised his voice against geographers who draw the earth in the form of a circle.[12] The same criticism may still be found in Geminus (first century B.C.), and the circular picture of the earth was restored to predominance in the wheel-shaped maps of late antiquity and the early Middle Ages—only, at this point, what began as a new and youthful science had become frozen into a childish and rigid system.

Anaximander's geographical theory is inseparable from his general physical-astronomical world view. The circular map of the earth must, therefore, be envisaged as resting upon the surface of a column drum—for he believed the earth to be such a

drum suspended in the universe. We might perhaps mention that
the expression "hollowed" (κοῖλος) applies to the horizontal
surface of a column drum. Demokritos still conceived the earth
in a disklike shape; since he, too, did not merely construct a theory of the earth but also designed a map, he must have assigned
to the inhabited earth a rather precise place upon that surface.[13]
This was not difficult for Anaximander, to whom the earth was a
drum and the *oikoumene* approximately circular in shape. For
Demokritos, on the other hand, the proportion of length to
width in the *oikoumene* was 3 : 2; and it remains uncertain
whether he conceived of other inhabited islands besides it or,
like Anaximander, he thought of the *oikoumene* as the only island,
but seen in a different proportion to the circular edge of the
surface of the earth.

Another detail must be mentioned. If the body of the earth
was envisaged as a disk, and the *oikoumene* as well as the surrounding Okeanos plotted upon it, the youthful mind devising
this system must have raised the question of the exterior limit
of the construction. To put it bluntly, the ocean would flow off
over the edge if there were nothing to hold it back. In a way,
the *Nekyia* of the *Odyssey* with its region of the beyond had
already prepared a solution for this problem, and many of the
Ionian natural philosophers adopted it. Generally speaking,
Kleomedes presents the old theory and its obvious explanation
(*Circular Theory of the Heavenly Bodies* I 8 40). Some, he said,
thought the earth was flat, but others envisaged it as indented
and hollowed out (βαθεῖα καὶ κοίλη), since only in this shape
could water remain upon it.[14] Demokritos and Archelaos are
expressly named as representatives of this theory. That
Anaximenes probably shared this view may be concluded from
the fact that, like Archelaos, he believed that the sun did not
"go down" but was covered by the "higher parts of the earth,"
i.e., by a sort of peripheral mountain range. Archelaos used the
old conception for a new purpose: to explain the changeability
of the horizon. In the *Phaedo* (99B), the same conception of the
earth is attributed to "somebody" who "puts the air as a
supporting element underneath the earth, as if it were a flat tub".
(ὥσπερ καρδόπῳ πλατείᾳ).

It is now hardly necessary to point out how Plato's conception of the earth should be understood: it is a youthful and bold attempt to transfer the picture of the *oikoumene* from the disk to the sphere.[15] The "hollows" form the most conspicuous feature of this picture. They are no longer difficult to comprehend, for we have seen how the Ionians were led to their conception of the earth as a flat disk elevated on the edges and indented in the center. The term "hollowed" (κοῖλος) represented this idea; we find the same expression in Plato. The scientific project of combining the theory of the earth as a sphere with the map of the earth, so persistently developed by the Ionians, was bound to arise. To achieve this end, nothing was more plausible than to retain the hollow and to infer, by probable reasoning, the existence of numerous analogous hollows. This view also eliminated a difficulty that must have occurred to some people in the early stages of spherical geography: the question of how a place of habitation could be found on the curved surface, and, at least, how it happened that the curvature could not be seen or felt.

It remains uncertain who is responsible for this step, which must be regarded as a scientifically important advance. We might think that it was Plato himself; but the manner in which Socrates refers to "somebody" does not speak for this view. It is perhaps more likely that it was a Pythagorean from the circle of Archytas, who, as a result of an ingenious intellectual combination, created this cosmological-physical structure, which was subsequently adopted by Plato so that it might serve his eschatological-metaphysical purposes.[16]

III

The *Phaedo* is not the only dialogue that contains a geophysical construction. We find a sharp contrast to it at the beginning of the *Timaeus* (24E–25D), where a geographical foundation is laid for the legend of Atlantis. This has nothing to do with the cosmology of the *Timaeus*, because it belongs, in content, to an entirely different sphere of thought, that of the *Critias*.

Our inhabited world, called Europe and Asia, is surrounded

by the ocean. Beyond the Pillars of Hercules, there once rose the island of Atlantis. It perished as a result of mighty earthquakes and storm tides, which made the sea in these regions too shallow for navigation. Prior to the island's destruction, however, there was traffic from Atlantis to our *oikoumene*, to the other islands in the sea, and even to the "true continent" that surrounds the "true ocean." The expression "true ocean" is chosen to express the contrast to the small Mediterranean, "true continent" in contrast to our *oikoumene*, which is envisaged as one of several islands.

This can be easily visualized and may be depicted in the form of a sketch (fig. 8): a large ocean containing a number of larger and smaller islands, of which our *oikoumene* is one; the vast ocean is surrounded by an enormous expanse of land. This land extends around the entire sphere of the earth; the ocean, large as it is, appears to be imbedded in it like an inland sea. And it is quite consistent with this picture to assume that there may be other closed ocean basins elsewhere inside the "true land."

It may, of course, be asked whether this is not a play of fantasy rather than a geographical hypothesis. We may answer that *oikoumene* and Atlantis are necessary parts of the legend; but, as far as we can see, islands, the true ocean, and the true continent are superfluous. All these details, however, including the superfluous features, combine to form a unit, which must mean that they have been conceived of independently of the legend; in other words, that they are aspects of physical geography, not the playful invention of a poet. And, indeed, it is hard to imagine that what represents a great advance in scientific thought as compared with the *Phaedo* was a playful invention.

The principal contrast between the two conceptions of the earth may be formulated as follows.[17] The individual "hollows" of the *Phaedo* are separated by insuperable boundaries. It is as if Plato erected transcendent worlds as barriers between our "hollow" and the others. But even if we concentrate exclusively on the physical side, the idea of passing from our *oikoumene* to a neighboring one appears fantastic and nonsensical. In order to leave our own habitation, we would have to be differently constituted human beings, breathing ether instead of air. The picture of the earth developed in the *Timaeus* no longer confines us to a small spot on the sphere by setting up permanent barriers. That the Atlantic Ocean has become too shallow for passage is a purely practical obstacle. On the basis of this geographical view, it is not implausible to think that what this practical obstacle prevented in the West might perhaps be

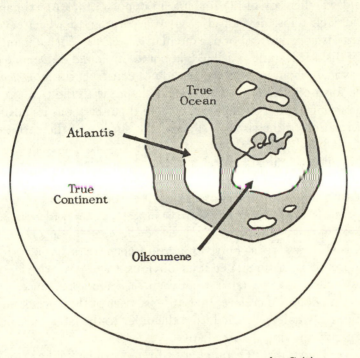

Fig. 8. Terrestrial sphere according to the *Critias*

ventured in the East. The absolute barriers by which the *Phaedo* had divided our earth's surface into individual regions permanently separated from one another are now broken down. The earth's surface has become a unit, open to further exploration and discovery.

That the science of geography was substantially advanced by this theory is not open to doubt, particularly in the light of further developments. What remains uncertain is the extent to which the Academy contributed to this advance. On the one hand, we may say that analogies to the geographical conception of the *Timaeus* are not entirely lacking. The "true ocean" is ultimately the old Okeanos—greatly enlarged. The "true continent" is foreshadowed by the land situated beyond Okeanos, as it was described in the *Nekyia* of the *Odyssey*, and as it still survived, among the Ionian philosophers of nature, in the notion of a high-towering edge of the earth.[18] It cannot be said whether any of the Ionians, in opposition to Anaximander and Hekataios, developed a view according to which several large islands, instead of one circular *oikoumene*, existed upon the flat disk. It is quite possible that some of them did. Demokritos may have thought so; since he did not construct the *oikoumene* in the form of a circle, but in an oval shape, with the two axes in the proportion of 3 : 2, he must have thought about its position in relation to the circular edge of the surface of the earth; but this is purely speculative.

While preliminary stages are thus demonstrable, or, at least, partly conceivable, there is one point that clearly conveys Plato's own spirit: the expressions "true ocean" and "true continent" (ὁ ἀληθινὸς πόντος. ἐκεῖνο δὲ πέλαγος ὄντως ἥ τε περιέχουσα αὐτὸ γῆ παντελῶς ἀληθῶς ὀρθότατ' ἂν λέγοιτο ἤπειρος). In the context, they refer only to a difference in size, not to a difference in nature. Yet it is obvious that, however faintly, they reflect Plato's contrast between *Idea* and appearance.[19] We have no doubt, therefore, that at least part of the development, if not the whole, which led from the older to the later conception took place within the Academy.

We know that Theopompos, in a Utopian annex to his history, incorporated the picture of the earth presented in the *Timaeus*, together with the fictional themes of the *Critias*.[20] He retained the expression "true continent"; the "true ocean" he called Okeanos; and, if Aelian's report (*Variae Historiae* III 18) is complete, he recognized only three of the many islands: Europe, Asia, and Africa. Thus he seems to have returned, in some respects, to simpler conceptions; he dismissed the many islands of the world ocean as unproven hypotheses, and he constructed his picture of the earth out of the three traditional elements: our *oikoumene*, the surrounding Okeanos, and the true continent. Unfortunately, we do not know the details of his theory, nor do we know how seriously he took it. At any rate, he must have considered Plato's geographical hypotheses as plausible.[21]

I V

The history of the science of antiquity resembles a subterranean stream; only now and then, for shorter or longer stretches of its course, does it emerge on the surface. When we encountered the problem of spherical geography in the *Phaedo*, this stream was obviously just a short distance away from its source. Subsequently, however, its impetus must have greatly increased. In the *Timaeus*, only a few decades later, we find the approach to this problem greatly advanced; and Aristotle, by taking an entirely new point of view, shows that once the question was raised, it did not come to rest again.

After the arguments in favor of the spherical shape of the earth in *De caelo*, Aristotle proceeds as follows (II 14 297ᵇ 30). from the heavenly phenomena it may be concluded, not only that the earth is a sphere, but also that it is not a very large sphere; for if we slightly change our location in a northerly or southerly direction, the meridian altitudes of the stars change. Stars visible in Egypt or Cyprus cannot be seen farther north, i.e., in Greece; others, which are circumpolar stars in the north, rise and set farther south. The conclusion that the earth is small, expressly emphasized, appears to be a correction of the older view as found in Plato. When the earth was first conceived as a sphere, and an attempt was made to place the countries known to us within its confines, it necessarily appeared of tremendous size in relation to these countries. Our inhabited world seemed like a tiny spot, which one did not know how to locate upon the enormous surface. It is understandable that the pendulum later swung to the other extreme. The progress is to be measured by the fact that the first stage did not enable people to raise the questions of the location of our countries and their relation to the size of the whole. This became possible only when the globe was made accessible to a comprehensive view.

Aristotle regarded the relatively small size of our earth as a proven fact. He was not equally sure of the conclusion—drawn

by others and at least plausible to him—that the region of the
Pillars of Hercules on the one side, i.e., the western end of the
oikoumene, and India on the other, i.e., its eastern end, come
together and that, therefore, the Atlantic and the Indian Oceans
are actually a single body of water.[22] His general view is quite
clear and may again be shown in a sketch (fig. 9).[23] What
remains doubtful and what has frequently been discussed—
though it is not too important for our purposes—is the question
how this "coming together" (συνάπτειν) is to be understood
precisely: whether the theory recorded by Aristotle assumed the
existence of a dividing ocean or actual contact, that is, a land
bridge (or several land bridges) from East Asia to western
Europe and Libya. Both interpretations are possible from the
linguistic point of view.[24] And his following sentence, which, in
support of this theory, mentions the appearance of elephants in
each of the "extreme regions," cannot be used either for
deciding the issue.[25] Aristotle would have expressed himself
more unequivocally if a decision one way or the other had been
significant for his problem.

A single land mass in the temperate zone, the rest filled with
ocean—that is the Aristotelian view, judging from two passages
of the *Meteorology*. In one of these (II 1 354[a] 1), we find the
following argument intended to prove that, unlike rivers, oceans
have no sources. Experience proves the point in the case of
inland seas whose entire shoreline we can trace. Among these
inland seas, the "Red Sea" is connected at one point with the
"ocean outside the Pillars"; the Hyrcanian and the Caspian
Seas, on the other hand, are surrounded by land, and completely
separated from that ocean. The classification of the Red Sea as
an inland sea is, strictly speaking, not quite correct; but since it
is "almost" an inland sea, with the exception of a small connecting area, it may be regarded as such for our purposes. This
characterization applies perfectly to the body of water that we
still call the Red Sea, and can only refer to it; for the entire
discussion is based on something empirically known and explored. The Indian Ocean, however, or the sea between Arabia
and India, which conceivably might be meant by the "Red Sea,"
had not been sufficiently explored and would not support this

description. Aristotle's assumption, then, that the "Red Sea" is connected with the "sea outside the Pillars," presupposes the view formulated in *De caelo*; namely, that the Atlantic Ocean meets and merges with the sea to the east of India.[26]

A later passage of the *Meteorology* (II 6 362[b] 21) discusses the view that the earth is habitable only in the temperate zones.

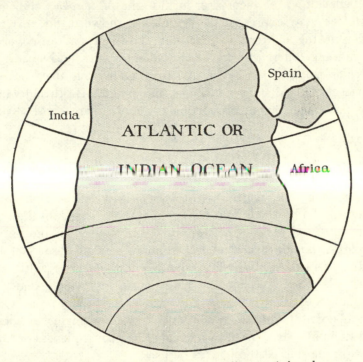

India · ATLANTIC OR INDIAN OCEAN · Spain · Africa

Fig. 9. Terrestrial sphere according to Aristotle

Thus, there are two inhabited regions, separated by the tropical zone, and bounded by uninhabitable regions to the north and south. In the east-west direction, on the other hand, there are, in principle, no boundaries; only the size of the ocean constitutes a practical obstacle to a journey around the earth (ὥστ᾽ εἰ μή που κωλύει θαλάττης πλῆθος, ἅπαν εἶναι πορεύσιμον). Between eastern Asia and the Pillars of Hercules, the ocean appears to interrupt the continuity. Without this interruption, our temperate zone would form a continuous habitable land belt (τὰ δὲ τῆς Ἰνδικῆς ἔξω καὶ τῶν στηλῶν τῶν Ἡρακλείων διὰ τὴν θάλατταν οὐ φαίνεται συνείρειν τῷ συνεχῶς εἶναι πᾶσαν οἰκουμένην). Several possibilities may have been considered in this context, barely touched upon by Aristotle, including, perhaps, the theory of a continent situated between eastern Asia and western Europe, i.e., of an "America." But, again, Aristotle seems to have thought that our zone consisted of a single land mass. Thus, we are first led to believe that the theory set forth in the *Meteorology* coincides with the view expressed in *De caelo*, as shown in fig. 9. Considering the matter more closely, however, we discover a significant difference. In order to show the inadequacy of circular maps of the earth, Aristotle points out that the experiences of land and sea voyages suggest that length and width are not equal, but in proportion of "more than 5 to 3," i.e.,

$$6 : 3 > L : W > 5 : 3$$

We do not know the width Aristotle assigned to the temperate zone.[27] If we choose the familiar 43° (an arbitrary assumption) and measure the length on the thirty-sixth degree of latitude (the parallel of Rhodes), it turns out that the length of the land mass amounts to one quarter, or a little more, of the entire circle. Although this calculation contains several vague factors, it is certain that, given the proportion of length to width, the land fills much less, and the water much more than, one half of the zone, or that fig. 9 does not correspond to the view presupposed by Aristotle's *Meteorology*. It remains an open question how far he tried to calculate these consequences or how final he considered the figures he used.

While it appears that we were faced with an undeniable contradiction in that the land mass, according to one theory, occupied far more than half of the globe and far less than half according to the other, these contradictory views, placed against the background of the geography of the *Timaeus*, may be seen as variations on the same basic thesis: the globe is small, and the land mass known to us—Europe, Asia, Libya—occupies a very considerable portion of the temperate zone. That there are additional land masses between western Europe and eastern Asia is practically impossible according to the view expressed in *De caelo*; according to the *Meteorology* it is theoretically possible, but does not seem to express Aristotle's opinion.

How did Aristotle envisage the shape of the continent extending toward the south, of which our *oikoumene* is a section? In the southern temperate zone he assumed an inhabited world corresponding to our own. Did his theory provide for a land mass uniting the two into a homogeneous continent, thus approximately corresponding to reality, or did he envisage the tropical zone as filled by an ocean encircling the equator, thus anticipating, in a way, the theory later held by Kleanthes and Krates? [28]

The second view appears to be supported by a passage in the *Meteorology* (II 5 363ª 5) that deals with the east and west winds "on the southern sea outside of Libya" (περὶ τὴν ἔξω Λιβύης θάλατταν τὴν νοτίαν).[29] Upon closer examination, however, these words appear in an altogether different light. Aristotle points out that the south wind does not originate at the South Pole. If it did, the north wind would have to spread to the southern hemisphere, since there must be a correspondence between the essential natural phenomena in the southern and the northern hemispheres. But this is, in fact, not the case. Rather, the north wind ends here (i.e., in our temperate zone) and cannot penetrate farther south, since east and west winds prevail "upon the southern sea outside of Libya" just as north and south winds prevail in our own region. (The idea seems to be that the east and west winds, like a horizontal bar, check the course of the north wind). This part of the argument evidently deals with an empirically established fact. But if this is so, Aristotle did not have an equatorial ocean in mind; for even if we assume that the theory, for one reason or another, required such an ocean, its location in the tropical zone would have placed it beyond all possible experience, and it would have been impossible to state, as a matter of course, what sort of winds prevailed on it. In the light of these considerations, Aristotle must have meant "the southern sea on Africa's east and west coasts" (still within our zone), and the wording of the passage seems to bear out this assumption.[30]

The material used so far does not seem to enable us to determine whether or not Aristotle assumed the existence of an equatorial ocean. We are helped, however, in this connection, by the treatise *On the Inundation of the Nile*. In an excellent analysis, Partsch proved that "the *Liber de inundacione Nili*, preserved to us in a medieval translation, justifiably bears the name of Aristotle; as a matter of fact, it represents an authentic though abridged treatise by the great philosopher, which must have been available to Eratosthenes in its original form." [31] Even if one wishes to be very skeptical, one must at least admit that the treatise was written under the master's eyes, which means that its essential aspects must still be traced to him. This treatise includes, among others, the theory of Nikagoras of Cyprus: the Nile rises in the summer because it originates in a part of the earth where winter prevails when we have summer. Put more precisely, says Aristotle, this leads to the conclusion that the sources are located in the southern temperate zone. The theory is refuted, not by reference to an ocean circling the equator, which would cut off the river's course from the southern to the northern hemisphere, but by the consideration that the river, between the tropics, would have to flow through a zone twice as wide as the temperate zone (a course of such length had been previously rejected as incompatible with appearances), and that this would be the "burned zone" (in which the water would evidently evaporate rather than come to us in such great abundance). This twofold argument is used to refute the theory; but, in principle, the refutation takes the same geographical point of view as the theory. We now know that Aristotle's conception of the earth presented a continental mass extending uninterruptedly from the zone of the North Pole at least as far as the southern temperate zone.

We do not know which scientists Aristotle followed in his geographical theories; however, more than one indication points to Eudoxos, the great mathematician and natural scientist. Let us therefore attempt to use, for purposes of comparison, what little has been preserved of the latter's geographical theories.[32]

There are general considerations of sufficient strength to suggest that Eudoxos advocated the theory of a spherical earth.

We also have historical evidence to that effect in a passage of Aëtios which informs us of Eudoxos' view concerning the inundation of the Nile. He explained these inundations, invoking the support of "the priests," in terms of heavy rains that were caused by the "alternation of the seasons" (κατὰ τὴν ἀντιπερίστασιν τῶν ὡρῶν).[33] When summer prevails in our region, under the Tropic of Cancer (i.e., in the northern temperate zone), the "dwellers opposite us" (ἄντοικοι), under the Tropic of Capricorn (i.e., in the southern temperate zone), have their winter. It is there that the flood waters of the stream originate. This hypothesis—which we encountered in Aristotle's treatise *On the Inundation of the Nile* [34]—obviously presupposes a fully developed spherical and zonal theory of the earth.

If Aristotle, in support of his view that the globe is relatively small, points out that stars visible in Egypt and Cyprus vanish farther north, i.e., in the latitude of Greece, we may recall that it was Eudoxos who made the most celebrated observation of antiquity in this respect, in connection with the star called Canopus. We know that Eudoxos first perceived this bright star in Egypt and subsequently, in his observatory above the city of Knidos, was just barely able to identify it on the horizon. Poseidonios remembered this discovery while he was in Spain (Strabo II 119), and we may well ask whether Aristotle did not have the same discovery in mind.[35] At the same time, it is not at all unlikely—though not supported by historical tradition—that Eudoxos, on the basis of this fact, drew the same conclusion as Aristotle with regard to the smallness of the earth. That Eudoxos actually did not envisage the earth as particularly large will become clear in the following remarks.

We previously concluded that Aristotle did not think of the torrid zone as cut by an ocean circling the equator, but that he saw the Old World, quite correctly, as a continental mass extending to the southern hemisphere. The same may be shown for Eudoxos. We know his views about the source of the Nile in the southern temperate zone. This means that the river had to cross the tropical zone, and Africa for Eudoxos extended from the northern temperate zone at least as far as the southern temperate zone.[36] This distribution of land areas corresponds to

Aristotle's and proves, as mentioned before, the relatively small size of the sphere according to Eudoxos.

In Aristotle, two views on the distribution of water and land may be found side by side. The first envisaged a continent of such "length" that western Europe and eastern Asia were separated only by a narrow sea. The second, to which Aristotle seems to have given greater weight, considerably limited the east-west expansion, and apparently assigned to it less than a quarter of the total length in the only zone known to us. This view theoretically allowed space for an "America," but there is little in Aristotle to point to such a theory. Eudoxos presents a very similar relationship, and if we place the two proportions side by side,

Eudoxos [37]   length : width = 2 : 1
Aristotle   6 : 3 = (2 : 1) > length : width > 5 : 3

Aristotle's view appears almost as a correction of Eudoxos', and shows its kinship even where it deviates.

Whether Eudoxos conceived of the rest of the surface as filled by ocean or assumed the existence of additional land masses, we do not know. What he held in common with Aristotle, however, may once more be emphasized. Both thought of the earth as relatively small. As evidence Aristotle cites the change of the meridian altitudes, with regard to which Eudoxos had made the most famous discovery in antiquity. For the land mass of Europe, Asia, and Africa extends on this sphere from the northern cold region at least to the southern temperate zone. They do not agree on the proportion of length to width as far as our inhabited world is concerned, but this difference speaks more for a connection between their views than against it.

That Eudoxos, while teaching and studying in the Academy, should not have discussed the subject of spherical geography with anybody is most improbable. Evidence to this effect, however, is not available; and we must therefore be satisfied with the fact that, in Eudoxos and Aristotle's other authorities, we find the decisive steps beyond Plato in the exploration and knowledge of the earth's surface. The same line of development was later continued by Eratosthenes, Poseidonios, and, under the Antonines, by Marinus and Ptolemy.[38] They, too, envisaged a single vast land mass extending through the northern and southern hemispheres, but with a much greater east-west extension than allowed for by Eudoxos and at least one of Aristotle's theories. The known length, according to Marinus, was 225°; according to Ptolemy, 180°. As to how far the continental mass might extend in the east beyond Sera (China) and Kattigara (Ceylon), these scientists, advanced in knowledge, but wisely conscious of their limits, did not speculate.

Postscript (1968)

The two pictures of the globe that antiquity passed on to the Renaissance were of the greatest historical significance. Aristotle's picture became, as we know, the basis for Columbus' voyages of discovery: he sailed to the west in order to reach East Asia by the shortest route [39*] That this could not be possible, however, was revealed only a few decades later through the discoveries of Magellan, Balboa, and Cortez. Then for the sixteenth century and its chroniclers, the picture of the earth in Plato's *Timaeus* and *Critias* became significant.[40*] According to this view, the Antilles appeared to be remnants of the continent of Atlantis, and the American continent could be seen either as a part of Atlantis or as the "true earth," with the Pacific Ocean the "true ocean." Against historical reality, it was assumed that Columbus himself had read the *Timaeus* and the *Critias*. Thus, there were attempts of the most varied kind to make the new world discoveries comprehensible through Plato, until finally, toward the end of the century (1589), the Jesuit José de Acosta insisted that Plato's picture of the earth was not meant to be real, but "symbolical."

CHAPTER SIXTEEN

Plato as Jurist[1]

BY HUNTINGTON CAIRNS

> Still, quotations from time to time met with, have led me to think
> that there are in Plato detached thoughts from which I might benefit
> had I the patience to seek them out.
>
> HERBERT SPENCER [2]

PLATO took the widest possible view of law. He held that it
was a product of reason and he identified it with Nature itself. Law was a subject which he kept constantly before him, and
there is scarcely a dialogue in which some aspect of it is not
treated explicitly. His theory of law is a fundamental part of his
general philosophy, and it illumines and is illumined by the entire Platonic corpus. Like the law of the Greeks, his legal
thought was never systematized as we have become accustomed
to regard system in law since the last century of the Roman Republic; yet it was remarkably coherent in relation to his major
philosophical ideas. He was a layman in the field, as were all the
Greeks, in the sense that there were no professional lawyers as
we conceive their function today. But in his juristic thinking, he
isolated a range of legal ideas among the most important in the
history of law and which have been the basis of much subsequent
speculation. His influence on the law has been large in both its
theoretic and its practical aspects. The Roman jurists "have
taken many ideas from Plato," said the learned Cujas; [3] and his
influence upon Hellenistic law, and through its practices upon
Roman law, and thus directly and indirectly upon much of the
law of modern times, has even yet not been fully appreciated.

This account of Plato's legal ideas is meant to include a description of his principal theories of law and his application of
them to the practical affairs of society. It endeavors to bring
together in one place the numerous suggestive ideas on the law

scattered throughout the dialogues. His principles are open to much criticism; but as that has been the main business of Platonists and others from Aristotle to the present day, it has here been kept to a minimum. To state as precisely as possible what he thought about a subject to which he gave so much reflection has appeared to be a task of sufficient value in itself. There are numerous points on which it would be profitable to have further information; but, as a general rule, conjectural attempts to repair omissions on the part of Plato have been left to the reader.

The Function of Law

Three hypotheses are assumed as the basis of Plato's thinking about law. They have been championed by influential schools of thought since his day; they have also been the source of much anguish in admirers whose political beliefs are of a different complexion than Plato's. He held that the end of law was to produce men who were "completely good"; that this could be done because, as the institutional idealists of the nineteenth century also asserted, human nature was capable of almost unlimited modification; the method to be used was a benevolent dictatorship: philosophers must become kings, or kings, philosophers. Those hypotheses have received as much attention as anything else in Plato, and it is necessary only that they be properly understood.

As a philosopher, Plato could not accept anything less than complete goodness in men; he therefore rejected all laws that did not incline to that end (630c). "Keep watch on my present lawmaking," says the Athenian, "in case I should enact any law either not tending to goodness at all, or tending only to a part of it" (705E). This is not the place to examine the role of ideals in legal thought, except to observe that the conception men have of a better condition of affairs has frequently been a potent element in lawmaking. Nor is it necessary to examine Plato's views on the relation of law and morals: his legal and moral views are so intertwined as to be inseparable, and lead him upon occasion even to assert that a bad law is no law (*Hippias Major* 284B–E; *Laws* 715B; *Minos* 314E). He was as aware as Hobbes and Aus-tin of the distinction between law and morals, of the idea of law as a command (723A), but he would have none of it (857CD). Although, if men would listen to him, his goals were possible of achievement, he understood fully that his proposal was visionary (632E, 712B), an old man's game of jurisprudence (685A), and he had no expectation that his ideal would be realized in practice. He was merely insisting upon the necessity of abstractions or hypotheses as controls in societal inquiry (739E).[4]

What is perhaps the best defense devised by Platonists for the doctrine of the philosopher-king argues that it represents the principle that government is an art or science as opposed to the politician's idea of government by oratory under law; [5] that it is a recognition of the demand that the state be ruled by the highest available intelligence (711A), and represents only the autocratic discretion of the true shepherd, pilot, or physician; and finally that, though Plato always insisted upon the proposition that it is better for the unwise, whether they consent or not, to be ruled by the wise, in practice he everywhere yields to the reign of law and the consent of the governed (684C; *Statesman* 290D, 296B). A marked feature of Plato's writings is the extraordinary care he takes to limit his proposals by explicit qualification or an ironical turn of phrase. The defense offered for him, therefore, is not an impossible one.

Was Plato hostile to law? That is a necessary question in any account of Plato's jurisprudence. There is no doubt that as a seeker after an ideal, the Plato of the *Republic* preferred the adaptable intelligence of the all-wise autocrat to the impersonality of the rule of law. Through the medium of the fixed, inflexible general rule, laws sought to direct men and actions which were constantly changing and always different. In such a system it was impossible to avoid the "hard case" (*Statesman* 294B). He knew well the simple truth, as the trial of Socrates had shown him, that the debating method of the courtroom was perhaps the least likely to lead to the discovery of truth.[6] Against this, Plato of the *Laws* and *Statesman* had come to realize that on this earth benevolent dictatorship was a counsel of perfection and that he would better propose a solution which had a possibility of realization. In the arts we trust the experts absolutely; but in the realm of government the expert is rarer than in any other art. Plato therefore believed that society should fall back upon law as a second best (875D; *Statesman* 300c), perhaps even as something in the nature of a *pis aller*—the supremacy of the rigid rule being adapted to the "average" man and the general situation and incapable of dispensing equity in the particular case.[7]

Plato thus came to his final view on the necessity of law. He insisted that it was indispensable; without it we were indistinguishable from animals. It was the instructor of youth. Its noblest work was to make men hate injustice and love justice. The laws are intended to make those who use them happy; and they confer every sort of good. It was hard, Plato pointed out, for men to perceive that the preoccupation of social science was with the community and not with the individual; loyalty to the community's interest bound a state together; the pursuit of the individual's interest tore it asunder. Plato stated that it was hard for men to see also that the interests of both alike were better served by the community's prosperity than by that of the individual. There was not a man among us whose natural equipment enabled him both to see what was good for men as members of a community, and, on seeing it, always to be both able and willing to act for the best. Irresponsible power for mortal men always led to grasping and self-interested action; or, as Acton was to rephrase it later, "all power corrupts and absolute power corrupts absolutely." If ever a man were providentially endowed with a native capacity to apprehend the true power and position of the ruler responsible only to Reason he would need no laws to govern him; for no law had the right to dictate to true knowledge. But, as things were, such insight nowhere existed, except in small amounts; that was why we had to take the second best solution—law the generality of which could not always do justice to particular cases.[8]

Anticipating subsequent analysis, Plato considered the suggestions that law is of divine origin and that man's function is to discover its true rules (624A, 835C); [9] that it is a product of impersonal social and natural forces—economic, geographical, and sociological or, as he expressed it, the result of chance and occasion (709A); and that it is an invention of man to meet the needs of society, Art co-operating with Occasion.[10] He accepted all these views as being in some sense partly true; but his ultimate idea was in the nature of a compromise. In his final position he regarded law as the art of adjusting human conduct to the circumstances of the external world. Sometimes, as Montesquieu was later to insist, the conditions of society shape the laws and sometimes, as Condorcet urged, the laws shape the conditions. Plato thus regarded law as both a genetic and teleologic process whose primary function as an art is to correct the inequalities in the relationship between society and its environment (709). Stated concretely, the precise end of law is the achievement of group unity, which cannot be obtained if minority groups are disregarded or by legislating for single classes (664A, 739C–E; *Republic* 419 *et seq.*, 423B, 462CD, 466A). This is the philosophic or highest view, and it leads to the position that if the function of law as the interest of the entire community is observed faithfully, in the end it will yield an understanding of the ideal laws in the world of forms which may then be utilized as models. It is Socrates' opponent in the *Republic* who insists that group unity may be achieved only by means of laws devised in the interest of the governing or stronger group (*Republic* 343B *et seq.*).

Theory of Legislation

At the root of Plato's theory of legislation is the idea, developed later by the proponents of natural law, that the legislator through reason alone is able to formulate a set of rules which will be adequate for the needs of the community. For Plato the legislator is the philosopher in action. He is the man who has seen the reality of the just, the beautiful, and the good. Although the better life of reality is within his power, he must be compelled to live an inferior life and rule the state; this is so since the law is not concerned with the special happiness of any class, but with the happiness of the whole society. Furthermore, he has been engendered as a king-bee and leader of the hive; he has received a better education than the others and is therefore more capable of sharing both ways of life. Down from the clouds he therefore must come. He will obey the command since it is a just one and he is a just man. He will take office as an unavoidable necessity (*Republic* 519c, 521b). The spectacle of a Henry Adams assuming the role of excluded aristocrat and remaining aloof from public office is the antithesis of this view.

In thinking of legislation, Plato followed the traditional Greek distinction between written and unwritten law. Antigone's rebuff to Creon was based upon "the immutable unwritten law"; in *Oedipus Tyrannus* the chorus refers to the "laws ordained from above"; in Xenophon unwritten laws are defined as those uniformly observed in every country, and he observes that they must have been made by the gods inasmuch as men could not all meet together and do not speak the same language.[11] Plato thought the unwritten law was not law strictly so called but that it was nevertheless important.[12] The Anglo-American conception of the unwritten common law and the Continental doctrine of unwritten law, which attaches to the monarchical tradition and is administered by the executive department as distinguished from the courts, approximate but do not equal Plato's idea. Unwritten law represents specifically the rules or regulations founded upon immemorial tradition and social usage. Law is like a stubborn and ignorant man who allows no one to do anything contrary to his command, or even to ask a question, not even if something new occurs to someone which is better than the rule he has himself ordained. Human life is not simple, but the law, which is persistently simple, aims, nevertheless, to control that which is never simple. Unwritten law helps to make up this deficiency. Plato indulged in a riot of metaphors to describe it. It is the mortise of legislation, the connecting link between the statute laws already enacted and those yet to come, a true *corpus* of tradition, which, rightly instituted and duly followed in practice, will serve as a screen for the statutes already enacted. Unwritten laws are the braces or clamps of metal which keep building stones in position; they are also the main supports on which a superstructure rests.

Plato saw an advantage in reducing these basic laws to writing; for, once put on record in writing, they stay written. It does not matter if a man misunderstands them at first sight, he can study them till he does understand them. The new city which Plato is establishing in the *Laws* will not have an inheritance of immemorial tradition; therefore its legislation must go into petty detail so that the enacted laws will not fail of their purpose.

Thus the legislation of a whole community can be framed by an effort of reason. In later times this doctrine was to appear in modified forms in the theories of Hume, Helvétius, and Bentham. Plato had no doubt that reason could arrive at absolute knowledge and that our errors are the product of our senses and are not due to any infirmity in our reason. Reason is the lord of all things and has produced everything, including law (875D, 890D). Plato liked to believe that the word for "human reason" was etymologically connected with the word for "law" (714A, 957C 4–7). In the sense of the trained philosophic intellect reason is the supreme authority in law. In a metaphor he suggests that men are puppets activated by the strings of desire. The leading string is the golden and holy cord of reason entitled the public law of the state. Man must always co-operate with the golden cord of reason. By this he meant that a careful calculation by the state of the end in view through an estimate of the probable pleasures and pains would result in a law. That is to say, the legislative process, including debate and ultimate agreement, concludes in statutory enactment. Law will thus guide man when he is attracted by the delights of pleasure or repelled by the fear of pain. Law is therefore in a sense the conscience of the state and possesses a direct educational influence. But behind it, as behind education, is the force of reason. It has been conjectured that Homer's picture of Zeus at one end of the golden rope, successfully resisting the pull of all the other gods and goddesses at the other, was perhaps here present in Plato's mind (644–45).

Plato took the traditional moralist's view of legislation: it was to regulate the whole of life. At the same time he recognized that mischief is done by making trifles penal, thus bringing fundamental laws into contempt (788B; *Republic* 425B). Nevertheless, there was little that was not subject to legal regulation in Plato's opinion: marriage, procreation, development of the citizen from infancy to old age, distribution of wealth, price-fixing, all relations between the citizens, shipping, merchandising, peddling, the control of emotions, innkeeping, the regulation of playgrounds, mines, loans and usury, the supervision of farmers, shepherds, and beekeepers, including the preservation and supervision of their instruments, the appointment of magistrates, every activity in fact that entered Plato's mind, concluding with the burial of the citizen and the celebration of the appropriate funeral rites and the assignment of proper marks of respect (780A, 631–32, 842CD). Plato found it unnecessary to enumerate all the laws which the legislator must promulgate. The enactments he proposed were in part intended to illustrate a theory of legislation. "I want to show," the Athenian says,"that there is a philosophy of law, a system, in the ordered code, to be discerned by the philosopher, and even by those who have lived under a perfect code: how it enables a man to judge of the relative importance and proper function of various enactments" (632D).

At this point in his thinking Plato made a great leap into the future. He clasped hands firmly with Bentham. Under the influence of Newton, Bentham attempted to discover principles which would direct him in the construction of a complete and systematic code. In that field he believed that the equivalent of the Newtonian physical laws were the principle of utility and the principle of the association of ideas. Plato had precisely the same objective in view, and the results of his efforts are an extraordinary anticipation of Bentham. He pointed out that existing codes were arranged by topics and that consequently the legislator, when he wished to provide for a situation which the code did not cover, was compelled to confine himself merely to tacking new provisions on to the appropriate chapter. In the matter of fraud, for example, the legislator in utilizing this method was in very truth trying to cut off a Hydra's head (*Republic* 426E). "Whatever kind of law any lawmaker finds to be needed," the Athenian remarks, "nowadays he devises, and adds it to its class: one adds a section on estates and their heiresses, another on unlawful beatings" (630E). Plato thought, as Bentham was to do later, that an orderly and exhaustive code could be framed on the basis of a principle rather than by the hit-and-miss method of existing procedures. As that principle he proposed nothing less than a form of the felicific calculus itself. "Two considerations," he wrote, "go to the foundation of the philosophy of law: (1) What pleasures ought not to be sought? (2) What pains ought not to be avoided?" (636DE). The measure of the legislator's ability was a direct function of his capacity to answer those two questions. Furthermore, the legislator was to keep his feet on the ground. His legislation must be definite. "He must often ask himself these two questions: first, 'What am I aiming at?' and secondly, 'Am I hitting the mark or missing it?' In this way, and this only, he may possibly so discharge his task as to leave nothing for others to do after him" (744A, 719, 769D, 885B, 916E). Pleasure and pain were the stuff with which the legislator had to work; it was to be controlled through habits created by his legislation. It is scarcely necessary to state that the idea of principle in code-making, to the extent envisaged by Plato, still remains in the realm of the philosopher's stone.

As an end the legislator was to have three objectives in view: freedom, unity of the state, and intelligence or temperance among the citizens (701B). Plato thought that liberty and despotism in the extreme were both bad. He concluded that a mixed government was the only salvation. He observed that there were two forms in which statutes could be enacted: a peremptory mandate accompanied with provisions for pains and penalties in the event of noncompliance, or a statute prefaced by a preamble, preparing the citizen's mind for the directions contained in the statute and making him understand its reasonableness so that he will be encouraged to obey it. He compares the preamble to the prelude of a musical composition or song (722D). Statutes will thus have two parts: the "despotic prescription," corresponding to the prescription of the autocratic doctor, which is pure law; and, in addition, the prelude, which is not the text of the law, but its preamble. (The same idea is given explicit application in some of the decree laws of present-day Spain.) The legislator should take constant care to see that all laws have their preambles appropriate to the subject. It would be a mistake, however, to insist on a preamble for minor laws, just as one does not treat every song in that fashion. Whether a particular law needs a preamble must be left to the discretion of the legislator (723).

All this, however, was confusing to fourth-century B.C. Austinians and realists who regarded law as a command and who wanted to know what the law was in fact. The Athenian makes their point fairly. He suggests that if one of the low-class physicians should overhear the educated physician explaining the method of his treatment to a patient his merriment would be instantaneous and loud. "How silly of you! You are *teaching* your patient instead of curing him; he doesn't want to be made into a doctor, he wants to be made whole" (857D). There may be a certain merit in that view; but Plato is not merely legislating; as a matter of fact, he is also teaching. Law for Plato is a form of literature, and the legislator's responsibility is greater than the poet's (858–59).[13] The legislator is himself the author of the finest and best tragedy he knows how to make. In fact, all his polity has been constructed as a dramatization of the fairest and best life, which is in truth the most real of tragedies (817B). Plato apparently intended his code to be studied as a textbook (810B, 811D). Bentham also suggested that the father of a family might teach Bentham's code to his children and give to the precepts of private morality the force and dignity of public morals.

Plato based the duty of obedience to law on the idea of good faith and, to some extent, on the notion of honor, i.e., the moral worth a man possesses in his own eyes and in the opinion of society. He valued obedience to legislation highly, for he held that the man whose victory over his fellow citizens took that form had the best claim to rule (715C, 762E). This view differs radically from a modern one, which, however, is still a paper expression in the attitude of governments generally, that legislation must secure allegiance through its inherent qualities. For Plato the issue was raised in a concrete case by the trial and condemnation of Socrates (*Crito* 49E *et seq.*). Kriton suggests to his friend, Socrates, who is in prison awaiting execution, that his escape can be arranged. Socrates refuses to disobey the law and thus wrong his country, even though the law has wronged him. He states simply that a man ought to do what he has agreed to do, provided it is right; he ought not to violate his agreements. The state cannot exist if its laws are flouted and the decisions of its courts made invalid and annulled by private persons. That is true even if the state has wronged the citizen and has not judged the case rightly. By his lifelong residence in Athens, Socrates has impliedly promised obedience to the laws. There is no equality of right between legislation and the citizen, any more than between the father and child, the master and servant. The child if he is punished does not hit the father in return; nor does the good citizen undertake to destroy the laws if his country undertakes to destroy him. Socrates has always had the opportunity to move to another country if the Athenian laws displeased him; failing to do that he has confirmed his promise to obey. If he disobeyed the laws of his country and escaped to Thebes or Megara, he would properly be regarded as the enemy of law everywhere. This argument, it has been observed, leaves open the question whether it is wrong to disregard the sentence of an incompetent court. In Socrates' case the court was without jurisdiction; but the court thought itself competent, and Athenian law had no provision for the quashing of findings as ultra vires; apparently Socrates thought that private judgment should not pass on the question of jurisdiction.

Elsewhere, Plato gives full expression to the idea, and fights against it most vigorously, that law is a convention devised by the weak to suppress the strong and regulate their conduct (714, 890A; *Gorgias* 483D, 488E; *Republic* 359A). Law in that view is nothing but arbitrary power, and whether it should be obeyed is dependent solely upon one's capacity to flout it. Again, Plato suggests that when the citizens consent to the authority of a code of laws as a substitute for the personal rule of the minority, there is apt to be greater unity in the state (627DE). That unity implies that the majority realize that it is in their own interest to obey the laws. Society does not act against its own will when it obeys its laws; when it does obey unwillingly they will be soon abolished (*Republic* 359 *et seq.*). He believed that once general respect was secured for a particular law, it would be implicitly obeyed. The difficulty was that public opinion is apt to stop halfway, when the progress of the law in question is thwarted by some passionate feeling on the part of large numbers of the population. For instance, the difficulties attending the establishment of common meals were overcome in Sparta for men; but the obstinate hostility of the women made its extension to them seem an impossibility (839CD).

In the myth of the ring of Gyges, which made its wearer invisible, Plato attempted to answer the current argument that everyone would break the law if he dared, that law observance rests entirely upon force. If two men were each given such a ring, the honorable man could readily be distinguished from the dishonorable one (*Republic* 359D *et seq.*). It is the ideal which makes all the difference for Plato. Without it law becomes merely a matter of force; with it the noblest and best life is possible for all members of the community and law itself becomes, in the Platonic scheme, in itself a good. As a practical philosopher, however, he knew how much depended upon the co-operation of the citizen. "Unless private affairs in a state are rightly managed," he wrote, "it is vain to suppose that any stable code of laws can exist for public affairs" (790B).

The Judicial and Administrative System

Athenian justice was held in great contempt by Plato, and there are many indications throughout his writings that he gave much thought to its reform. He had grown to manhood in the atmosphere produced by the disastrous Sicilian expedition, when the Athenian Empire was falling apart. The large jury courts of Athens were judges of both law and fact, were unrestrained by precedent, and were swayed by the gusts of sentiment which moved the populace. In the end they became instruments of political blackmail and judicial murder—evidence of the disintegration of the state. Plato was present at the condemnation of Socrates, and the failure of the court to observe even the ordinary decencies of a fair trial, such as patience and the preservation of order in the courtroom, did not pass unnoticed in his description of the proceedings. When the multitude—that great beast, as Plato calls it—are seated together in the courtroom, and with loud uproar censure some of the things that are said and done and approve others, both in excess, with full-throated clamor and clapping of hands, in such a case, asks Plato, what is the plight of the young man? What private teaching will hold out and not be swept away by the torrent of censure and applause, and borne off on its current, so that he will affirm the same things that they do to be honorable and base, and will do as they do, and be even such as they? A chief count against courts was that they were exclusively places of punishment and not of instruction (*Apology* 26A; *Republic* 492B–D). Plato, after long experience with the Athenian courts, became convinced that only drastic remedies could eliminate the evils which he observed.

As a matter of general principle, Plato held that judges must be men of superior intellect, and that the judicial system must be so constructed that there will be a clear presentation of issues and time for due deliberation (766DE). A true judge, in deciding a matter, ought not to content himself with a safe legal yes or no, but ought to state the principles of his decision. He had no use for courts which were mean-spirited and inarticulate, where the judges never told each other what they thought, and hid their opinions from the public (876B).

Plato followed the distinction of Attic law and divided causes into private suits—where the dispute was between individuals—and public suits—where the wrong was to the state (767B).[14] For private disputes, he proposed a system of three courts: a court of first instance, an intermediate appellate court, and a court of final appeal. The court of first instance was to be arranged by the parties themselves. They selected the judges from among their neighbors and common friends, the people who know most about the matter in dispute. This proposal was no doubt suggested to Plato by the excellent system of public arbitration which prevailed in Athens. The bulk of private suits were assigned to public arbitrators who were selected by lot. They were men in their sixtieth year, experienced and impartial, and their first duty was to effect a compromise. If they failed in this task, they heard the arguments and received the evidence.

An appeal lay from their decisions, but was confined to the record made before the arbitrators, which was placed in a sealed casket until the day of the appellate hearing. Altogether it was an easy and inexpensive method of settling disputes, and the only innovation which Plato introduced was to permit the plaintiff and defendant to select their own arbitrator rather than to depend upon choice by lot. Undoubtedly the capacities of the Athenian public arbitrators varied, and Plato's modification of the system perhaps represented an effort to equalize the inequalities of chance. Plato remarked that if litigants were compelled first to resort to arbitration the issue between them would be sharpened, thus facilitating the work of the courts (767c, 956).

From the arbitrators an appeal, as in Athenian practice, could be taken to an intermediate court composed of villagers and tribesmen. Apparently in these tribal courts Plato had in mind, as a model, the Athenian Dicastery. He insists that all citizens have a share in the settlement of even private disputes; for the man that has no share in helping to judge imagines that he has no part or lot in the state at all. The courts will, therefore, be popular ones, but at the same time they should be neither too large nor too small: "it is not easy for a large body of men to judge well, nor yet for a small one, if of poor ability."

No appeal could be had from the Athenian Dicastery. Plato, however, provided for an appeal from his popular court to a tribunal which was "to be organized in the most incorruptible way that is humanly possible, specially for the benefit of those who have failed to obtain a settlement of their case either before the neighbors or in the tribal courts." The judges were to be selected by the public officials, who were to assemble in a temple and choose from among their own ranks those who had most competently discharged their duties and who appeared the most likely to decide the suits for their fellow citizens during the ensuing year in the best way. When the selection had been made, there should be a re-examination by the electing body itself, and if any name be rejected, another should be chosen in like manner. The hearings of the court should be held publicly, in the presence of the officials who elected it, and any others who wished to attend, and the judge's vote should be a matter of record. This latter provision was a departure from Attic practice, the vote of each dicast being secret. Elsewhere, Plato names thirty-five as the number of judges which should constitute the court (*Letter VIII*, 356DE), but the scheme of the *Laws* apparently contemplated a much smaller court.

Plato's proposals are, with the principal exception of the appellate procedure, an adaptation of Athenian theory and practice. He was convinced of the soundness of the conception that the law could be stated simply enough to be understood by the average man. He believed also that a popular court—one composed, that is, of a fairly large number of citizens—was perhaps the best insurance of justice; and, as Machiavelli was to remark later, a court consisting of numerous judges was a guaranty against bribery. A court as large as the one which tried Socrates, possessing a membership of probably 501, was perhaps too unwieldy for Plato. He compromised by reducing the membership and by adding the element of publicity. To permit an appeal to a court of select judges from the large popular courts, which in Athenian democratic theory were supreme since they were a committee of the sovereign people, was a decided innovation, and Plato endeavored to provide what he thought were necessary safeguards. The judges were subject to fines or impeachment for improper decisions and could be compelled to correct their wrongs. Their one-year tenure of office, while inapplicable to our own professionalized system of law which demands an expertness acquired only after a long period of application, was no detriment to the nonprofessionalized system envisaged by Plato, and which obtained in the Attic world, inasmuch as the emphasis there was on the ascertainment of fact and upon decision according to common-sense ideas of justice.

In matters involving wrongs against the state, Plato thought it was necessary, first of all, to admit the public to a share in the trial; for when a wrong was done the state, it was the whole of the people who were wronged (768A). But, before the case came before the popular court for decision, Plato desired to make certain that it was properly presented and prepared, a situation which did not always exist in the Attic legal system.

So, while it was right that both the beginning and the ending of such a suit should be assigned to the people, the examination should take place before three of the highest officials, mutually agreed upon by both defendant and plaintiff, or by the Public Council if they were unable to agree. The three commissioners would conduct the inquiry and develop the issues by searching questions (766D).

Plato did not overlook procedure (855D–66A). The judges should be seated, facing the plaintiff and defendant, in a closely-packed row in order of seniority, and all the citizens who had leisure to do so should attend and listen attentively to the trials. The prosecutor should state his case and the defendant reply to it, each in a single speech. When the speeches had been delivered the senior judge should first state his view of the case, in which he should review in detail the statements made. When he had finished, the rest of the judges, each in his order, should review any omissions or errors they found to complain of in the pleadings of either party, a judge who had no complaint to make leaving the right of speech to his neighbor. The written record of all statements pronounced to be relevant should be confirmed by the seals of all the judges and deposited on the sacred hearth of the courtroom. They should meet again the next day at the same place to continue the review of the case, and once more affix their seals to the documents. When this had been done for a third time, due weight being allowed to the evidence and witnesses, each judge should give a solemn vote, swearing by the altar to pronounce just and true judgment to the best of his power, and that should be the end of the trial.

Plato evolved a rule of thumb for testing the veracity of witnesses (937C). A single lapse from truth might be due to an unavoidable mistake; two such lapses indicated carelessness—such a man was no good as a witness; three lapses made him a knave. If anyone were unwilling to act as witness, he might be summoned and had to obey under penalty of damages. If he knew the facts and were willing to give evidence, he should give it; if he lacked knowledge, he should take an oath that he had no knowledge and he might then be dismissed. A judge summoned as a witness should not vote at the trial. A woman might act as a witness if over forty; and, if unmarried, might bring an action. If she had a husband alive, she should only be allowed to give evidence. In murder trials, slaves and children might be witnesses provided they furnished bond that they would stand trial for perjury. Evidence might be denounced as perjured provided it was done before the trial was concluded. A new trial should be awarded if found to have been decided on false evidence which influenced the verdict.

Plato thought that life abounded in good things and that a fair judicial proceeding was one of mankind's boons. It was cursed, however, by the art of professional advocacy, which begins by asserting that there is a device for managing one's legal business and that this device would ensure victory equally whether the conduct at issue in the case had been rightful or not. The advocate who defended anyone for pay must be silenced and banished. If any attempted to pervert the influence of justice upon the mind of a judge, or wrongfully multiplied suits at law, or wrongfully aided others to such suits, they should be duly tried and punished. If the culprit acted for the sake of fame, he should be excluded from taking part in any trial, or maintaining a suit of his own, unless twice convicted, in which case he should be put to death; if he acted for money, he should be put to death if a citizen, or banished if a foreigner.

From Attic practice Plato borrowed the idea of a Board of Examiners to watch over the conduct and audit the proceedings of administrative officials and judges (945B–48B). Modern parallels, to some extent, are the American practice of the office of the Comptroller General and the theory behind some congressional investigating committees, but the Platonic suggestion was on a much more elaborate scale. Some officials in Plato's state were chosen by lot, some by election, some for a year, some for a longer period. There were hazards in that method of selection, and the state must have competent examiners in the event any of them acts at all crookedly through being burdened by the weight of his office and his own inability to support it worthily. Plato provides for the election of examiners by a carefully circumscribed method. The examiners, by means of honorable tests, were to judge the official acts and life of public servants. An appeal from their rulings might be taken to the court of select judges which heard final appeals; but if the appeal failed, the penalty (if short of death) was doubled. The examiners themselves were not, however, above suspicion, and Plato provides for an examiner of examiners. That was a special tribunal before which any citizen could bring impeachment proceedings. Conviction involved loss of all rank while alive and loss of the state funeral when dead. If the impeachment proceedings failed to gain one-fifth of the tribunal's votes, the prosecutor was subject to fine. It may be well to emphasize that the judiciary were subject to scrutiny by the examiners and were liable also to actions for damages by suitors for abuse of judicial power—an idea which was to appear later in Roman law and other systems.

Contract and Property

Plato allowed recovery for failure to carry out the terms of an agreement (920D) unless the agreement were contrary to law, or made under duress, or frustrated by unforeseen circumstances beyond the control of the parties—the latter ground being, perhaps, an anticipation of the modern doctrine of "frustration of adventure," which came into being as a result of the circumstances created by the first World War. An action for nonfulfillment of agreement would lie in the tribal courts unless previously settled by the arbitrators. Agreements made with aliens were to be regarded as specially sacred (729E). If a craftsman culpably failed to complete work he had undertaken, he had to produce double value. If work was received which had been contracted for, and the price was not paid within the stipulated time, the price was recoverable twofold with interest for each month that payment was deferred (921).

Plato was never able to develop a law of property adapted to a going society. He knew that the proper distribution of property was vital to the welfare of the state (736E), but his solutions of the problem were limited to the artificial conditions of ideal communities. In the strength of middle age he proposed to abolish private property for the guardians of his ideal state to ensure disinterestedness on the part of the ruling class (*Republic* 416D, 420A, 422D, 464C, 543BC). For the second best state of his old age, he felt that the rule of community property was beyond the capacity of the people who inhabit it and he therefore arranged for the portioning out of the land and houses (740A). He was well aware of the passions which would be aroused in any attempt at redistribution of property; if the legislator endeavored to disturb such things, everyone would confront him with the cry "Hands off" and with curses, with the result that he would be rendered powerless (684E, 736D). To regard other people's property as sacred was, he believed, the basis of mutual trust, and he therefore proposed the following as a comprehensive rule: So far as possible no one shall touch my goods nor move them in the slightest degree, if he has not my consent; and I must act in like manner regarding the goods of all other men, keeping a prudent mind. He laid down the doctrine that the citizen held his lands of the state (740A, 923A), a rule which though latent still obtains in American law. He recognized that the state could impose restrictions on the transfer of property (923A), and he provided for a record office and the registration of title so that legal rights pertaining to all matters of property might be easy to decide and perfectly clear; his system included also the valuation of the property (745A, 754E, 850A, 855B, 914C; 955D).

Plato's fumbling effort at a classification of property was probably caused by the absence of a tradition of theoretical analysis, one of the rewards of professionalization. He was unable to perceive any place for the application of his favorite principle of bifurcation, something which was readily apparent to the Roman and common-law lawyer though that perception was not grounded on a necessarily scientific basis. Since he could not bisect, he divided property "like an animal that is sacrificed, by joints" (*Statesman* 287–89). By this method he obtained a sevenfold classification: implements, materials from which things are manufactured, receptacles, vehicles, articles for defense, playthings, and articles which provide nourishment. Plato observes that "the classification is somewhat forced" but that it took care of all property except tame animals including slaves (776C). He objected to the oligarchic system because it inevitably tended to make property a test of office (698B, 774A; *Republic* 551B).

He attempted no systematic survey of the law of property, but he had made a thorough study of the traditional rules and practices, particularly in the Athenian state. He ventures numerous suggestions. On the troublesome question of boundaries, he provides simply that no man shall move boundary marks of land (842E–44D) [15]; if he does so, anyone may report him, and if convicted, the court shall estimate the damages. Petty acts of annoyance on the part of a neighbor, Plato thought, particularly when they are frequently repeated, engender an immense amount of enmity. Invasions of real property, in Plato's view, were such a source of irritation that he provided that a man must, above all things, take special care not to encroach in the least degree on his neighbor's land. Whoever encroached on his neighbor's ground, overstepping the boundaries, should pay for the damage and, by way of penalty, should also pay twice the cost of the damage. Similarly, a man should be fined for the theft of bee swarms by the rattling of pans, and for injuries caused by fire or by the planting of trees too close to a neighbor's boundary. He also laid down elaborate rules, borrowed from the old laws, on irrigation, well-digging, and damage by flood. If the ownership of lost property was in controversy, it should be produced in court, and the magistrates should try the dispute with the help of the state register of property in case of registry; if it was not registered, the magistrate had to decide the case within three days (914CD).

Plato proposed to abolish the power of testation on the ground that too much indulgence had been paid the dying man's desire to keep his possessions (923A *et seq.*). Let the preamble of the law state: "Poor creature of a day, in your present state you do not know what you have or what you are: you and yours belong not to yourself so much as to your family past and present, and both you and they belong to the state. So I will not suffer you to be cajoled by flattery, or reduced by sickness, into making a bad will: the state's interest must count before that of any individual. Depart from life in peace and charity: leave the rest to us lawgivers." He thereafter makes elaborate provision for the distribution of the deceased's property.

Sale of Goods

Plato's proposals for regulating sales of goods lack the concrete richness of the case law of sales. Human conduct, when confronted with the complex situation known as the transfer of property in goods, is so charged with the unexpected and the necessary that legislative devices to control it, unless grounded upon an intimate familiarity with actual practice, are apt to miss the mark. Plato saved himself by legislating for a small city-state of quasi-utopian construction, and by confining all transactions to an area of narrow dimensions.

He prohibits altogether certain transactions and methods of acquiring property. No finder of treasure trove shall disturb it, and penalties are laid down for the violation of the rule (913–14B). Similarly, anyone who finds property which has been left behind by another, whether voluntarily or not, shall leave it undisturbed, under penalty; such goods are under the protection of the Goddess of the Wayside (914B–D). Plato's rule of treasure trove and lost property (914E, 916A–C) is regarded by him as applications of the purportedly Solonic maxim: "What thou hath not laid down, take not up" (913C). A contributor to a mutual benefit association may not maintain an action with respect to any dispute arising out of his contribution (915E).[16] Credit sales are frowned upon, and a man must not hand over to the other party his part of the transaction, whether it be goods or money, without getting the equivalent. Thus, a vendor making a sale on credit had to rely upon the good faith of the purchaser for payment. It has been suggested that that is the best way to prevent the creation of debt in a state (742C, 849E, 915E; *Republic* 556A). Runaway slaves may be seized by the owner or by friends or kinsmen of the owner. If a slave is sold and is found within six months to be diseased, or within twelve months to be epileptic, he may be returned unless the purchaser is a physician or a trainer or was informed of the disease at the time of the sale. The purchaser of a murderer had the right to return the slave upon discovery of the fact. If the vendor of a diseased slave was an expert, who could be presumed to have knowledge, he must pay as damages twice the purchase price; if a layman, only the actual price received (914E, 916A–C).

Although Plato believes that the practice of selling goods gives rise to lying and cheating, and that retailers, businessmen, and innkeepers are never content with a reasonable profit, but always prefer to make an exorbitant one, he nevertheless recognizes the necessity of such business; however, this practice is limited to noncitizens (917B, 918D, 920A). Market stewards are to have full charge of all matters which concern the markets, including keeping an eye on outrageous behavior (849A). There must be one fixed price for every article, and that price must be neither increased nor decreased during the day on which it is announced (916–17). The law wardens are instructed to meet in consultation with experts in every branch of retail trade and fix a standard of profits and expenses which is to be prescribed in writing (920C). Retailers must not engage in putting or taking of oaths about anything offered for sale, under severe penalty (917C). Anyone who exchanges for money either money or anything else, living or not living, shall give every such article unadulterated. If anyone gives a security, it must be given in express terms, setting forth the whole transaction in a written record before at least three witnesses if the amount be under 1,000 drachmae, and before not less than five, if over 1,000. The broker in a sale may be held as surety for a seller who does not have good title to the goods sold, or who cannot guaranty delivery, and an action may lie against the broker equally with the seller (954A). Plato's views on those matters represent an attempt to find a compromise between what he felt were the evils of Athenian trade and the necessity, in any state, of permitting the sale of goods. His solution was rigorous supervision, careful limitations, and increased penalties.

Notes on a Penal Code

By the time Plato had come to formulate the penal principles of the *Laws*, he had given much thought to the circumstances under which punishment was justified. His general view was that punishment was warranted only on the assumption that virtue can and must be taught. No one reproves another for an affliction which has come to him by nature or by accident; we have only pity for the ugly, the small, or the weak. But we are wrathful and reproving in the case of those who do not possess the qualities that people are supposed to acquire by application, practice, and teaching. That is the idea of punishment. No rational man, he maintained, undertakes to punish in order to avenge himself for a past offense, since he cannot make what was done as though it had not come to pass. He looks rather to the future, and aims at preventing that particular person, and others who see him punished, from doing wrong again. His object in punishing must therefore be both reformation and deterrence; and by necessary implication we must draw the conclusion that virtue can be produced by training (*Protagoras* 323–24c).[17] Plato also insists, from the sociological standpoint, that the wrongdoer is not alone in his guilt; that the entire community, because of its tolerance of bad government and faulty educational practices, is also guilty (*Timaeus* 87B)—a notion which sometimes is put into practice in the execution of Chinese criminal justice.[18] In devising his penal principles, Plato had also to face the difficulty of the proposition which he had maintained a score or more times: that all wrongdoing is involuntary and arises from ignorance since right conduct is happiness, and wrong conduct is unhappiness, and no one therefore would willingly choose wrong conduct which would lead to unhappiness.[19]

Plato felt that it was a shameful thing to have to make criminal laws, since it assumed that the citizens of his state would grow up to share in the worst forms of depravity practiced in other states.[20] The Golden Age was past, however, and he was legislating for mortal men; besides there would be foreigners and slaves in his state who would not have the benefit of a sound education.

Plato's main argument appears to turn on what a present-day lawyer would regard as a distinction between tort and crime; but it is complicated, because the idea was a new one.[21] He was driven to make the distinction because of his assertion that all bad men were unwillingly bad. He found himself differing from popular opinion on that point and on another: it is just, and therefore beautiful, to punish the temple-robber by putting him to death; but punishment is shameful. Plato asserts, however, that if it is proper that the punishment should be imposed, it cannot be improper for it to be suffered. At all times and everywhere legal systems have made the necessary distinction between voluntary and involuntary wrongdoing. Plato could not accept this distinction because it ran counter to his philosophical position that wrongdoing could not be voluntary. What he must do, therefore, is to make clear what jurists really have in mind when they distinguish between voluntary and involuntary acts. His views and those of the jurists would then be reconciled. Plato's resolution of the difficulty was to make a distinction between acts which were remediable in damages and acts which required punishment, between injury and wrongdoing. If an injury had been inflicted, the court must make it good so far as possible; it must conserve what was lost, restore what was broken down, make whole what was wounded or dead. And when the injury had been atoned for by compensation the court must endeavor always, by means of the laws, to convert the parties who had inflicted it and those who had suffered it from a state of discord to a state of unity. If there had been wrongdoing, the guilty person must not only pay for the injury, but must also be punished so that he would not repeat the deed in the future; in other words, the court must teach him virtue, which for Plato is the basis of punishment.

In using the terms "voluntary" and "involuntary," Plato said that he meant something different from their popular usage. He would never call an unintended injury wrongdoing, as the public did. When someone had involuntarily caused a loss to another, it was a misnomer to describe his action as an "involuntary wrong"; he had merely damaged another. Once this distinction was grasped, it was, of course, important to consider the state of mind of the actor. The degree of his culpable intention must be taken into account. To make the matter clearer, Plato turned to psychology and classified offenses as follows: (1) those due to passion and fear; (2) those produced by pleasure and desire; (3) those prompted by a mistaken belief in what was for the best—which may come from simple ignorance, or from the false knowledge of the powerful or the insignificant. It is plain to perceive in all this, in spite of the obscurities, that Plato was endeavoring to extend his ideas of code-making from the civil to the criminal field, and to devise a penal code based upon rational principles.

He met the weakness of the reformation and deterrent theories—that they justify the punishment of innocent men—by maintaining that before a man can be punished he must by his conduct have done or failed to do some act which in itself called for the application of penal measures (862DE; *Statesman* 297–300). A man should not be punished merely because it might deter those who are likely to be criminals in the future, or merely because it might transform a bad man into a good man. Before a punishment could be imposed there must have been an offense. This view itself ends in difficulties which are still unresolved in penology. The measure of punishment is basically the offense and not the personality of the criminal. If the measurement of punishment is shifted to the criminal's personality, then there is a return to the position that the bad, though innocent, man ought to be punished for his own good; but that is a proposal which few have had the temerity to advocate.

At the head of his list of crimes came sacrilege and treason. The punishment was to be death or a lesser penalty in the discretion of the court, but the punishment should not descend upon the children, unless the father, grandfather, and great-grandfather had been condemned on a capital charge, in which case the children should be deported. For theft, the culprit should pay twice the value of the stolen article; if he was unable to comply with this rule, he must stay in prison until he did so or was released by the prosecutor. In dealing with homicide, Plato distinguished between voluntary, involuntary, and justifiable homicide—the latter class embracing the killing of burglars, robbers, and rapists. He also provided penalties for wounding and beating. He devoted extensive treatment to the crime of outrage, which was generally committed by young men and fell into five groups: outrages against sacred things or places, private shrines and tombs, parents, magistrates, and civil rights of private citizens (884–85A). It was here, for the first time in the Western world, that the idea of the Inquisition was proposed, an institution which would seek out, examine, and punish heretics (885B, 907D–910E).

The Lawyer

The case against the lawyer has not been stated more bitterly than by Plato.[22] Lawyers abounded, he observed, when wealth increased. It was a dishonor to go to court at all. What surer proof could there be of an evil and shameful state of education than the necessity of first-rate judges, not only for the uneducated, but also for those who profess to have had a liberal training? Is it not disgraceful for a man to have to go to others for his justice from lack of such qualities in himself, and thus put himself into the hands of men who become his masters and judges?

A philosopher has his talk out in peace, and wanders at will from one subject to another, not caring whether his words are many or few, if only he attains the truth. But the lawyer is always in a hurry; there is the water flowing through the water-clock to drive him on and not allow him to develop his points at will; there is his adversary standing over him, enforcing his rights; there is the pleading to be read, from which he must not deviate. He is a servant continually disputing before his master, who is seated and has the cause in his hands. As a consequence, he has become tense and shrewd; he has learned how to wheedle his master with words and indulge him in deed; and his character becomes small and warped. His thoughts are never disinterested, because of the issue at stake, which is sometimes life itself. From his youth upward he has been a slave, and that has deprived him of growth, straightforwardness, and independence. Dangers and fears, which were too much for his truth and honesty, came upon him in early years, when the tenderness of youth was unequal to them, and he has been driven into crooked ways; from the first he has practiced deception and retaliation, and has become bent and stunted. Conse-

quently, he has passed from youth to manhood with no soundness of mind in him; but he thinks he has become clever and
wise. His narrow, keen, pettifogging mind reveals its help-
lessness when, divorced from its pleas and rejoinders, it is
brought to the contemplation of the nature of right and wrong
or of human happiness and misery. He can make a fawning
speech smartly and neatly, but he cannot discourse intelligently
on the meaning of the good life.

Conclusion

Kant's comparison of Plato with the light dove piercing the air
in her easy flight and imagining, upon perceiving its resistance,
that flight would be easier still in empty space,[23] has little rele-
vance to Plato's legal ideas. He knew in the long run that practice, at least in the legal world, outweighed theory. His study of
actual laws and procedures was comprehensive and profound; its
penetration is particularly evident in his continued insistence upon the limits of effective legal action. In the history of jurisprudence, however, no one has been more fully aware of the necessity of the reign of law for any state which desires to realize the
ultimate values of happiness and well-being for its citizens. He
had a complete understanding of the function of law as an agency
of social control. His concrete proposals must always be understood in terms of the problems created by his age, and particularly against the background of the waste stretch in Crete, where
his Model City was to be placed. His philosophical statements
about law are another matter. They are theories of law in its
generality and, if they have validity in whole or in part, the
measure of truth they contain is independent of their local setting. Some of his thoughts were never completely expressed,
some were mere asides. Aristotle brought a number of his ideas
into sharper focus; but others were to wait more than two thousand years for their validity to be urged again, occasionally by
men who believed they were stating new doctrines. Whatever
may be the attitude toward the "mystical" or "spiritual" aspects of Platonism, the questions raised by Plato have been
among the most useful ever formulated for jurisprudence. Per-

haps the best evidence of their suggestiveness is the fact that we must go beyond Platonism for the answers. His grasp of legal problems was so acute that it is enough to venture the paraphrase that Western jurisprudence has consisted of a series of footnotes to Plato. The extent of his practical effect on the legal institutions of the thousand or more city-states founded during Hellenic times is still locked in the mysteries of Hellenic jurisprudence. But it is reasonable to suppose that it was considerable. Until Rome conquered, it was a period of great dreams; but, under Roman rule, as has been observed, there was no place for dreams.

CHAPTER SEVENTEEN

Plato as City Planner

THE IDEAL CITY OF ATLANTIS

The Coastal Plain of Atlantis (fig. 10)

WIDTH 3,000 stadia, depth in the inland direction 2,000 stadia (*Critias* 118A). Surrounded by the large irrigation canal (τάφρος), 1 plethron in depth, 1 stadium wide, 10,000 stadia long, i.e., 2 × 3000 + 2 × 2000. This canal meets the city on both sides (ἔνθεν καὶ ἔνθεν) and goes into the sea (118D).

"On both sides" may be interpreted to mean that the town wall touches the main canal; if this were the case, provision would have had to be made for channeling into the ocean, and since a large connecting channel leads from the ocean into the interior of the city (see below), it was sensible to extend this connecting canal through the entire city until it met the main canal surrounding the plain. "On both sides," however, could also be understood to mean that the city cuts into the system of canals rather than touches it tangentially. A. E. Brinckmann (orally) took exception to the latter interpretation because it contains a "penetration," i.e., a baroque and nonclassical motif. Decisive in the same sense is the practical consideration that such a cut would disturb the system of the fiefs (leaseholds). This system (see below) requires an unbroken line of the canal net in pure rectangles.[1]

The rectangular plain surrounded by the great canal is traversed by ditches (διώρυχες). The distance from one to the other is 100 stadia; the width of each ditch approximately 100 feet. The number, therefore, must be 29. In this calculation, Plato did not take into account the space that the widths of the canals would yield (20 × approximately 100 feet).

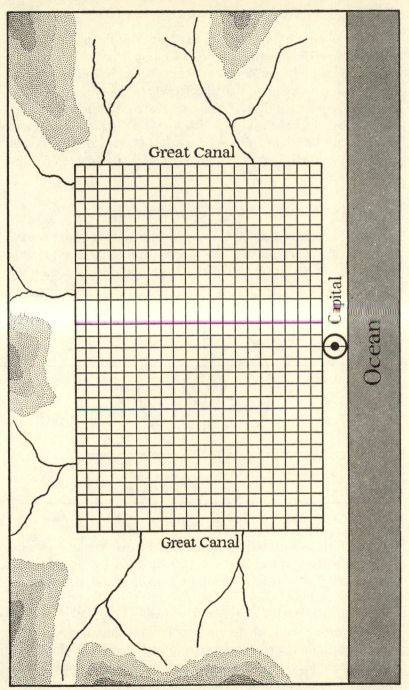

Great Canal

Capital

Ocean

Great Canal

Fig. 10. The coastal plain of Atlantis

Of the ditches going through the length of the plain (διάπλοι πλάγιαι), we know neither the exact number nor whether they extend through the entire plain. It is probable, however, because it is simplest to assume, that they traverse the entire plain and that Plato conceived them at the same distance from one another as the cross-ditches through which they cut. If such is the case, there would be 19 ditches, i.e., a total of 600 squares. Since the entire plain holds 60,000 lots (κλῆροι), each square would comprise 100 such lots.

The City of the Atlantides (fig. 11)

The low mountain that later becomes the middle island is at a distance of "approximately 50 stadia" from the sea (113c). According to an exact calculation, the distance is somewhat

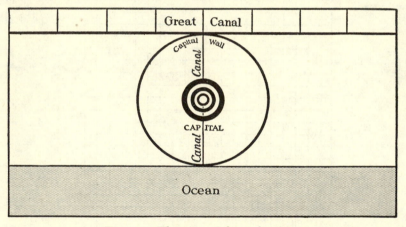

Fig. 11. The city of the Atlantides

greater; for the wall circling the city is at a distance of 50 stadia from the outermost and largest of the three ring-shaped harbor basins (117E). The distance from the middle island, therefore, is exactly 61 stadia.

The circular wall "starts at the sea" (117E); it "closes" (συνέκλειεν ἐς ταὐτόν) where the canal flows into the sea. The circular wall, therefore, touches the coast and at that point, from both sides, approaches the canal, which finds its way into the sea through an opening in the wall.

Interior of the City (fig. 12)

From the sea, a canal 3 plethra wide, 100 feet deep, and 50 stadia long leads to the outermost ring of the harbor. Like the next island ring, the latter is 3 stadia wide, the next water and land ring are each 2 stadia wide, and the innermost water ring is 1 stadium wide (115E). The diameter of the middle island is 5 stadia (116A).

BRIDGES. Bridges extend over the rings of water (115C). It is not immediately clear how many series of bridges there are. It

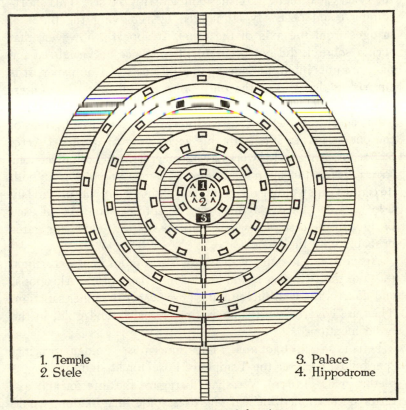

1. Temple   3. Palace
2. Stele   4. Hippodrome

Fig. 12. Interior of the city

is conceivable that there are several, so that the entire system would have the shape of a star. But 116A makes mention of "the bridge" in contrast to "the rings." In this context, then, the entire group is conceived as a single bridge. It is, of course, no contradiction if 115E refers to the three bridges of this tract. But the one reference in the singular that we previously mentioned prevents us from multiplying the number of series.

In the series of bridges (κατὰ τὰς γεφύρας), there is a breakthrough of the earth rings, allowing passage of one galley (trireme).

At this point, we should refer to a passage in which Plato's otherwise so accurately conceived picture lacks accuracy. According to our reconstruction, the last bridge leads straight to the great canal that establishes contact with the sea. This shortcoming could be easily eliminated by removing the flight of bridges from the axis of the canal. It appears, however, that such a solution did not occur to Plato. Since he visualized the picture in his mind, of course, and did not see it on paper, it is surprising that this is the only impracticability we encounter.

WALLS. They surround the central island, the island rings, and "the bridge" (116A), i.e., as we interpret it, the three bridges of the one series. In line with this series (κατὰ τὰς τῆς θαλάττης διαβάσεις), gates and towers have been erected in both directions (ἑκασταχόσε) at or upon the bridges (ἐπὶ τῶν γεφυρῶν). "In both directions" may either mean left and right (what was previously ἔνθεν καὶ ἔνθεν), or it may mean at the entrance and exit of each bridge. In the case of towers, both possibilities exist, for gates probably only the second.[2]

Apart from the outer wall, there is a total of four wall rings, those of the two-ring island and of the island of the Akropolis, and, fourth, the wall surrounding (περίβολος) the inner sanctum. They are covered with copper, tin, orichalch, and gold, in the order mentioned.

BUILDINGS AND GROUNDS. The innermost golden precinct (peribolos) encloses the Temple of Poseidon, 1 stadium long, 3 plethra wide (116CD). We shall disregard the interior and exterior decoration, which, if one uses some imagination, would allow pictorial reconstruction of its own. In front of the Temple is the great altar. The royal palace is situated in the ring between the two walls covered with gold and orichalch respectively.[3]

In the center of the circular island, i.e., the center of town, the sacred law of the state is placed upon a stele or slab of orichalch (119CD).

The central island holds the sources of a warm and a cold spring (113E). Both of them have been made into wells and are surrounded by trees and bathhouses (117A). The water is piped into the grove of Poseidon and across the bridges to the ring islands. (The aqueducts are not included in the sketch.)

Upon the ring islands there are sanctuaries, gardens, and gymnasia. The larger island is subdivided into three rings. The middle ring is the large hippodrome. The houses of the body-guards are located upon the two outer rings. A group of even more faithful guards lives upon the inner ring island, and the most loyal dwell on the Akropolis in the immediate vicinity of the royal palace.

Our illustration does not show the boathouses, which have been worked into the natural rock as chambers, so to speak, on both sides of the ring canals (116A, 117D).[4]

At this point, we shall attempt to support the thesis that Plato's picture of Atlantis is "ideated Orient" (page 203). By way of comparison, let us point to Herodotos' and Ktesias' descriptions of Babylon and Ecbatana or the Egyptian stories of Hekataios of Abdera.[5] In the center of the city of Atlantis, the circular golden wall surrounds the royal palace and the sanctuary. The Temple holds golden statues of gods and is surrounded by statuary and numerous devotional offerings. In front of the Temple is an altar whose size and fine workmanship harmonize with the rest. Babylon consists of two parts. In the center of one of the sections of the city is the royal palace, surrounded by a sturdy circular wall; the other half holds the Temple of Bel with its bronze gate. Inside the Temple is the golden statue of the god; outside, a gold altar and many devotional offerings. The tomb monument of the Egyptian king Ozymandias (Ramses II) includes an altar, built of the finest stone, exquisite in artistic design and execution, and admirable for its size. According to Herodotos, Ecbatana had seven circles of walls, whose turrets were black, white, red, blue, vermilion, silver, and gold; Plato uses the colors black, white, and red for the stones of his buildings and four metals of increasing value, with silver and gold at the end, to cover his wall rings. Like Solomon's Temple of Jehovah or the sanctuaries of Nebuchadrezzar, the Temple of Poseidon is covered with silver and gold.[6] The canal leading from the sea to the city also has a parallel in the canal that, according to Diodoros (Ktesias), Semiramis built from one palace to the other. In both instances, exact measurements of length, width, and depth are given. Many other similarities between individual features of the two cities could be pointed out. More important, however, are the general lines of the blueprint. What distinguishes Babylon, according to Herodotos', or even more Diodoros', description, from all, or at least all the older, Greek cities is the geometric regularity of the ground plan.[7] In the capital of the Atlantides, there is even greater emphasis on this feature, and the square is largely replaced by the more perfect form of the circle. If the regularity of the building plan here extends to the plain with its canals, we are reminded of the canal systems of Babylon and Egypt (Herodotos I 193).

We know that the circular city has a long Oriental tradition. According to Arabic descriptions, Baghdad was a city of circular shape in the early Islamic period. Compare the reconstruction of Herzfeld and Sarre, in whose work (p. 132) the circular city plan is traced back to the Persian ruin Quala i Darad from the Arsacid period, and further to Hatra in the first century B.C., and to Zinjirli approximately 1000 B.C. The circular army camps of the Assyrians fit into the gap between the periods of Zinjirli and Hatra. Still much earlier than Zinjirli is Tepe Gawra in northwestern Iraq, "a mound that had already been abandoned by 1500 B.C. and twenty occupational levels below it. At the eleventh level a circular citadel in excellent condition was found that combined the purposes of fortress and temple."[8] Herodotos describes the walls of Ecbatana as "rising in circles, one within the other. . . . The number of the circles is seven, the royal palace and the treasuries standing within the last." The similarity with Plato's imaginary construction is obvious.[9]

It would be impossible to determine with certainty whether the system of Hippodamos of Miletus has any connection with these Oriental city constructions.[10] But is it not rather improbable that a Milesian architect should have overlooked such Oriental models, on which, after all, Herodotos of Halicarnassus reported? Aristophanes has the Athenian emigrant counseling the birds to build one city and "to encircle the air with large bricks after the model of Babylon" (*Birds* 550ff.). Then the mathematician and astronomer Meton holds forth on the circular-square plan according to which the birds' city is to be constructed, with a radial system of streets focused in the central market place (1004ff.). Aristophanes felt justified in expecting his audience to recognize the Hippodamic principle of architecture and even to understand the reference to its Oriental model. The principle, after all, was known to every Athenian, since it had found practical application in the Piraeus. Aristotle calls it "the modern or Hippodamic style of architecture" (*Politics* VII 11 1330[b] 17 *et seq.*) and regards it—we in the United States might agree—as an expression of the democratic spirit in contrast to the "oligarchical" city plans of older periods. Aristophanes' comedy was written during Plato's youth (414), and Hippodamos certainly must have impressed Plato as much as he later impressed Aristotle—Hippodamos, whose mind combined mathematical constructions of cities and Utopian state planning, so that the Pythagoreans of southern Italy had good reason for regarding him as one of them.[11] The Hippodamic system, to be sure, is as far removed from what Plato, the Utopian builder of cities, visualized with such remarkable clarity as was the democracy of the fifth century from the imaginary picture of a centralized monarchy, in a fantastic distance of space and time.[12]

The city of Atlantis is a strictly Platonic construction; yet it cannot be understood if one does not at least try to place it in the history of architecture. Just as it must have its predecessors, so it must have had its repercussions. Herter has called attention to such a later model in the Villa of the Emperor Hadrian at Tivoli.[13] "The so-called Natatorio or Teatro Marittimo of Hadrian's Villa is a circular stone island, surrounded by a circular canal, which, in turn, is surrounded by a circular hall of about the same width. The island character of the center was accentuated by the fact that there were only drawbridges, two of them, which when pulled up left the Ritiro in complete seclusion.". This is a significant analogy, and it is most unlikely that the similarity is merely accidental, even though "Hadrian's work remains a romantic play which reduces the gigantic dimensions of Plato's fantasy to very small proportions." The only possibility of interpreting Herter's discovery differently would be to suppose that Plato's construction did not have a direct effect upon Hadrian or his architects, but that some unknown monuments of Hellenistic architecture may have been intermediaries between Plato's model and this miniature copy. The palace of King Herod at Masada west of the Dead Sea contains a strange construction of a not quite dissimilar kind: two circular homocentric walls are surrounded by rectangular building foundations.[14]

In conclusion, we should at least raise the question whether Plato's Atlantis influenced the Renaissance constructions of the ideal city. Brinckmann thinks it probable that it did.[15] If we look at his illustrations, we are struck a great deal more by the affinity of spirit animating the styles than by the adoption of individual motifs. Nor have I found any specific resemblance in Filarete's theoretical writings. What the architects of the Renaissance have in common with Plato is the subjection of pure geometrical form to a ruler's will. In their constructions, for example, a dome-topped building or a fortification tower dominating the radial system of streets may correspond to the slab bearing the sacred law in the center of the whole. The analogies are as characteristic as the differences. If we consider, however, that Plato's architectural constructions were not ends in themselves but tools for his political Utopia, we shall not be able to separate the Renaissance architectural plans for ideal cities entirely from the Utopias of More, Bacon, and Campanella. In another sense, then, the architects too may be said to form part of the Platonic succession.

CHAPTER EIGHTEEN

Socrates Enters Rome[1]

Georgio Lincoln Hendrickson
hoc caput manet dedicatum

I

IT IS our great fortune, and certainly no mere accident, that Polybios' famous pages on the education and character of the young Roman who later became Scipio Africanus Minor are preserved among the excerpts, made at the command of Konstantinos Porphyrogennetos, in the volume *On Virtues and Vices*.[2] If they were lost we should still possess a shadowy reflection of them in Diodoros (XXXI 26 *et seq.*) and perhaps a still more shadowy and distorted one in Pausanias (VII 30 9). We should have found reflections in Plutarch's biography of Scipio and in Livy's and Cassius Dio's relevant chapters, had they come down to us. For the impression made by those pages of Polybios must have been deep. Though formally a "digression" (παρέκβασις, XXXI 30 – XXXII 16), they were meant to impress upon the reader the conviction that without this formative influence on Scipio's personality the course of the Scipionic period would have been different. Their importance is made clear by two facts: the author had already prepared for them in an earlier passage, now lost, to which he deliberately refers at the beginning; and at the end of the episode he emphasizes that it is meant to enhance the credibility of what he is going to narrate in the following books—achievements that one might easily, if wrongly, attribute to chance, though they were founded on principles (κατὰ λόγον γεγονότα). There can be no doubt that in these later parts Polybios must have pointed back, at least implicitly, to the pages under discussion, and we have actually one chapter (XXXV 4) treating of young Scipio's early deeds in Spain: here he is praised for exactly the same virtues—self-control and fortitude—that we shall presently find in our "digression." It is quite possible that a passage in Cassius Dio's *History* (XXI 70 4) on Scipio's character and achievements also preserves something from those later books of Polybios, who may have spoken with similar words of Scipio's planning at leisure and his acting on the spur of a moment, his devising comprehensive plans of war and his personal boldness in action, his scrupulous rectitude, his moderation and amiability, his readiness for all occasions.

The theme of the digression is twofold, as Polybios himself states at its beginning, and as he must already have made clear when he prepared for it in the preceding book. The first point is "how Scipio's reputation in Rome spread so far and became so brilliant at an unusually early time of his life"; the second, "how this friendship with Polybios grew so great that it became known in Italy and Greece and even beyond." According to these outlines—though in reverse order—the author gives first his famous conversation with young Scipio, then a detailed analysis of Scipio's character and its unfolding.

These two parts are joined together by a double link, the first element of which is with good reason considered as the conclusion of Part I, the second element as the beginning of Part II. In both linking sentences the emphasis is first on the beginning of the friendship: "from this mutual agreement on" and "from this time on"; in both he goes on to stress the continuity of the intercourse: "the young man was inseparable from Polybios" and "they constantly lived in an active communion"; and finally, while the first dwells on the highest value of this companionship for young Scipio, the second characterizes their mutual love as one between father and son or near relatives. Immediately afterward, the analysis of Scipio's character begins. One can hardly doubt that the foundation of the friendship between the older and the younger man and the formation of the latter's character are meant to be closely connected. A symbol of this connection may be the fact that the above-mentioned starting point "from this agreement on" and "from this time on" is later referred to by the comment: "during the first five years Scipio's renown for *sophrosyne* became widespread," the "five years" apparently being counted "from that agreement on."

What is the main point in this first decisive conversation? The young Roman asks the Greek gentleman whether he, too—like most of the others—thinks of him as overquiet and inactive; in a word, as un-Roman. Polybios answers that his very concern proves his "high-mindedness." He presents himself as the one who could help the young man "to speak and to act in a manner worthy of his ancestors"—he might well have said, who could help him to consummate that "high-mindedness." And Scipio emphatically echoes the very words his friend had chosen: "worthy of family and ancestors."

So much for the leading concept in Polybios' conversation with Scipio. Now what are the main points in the following analysis of Scipio's character? It divides into three parts, dealing first with his moderation or self-control or however one may render the untranslatable σωφροσύνη; second, with his high-mindedness in money affairs; and third, with his fortitude. Σωφροσύνη, identified with εὐταξία, good order (of the soul), (inner) discipline,[3] apparently is the foundation of virtue in general; and this is the reason why, after contrasting Scipio's self-control with the ruling dissoluteness of his period, Polybios ends this part of his analysis by borrowing the words ὁμολογού-μενος, "co-ordinated," and σύμφωνος, "harmonious," from the Stoic vocabulary, in which both were used to define "virtue."[4]

The second part of the moral analysis deals with Scipio's high-mindedness and integrity in money affairs. This virtue Polybios traces back, first to his natural gift, and then to the influence of Aemilius Paulus, and, at the end, he identifies it with *sophrosyne* and *kalokagathia*, so that the second part appears closely connected with the first; after all, it is the same virtue which shows in his hatred of lust and in his quite un-Roman generosity.

In the third part, Scipio's fortitude becomes the leading concept. The practice of this virtue is traced back to the young man's passion for the hunt, and here again, as in the field of high-mindedness, the father is the guiding force. But toward the end, Polybios himself steps in as the one who shared, and therefore strengthened, that enthusiasm.

This short survey will have revealed one apparent lacuna in the author's analysis. At its very beginning, in dealing with *sophrosyne*, he refrains from stating who was responsible for Scipio's devotion to this first and basic virtue. But he need not have done so expressly; he had just spoken about the young Roman's inseparableness from himself and about their mutual love as between father and son. Probably no one has ever failed to realize, when he read the next sentence, that it was Polybios himself who had guided Scipio's zeal for *sophrosyne*. It now becomes evident, if it was not so to begin with, how the two main parts of the digression—the establishment of Polybios' and Scipio's friendship and the analysis of Scipio's virtues—are linked together. Polybios' educational influence accounts more than anything else for the consummation of Scipio's natural gifts.

II

It was Mommsen's opinion that "Plato and Aristotle . . . remained without essential influence on the Roman culture." [5] This study, however, will add new evidence to E. K. Rand's conclusion, so surprising at first sight: "Plato was invisibly but potently one of the builders of Rome." [6]

I wish to point out a marked resemblance between that colloquy of Polybios and Socrates' unforgettable conversation with young Alkibiades in Plato's dialogue, the *Alcibiades Major*. Before I call attention to the main points of similarity, let it be made clear that this harmony is to a high degree one of opposites. In both cases we find a colloquy of the experienced teacher with the young man who is to be his pupil—the most extraordinary of his pupils. The teacher is, in the one case, the man of action whom fate turned into an observer and historian; in the other case, Socrates. The young men are destined to be, the one the greatest statesman of the Roman republic, the other both the most brilliant political figure of Athens and its destroyer.

1. In both cases there is a resolution of a remarkable tension. Polybios' intercourse with the two sons of Aemilius Paulus had

already lasted some time, yet young Scipio felt neglected and one day asked Polybios why he always conversed with his elder brother and paid no attention to him. In Plato's dialogue the conversation is opened by Socrates, but he anticipates Alkibiades only by a moment, as the latter is presently made to say. Socrates points out the contrast between the young man's other admirers, who have dropped away, and himself, who has not so much as spoken to him. Alkibiades answers that he was about to ask Socrates why he persecutes him with his attention. It is a decisive moment: in Plato, a long, tense silence is broken by the first colloquy; in Polybios, this first serious colloquy transforms a long and friendly, but in Scipio's opinion quite unsatisfactory, relationship.

2. A characterization of the younger interlocutor follows in both cases. Scipio feels himself looked down upon as unworthy of the family he springs from and asks whether Polybios shares this opinion; whereupon the latter answers that Scipio's very words prove how high-minded (μέγα φρονῶν) he is, and thus Polybios helps Scipio to gain a first insight into his own aims. Alkibiades is characterized by Socrates: he is not only high-minded (μέγα φρονῶν), but he fancies himself to be more than the high-minded ones (μεγαλόφρονες); among other things, he springs from a mighty family; he is also rich, "though this is something of which you seem to be the least proud" (high-minded)—words which (in an opposite vein, to be sure) are similar, even in sound and rhythm, to those in which Scipio is addressed by Polybios: "for it is apparent that you are high-minded because of these things" (Plato, δοκεῖς δέ μοι/ἐπὶ τούτῳ/ἥκιστα μέγα φρονεῖν; Polybios, δῆλος γὰρ εἶ/διὰ τούτων/μέγα φρονῶν).

3. After having characterized Scipio in this manner, Polybios adds: "I wish to dedicate myself to you and to become your helper (σύνεργος) in reaching your goal, which is education toward speaking and acting worthily of your ancestors." And again: "In your present situation you can find no better helper and fellow-combatant than I am." Socrates, after having revealed to Alkibiades his ambitious aspirations, adds in a similar though ironical manner: "You cannot reach your goal without me; nobody else can help you to the power for which you are

striving except me." The expression "helper and fellow-combatant" used by Polybios has its exact analogy not in the *Alcibiades* but in the *Symposium*, where it is again Alkibiades who says to Socrates: "I am striving to perfect myself as much as possible (ὡς βέλτιστον γενέσθαι), and nobody can lend a helping hand better than you." (Plato, τούτου δὲ οἶμαι συλλήπτορα οὐδένα κυριώτερον εἶναι σοῦ; Polybios, δοκῶ μηδένα συναγωνιστὴν καὶ σύνεργον ἄλλον εὑρεῖν ἂν ἡμῶν ἐπιτηδειότερον.) [7]

4. Scipio, seizing Polybios' hand, expresses his fervent assent: "May I see the day on which you dedicate yourself to me alone and live together with me!" Then, with the repeated "from this encounter on" (ἀπὸ ταύτης τῆς ἀνθομολογήσεως) and "from this time onward" (ἀπὸ τούτων τῶν καιρῶν), their inseparability and mutual affection are made manifest. In Plato's *Alcibiades* one must look to the end of the dialogue for the corresponding moment, as pathetic and enthusiastic as the one in Polybios' *History*—even more so, since it occurs not in second-century Rome but in fifth-century Athens. "From this day on" (ἀπὸ ταύτης τῆς ἡμέρας), says Alkibiades, "I shall be your inseparable companion" (παιδαγωγός), and Socrates confirms this promise with the strong metaphor of the stork's love that hatches love in the stork's children. [8]

5. The new fellowship is directed toward the same aim in Polybios and in Plato, and in both cases it is the young man who expresses the aim. Scipio: "From that moment on (αὐτόθεν) I shall at once think to be worthy of my house and my forefathers." Alkibiades: "I shall begin from now on (ἐντεῦθεν) to strive for justice." The difference of the expression is that between Rome and Athens—the one thinking in terms of ancestry, the other in terms of virtue; but the meaning and even the form are essentially the same.

6. Polybios, in spite of all that had gone before, had yet one scruple "when he reflected on the high position of Scipio's family and the wealth of its members." It is not made clear whether the rank and the riches of the Aemilii might contain a hindrance for Polybios or a danger for young Scipio; probably one as well as the other is meant. Socrates expresses his apprehension unambiguously: "I am afraid," says he, "lest the might

of the state may overpower you and me." Plato puts in Socrates' mouth a prophecy which was fulfilled. Polybios' words sound like a soft echo—they hint at a possible danger that never became reality.

At this point I should like to note that the second part of Polybios' digression also contains at least one strange similarity to Plato. To be sure, it may be accidental that those three virtues in which Scipio is educated—self-control, magnanimity, and fortitude—occur again in the *Alcibiades* (122c) among others in a long series of virtues that are attributed to the Spartans. The Stoics had similar lists.[9] But it cannot be due to chance that Polybios compares young Scipio's nature with that of a well-bred hound (κατὰ φύσιν οἰκείως διακειμένου καθάπερ εὐγενοῦς σκύλακος), whereas in Plato's *Republic* (375A) the nature of a well-bred watchdog is likened to that of young men of good stock (οἴει οὖν τι διαφέρειν φύσιν γενναίου σκύλακος εἰς φυλακὴν νεανίσκου εὐγενοῦς). Polybios had this passage well in mind. There are others from the *Republic* that he quotes with or without the express remark "as Plato says,"[10] and it is well known that he abundantly uses and criticizes theories from the *Republic* and the *Laws*.[11]

III

The similarities that we have pointed out between the two episodes in Plato and Polybios do exist. How, then, is this relationship to be accounted for? One cannot explain it in terms of literary tradition or literary imitation. For what Polybios tells his readers is not the less but rather the more an exact and highly reliable report because the historian is a participant in the event that he reports.

Two questions must be asked: Can it be established as probable that Polybios knew Plato's *Alcibiades Major*, or at least as improbable that he did not know the dialogue? And in this case, how can one understand the strange fact that an unquestionably historical event bears definite resemblance to a literary model?

To turn to the first question first, it is known—and we have already stated before—that Polybios was well acquainted with Plato's philosophy, most of all with his great political works, probably at an early period of his life. His intimacy with the Academy dates back to his years in Arcadia, whereas he probably was not steeped in the Stoic doctrine before he met, in the Scipionic circle, that great Stoic and humanistic philosopher, Panaitios.[12]

But Polybios not only quotes, uses, and criticizes Plato freely; he enters into a competition with him. Referring to the central postulate of the *Republic* (473CD, 479BC), the identity of ruler and philosopher, he demands in almost the same words that the active statesman write history or that the historian have an active role in the state: "Until this happens there will be no end to the ignorance of the historians." He himself is convinced that in his person are merged the philosopher and the statesman, the statesman and the historian, and his very wording shows how strongly he felt himself to be on a par with Plato—whereas his antagonist Timaios was in his judgment "an unphilosophical and entirely uneducated writer" (ἀφιλόσοφος καὶ συλλήβδην ἀνάγωγος συγγραφεύς, XII 25 6).

It seems to be a modern point of view to single out the statesmanship and generalship of Polybios and to minimize his philosophic thought.[13] He himself felt differently; and it may be said in general that there has never been a great historian without a metahistoric philosophy.

Philosophy, for Polybios, is linked, almost to the point of identity, with education, culture, παιδεία. Censuring King Prusias as "cowardly and wanton" (δειλὸς καὶ ἀσελγής),[14] he traces these defects to a lack of "education and philosophy" (παιδείας καὶ φιλοσοφίας), for Prusias knows nothing of the theorems, or visions, or intuitions (θεωρήματα)—which apparently are the result of philosophic training—and has no notion of "what the beautiful is" (καλὸν τί ποτ' ἔστιν), where the very formula testifies to the philosophic, in the last instance Platonic, schooling of the man who uses it. Scipio, in sharp contrast to Prusias, combines the virtues of self-control (σωφροσύνη) and valor (ἀνδρεία). He owes them, after his natural gifts and the example of his father, to the formative influence of the historian's "education and philosophy." Thus we must judge in reading Polybios, and this was the judgment of Diodoros (XXXI 26), who still possessed his entire work. Scipio, he relates, was from his youth steeped in Greek education. At eighteen he began to devote himself to philosophy, having as his "tutor" (ἐπιστάτης) Polybios of Megalopolis, the historian. Appian, too (*Punica* 132), commenting on the conversation of the two men in view of Carthage's smoking ruins, simply calls Polybios the "teacher" (διδάσκαλος) of Scipio.[15]

Polybios, the admirer of Rome, the first to carry to the world abroad the right estimate of Rome, nevertheless criticized one thing in Roman life: the lack of education (Cicero, *De re publica* IV 3 3: "*disciplinam puerilem ingenuis . . . in qua una Polybius noster hospes nostrorum institutorum neglegentiam accusat*"). But in what sense could he speak thus? He knew very well the training of the young Roman in the juridical and political life of the forum under the supervision of an elder statesman. This, consequently, was not the thing he felt to be missing. This sort of practical training, culminating in lawsuits and political handshaking, he directly contrasts with the form of life of young Scipio. What the Romans lacked and what Scipio was the first to be imbued with are "philosophy and culture." His education, then, was not an isolated happening. It was a work that Polybios, aided by Panaitios, carried on among the young generation of the Roman nobility. "Your Plato," says Laelius to Scipio in Cicero's dialogue *De re publica*, exactly where Roman education is the point in question (IV 4); "our Plato," says another person of the dialogue, probably Scipio, still in the same context (IV 5). For, after all, it was Plato—though Plato himself would have said, "Not I but Socrates"—who was still the highest educational force in Greece and who became this force in Rome through the agency of Polybios. One cannot express it with plainer words than Cicero does again in the same work (III 5 3), when he puts in the mouth of one of the interlocutors the formula: "Scipio and his friends added to the native usage of our ancestors the teaching of Socrates coming from abroad" ("*ad domesticum maiorumque morem etiam hanc a Socrate adventiciam doctrinam adhibuerunt*").

Philosophic communication—this was what Polybios himself had absorbed as a living Greek tradition. Its greatest representation in literature was for him, as for everyone, the work of Plato; its unequaled living master had been—no, still was—Socrates. Is it, after all, likely that Polybios had studied not only the *Republic* and the *Symposium* but also the *Alcibiades Major?* One ought to prove rather that the widely read historian did *not* know the work among Plato's dialogues which bears the most fatal name of Greek history, a name so famous even among the Romans that at an early period they erected the bronze statue of Alkibiades when an oracle had told them to honor the most valiant of Greeks (Plutarch, *Numa* 8). Polybios must have seen this monument in the forum. He could not have overlooked the dialogue that the entire classical world read among Plato's writings, and that the Academy, at least the later Academy, used as the "entrance gate" to Plato's philosophy: *Alcibiades, or Concerning the Nature of Man.*[16]

How, then, can one explain the strange similarity between the historical event that Polybios narrates and the scene shaped in Plato's imagination? That conversation of the year 167/6 B.C. remained sharply outlined in the memory of the historian. Is it necessary to say that, fortunately, we have no phonographic record of it, but its condensation in a great piece of historic art? The event, probably at the very moment when it happened, and certainly at a later time when it was written down, evoked the scene from Plato's dialogue in Polybios' mind. He saw Scipio and himself as the more fortunate counterparts of Alkibiades and Socrates. The educational work that he accomplished with the son of Aemilius and consequently with the young Roman nobility he felt to be initiated, directed, and sanctioned by the great example. And he was not mistaken, of course. The power that was Socrates, recorded by Plato's art, had engendered both an event of the highest historical importance and "one of the most delightful passages in all ancient history."[17] Polybios was at once the Socrates who acted in this event and the Plato who described it.

For the first time, the Socratic-Platonic force had crossed beyond the borders of the Hellenic world.

NOTES AND ABBREVIATIONS

ABBREVIATIONS
with List of Periodicals

AA = Archäologischer Anzeiger (Supplement to the *Jahrbuch des Deutschen Archäologischen Instituts*). Berlin.

AbhBerl = Abhandlungen der Preussischen Akademie, Phil.-hist. Kl. Berlin.

AbhLeipz = Abhandlungen der Sächsischen Akademie der Wissenschaften. Leipzig.

AbhMun = Abhandlungen der königlichen Akademie der Wissenschaften. Munich.

AeR = Atene e Roma. Florence.

AfB = Archiv für Begriffsgeschichte. Bonn.

AfP = Archiv für Philosophie. Berlin.

AJP = American Journal of Philology. Baltimore.

AM = Athenische Mitteilungen (*Mitteilungen des kaiserlich deutschen Archäologischen Instituts,* Athenische Abteilung). Athens.

Ancilla = Kathleen Freeman, Ancilla to the Pre-Socratic Philosophers. Oxford and Cambridge, Mass., 1948.

Antike, Die. Berlin.

ArchRW = Archiv für Religionswissenschaft. Freiburg i. B.

BCH = Bulletin de correspondance hellénique (École française d'Athènes). Athens.

BerLeipz = Berichte der Sächsischen Akademie der Wissenschaften, Phil.-hist. Kl. Leipzig.

Bulletin de l'Association Guillaume Budé. Paris.

CP = Classical Philology. Chicago.

CQ = Classical Quarterly. London and Boston.

CW = Classical Weekly. Pittsburgh.

DLZ = Deutsche Literaturzeitung. Berlin.

Ethics. Philadelphia.

Gnomon. Berlin.

Gymnasium, Das. Heidelberg.

Hermaion. Lwow.

Hermes. Berlin.

Imago. Leipzig and Vienna.

HJGörres = Historisches Jahrbuch des Görres-Gesellschaft. Munich.

HSCP = Harvard Studies in Classical Philology. Cambridge, Mass.

JDAI = Jahrbuch des Deutschen Archäologischen Instituts. Berlin.

JHistId = Journal of the History of Ideas. Lancaster, Pennsylvania.
JHS = Journal of Hellenic Studies. London.
JPhilos = Journal of Philosophy. Lancaster, Pennsylvania.
Klio. Leipzig.
LCL = Loeb Classical Library. London and Cambridge, Mass.
Lexis. Lahr in Bavaria.
Logos. Tübingen.
MémAcInscr = Mémoires présentés par divers savants à l'Académie des inscriptions et belles lettres. Paris.
Migne, *PG* = J. P. Migne, *Patrologiae cursus completus.* Greek Series. Paris, 1857–66. 166 vols. References are to column.
Mind. London.
Mnemosyne. Leyden.
MusHelv = Museum Helveticum. Basel.
Neue Jahrbücher für das klassische Altertum. Leipzig.
NGG = Nachrichten der Göttinger Gelehrten Gesellschaft (der Wissenschaft). Göttingen.
Orientalische Literatur-Zeitung. Leipzig.
PAPS = Proceedings of the American Philosophical Society. Philadelphia.
ParPass = La Parola del Passato. Naples.
PhA = Philosophischer Anzeiger. Tübingen.
Philologus. Leipzig and Göttingen.
Phronesis = Phronesis. A Journal for Ancient Philosophy. Assen, Netherlands.
PhU = Philologische Untersuchungen. Berlin.
Plato 2 = Paul Friedländer, *The Dialogues . . . First Period* (1964).
Plato 3 = Paul Friedländer, *The Dialogues . . . Second and Third Periods* (1969).
PR = Philosophical Review. Ithaca, New York.
RE = August Pauly and Georg Wissowa, eds., *Real-Encyclopädie der classischen Altertumswissenschaft.* Stuttgart, 1894ff. This work, as yet incomplete, is issued in two series, the volumes of the first series (entries beginning A-Q inclusive) numbered consecutively from I onward, those of the second series (entries beginning R-Z inclusive) also numbered consecutively from I onward. References to the A-Q series are given by number of volume only; those to the R-Z series by number of volume preceded by "Second Series"; those to the Supplement by number of volume preceded by "Suppl." References are to columns, not to pages.
RevÉtGr = Revue des Études Grecques. Paris.
RevMet = Review of Metaphysics. New Haven.
RevPhil = Revue de Philologie. Paris.
RhM = Rheinisches Museum. Frankfurt a. M.
RTP = Revue de Théologie et de Philosophie. Lausanne.

SBBerl = *Sitzungsberichte der königlichen Akademie der Wissenschaften* [*Berliner Akademie*]. Berlin.

SBHeid = *Sitzungsberichte der Heidelberger Akademie der Wissenschaften*, Phil.-hist. Kl.

Sokrates = *Sokrates, Jahresberichte des philologischen Vereins zu Berlin*.

StudItal = *Studi Italiani di Filologia Classica*. Florence.

ThLZ = *Theologische Literaturzeitung*. Leipzig.

Vorsokr. = Hermann Diels, *Die Fragmente der Vorsokratiker* 5. 3 vols., Berlin, 1934–38.

WVDOG = *Wissenschaftliche Veröffentlichungen der deutschen Orient Gesellschaft* (Berlin).

ZBud = *Zeitschrift für Buddhismus*. Munich.

ZgN = *Zeitschrift für die gesamte Naturwissenschaft*. Halle.

ZII = *Zeitschrift für Indologie und Iranistik*. Leipzig.

NOTES

A bracketed reference of the style [I²] indicates a previous note where the citation in question is given fully. See also the foregoing list of abbreviations. An asterisk indicates new information, or a new note, in the Addenda to the Second Edition, below, pp. 398ff. Addenda are indexed on pp. 430f.

CHAPTER I

1. *Letter VII* 324B–326B.
2. Goethe, in the essay, "Albert Stapfer, Notices sur la vie et les ouvrages de Goethe," *Werke* (Vollständige Ausgabe letzter Hand, Stuttgart and Tübingen, 1827–34) XLVI, 199; Nietzsche, *The Joyful Wisdom*, § 91, tr. Thomas Common (Works, X, London, 1910), p. 125. / See ch. XIII, "Plato's Letters."
3. Erich Frank, *Plato und die sogenannten Pythagoreer* (Halle, 1923), p. 122. Harold Cherniss, "Aristotle, *Metaphysics*, 987a 32 – b 7," *AJP*, LXXVI (1955), 184ff., correctly upholds the interpretation of πρῶτον in Aristotle *Metaphysics* I 987a 32, as stating a biographical or historical priority, against D. J. Allan, *AJP*, LXXV (1954), 271ff., who finds in it a "logical" priority. In a wider sense, to be sure, Aristotle writes his historical chapters (*Metaphysics* I chs. 3–6) because he is searching for causes and principles, and because he wants to make clear both the discoveries and the shortcomings of his predecessors. See Richard McKeon, "Plato and Aristotle as Historians," *Ethics*, LI (1941), 66ff., esp. 97: "Neither Plato nor Aristotle wrote as historians. . . . Both, as philosophers, tried to relate the philosophers they quoted, not to times and circumstances, but to truth." *
4. Jacob Burckhardt, *Griechische Kulturgeschichte* (4 vols., Berlin and Stuttgart, 1898–1902), III, 393; similarly, the malicious criticism of Plato in antiquity: Athenaeus XI 507D: καὶ τὸ πόλιν δὲ θελῆσαι κτίσαι καὶ τὸ νομοθετῆσαι τίς οὐ φήσει πάθος εἶναι φιλοδοξίας; See on this Johannes Geffcken, "Antiplatonica," *Hermes*, LXIV (1929), 87ff.
5. See Erich Frank, "Plato's View of the State" (1941), in *Knowledge, Will and Belief* (Zurich and Stuttgart, 1955), pp. 120ff. / Ernst Howald, *Die Briefe Platons* (Zurich, 1923), Introd., pp. 39ff., and *Platons Leben* (Zurich, 1923), acknowledges the consistency of Plato's life, but considers it, taken as a whole, to be "a false and erroneous life."

6. Homer, *Iliad* IX 98ff.; Hesiod, *Theogony* 901ff.; *Erga* 256ff.; Herakleitos, in *Vorsokr.* 22 [12] B 44, 114 (tr. *Ancilla*, p. 32): ἐξαρκεῖ πᾶσι καὶ περιγίγνεται probably means 'satis superque,' i.e., the *nomos* is inexhaustible. Perhaps we might compare Aeschylus, frag. 10: Ζεύς τοι τὰ πάντα χὤτι τῶνδ᾽ ὑπέρτερον, and also St. Augustine, *Confessions* I 3: *"an imples et restat quoniam non te capiunt?"* / See Wilhelm Dilthey, *Gesammelte Schriften* (8 vols., Leipzig and Berlin, 1914–29), I, 46ff.; Rudolf Hirzel, *Themis, Dike und Verwandtes* (Leipzig and Berlin, 1907); N. D. Fustel de Coulanges, *The Ancient City*, tr. Willard Small (12th edn., Boston, 1901); Werner Jaeger, "Die griechische Staatsidee im Zeitalter des Platon," *Humanistische Vorträge* (Berlin, 1937), pp. 93ff.; M. P. Nilsson, *Greek Piety*, tr. Herbert J. Rose (Oxford, 1948), pp. 55ff.; Friedrich Solmsen, *Hesiod and Aeschylus* (Ithaca, N. Y., 1949), pp. 89ff.; A. E. Zimmern, *The Greek Commonwealth*[5] (Oxford, 1931), p. 86: "They [men] came together not so much for safety as for Justice. This is the oldest and perhaps the strongest of the city's claims to men's devotion."

7. Anaximander: *Vorsokr.* 12 [2] A 9, B 1 (tr. *Ancilla*, p. 19); Parmenides: *Vorsokr.* 28 [18] B 1, 14; 8, 13ff. (*Ancilla*, p. 41); Herakleitos: *Vorsokr.* 22 [12] B 80, 94 (*Ancilla*, pp. 31, 30).

8. *Dialexeis* ch. 3: *Vorsokr.* 90 [83]; Kritias: *Vorsokr.* 88 [81] B 25; Antiphon: *Vorsokr.* 87 [80] B 44.

9. See Ferdinand Dümmler, *Kleine Schriften* (3 vols., Leipzig, 1901), I, 159ff.; Jaeger, "Die griech. Staatsidee" [I[6]].

10. Dilthey [I[6]], I, 178: "Socrates proved that scientific knowledge did not yet exist in any field." Wilhelm Windelband, *Lehrbuch der Geschichte der Philosophie*[5] (Tübingen, 1910), p. 76, has a chapter heading, "The Problem of Science—Socrates."

11. Theodor Gomperz, *Die Apologie der Heilkunst*[2] (Leipzig, 1910), pp. 3, 134, 155, has collected some material for the history of this simile. But, to be accurate, there is only one instance in Aristotle: *Nicomachean Ethics* VI 1144a 30 (see n. 14 below). In general, see Bernhard Schweitzer, *Platon und die bildende Kunst der Griechen* (Tübingen, 1953), pp. 13f.*

12. Aeschylus, *Choephori* 854 (cf. *Eumenides* 103f.); Pindar, *Nemean Odes* vii 23f.; Parmenides in *Vorsokr.* 28 [18] B 4; Empedokles in *Vorsokr.* 31 [21] B 17; Epicharmos in *Vorsokr.* 23 [13] B 12; Gorgias in *Vorsokr.* 82 [76] B 11 § 13; Ps-Hippokrates, Περὶ Τέχνης § 11 in: Gomperz, p. 52.

13. See my *Der Grosse Alcibiades* (2 pts., Bonn, 1921–23), I, 27f.

14. Aristotle, *Nicomachean Ethics*, VI 1144a 28: ἔστι δ᾽ ἡ φρόνησις οὐχ ἡ δύναμις, ἀλλ᾽ οὐκ ἄνευ τῆς δυνάμεως ταύτης. ἡ δὲ ἕξις τῷ ὄμματι τούτῳ γίνεται τῆς ψυχῆς οὐκ ἄνευ ἀρετῆς. . . . ὥστε φανερὸν ὅτι ἀδύνατον φρόνιμον εἶναι μὴ ἀγαθόν.

15. On the ὄμμα ᾧ ἡ ἱππότης θεωρεῖται, the νοῦς ᾧ τραπεζότης καὶ κυαθότης βλέπεται, in the jocular stories about Plato's arguments with

Antisthenes and Diogenes, see Eduard Zeller, *Die Philosophie der Griechen*⁴ (3 pts., Leipzig, 1888), II, I, 295; Diogenes Laërtius VI 53. There is a similar jest in Lucian's Βίων πρᾶσις § 18, where Socrates behaves as a genuine pseudo-Platonist. Epicurus in Cicero, *De natura deorum* I 8 19 = Hermann Usener (ed.), *Epicurea* (Leipzig, 1887), frag. 367: *"Quibus enim oculis animi intueri potuit vester Plato fabricam illam tanti operis. . . ."* If one deletes *animi*, the edge is taken off the sentence. See Cicero, *Orator* 3 9: ". . . *perfectae eloquentiae speciem animo videmus . . ."*

16. Some material is to be found in Gomperz, *Heilkunst* [I¹¹]. See also Rudolf Bultmann, "Zur Geschichte der Lichtsymbolik im Altertum," *Philologus*, XCVII (1948), 17ff.; Ernst Robert Curtius, *European Literature and the Latin Middle Ages*, tr. Willard R. Trask (Bollingen Series XXXVI, New York, 1953), pp. 145f. Cf. e.g. Cicero, *Orator* § 101, in a Platonizing sentence: *"eloquentia ipsa, quam nullis nisi mentis oculis videre possumus"*; Ovid, *Metamorphoses* XV 63 about Pythagoras: *"quae natura negabat visibus humanis, oculis ea pectoris hausit"*; Ptolemy, *To Flora* 1 7: μὴ μόνον τὸ τῆς ψυχῆς ὄμμα ἀλλὰ καὶ τὸ τοῦ σώματος πεπηρωμένον. (This author also uses Neoplatonic language elsewhere, e.g., 5 7: φῶς αὐτοόν.) I am indebted to Bultmann for this reference, as well as for the following: that in this context the expression ὀφθαλμὸς τῆς καρδίας should be noted, which occurs in the Epistle to the Ephesians 1:18; in St. Clement's First Epistle to the Corinthians; and in the *Hermetica* (here also νοῦ ὀφθαλμοί); see Josef Kroll, *Die Lehren des Hermes Trismegistos* (Münster, 1914), p. 352. Here the East comes into contact with Greece.* For documentation from the mysticism of the Middle Ages, see Grete Lüers, *Die Sprache der deutschen Mystik des Mittelalters im Werke der Mechthild von Magdeburg* (Munich, 1926), p. 129. For a few references from more recent German literature, see Jakob and Wilhelm Grimm, *Deutsches Wörterbuch* (16 vols., Leipzig, 1852–1954), IX, 2863f. See also Hans Leisegang, *Der Heilige Geist* (Leipzig, 1919), I, 216ff.

17. In reference to the following see A. E. Taylor, "The words Εἶδος 'Ιδέα in pre-Platonic Literature," *Varia Socratica* (Oxford, 1911), pp. 178ff. Taylor has collected abundant material for the history of these words; for legitimate objections to some of his interpretations and conclusions see R. C. M. Gillespie, "The Use of εἶδος and ἰδέα in Hippocrates," *CQ*, VI (1912), 179–203. See also Constantin Ritter, *Neue Untersuchungen über Platon* (Munich, 1910), pp. 228ff., and U. von Wilamowitz-Moellendorff, *Platon* (2 vols., Berlin, 1919), II, 248ff. In contrast to the latter, I have attempted to understand Plato's concepts in their most concrete sense rather than in a generalizing meaning.* / Peter Brommer, ΕΙΔΟΣ *et* ΙΔΕΑ, *Étude sémantique et chronologique des œuvres de Platon* (Assen, 1940), tries to prove that the meaning of the two words is quite different, and that they can be used as evidence for a

chronological development of Plato's thought. There is some slight reason for the first point, but no justification for the second. See the reviews of Brommer's book by Harold Cherniss, *AJP*, LXVIII (1947), 126ff. and Bultmann, *ThLZ*, LXXII (1947), 79ff. / On the pre-Platonic use of *Eidos and Idea*, and the "new creation of their meaning by Plato," see Kurt von Fritz, *Philosophie und sprachlicher Ausdruck bei Demokrit, Platon und Aristoteles* (New York and London, 1938), pp. 43ff.

18. These refs. are to Hippocrates, *Œuvres complètes*, tr. (into French) M. P. E. Littré (10 vols., Paris, 1839–61).

19. See Thucydides I 109, with the commentaries.

20. In reference to this passage and what follows see ch. X.

21. Paul Shorey, *The Unity of Plato's Thought* (Chicago, 1903), p. 28: "Except in purely mythical passages, Plato does not attempt to describe the ideas any more than Kant describes the Ding-an-sich or Spencer the 'Unknowable.' He does not tell us what they are, but that they are." Among modern authors Paul Natorp has perhaps given the most profound and impressive interpretation of the *Idea*, in *Platos Ideenlehre*² (Leipzig, 1921), pp. 471ff. Such an interpretation is justified even when, as in this case, the philosophical views of the interpreter are, necessarily, blended with the object of his interpretation.* / On the development of the concept of intuition itself see Richard Hönigswald, *Die Philosophie des Altertums* (Munich, 1917), p. 176.

22. Arthur Schopenhauer, *The World as Will and Idea*, tr. R. B. Haldane and J. Kemp (3 vols., London, 1883), I § 49, p. 302.

23. The following is based on Goethe's paper, "Erste Bekanntschaft mit Schiller," to be found in the "Morphologie" and in the "Annalen," *Werke*, ed. G. von Loeper and others (143 vols. in 4 sections, Weimar, 1887–1919), sec. I, xxxvi, 246ff., 437ff. See Ernst Cassirer, *Idee und Gestalt* (Berlin, 1921). The difference between the *Idea* according to Goethe and according to Plato (emphasized by Cassirer, p. 17) is probably a difference of expression rather than of substance. See also Gottfried Wilhelm Hertz, *Natur und Geist in Goethes Faust* (Frankfurt a. M., 1931), pp. 200f. / See Rupert C. Lodge, *The Philosophy of Plato* (London, 1956), p. 296: ". . . biological science, as such, has finally dropped the Platonic idea from its list of approved principles." —But, maybe, morphology raises its head again? See Wilhelm Troll, *Praktische Einführung in die Pflanzenmorphologie* I II (Jena, 1954, 1957).—"The present-day scientist tries to describe how things behave."—Only?

24. In the section, "Bildung und Umbildung organischer Naturen," under the heading, "Entdeckung eines trefflichen Vorarbeiters," *Werke* (Weimar edn., see n. 23), II, vi, 156.

25. D. J. Allan, "The Problem of *Cratylus*," *AJP*, LXXV (1954), 271ff.

26. Wilamowitz-Moellendorff, *Euripides Herakles*² (2 vols., Berlin, 1895), II, in reference to v. 106.

27. See *Republic* 507ʙ and 597ᴀ. From ὃ δή φαμεν εἶναι ὃ ἔστι κλίνη it is to be inferred that τοῦ ὃ ἔστι ἴσον and αὐτοῦ τοῦ ἴσον ὃ ἔστιν are to be understood as "what the equal [really] is," not "the equal that [really] is."

28. Plato, *Phaedrus* 250c: ὁλόκληρα ἁπλᾶ ἀτρεμῆ. Parmenides: οὖλον ἀδιαίρετον ἀτρεμές. See Natorp, p. 72.

29. *Parmenides* 127ᴅᴇ.

30. Parmenides, *Vorsokr.* 28 [18] ʙ 4 (*Ancilla*, p. 43, nos. 7, 8).

31. Parmenides, *Vorsokr.* 28 [18] ʙ 8, 40 (*Ancilla*, p. 44). The parallelism of this section in Plato with Parmenides seems to prove that Plato understood Parmenides in the same way as Karl Reinhardt does (*Parmenides und die Geschichte der griechischen Philosophie*, Bonn, 1916, pp. 64ff.), not as Parmenides has generally been understood since Jakob Bernays' *Gesammelte Abhandlungen* (ed. H. Usener, 2 vols., Berlin, 1885), I, 62ff. Therefore (in opposition to Diels and Kranz, *Vorsokr.*⁵, note to frag. 6, 2, p. 233) the opinion that frag. 6 refers to Herakleitos can be maintained only in so far as we consider him one of the representatives of the common view of men ("all men, common men and philosophers alike": F. M. Cornford, *Plato and Parmenides*, London, 1939, pp. 32f.). Walther Kranz ("Über Aufbau und Bedeutung des Parmenideischen Gedichtes," *SBBerl*, 1916, p. 1175) claims, with the assent of Diels, that Parmenides' remarks on the double-headed men who regard being and not-being as identical cannot refer to the common view of men, because men do not formulate their views in this way. The judgment seems to start from a wrong premise: the question is not how men formulate their common view themselves, but how it is seen by Parmenides from the standpoint of pure being. And from this standpoint no more pertinent expression could be found. Kranz's argument is based on another false inference. The word παλίντροπος does not refer to Herakleitos, because the genuine reading of Herakleitos (*Vorsokr.* 22 [12] ʙ 51) is παλίντονος [not παλίντροπος] ἁρμονίη λύρης καὶ τόξου. If we ask why Diels chose παλίντροπος "among variants of equal value," we find—see Hermann Diels, tr. and ed., *Herakleitos von Ephesus* (Berlin, 1901), p. 13—that it was the passage in Parmenides which determined his choice: an obvious circle. (Correctly seen by Gregory Vlastos, "On Heraclitus," *AJP*, LXXVI, 1955, 350, note 30). τρέπειν and τροπή go with path; τείνειν and τόνος go with lyre, bow, and string, not vice versa. / See now the thorough discussion in favor of παλίντονος ἁρμονίη by G. S. Kirk, *Heraclitus: The Cosmic Fragments* (Cambridge, 1954), pp. 210ff.* / It follows, incidentally, that Diels, in his edition of the pre-Socratics, put Parmenides in the wrong place.

32. On the subjective and objective meaning of the term δόξα see Bruno

Snell, "Die Ausdrücke für den Begriff des Wissens in der vorplato-nischen Philosophie," *PhU*, XXIX (1924), 53.

33. *Phaedrus* 249c: ὑπεριδοῦσα ἅπερ νῦν εἶναί φαμεν, 247e: ὧν ἡμεῖς νῦν ὄντων καλοῦμεν. *Theaetetus* 152d: πάντα ἃ δή φαμεν εἶναι οὐκ ὀρθῶς προσαγορεύοντες.

34. Cf. *Symposium* 211a: ἀεὶ ὂν καὶ οὔτε γιγνόμενον οὔτε ἀπολλύμενον οὔτε αὐξανόμενον οὔτε φθῖνον with Parmenides in *Vorsokr.* 28 [18] B 8, 13. 14: τοῦ εἴνεκα οὔτε γενέσθαι οὔτ' ὄλλυσθαι ἀνῆκε Δίκη. B 8, 6–7: τίνα γὰρ γένναν διζήσεαι αὐτοῦ; πῇ πόθεν αὐξηθέν; B 8, 38–40: τῷ πάντ' ὄνομ' ἔσται. . . . γίγνεσθαί τε καὶ ὄλλυσθαι, εἶναί τε καὶ οὐχί.

35. For this question and for a part of the answer I am indebted to Natorp's penetrating essay "Logos–Psyche–Eros" in the Appendix to *Platos Ideenlehre*[2]. But it is one-sided to see, as Natorp does, Plato (against his will) as an almost complete Herakleitean. Therefore, my attempt to make Herakleitos and Parmenides coalesce in Plato may be justified. / In favor of this view see also Kurt Riezler, *Parmenides* (Frankfurt a. M., 1934). / Victor Goldschmidt, *Essai sur le "Cratyle"* (Paris, 1940), p. 34, seems to think that Plato knew Herakleitos only by way of Kratylos.

36. See Kurt von Fritz, *Pythagorean Politics in Southern Italy* (New York, 1940) and the review by Erich Frank, *AJP*, LXIV (1943), 220ff. In reference to the following see Cornford, "The Harmony of Spheres," *The Unwritten Philosophy and Other Essays*, ed. W. K. C. Guthrie (Cambridge, 1950), pp. 14ff.

37. Erwin Rohde, *Psyche*, tr. W. B. Hillis (London and New York, 1925), p. 484, n. 44; Windelband, *Platon*[3] (Stuttgart, 1900), ch. V, "Der Theologe." / Wilamowitz-Moellendorff, *Der Glaube der Hellenen* (2 vols., Berlin, 1932), II, 182ff., and Ivan Mortimer Linforth, *The Arts of Orpheus* (Berkeley and Los Angeles, 1941), have taught us to be more careful in the use of the term "Orphic religion." But there would be a vacuum if we adopted completely the skeptical view of these authors; see the review of Linforth's book by A. D. Nock, *CW*, 35 (1942), 161–63: "the modern concept, which Linforth attacks, does not spring from simple wrong-headedness: it rests on certain facts."

38. See Julius Stenzel, *Über zwei Begriffe der platonischen Mystik:* ΖΩΙΟΝ *und* ΚΙΝΗΣΙΣ (Breslau, 1914) = *Kleine Schriften zur griechischen Philosophie* (Darmstadt, 1957), pp. 1ff. / These Platonic concepts should not be confused with the kind of Oriental speculations on the microcosm discussed by Richard Reitzenstein, *Studien zum antiken Synkretismus* (Studien der Bibliothek Warburg, Leipzig, 1926). The pseudo-Hippokratean *De Hebdomadibus* transfers these Oriental specu-lations to Greek soil; but this treatise, according to Albrecht Goetze, "Persische Weisheit im griechischen Gewande?" *ZII*, II (1923), 79, is "an erratic block" in Hellas. See Walther Kranz, "Kosmos und

Mensch in den Vorstellungen des frühen Griechentums," *NGG*, 1938, pp. 131ff.; "Kosmos," *AfB*, II (1955), 7ff.

39. *Sophist* 248E *et seq.*, *Letter VII* 342D. / See John Elof Boodin, "The Discovery of Form," *JHistId*, IV (1943), 177ff.

CHAPTER II

1. Albinus (= Ἀλκινόου Εἰσαγωγή) ch. 15; Diogenes Laërtius III 79; Apuleius, *De Platone* I 15; Hermann Diels, *Doxographi Graeci* (Berlin and Leipzig, 1879), p. 568, l. 9. With reference to ch. II see Hermann Gundert, "Platon und das Daimonion des Sokrates," *Gymnasium*, LXI (1954), 514f.; Erich Frank, "Begriff und Bedeutung des Dämonischen," *Knowledge, Will and Belief* [I⁵], pp. 51ff.

2. Schopenhauer, "Versuch über Geistersehen," *Sämtliche Werke* (7 vols., Wiesbaden, 1946–50), V, 274ff.

3. Eduard Zeller, *Die Philosophie der Griechen*⁴ (3 pts., Leipzig, 1888), II, 89; Edmund Pfleiderer, *Sokrates und Plato* (Tübingen, 1896), p. 44.

4. *Memorabilia* I 4 15, IV 3 12, IV 8 1.

5. *Gespräche mit Eckermann*¹³, ed. von Houben (Leipzig, 1913), p. 362. (Cf. tr. John Oxenford, London, 1879, p. 514.) The "retarding demons" (p. 553) are different, as is the statement that the demonic is "not negative" (p. 373, conv. of March 2, 1831).*

6. *Phaedrus* 242B 9 should read τὸ δαιμόνιόν τε καὶ [τὸ] εἰωθὸς σημεῖόν μοι γίγνεσθαι. Thus Codex Laurentianus IX 85 and Friedrich Ast, ed., *Phaedrus* (Leipzig, 1810).*

7. Cf. tr. Oxenford, p. 379.

8. In the *Apology* 31D: θεῖόν τι καὶ δαιμόνιον are connected. In 40B: τὸ τοῦ θεοῦ σημεῖον designates the *daimonion*. This may answer the argument which Ernst Hoffmann—see *Platonismus und Mittelalter* (*Vorträge der Bibliothek Warburg*, Leipzig, 1923/24), p. 57—again raised against the authenticity of the *Alcibiades Major* (because of 105E *et seq.*). See my *Der Grosse Alcibiades*, II, 23ff.

9. *Procli Opera Inedita*², ed. Victor Cousin (Paris, 1864), pp. 377ff.*

10. W. R. Inge, *The Philosophy of Plotinus* (2 vols., London and New York, 1918), II, 199: "The whole belief in intermediate beings is part of the current religion of the time, and has no inner connection with the philosophy which we are considering." It would be more plausible to say that meaning and connection ought to be sought.

11. Karl Jaspers, *Psychologie der Weltanschauungen*³ (Berlin, 1925), pp. 193ff., 198: "Goethe did not seek the demonic: he merely experienced and respected it as the limit of his experience. This explains the contrast between his conception of the world and the theosophic constructions of those who use the demonic as material, seeking it to

satisfy their lusts, their need for edification, or their horror, making an object of it instead of accepting it as the limit." The same words may be used to describe the contrast between Plato and many a dogmatic Platonist.

12. *De genio Socratis* ch. 20; Karl Reinhardt, *Poseidonios* (Munich, 1921), pp. 464ff., and *Kosmos und Sympathie* (Munich, 1926), pp. 259, 289.

13. Proklos in his Commentary on the *First Alcibiades* (ed. Creuzer p. 73 = ed. Cousin² p. 383 = ed. Westerink p. 32) opposes the identification of λογική ψυχή with "our demon." He considers it μέχρι τῆς ἀναλογίας μόνον ἀληθές because it contradicts the system distilled out of other passages in Plato.

14. Karl Jaspers, *Philosophie* (3 vols., Berlin, 1932), II, ch. 5, "Wille"; ch. 6, "Freiheit." The passages quoted are on pp. 197–98.

15. *Geschichte der Farbenlehre, Werke* (Stuttgart and Tübingen, 1827–34), LIII, 1, 19.

16. See my *Der Grosse Alcibiades*, II, 15.

17. Concerning the demon see Karl Lehrs, "Gott, Götter und Dämonen," *Populäre Aufsätze aus dem Altertum²* (Leipzig, 1875), pp. 141ff.; Andres, in *RE*, Suppl. III, cols. 267ff.; Wilamowitz-Moellendorff, *Der Glaube der Hellenen*, I, 362ff.; Otto Kern, *Die Religion der Griechen* (3 vols., Berlin, 1926–38), I, 60ff.; M. P. Nilsson, *Geschichte der griechischen Religion* (2 vols., Munich, 1941–50), I, 200ff., and *Greek Piety*, 59ff.; E. R. Dodds, *The Greeks and the Irrational* (Berkeley, 1951), pp. 39ff., 207ff.

18. Léon Robin, *La Théorie platonicienne de l'amour* (Paris, 1908), confuses myth and dogma, Plato and the Platonists. See particularly §§ 128ff.: "the reasonable soul is a demon. . . ." For reference to the following see Richard Heinze, *Xenokrates* (Leipzig, 1892), pp. 92ff.; Max Pohlenz, *Vom Zorne Gottes* (Göttingen, 1909), pp. 129ff. In both works Plotinos and Proklos are omitted. For further information see Andres, *RE*, Suppl. III, cols. 267ff.

19. Heinrich Wölfflin, *Principles of Art History*, tr. M. D. Hottinger (London, 1932), pp. 73ff.

20. With regard to this passage and the chapter as a whole see Ernst Hoffmann, "Methexis und Metaxy bei Platon," *Sokrates*, 7. Jahrg., LXXIII (1919), 48–78. Concerning the influence of the motif of σύνδεσμος see Werner Jaeger, *Nemesios von Emesa* (Berlin, 1914), pp. 96ff.; Reinhardt, *Poseidonios*, pp. 343ff. The theme occurs again in Thomas Aquinas (quoted by Étienne Gilson, *The Philosophy of St. Thomas Aquinas*, tr. Edward Bullough, Cambridge, 1929, p. 183): "*Ordo rerum talis esse invenitur, ut ab uno extremo ad alterum non perveniatur nisi per media.*"*

21. Friedrich Hölderlin, "The Only One" ("Der Einzige"). (Cf. tr. Michael Hamburger, New York, 1952, pp. 214f.)

22. See my *Der Grosse Alcibiades*, I, 20. For reference to the following

see Ivo Bruns, "Attische Liebestheorien," *Vorträge und Aufsätze* (Munich, 1905), pp. 118ff.; Léon Robin, op. cit.; Erich Bethe, "Die dorische Knabenliebe, ihre Ethik und ihre Idee," *RhM*, LXII (1907), 438–75; Julius Stenzel, *Platon Der Erzieher* (Leipzig, 1928), ch. V, "Eros"; Hans Kelsen, "Die platonische Liebe," *Imago*, XIX (1933), 34ff.; M. A. Grube, *Plato's Thought* (London, 1935), ch. III, "Eros"; Raphael Demos, "Eros," *JPhilos*, XXXI (1934), 337–45; Gerhard Krüger, *Einsicht und Leidenschaft* (Frankfurt a. M., 1939); Renata von Scheliha, *Patroklos* (Basel, 1943), pp. 306ff.; F. M. Cornford, "The Doctrine of Eros in Plato's Symposium" (1937) in *The Unwritten Philosophy and Other Essays* (Cambridge, 1950), pp. 68ff.*

23. Proclus, *Opera* (ed. Cousin), col. 369, l. 33; col. 372, l. 18.

24. Tr. Oxenford, p. 446.

25. *Scriptores physiognomici graeci et latini*, ed. Richardus Foerster (2 vols., Leipzig, 1900), I, viiff.

26. According to Ernst Howald, *Platons Leben* (Zurich, 1923).

27. Frag. 11, Dittmar (Heinrich Dittmar, *Aeschines von Sphettos*, Berlin, 1912) = frag. 4, Krauss (Heinrich Krauss, *Aeschinis Socratici Reliquiae*, Leipzig, 1911).

28. Bruns, p. 197, noticed neither ἐν τῇ ψυχῇ nor ἐνωμφω in §§ 21, 28.

29. It ought to be stated, in opposition to the usual misconception, that this does not deal with magic, though perhaps with the "magic" of the great educator. See the chapter "Theages" in vol. 2 of the present work.

30. See Ernst Bertram, *Nietzsche: Versuch einer Mythologie* (Berlin, 1918), pp. 316f.

31. See the chapter "Lysis" in vol. 2.

32. For reference to this association see Julius Stenzel's review of Willy Theiler, "Zur Geschichte der teleologischen Naturbetrachtung bis auf Aristoteles," *Gnomon*, II (1926), 323.

CHAPTER III

1. Aristotle (*Aristotelis qui ferebantur librorum Fragmenta*, ed. Valentin Rose, Leipzig, 1886) frag. 49 is still very Platonizing: ὅτι γὰρ ἐννοεῖ τι καὶ ὑπὲρ τὸν νοῦν καὶ τὴν οὐσίαν ὁ Ἀριστοτέλης δῆλός ἐστι πρὸς τοῖς πέρασι τοῦ περὶ εὐχῆς βιβλίου σαφῶς εἰπὼν ὅτι ὁ θεὸς ἢ νοῦς ἐστιν ἢ ἐπέκεινά τι τοῦ νοῦ. Simplicius' explanation seems too precise and too explicit to justify Harold Cherniss' interpretation in *Aristotle's Criticism of Plato and the Academy* (Baltimore, 1944), I, 592, 609. See Werner Jaeger, *Aristotle*, tr. R. Robinson (Oxford, 1948), p. 160, n. 3; Erich Frank, "The Fundamental Opposition of Plato and Aristotle," *AJP*, LXI (1940), 34–53, 166–85, esp. p. 179; = *Knowledge, Will and Belief*, pp. 86–119, 470–85, esp. p. 480.

2. I find confirmation in Natorp, *Platos Ideenlehre*² [I²¹], p. 516. Ernst

Hoffmann's essay, "Die Sprache und die archaische Logik," *Heidelberger Abhandlungen zur Philosophie und ihrer Geschichte* (Tübingen), III (1925), does not seem to necessitate alteration of what I have said. Hoffmann (73ff.) makes a good case for the "archaic" unity of speech and thought, in Plato too; but I do not think that *Letter VII* represents a new point of departure in this respect. The letter merely makes explicit what appears throughout Plato's work and is indispensable for an understanding of his technique as a writer, particularly for the form of the dialogue. See chs. V and VIII.

3. Goethe, *Zur Morphologie, Aphoristisches* in *Werke* (Weimar edn.; [I²³]), II, VI, no. 354. A similar reference may be found in "Maximen und Reflexionen," *Jahrbuch der Goethe-Gesellschaft* (Weimar), XXI (1907), no. 577 ("Wanderjahre").

4. How unlike Plato, for example, is what Proklos says at the end of a lecture on the *Republic* (*Procli Diadochi in Platonis Rem publicam Commentarii* ed. Guilelmus Kroll, Leipzig, 1895, I, 205): ταῦτα, ὦ φίλοι ἑταῖροι, μνήμη κεχαρίσθω τῆς τοῦ καθηγεμόνος ἡμῶν συνουσίας, ἐμοὶ μὲν ὄντα ῥητὰ πρὸς ὑμᾶς, ὑμῖν δὲ ἄρρητα πρὸς τοὺς πολλούς.

5. See Otfried Becker, *Das Bild des Weges und verwandte Vorstellungen im frühgriechischen Denken* (*Hermes:* Einzelschriften 4, Berlin, 1937); Bruno Snell, *Die Entdeckung des Geistes³* (Hamburg, 1955), ch. 13, "Das Symbol des Weges."*

6. F. M. Cornford, *The Unwritten Philosophy and Other Essays* (Cambridge, 1950), pp. 77f.*

7. See Walther Kranz, "Diotima von Mantineia," *Hermes*, LXI (1926), 437–47, esp. 446 with bibliography.

8. Christian August Lobeck, *Aglaophamus* (2 vols., Regensburg, 1829), I, 111ff.; Ferdinand Noack, *Eleusis* (2 vols., Berlin and Leipzig, 1927), 277ff.; Nilsson, *Geschichte der griechischen Religion* [II¹⁷], I, 619ff.

9. A strange poem entitled "Eleusis," which young Hegel addressed to Hölderlin, sees the Eleusinian mysteries as a symbol of the *Arrheton*. See *Friedrich Hölderlins Werke*, ed. Norbert von Hellingrath (6 vols., Munich and Leipzig, 1913–23), VI, 253ff.

10. The following benefits from Schopenhauer, *The World as Will and Idea*, tr. Haldane and Kemp, I, Book IV, § 68; Evelyn Underhill, *Mysticism³* (London, 1911); R. A. Nicholson, *The Mystics of Islam* (London, 1914); and others. Since the historical element has been unduly neglected in more recent publications, Adalbert Merx, "Idee und Grundlinien einer allgemeinen Geschichte der Mystik," *Akademische Rede Heidelberg* (1893), is important for reference. See Rudolf Otto, *Mysticism East and West*, tr. B. L. Bracey and R. C. Payne (New York, 1932), particularly pp. 139ff., for a definition of mysticism; Henri Bergson, *The Two Sources of Morality and Religion*, tr. R. Ashley Audra and others (London, 1935), ch. III.

11. Rudolf Otto, *Vischnu-Narajana* (Jena, 1923), p. 135. For the ladder to heaven, see Johannes Klimakos, *Scala Paradisi* (in Migne, *PG*, vol. 88, cols. 631–1164; tr. Fr. Robert, *The Holy Ladder of Perfection*, by *which we may Ascend to Heaven*, London, 1858); for the stairway, Walter Hilton, *The Scale of Perfection*, ed. Evelyn Underhill (London, 1923). See also Underhill, *Mysticism*, p. 154; Josef Kroll, *Die Lehren des Hermes Trismegistos* (Münster, 1914), p. 380.

12. Edmund Hardy, *Indische Religionsgeschichte* (Leipzig, 1898), p. 113.

13. See Wilhelm Bousset, *Kyrios Christos*[3] (Göttingen, 1926), pp. 172ff.; G. A. P. Wetter, *Phos* (Uppsala, 1915). The Platonic influence is traced through the Middle Ages by Clemens Baeumker, *Witelo* (Beiträge zur Geschichte der Philosophie des Mittelalters, III, 2, Münster, 1908), pp. 357ff.; in the Renaissance by Ernst Goldbeck, *Der Mensch und sein Weltbild* (Leipzig, 1926), pp. 61ff. ("Plato und Copernicus"). For a nonhistorical point of view, see Gerda Walther, *Zur Phänomenologie der Mystik* (Halle, 1923), p. 136.

14. *Dante's Inferno—Purgatorio—Paradiso*, tr. Laurence Binyon (3 vols., London, 1933–43); *Inferno*, I, l. 2, p. 3; *Paradiso*, XXXIII, ll. 83–90, p. 391.

15. See Karl Holl, "Augustins innere Entwicklung," *Abh Berl*, 1922, no. 4 (pub. 1923), 25.

16. Otto, *Vischnu-Narajana*, p. 150.

17. Underhill, *Mysticism*, pp. 127f.

18. Plotinus, *Enneades* V 5 7; II 7 34, 36.

19. *The Complete Works of St Teresa*, tr. E. Allison Peers (3 vols., London, 1946), I, 120.

20. Julian Obermann, *Der philosophische und religiöse Subjektivismus Ghazalis* (Vienna and Leipzig, 1921), p. 91.

21. William James, *The Varieties of Religious Experience* (London and New York, 1905), p. 399.

22. Lüers, *Die Sprache der deutschen Mystik* [I[16]], pp. 72ff., 218ff.

23. *Ethics*, part V, propositions 35–36.

24. Otto, p. 72.

25. Plotinus, *Enneades* I 7 1, says of the *Agathón*; καὶ γὰρ ὅτι ἐπέκεινα οὐσίας, ἐπέκεινα καὶ ἐνεργείας καὶ ἐπέκεινα νοῦ καὶ νοήσεως. There is a much exaggerated account in Dionysius the Areopagite, *De divinis nominibus* II 2: ἀπάντων ἐπέκεινα τῆς ἐπέκεινα πάντων ὅλης ἰδιότητος ταυτότης.

26. *De mystica theologia* I 2. This motif runs through the entire work, and is particularly strong at the end. The preceding quotation is from *De divinis nominibus* I 7.

27. "I no longer see anything but the divine Nothing moving the world": Hasidic mysticism in Martin Buber, *Ekstatische Konfessionen* (Jena, 1909), p. 186. For reference to the old German mystics see Lüers, p. 232.

28. Alfred Hillebrandt, tr., *Aus Brahmanas und Upanischaden* (Jena, 1923), pp. 41, 125, 171; Paul Deussen, *Sechzig Upanischaden* (Leipzig, 1897), p. 445; Hermann Oldenberg, *Die Lehre der Upanischaden* (Göttingen, 1915), pp. 62ff.; Otto Strauss, *Indische Philosophie* (Munich, 1925), p. 58; Swami Nikhilananda, *The Upanishads* (New York, 1949), pp. 25ff.

29. See the 10th and 11th Tractates of Hermes Trismegistos in *Corpus Hermeticum*, ed. and tr. A. D. Nock and A.-J. Festugière (3 vols., Paris, 1945–54), I, 107ff.; Kroll [III¹¹], pp. 365ff.

30. *Quis rerum divinarum heres* 511M. Cf. Leisegang, *Der Heilige Geist* [I¹⁶], I, 163ff.; Eduard Norden, *Die Geburt des Kindes* (Leipzig, 1924), pp. 92f.; Arthur Allgeier, "Das gräco-ägyptische Mysterium im Lukasevangelium," *HJGörres*, XLV (1925), 1–20, esp. 6ff.

31. Numenius, in Eusebius, *Praeparationes* XI 22 (K. S. Guthrie, tr., *Numenius*, London, 1917), 5: ἀπελθόντα πόρρω τῶν αἰσθητῶν ὁμιλῆσαι τῷ ἀγαθῷ μόνῳ μόνον. Franz Cumont, *Le Culte égyptien et le mysticisme de Plotin* (Monuments Piot XXV, Paris, 1921–22), p. 87, called attention to this passage and to its agreement with Plotinos.*

32. An ecstasy shared by two people, however, may be found in the case of St. Catherine of Siena (see Buber, p. 137), likewise in the *Katharinentaler Chronik* (quoted by Lüers, p. 49). The more primitive the ecstasy, incidentally, the greater the possibility of "contagion." But this is not relevant to our purpose.

33. Mundaka Upanishad III 2 8, tr. S. Radhakrishnan, *The Principal Upanishads* (London, 1953), p. 691.

34. Nicholson, p. 168.

35. Alois Bernt, ed. and tr., *Meister Eckhart: Ein Breviarium aus seinen Schriften* (Leipzig, 1919), p. 20.

36. Underhill, p. 507.

37. κἀκείνου γενόμενος ἕν ἐστιν ὥσπερ κέντρῳ κέντρον συνάψας, § 10.

38. ἔκστασις καὶ ἅπλωσις καὶ ἐπίδοσις αὐτοῦ καὶ ἔφεσις πρὸς ἁφὴν καὶ στάσις καὶ περινόησις πρὸς ἐφαρμογήν, § 11.

39. Plotinus, *Enneades* I 2 6: ἡ σπουδὴ οὐκ ἔξω ἁμαρτίας εἶναι, ἀλλὰ θεὸν εἶναι. VI 9 9: θεὸν γενόμενον, μᾶλλον δὲ ὄντα. On the other hand, we have θεοειδές, *Phaedo* 95c; θεοφιλής, *Republic* 612E, *Symposium* 212A, and elsewhere; εἰς ὅσον δυνατὸν ἀνθρώπῳ ὁμοιοῦσθαι θεῷ, *Republic* 613B; ὁμοίωσις θεῷ κατὰ τὸ δυνατόν· ὁμοίωσις δὲ δίκαιον καὶ ὅσιον μετὰ φρονήσεως γενέσθαι, *Theaetetus* 176B. See Wilamowitz-Moellendorff, *Reden und Vorträge* (2 vols., Berlin, 1925–26), II, 185.*

40. "Plato's plastic will to recognize limits is opposed to any form of limitless enthusiasm." Heinrich Friedemann makes this statement in *Platon: Seine Gestalt* (Berlin, 1914), p. 74, in contrast to Franz Müller, "Dionysios Proklos Plotinos," *Baeumkers Beiträge zur Philosophie des Mittelalters* (Münster), XX (1911), who calls Plato "the greatest mystic among the Greeks" (p. 105) and asserts (p. 87): "a

common element of Platonic and Plotinian mysticism is the belief that knowledge consists in the essential union of the knower with the object of knowledge; that knowledge of God is union with God." Even Natorp, in his old age, was probably too much inclined to interpret Plato in terms of Plotinos, so that (p. 472) he twisted the words θεᾶσθαι μόνον καὶ συνεῖναι in the *Symposium* 211D. μόνον means "only," not "alone," and συνεῖναι does not mean "to be one," but rather the community of two separate beings. / For reference to this chapter as a whole see Hoffmann, pp. 64ff.;* Julius Stenzel, "Der Begriff der Erleuchtung bei Platon," *Antike*, II (1926), 235ff. = *Kleine Schriften* [I[38]], 151ff.; Hermann Gundert, "Enthusiasmos und Logos bei Platon," *Lexis*, II (1949), 25ff.; A.-J. Festugière, *Contemplation et vie contemplative selon Platon* [1,2] (Paris, 1936, 1950), the latter an outstanding work in which, however, the difference between Plato and Plotinos does not come out clearly. See Émile Bréhier, "Platonisme et Néoplatonisme," *RevÉtGr*, LI (1939), 489ff. Concerning Plotinos see Émile Bréhier, *La Philosophie de Plotin* (Paris, 1928) and Franz Josef Brecht, "Plotin und das Grundproblem der griechischen Philosophie," *Antike*, XVIII (1942), 81–94. Bréhier's comparison of Plotinian thought with the *Upanishads* is important even if an Indian influence on Plotinos cannot be strictly proved. See Eric R. Dodds's review of Bréhier's *La Philosophie de Plotin* in *Gnomon*, V (1929), 480f.

CHAPTER IV

1. On the legal status of the Academy, see Wilamowitz-Moellendorff, *Antigonos von Karystos* (Berlin, 1881), pp. 279ff.; Theodor Gomperz, *Greek Thinkers*, tr. Laurie Magnus and G. G. Berry (4 vols., London, 1901–12), III, 308; Guy Cromwell Field, *Plato and His Contemporaries* (London, 1930), pp. 47ff. On the topography of the Academy see Walther Judeich, *Topographie von Athen*[2] (*Handbuch der Altertumswissenschaft*, Sec. 3, Pt. 2, Vol. 2, Munich, 1931), pp. 404ff. On the excavations in the district of the Academy see Georg Karo, "Archäologische Funde 1932–3, Griechenland und Dodekanes," *AA*, 1933, cols. 208ff.; H. G. G. Payne, "Archaeology in Greece, 1930–31," *JHS*, LI (1934), 184–210, esp. 188f. The names on the inscription: Χαρμ[ίδες] Ἀρισ[τον] Ἀξι[οχος] Κριτον.

2. Cf. also 535A *et seq.* Isokrates also stresses φύσις as the basis of education, e.g., XIII 14, XV 185 *et seq.* Eduard Schwartz in *Ethik der Griechen*, ed. Will Richter (Stuttgart, 1951), pp. 50f., has shown how Pindar's antithesis of φυά and μάθος is carried on in the time of the Sophists in discussing whether φύσις or παιδεία should be pre-eminent. All this receives a new and special meaning in Plato.

3. Wilamowitz, reviewing Franz Egermann, *Die platonischen Briefe* 7

und 8, says in *Gnomon*, IV (1928), 362, of *Letter VII*, "of course it was published by the Academy, as were all the dialogues."

4. Recent literature on the Academy includes Otto Immisch, *Academia* (Freiburg i. B., 1924); Stenzel, *Platon Der Erzieher* [II²²], pp. 94ff.; Field, pp. 30ff.; Léon Robin, *Platon* (Paris, 1935), pp. 11ff.; Ernst Kapp, "Platon und die Akademie," *Mnemosyne*, III–IV (1936–37), 227ff.; Jaeger, *Aristotle*, [III¹], ch. II, and *Paideia*, tr. Gilbert Highet (3 vols., Oxford, 1939–45), II, 273ff.; Hans Herter, *Platons Akademie*¹,² (Bonn, 1946, 1952)—see review by Harold Cherniss, *CP*, XLIII (1948), 130–32; Hans Leisegang, "Platon," in *RE*, XX, col. 2352. The "most noteworthy recent attempt" is that of Harold Cherniss, *The Riddle of the Early Academy* (Berkeley and Los Angeles, (1945). See Sir David Ross, *Plato's Theory of Ideas* (Oxford, 1951), pp. 142ff.*

5. Antigonos of Karystos in Athenaeus XII 547ff.; Wilamowitz, *Antigonos*, pp. 84f., 264; Jaeger, *Aristotle*, p. 316.

6. The philosophical problem certainly cannot be solved by supposing "frequent changes of mood," as Paul Natorp says in *Platos Ideenlehre*², pp. 173f.

7. See ch. VI.

8. Ludwig von Sybel, in his edition of Plato's *Symposium* (Marburg, 1888), says (p. 102) that we hear Plato himself speak directly through Alkibiades' words. We must also realize how much of Alkibiades was in Plato.

9. Plutarch, *De genio Socratis* ch. 12: Σωκράτους ἀνδρὸς ἀτυφίᾳ καὶ ἀφελείᾳ μάλιστα τὴν φιλοσοφίαν ἐξανθρωπίσαντος. *Phaedrus* 230A: σκοπῶ οὐ ταῦτα ἀλλ᾽ ἐμαυτόν, εἴτε τι θηρίον ὂν τυγχάνω Τυφῶνος πολυπλοκώτερον καὶ μᾶλλον ἐπιτεθυμμένον, εἴτε ἡμερώτερόν τε καὶ ἁπλούστερον ζῷον θείας τινὸς καὶ ἀτύφου μοίρας φύσει μετέχον.

10. Wilamowitz, *Antigonos*, p. 268.

11. Diogenes Laërtius V 86; Cicero, *Tusculanae Disputationes* V 8.

12. On the poor testimonies (Elias, *Categoriae* 118, 18; Philoponus, *De anima* 117, 29; Tzetzes, *Chiliades* VIII 972) see Eduard Zeller, *Philosophie der Griechen*⁴, [II³], II, 1, 411, n. 3; I. Thomas, *Selections Illustrating the History of Greek Mathematics* (Cambridge, Mass., 1939), pp. 386f.

12a. Plutarch, *Dion* chs. 13, 14; see further p. 400, n. 12a, below.

13. Erich Frank, *Plato und die . . . Pythagoreer* [I³], pp. 150ff., 161ff.

14. Paul Tannery, "Le Nombre nuptial dans Platon," *Mémoires scientifiques* (Toulouse, 1876–1913), I, 12ff.; James Adam, *The Republic of Plato* (2 vols., London, 1902), II, 264ff.; Gustav Kafka, "Zu J. Adams Erklärung der platonischen Zahl," *Philologus*, LXXIII (1914), 109ff.; Auguste Diès, "Le Nombre de Platon," *MémAcInscr*, XIV (1936), 1, 1–139; F. A. Ahlvers, *Zahl und Klang bei Platon* (Noctes Romanae, no. 6, Bern, 1952), p. 11; Robert S. Brumbaugh, *Plato's Mathematical*

Imagination (Bloomington, 1954), pp. 107ff. On Plato's mathematics in general see Abel Rey, *La Science dans l'antiquité* (6 vols., Paris, 1930–48), III, 297ff.; Charles Mugler, *Platon et la recherche mathématique* (Strasbourg, 1948); Harold Cherniss, "Plato as a Mathematician," *RevMet*, IV (1951), 395ff., with a review of Mugler and older literature, little of which is quoted here.*

15. Simplicius, *In libros Aristotelis de caelo* 488 16 *et seq.*, from Sosigenes and by way of him from Eudemos. This need not be taken literally, as if Plato had offered a prize for a competition in which Eudoxos was victorious. If we take it in a more general sense, Hultsch's objection (s.v. "Eudoxos," *RE*, VI, 939) becomes untenable. The situation in astronomy was that formulated for mathematics in the *Academicorum philosophorum index Herculanensis* (ed. Siegfried Mekler, Berlin, 1902), pp. 15ff.: καὶ τῶν μαθημάτων ἐπίδοσις πολλὴ κατ' ἐκεῖνον τὸν χρόνον ἀρχιτεκτονοῦντος μὲν καὶ προβλήματα διδόντος τοῦ Πλάτωνος, ζητούντων δὲ μετὰ σπουδῆς αὐτὰ τῶν μαθηματικῶν. See also G. V. Schiaparelli, "Die homozentrischen Sphären des Eudoxos," *Abhandlungen zur Geschichte der mathematischen Wissenschaften mit Einschluss ihrer Anwendungen*, Pt. I (Leipzig, 1877), p. 110; Paul Tannery, *Recherches sur l'histoire de l'astronomie ancienne* (Paris, 1893), pp. 267ff.; Frank, *Plato und die sogenannten Pythagoreer* [1³], pp. 35f., 207ff.; J. L. Heiberg, *Geschichte der Mathematik und der Naturwissenschaften im Altertum* (Munich, 1925), pp. 7ff., 51ff.; A. Rehm and K. Vogel, "Exakte Wissenschaften," in Alfred Gercke and Eduard Norden, *Einleitung in die Altertumswissenschaften* (3 vols., Leipzig, 1933), II, 37. / Concerning the relation of Eudoxos to Plato, extremes of judgment oppose each other. Hermann Usener in *Vorträge und Aufsätze*, ed. A. Dieterich (Leipzig, 1907), portrays (p. 87) "the then first school of astronomy, striking its colors and marching, drums beating, into the Academy," whereas Hultsch would prefer to deny any relationship at all. On the one hand, the hypothesis of Felix Jacoby, *Apollodors Chronik* (Philologische Untersuchungen 16, Berlin, 1902), p. 324, and Eva Sachs, *De Theaeteto mathematico* (Berlin, 1914), p. 17, that during Plato's Sicilian journey Eudoxos held the presidency of the Academy, cannot be regarded as assured by tradition. (The *Vita* of Suidas makes the same claim for Herakleides.) On the other hand, the material which August Boeckh—*Über die vierjährigen Sonnenkreise der Alten* (Berlin, 1863), pp. 155ff.—collected and examined with his wonted acumen and caution cannot be so disregarded that the clearly attested connection of the two men is simply denied. Eudoxos is often called ἑταῖρος τῶν περὶ Πλάτωνα γενόμενος, συνήθης, ἀκροατής, γνώριμος Πλάτωνος, *auditor Platonis* (Zeller, II, 1, 933), just as Helikon of Kyzikos is called εἷς τῶν Πλάτωνος συνήθων in Plutarch's *Dion* ch. 19. See Wilamowitz-Moellendorff, *Platon* [1¹⁷], I, 496ff.; Jaeger, *Aristotle*, pp. 16ff.;

Joseph Bidez, *Eos, ou Platon et l'Orient* (Brussels, 1945), pp. 24ff.; Erich Frank, "Die Begründung der mathematischen Naturwissenschaft durch Eudoxus," *Knowledge, Will and Belief* [I⁵], pp. 134ff.

16. Plato, *Protagoras* 318E.

17. Usener's essay, "Organisation der wissenschaftlichen Arbeit," *Vorträge und Aufsätze*, pp. 67ff., is still well worth reading. Of the opponents of Usener's view, Jaeger (*Aristotle*, pp. 17f.) weighs his words most cautiously, while some of Frank's statements are more negative. Completely in error are Ernst Howald, *Die platonische Akademie und die moderne Universitas Literarum* (Zurich, 1921), and P. L. Landsberg, *Wesen und Bedeutung der platonischen Akademie* (Bonn, 1923).

18. See Paulus Lang, *De Speusippi Academici scriptis* (Bonn, 1911), pp. 7ff. on the Ὅμοια. Tradition mentions only the names of the genera μαλακόστρακα and πολύποδες. But these "characteristic fragments" furnish conclusive evidence. See Ernst Hambruch, *Logische Lehren der platonischen Schule* (Breslau, 1904), pp. 7ff.; Julius Stenzel, *Zahl und Gestalt bei Platon und Aristoteles*² (Leipzig, 1933), p. 11, and "Speusippos," *RE*, 2d ser., III, cols. 1638ff.

19. See ch. XIV. / Aristotle, *De generatione et corruptione* 330b 16: Πλάτων ἐν ταῖς διαιρέσεσιν. Heinze, *Xenokrates* [II¹⁸], pp. 68f., 179 (frag. 53); Hermann Diels, *Elementum: eine Vorarbeit zum griechischen und lateinischen Thesaurus* (Leipzig, 1899), p. 21; Jaeger, *Aristotle*, p. 308; Cherniss, *Aristotle's Criticism of Plato* [III¹], I, 145ff. / Rey, IV, 24, says on the optics of reflection in the *Timaeus* 46AC: "This fact seems to be of great historical interest. It suggests that the apriority of Plato's mathematical constructions was preceded by a very careful examination of observation and experience."

20. The fundamental principles of this discussion are stated in ch. XV.*

21. Wilamowitz, *Platon*, II, 388, interpreting *Timaeus* 40D 2: "It would be useless to speak of eclipses of the sun and moon without demonstrations on a model," and adds, "therefore such a model existed in the Academy." The σφαιρίον criticized in *Letter II* 312D 2 may refer to this matter.*

22. Schweitzer, *Platon und die bildende Kunst der Griechen* [I¹¹], has recently undertaken to answer the question; see particularly pp. 67ff.

23. Antiphanes in "Antaios" and Ephippos in "Nauagos," Athenaeus XII 544E, XI 509B; Alexis in "Meropis" and Amphis in "Dexidemos," Diogenes Laërtius III 27f. In the words of Amphis—ὥσπερ κοχλίας σεμνῶς ἐπηρκὼς τὰς ὀφρῦς—translated in the text, there is a grotesquely exaggerated comparison of Plato's contracted eyebrows with the feelers of a snail; I point this out on account of the comical misunderstandings patiently reported on by Johann Jakob Bernoulli, *Griechische Ikonographie* (2 pts., Munich, 1901) II 19. / We read in

Plutarch, *De adulatore* ch. 9 and *De audiendis poetis* ch. 8, that some of Plato's disciples liked to imitate their master's stoop.

24. *Letter VII* 326A; cf. ch. I, pp. 3ff.

25. Jaeger, *Aristotle*, pp. 259ff. How much of that stratum always subsisted in Aristotle remains the question.

26. Karl Friedrich Hermann's two Universitätsprogramme (Marburg, 1836). Also *Dikaiomata*, ed. Graeca Halensis (Halle, 1913) 67 passim (see index); Immisch, p. 12; Walter G. Becker, *Platons Gesetze und das griechische Familienrecht* (Münchener Beiträge zur Papyrusforschung und antiker Rechtsgeschichte, XIV, 1932); Huntington Cairns' contribution to the present volume, ch. XVI below; Pärtel Haliste, "Zwei Fragen zum Katasterwesen in Platons 'Gesetzen' " and "Das Servitut der Wasserleitung in Platons 'Gesetzen,' " *Eranos* (Uppsala), XLVIII (1950), 93ff., 142ff.

27. Most of this can be read in Plutarch, *Adversus Colotem* ch. 32. On Cyrene, see Plutarch, *Ad principem ineruditum* 1; Aelian, *Varia Historia* XII 30. On Megalopolis, see Aelian II 42; Diogenes Laërtius III 23. On Elis, see Plutarch, *Praecepta gerendae reipublicae* 10, 15. See Eduard Meyer, *Geschichte des Altertums* (5 vols., Stuttgart, 1889-1902), V, §§ 800A, 870, 909; Jakob Bernays, *Phokion und seine neueren Beurteiler* (Berlin, 1881), pp. 36ff.; Wilamowitz, *Platon*, I, 698ff. In reference to the problem of the Academy and the state see also Paul Wendland, "Die Aufgaben der platonischen Forschung," *NGG*, 1910, p. 100; Jaeger, *Aristotle*, pp. 111ff.; Glenn R. Morrow, *Studies in the Platonic Epistles* (Illinois Studies in Language and Literature, XVIII, nos. 3 and 4, Urbana, 1935); Snell, *Entdeckung des Geistes³* [III⁵], p. 407; Philip Merlan, "Isocrates, Aristotle and Alexander the Great," *Historia*, III (1954), 60ff.

28. τὴν ἀρχὴν τῆς βασιλείας Φίλιππος διὰ Πλάτωνος ἔσχεν, Athenaeus XI 506E.

29. Plato, *Letter VI*. The quotation in Pollux X 150 is taken from a letter addressed to Plato in the course of that correspondence. See Didymos, *In Demosthenem* 4, 60ff. Jaeger, *Aristotle*, p. 114: "in the milder form of constitution we may recognize the ideas of Plato and Dion." A. E. Taylor, *Plato, the Man and His Work* (New York, 1927), pp. 7ff.

30. *Bernays, pp. 45ff. On what precedes in the text see Athenaeus XI 508E *et seq.* and *Academicorum Index* p. 35. See, moreover, Ingemar Düring, "Chion of Heraclea, A Novel in Letters," *Acta Universitatis Gotoburgensis*, LVIII (Göteborg, 1951). / It is worth mentioning that political endeavor was still alive in the Academy of Arkesilaos: Ekdemos and Megalophanes, in their home town Megalopolis and in Sikyon, accomplished the overthrow of the tyranny, and in Cyrene the establishment of εὐνομία. See Plutarch, *Philopoemen* 1; *Academicorum Index* p. 11. This political tradition persists even into late

times. One should think of Plotinos' Platonopolis, and should read Agathias II 30 on the emigration of Damaskios and his companions to the empire of the Sassanidae because they ᾤοντο τὴν Περσικὴν πολιτείαν πολλῷ εἶναι ἀμείνονα. See Gunnar Rudberg, "Neuplatonismus und Politik," *Symbolae Osloenses* (Oslo, 1922), pp. 1ff.

31. Meyer, *Geschichte des Altertums*, V, 500ff.; Eduard Schwartz, *Charakterköpfe aus der antiken Literatur* (Leipzig, 1903), pp. 64ff.; Constantin Ritter, *Platon* (2 vols., Munich, 1910–23), I, 136ff.; Wilamowitz, *Platon*, I, 351ff.; Renata von Scheliha, *Dion, Die platonische Staatsgründung in Sizilien* (Leipzig, 1934).*

32. Zeller, II, 431: "But it was a mistake that the philosopher was enticed, by the prospect of political activity, to go to Syracuse; and for this mistake he had to atone severely enough." The most exaggerated statements are to be found in Howald, *Platons Leben*. Karl Friedrich Hermann, *Geschichte und System der platonischen Philosophie* (Heidelberg, 1839), pp. 66ff., had a much sounder judgment than many of the moderns. See Jaeger, *Paideia*, III, 197ff.; L. Wickert, "Platon und Syrakus," *RhM*, n.s., XCIII (1950), 27ff.

33. See C. M. Bowra, "Plato's Epigram on Dion's Death," *AJP*, LIX (1938), 394ff. = *Problems in Greek Poetry* (Oxford, 1953), ch. VIII; Hans Herter, "Platons Dionepigramm," *RhM*, n.s., XCII (1944), 289ff.

CHAPTER V

1. *Dialogues*, tr. William McCausland Stewart (Collected Works of Paul Valéry, vol. 4; Bollingen Series XLV, New York, 1956), p. 107.

2. See Uvo Hölscher, "Der Logos bei Heraklit," *Varia Variorum, Festgabe für Karl Reinhardt* (Münster and Cologne, 1952), pp. 69ff., with discussion of previous literature. That the word *logos* should have an "unambiguous sense" is least valid for Herakleitos of all people.

3. See my *Der Grosse Alcibiades*, II, 29. For other passages see Paul Shorey, *What Plato Said* (Chicago, 1933), p. 500; Pierre Louis, *Les Métaphores de Platon* (Paris, 1945), pp. 43ff. In *Protagoras* 361A: ἡ ἄρτι ἔξοδος τῶν λόγων is a variant of the usual ὁ λόγος or οἱ λόγοι. In *Theaetetus* 173C it is not Socrates but Theodoros who says, "We are masters of the *logos*."

4. On the attitude of the Greeks and Orientals to books, see Oswald Spengler, *The Decline of the West*, tr. Charles Francis Atkinson (2 vols., London, 1926–29), II, 243ff.; Richard Harder, "Bemerkungen zur griechischen Schriftlichkeit," *Antike*, XIX (1943), 86–108; Ernst Robert Curtius, *European Literature and the Latin Middle Ages* [I[16]], ch. 16; Walther Kranz, "Welt und Menschenleben im Gleichnis," in G. Eisenmann, ed., *Wirtschaft und Kultursysteme* (Zurich and Stutt-

gart, 1955), pp. 181ff.; Franz Dornseiff, *Das Alphabet in Mystik und Magie*[2] (*Stoicheia*, Heft 7, Leipzig and Berlin, 1925). On book and script in Orphic doctrine, see Euripides, *Hippolytus* 954: πολλῶν γραμμάτων τιμῶν καπνούς. *Alcestis* 967: Θρήισσαις ἐν σανίσιν τὰς Ὀρφεὺς κατέγραψεν, with Herakleides Pontikos in the scholion. Demosthenes, *De Corona* 259: τῇ μητρὶ τελούσῃ τὰς βίβλους ἀνεγίγνωσκες. Plato, *Republic* 364E: βίβλων ὅμαδον παρέχονται Μουσαίου καὶ Ὀρφέως. Diogenes Laërtius X 4 on Epicurus: σὺν τῇ μητρὶ περιιόντα αὐτὸν εἰς τὰ οἰκίδια καθαρμοὺς ἀναγινώσκειν. (Albrecht Dieterich, *Kleine Schriften*, Leipzig, 1911, p. 452.) In this line are the books of oracles, Bakis, and the Sibyllines. / See also Albert Thibaudet, *La Campagne avec Thucydide*[6] (Paris, 1922), pp. 58f.: "Greece . . . the civilization without books." Thibaudet mentions the *Phaedrus* and the contrast between Plato and Platonism. / In reference to the following see Wilamowitz-Moellendorff, *Hellenistische Dichtung in der Zeit des Kallimachos* (2 vols., Berlin, 1924), I, 98.

5. See Hans von Arnim, *Leben und Werke des Dio von Prusa* (Berlin, 1898), p. 14.

6. On the extensive literature in which the discussion has often been connected with the chronology of the *Phaedrus*, see Gomperz, *Greek Thinkers* [IV[1]], III, 27, 325; Robin, *La Théorie platonicienne de l'amour*, §§ 96ff.; Wilamowitz, *Platon*, II, ch. 10; Gunnar Rudberg, "Isokrates und Platon," *Symbolae Osloenses* (Oslo, 1924); Marjorie Josephine Milne, *A Study in Alcidamas* (Bryn Mawr diss., 1924). Wilhelm Suess, *Ethos* (Leipzig, 1910), pp. 34ff., reconstructs the system of Gorgias from alleged and real common traits of Isokrates, Alkidamas, and Plato. In this way he antedates by half a century what was meaningful about 380 B.C.

7. See *Letter VII* 343A: εἰς ἀμετακίνητον, ὃ δὴ πάσχει τὰ γεγραμμένα τύποις.

8. Isokrates, *Epistula* I § 3. / Isokrates, in his principal demand that nothing of the necessary quality of things should be omitted (μηδὲν τῶν ἐνόντων τοῖς πράγμασι παραλιπεῖν, XIII 9), agrees with young Phaidros' praise of his master Lysias in Plato's *Phaedrus* 235B: τῶν ἐνόντων ἀξίως ῥηθῆναι ἐν τῷ πράγματι οὐδὲν παραλέλοιπεν.

9. Thus Stenzel, "Der Begriff der Erleuchtung bei Platon," [III[40]], 235ff., esp. 255.

10. See ch. XIII.

11. The scholion on *Letter II* 314C (*Appendix Platonica*, ed. K. F. Hermann, Leipzig, 1920, 390) is excellent, missing in *Scholia Platonica*, ed. W. C. Greene (Philological Monographs, 8, Haverford, Pa., 1938): ἐντεῦθεν δηλοῦται διὰ τί ὁ Πλάτων ἐν ταῖς βίβλοις αὐτοῦ μηδὲν διαλέγεται.* This passage in *Letter II* is quoted at the end of *Letter XV* in "Socratis et Socraticorum Epistulae," *Epistolographi Graeci*, ed. Rudolf Hercher (Paris, 1873), p. 622, with the arbitrary judgment,

θρυπτόμενος πρὸς τοὺς καλούς φησι, which cannot affect our interpretation.

12. κεῖται δέ που ἐν χώρᾳ τῇ καλλίστῃ τῶν τούτου. The subject of the sentence is τὸ σπουδαιότατον. See Aristotle, *De part. anim.* I 5 645a 25: οὗ δ' ἕνεκα συνέστηκεν ἢ γέγονε τέλους [namely, the objects of nature] τὴν τοῦ καλοῦ χώραν εἴληφε.

13. See also *Phaedrus* 258A *et seq.*, where in a similar context the sense of λογογράφος is widened to "lawgiver."

14. ἐπιστήμη καὶ τῷ δικαίῳ προσχρώμενοι, 293D. τὸ μετὰ νοῦ καὶ τέχνης δικαιότατον ἀεὶ διανέμοντες τοῖς ἐν τῇ πόλει. . . . σῴζειν τε αὐτοὺς καὶ ἀμείνους ἐκ χειρόνων ἀποτελεῖν κατὰ τὸ δυνατόν, 297B.

15. οὐκοῦν ἀδύνατον εὖ ἔχειν πρὸς τὰ μηδέποτε ἁπλᾶ τὸ διὰ παντὸς γιγνόμενον ἁπλοῦν, 294C.

16. δῆλον ὅτι πᾶσαί τε αἱ τέχναι παντελῶς ἂν ἀπόλοιντο ἡμῖν καὶ οὐδ' εἰσαῦθις γένοιντ' ἂν ποτε διὰ τὸν ἀποκωλύοντα τοῦτον ζητεῖν νόμον· ὥστε ὁ βίος ὢν καὶ νῦν χαλεπὸς εἰς τὸν χρόνον ἐκεῖνον ἀβίωτος γίγνοιτ' ἂν τὸ παράπαν, 299E.

17. γράψαντι καὶ ἄγραφα νομοθετήσαντι, 295E. γράψαντας ἐν κύρβεσί τισι καὶ στήλαις, τὰ δὲ καὶ ἄγραφα πάτρια θεμένους ἔθη, 298D. γεγραμμένα καὶ πάτρια ἔθη κείμενα, 299D. See Rudolf Hirzel, *Agraphos Nomos* (*AbhLeipz*, 1903), XX, 1, 19.

18. Nietzsche, *Beyond Good and Evil*, tr. Helen Zimmern (Complete Works, vol. 12, Edinburgh and London, 1909), p. 89, no. 94: "The maturity of man: that means, to have reacquired the seriousness that one had as a child at play."

19. The confusion of interpreters is shown in the note of J. Adam on *Republic* 595A (*The Republic of Plato*, ed. with crit. notes, etc., 2 vols., Cambridge, 1921, 1926). The interpretation of the episode by Eduard Zeller (*Philosophie der Griechen* [II³], II, 1, 556) and others, as an appendix in which Plato answers censure of the second and third books, goes beyond the work of art itself and is as such an attempt to explain by unsuitable methods. In contrast to this, Georg A. Finsler (*Platon und die aristotelische Poetik*, Leipzig, 1900, p. 227) tries to understand the immanent meaning of the episode. In reference to the two kinds of mimesis see James Tate, "Imitation in Plato's *Republic*," *CQ*, XXII (1928), 16-23.

20. This has often been stated, e.g., by Eduard Müller, *Geschichte der Theorie der Kunst bei den Alten* (2 vols., Breslau, 1834-37), I, 27; Julius Walter, *Die Geschichte der Ästhetik im Altertum* (Leipzig, 1893), pp. 169f.; Ernst Cassirer, *Eidos and Eidolon* (Vorträge der Bibliothek Warburg, Leipzig, 1922-23), p. 26; Schweitzer, *Platon und die bildende Kunst* [I¹¹], pp. 11f. See Erwin Panofsky, *Idea* (Studien der Bibliothek Warburg Heft 5, Leipzig, 1924), pp. 1ff.; André Jolles, *Vitruvs Ästhetik* (Freiburg i. B., 1905), pp. 51ff.; B. Schweitzer, "Xenokrates von Athen," *Jahresbericht der Königsberger Gelehrten*

Gesellschaft, IX (1932), Pt. 1, 9f.; P.-M. Schuhl, *Platon et l'art de son temps* (2d edn., Paris, 1952); W. J. Verdenius, "Platon et la poésie," *Mnemosyne*, 3d ser., XII (1945), 118ff., and *Mimesis* (2d edn., Leyden, 1962); H. Broos, "Plato and Art," *Mnemosyne*, 4th ser., IV (1951), 113ff.; Rupert Clendon Lodge, *Plato's Theory of Art* (London, 1953); T. Moretti-Constanzi, *L'Estetica di Platone* (Rome, 1948); Elfriede Huber-Abrahamowicz, *Das Problem der Kunst bei Platon* (Winterthur, 1954).* R. G. Collingwood's detailed analysis in "Plato's Philosophy of Art," *Mind*, XXXIV (1925), 154ff., is an almost complete contradiction of the general view taken in my text.

21. Cf. 484CD, 500E. Aristotle, *Politics* VIII 5 7 1340a 36: δεῖ μὴ τὰ Παύσωνος θεωρεῖν τοὺς νέους ἀλλὰ τὰ Πολυγνώτου κἂν εἴ τις ἄλλος τῶν γραφέων ἢ τῶν ἀγαλματοποιῶν ἐστιν ἠθικός.

22. See Wolfgang Helbig, "Zeuxis und Parrhasios," *Jahrbuch für Philologie* (Munich), 1867, 649ff.: "They appear altogether as men of that transitional epoch, and remind us vividly of the most typical and many-sided representatives of the new trend, the Sophists" (p. 662). See also Ernst Pfuhl, *Malerei und Zeichnung der Griechen* (Munich, 1923), pp. 620f., 674ff.

23. See my "Die griechische Tragödie und das Tragische," *Antike*, I (1925), 5–35, 295–318; II (1926), 79–112.

24. The excellent and by no means fully exploited ch. XIII of the treatise Περὶ ὕψους should be carefully considered. In the *Republic* 378E Socrates says: Ὦ Ἀδείμαντε, οὐκ ἐσμὲν ποιηταὶ ἐγώ τε καὶ σὺ ἐν τῷ παρόντι, ἀλλ᾽ οἰκισταὶ πόλεως. Here the phrase "at present" might point to another time, when Socrates is indeed a "poet."

25. The *Timaeus* contains much of such "play," and it is not rightly understood if one finds "the character of παιδιά completely absent" from this dialogue, as does Reitzenstein, *Studien zum antiken Synkretismus* [I³⁸], pp. 35, 145.

26. See *Laws* VII 803B: ἔστι δὴ τοίνυν τὰ τῶν ἀνθρώπων πράγματα μεγάλης μὲν σπουδῆς οὐκ ἄξια. Cf. I 644D. *Republic* X 604B: οὔτε τι τῶν ἀνθρωπίνων ἄξιον ὂν μεγάλης σπουδῆς. On this problem see Eduard Zeller, *Platonische Studien* (Tübingen, 1839), p. 73; Wilamowitz, *Platon*, I, 448, 686. Ivo Bruns, *Plato's Gesetze* (Weimar, 1880), pp. 83ff., considered this attitude as not Platonic but characteristic of Philippos of Opus.

27. On the following see the Προλεγόμενα τῆς Πλάτωνος φιλοσοφίας, ch. 15 (Hermann, *Appendix*), p. 209. Perhaps the treatise Περὶ τοῦ γράφειν, listed among the works of Xenokrates in Diogenes Laërtius IV 12, discussed this matter.

28. In reference to this chapter see Hermann's excellent lecture "Über Platos schriftstellerische Motive" (1839), *Gesammelte Abhandlungen*

(Göttingen, 1849), pp. 281ff. Even Hermann's ordering of the Platonic dialogues is surprisingly correct; thus, he assigned the *Phaedrus* to the period of Plato's later creativity. / A. E. Chaignet, *La Vie et les écrits de Platon* (Paris, 1871), pp. 469ff., pins down the weak points of Hermann's view. But his own *"simplicité naïve et gauloise"* (*"Platon a écrit parce qu'il lui a plu d'écrire"*) will appear unsatisfactory not only to the *"gravité allemande,"* for Thibaudet (n. 4, above) goes far beyond that. / For ch. V see: William Chase Greene, "Plato's View of Poetry," *HSCP*, XXIX (1918), 1 ff.; Luigia Achillea Stella, "Influssi di poesia e d'arte Ellenica nell'opera di Platone," *Historia*, VI (1932), 433ff.; VII (1933), 75ff.; VIII (1934), 3ff.; Hans-Georg Gadamer, *Platon und die Dichter* (Frankfort, 1934); much in René Schaerer, *La Question platonicienne* (Neuchâtel, 1938); Philip Merlan, "Form and Content in Plato's Philosophy," *JHistId*, VIII (1947), 406-30; G. J. de Vries, *Spel bij Plato* (Amsterdam, 1949).

CHAPTER VI

1. See Georg Misch, *History of Autobiography in Antiquity*[3], tr. E. W. Dickens (2 vols., London, 1950), ch. I; Albrecht Werner von Blumenthal, *Die Schätzung des Archilochos im Altertume* (Stuttgart, 1922), pp. 7f.; Bruno Snell, *Die Entdeckung des Geistes* [III[5]], ch. III; Hermann Fränkel, *Dichtung und Philosophie des frühen Griechentums* (New York, 1951), pp. 652, 658.

2. Archytas frag. 1: καλῶς μοι δοκοῦντι. . . . Diogenes of Apollonia frag. 1: λόγου παντὸς ἀρχόμενον δοκεῖ μοι χρεὼν εἶναι. . . . Hippokrates Περὶ ἀέρων ch. 3: ἐγὼ φράσω σαφέως. . . . Προγνωστικόν ch. 1: τὸν ἰητρὸν δοκεῖ μοι ἄριστον εἶναι. . . . Περὶ διαίτης ὀξέων ch. 2: πολλὰ ἑτεροίως γιγνώσκω ἢ ὡς ἐκεῖνοι ἐπεξήεσαν. . . . Hippias frag. 6: ἐγὼ δὲ ἐκ πάντων τούτων τὰ μέγιστα καὶ ὁμόφυλα συνθεὶς τοῦτον καινὸν καὶ πολυειδῆ τὸν λόγον ποιήσομαι.*

3. Probably the "treatises in a more Aristotelian style" to which Stenzel refers in *Zahl und Gestalt*[2] [IV[18]], relying on the treatment of these questions by Werner Jaeger (*Studien zur Entstehungsgeschichte der Metaphysik des Aristoteles*, Berlin, 1912, pp. 131ff.), never existed. If different editions of Plato's single lecture (Jaeger, p. 141; Stenzel, p. 94) existed, it seems to follow that there was no genuine Platonic written version accessible even to his disciples. Nor does Aristotle, *Physics* 209b 14—[Πλάτων] ἐν τοῖς λεγομένοις ἀγράφοις δόγμασιν—support Stenzel. See Harold Cherniss, *Riddle of the Early Academy*, pp. 1ff.; Hans Leisegang, "Platon," *RE*, XX, col. 2520; Sir David Ross, *Plato's Theory of Ideas* [IV[4]], pp. 147ff.*

4. Ernst Buschor, in Adolf Furtwängler and Karl Reichhold, *Griechische Vasenmalerei* (3d ser., Munich, 1910-32), III, 155: "Leading personalities apparently did not then engage in vase painting. They are also

rare in the plastic arts. Here too the pioneer's impetus is lacking, and neither single beautiful reliefs nor even masters like Timotheos or Kephisodotos can prevent us from realizing that something like a valley spreads out between the creations of the school of Phidias and the works of Skopas' and Praxiteles' youth. It is as if the art of the ancients had been holding its breath while in another field a great genius transformed the countenance of antiquity and of mankind: Plato."

5. "Detours certainly are, for creative natures, often the only possible road to their goal." Franz Marc, *Briefe* (Berlin, 1921), p. 43.

6. Howald, *Platons Leben* [I⁵], sees in Plato's encounter with Socrates the first deviation from the anticipated line of Plato's life. Howald is influenced in this by Nietzsche: "Did the wicked Socrates really corrupt him?" (Preface to *Beyond Good and Evil.*) See Kurt Hildebrandt, *Nietzsches Wettkampf mit Sokrates und Platon* (Dresden, 1923), pp. 73, 96. / In reference to this chapter in general see Auguste Diès, *Autour de Platon* (2 vols., Paris, 1927), Livre II, "Socrate"; Julius Stenzel, "Sokrates," *RE*, 2d ser., III, cols. 811ff.; Eduard Spranger, "Sokrates," *Antike*, VII (1931), 271ff.; Alain (Émile Chartier), *Idees* (Paris, 1932), pp. 9ff; Arthur Kenyon Rogers, *The Socratic Problem* (New Haven, Conn., 1933); Helmut Kuhn, *Sokrates* (Berlin, 1934); Emma Edelstein, *Das Xenophontische und Platonische Bild des Sokrates* (Heidelberg, 1935); Victor Martin, "Le Problème du Socrate historique," *RTP*, XXIII (1933), 217–42; René Schaerer, "Le Portrait de Socrate," *La Question platonicienne* [V²³], pp. 170ff.; Jaeger, *Paideia* [IV⁴], II, 13ff.; Victor de Magelhães-Vilhena, *Le Problème de Socrate* (Paris, 1952), rev. by Olof Gigon, *Gnomon*, XXVII (1955), 255ff.*

A basic mistake of Gigon's remarkable book, *Sokrates. Sein Bild in Dichtung und Geschichte* (Bern, 1947), is its contrast of the dialogues of the Socratics as "literary creation" (*Dichtung*) with the so-called historical reports. In dealing with historic truth, however, Gigon's frame of reference is the authenticity of the dossier or police report—in that case, what is left of Thucydides?—while his idea of literary creation appears to coincide with what we call "fiction." As a result, what is alleged to be fact regarding the historic Socrates consists of a series of disconnected data, among them the fact that he "met his end, not exactly an ordinary one, in prison" (p. 14). According to Gigon, Plato must not be consulted at all as to the historic Socrates. For example, Socrates' attitude as Prytanis in the trial of the generals after the battle of Arginusai is history, but his refusal to obey the order of the Thirty to participate in the arrest of Leon of Salamis is not. Why? Because Xenophon's *Hellenica*, a historical work, contains three lines concerning the former fact, whereas the latter happens to be mentioned "only" in the *Apology* and in *Letter VII*. How can Gigon, though he knows that Socrates is an "elemental force," put aside "in determined resignation" the inquiry into the historic existence of that "elemental force" (14f.)? Furthermore, we should not forget, besides the written texts, the testimony of the plastic portraits: the picture of Socrates occupies an extremely important place in the history of Greek portraiture. See Karl Schefold, *Die Bildnisse der antiken Dichter, Redner und Denker* (Basel, 1943), pp. 63f., 82ff. We even know something about Socrates' manner of moving: βρενθυόμενος καὶ τὡφθαλμὼ παραβάλλων. Plato certainly would not have taken this characterization of his walk and look from Aristophanes' *Clouds* (v. 362) for his *Symposium* (221B) unless it hit off something of the real appearance of the man. The fact that the science of physiognomy links its origin with Socrates is also connected with these historic facts. See *Scriptores Physiognomici*, ed. Foerster, I, viiff.; Wilamowitz, *Antigonos von Karystos* [IV¹], p. 148. / See now C. J. de Vogel, "The Present State of the Socratic Problem," *Phronesis*, I (1955), 26ff.

7. Jean Paul Friedrich Richter, *Titan*, tr. Charles T. Brooks (2 vols., Boston, 1868), I, 7.

8. The following, therefore, are mistaken: Ernst Horneffer, *Platon gegen Sokrates* (Leipzig, 1904); S. Trubetzkoy, in "Zur Erklärung des Laches," *Hermes*, XL (1905), 66ff., referring to a remark by Vladimir Soloviev; Alfred Gercke, "Eine Niederlage des Sokrates," *Neue Jahrbücher für das klassische Altertum* (Leipzig, 1918). Julius Stenzel, "Zur Logik des Sokrates," *Studien zur Entwicklung der platonischen Dialektik von Sokrates zu Aristoteles²* (Leipzig, 1931), p. 152, has emphasized this thought in the most comprehensive terms: "The objective discussion of the Socratic problems must have been more important to Plato than literary controversy as such. Thus every Platonic dialogue remains a debate with Socrates himself." Generalized in this manner, the thought becomes meaningful: since every dialogue is a debate of Plato with himself, it is also one with the Socrates in him.

9. Grote believed that Plato intended to identify the Athenian of the *Laws* with Socrates, and that he only refrained from doing so because, as was common knowledge, Socrates had not been in Crete (quoted in W. D. Ross, ed., *Aristotle's Metaphysics*, 2 vols., Oxford, 1924, I, xl). I would say that it was not the shift of the conversation to Crete which caused the choice of the principal speaker. If Plato had wanted to introduce Socrates, he might well have been able to invent another setting. The shift of scene to Crete and the introduction of the Athenian are to be thought of as a single creative act.

10. Two formulations of the opposite opinion may stand for many others: Paul Wendland, "Die Aufgaben der platonischen Forschung," *NGG*, 1910, p. 104: "Certainly this change of participants betrays Plato's clear consciousness that his distance from the conceptual ethics of Socrates had become ever greater with his own growth, and that it

was no longer possible to make Socrates the mouthpiece of his own world of ideas." Gilbert Ryle, "Plato's Parmenides," *Mind*, XLVIII (1939), 130: "So slight a part does Socrates play in the *Parmenides*, *Sophist*, and *Politicus* . . . that the natural inference would surely be that Plato had discovered that certain important philosophic truths or methods were to be credited not to Socrates but to the Eleatics. Zeno is the teacher now and not Socrates."

11. See Louis Couturat, *De Platonicis mythis* (Paris, 1896), pp. 32ff.; Ernst Howald, "Εἰκὼς λόγος," *Hermes*, LVII (1922), 63ff.

CHAPTER VII

1. Goethe, at the end of the essay, "Plato als Mitgenosse einer christlichen Offenbarung" (1796), *Werke* (Stuttgart and Tübingen, 1827–34), XLVI, 28.*

2. See his "Ironie und Radikalismus," *Betrachtungen eines Unpolitischen* (Berlin, 1918), pp. 587ff.; *Bemühungen* (Berlin, 1925), pp. 56, 137f.; *Lotte in Weimar*, tr. H. T. Lowe-Porter (London, 1940), pp. 63ff. Mann wrote in a letter to the author on Aug. 21, 1949: "Die Ironie ich finde immer noch, dass Goethes Aussage darüber die beste ist. 'Ironie ist das Körnchen Salz, das das Aufgetischte überhaupt erst geniessbar macht.' "*

3. Jean Paul (Friedrich Richter), *Vorschule der Ästhetik, Werke*² (33 vols., Berlin, 1841), XVIII, § 38; *Wahlkapitulation zwischen Vulkan und Venus*, ch. 9 (in *Das heimliche Klaglied der Männer*, Munich, 1925). The most important aphorisms of Friedrich Schlegel will be quoted later. In Sören Kierkegaard's first work, *Om Begrebet Ironi med stadigt Hensyn til Socrates* (Copenhagen, 1841; German tr. by H. H. Schaeder, Munich, 1929), a profound insight into irony counterbalances the rigidity of Hegelian concepts such as "the infinite nothingness of irony," or irony as "infinite and absolute negativity." See Rudolf Schottländer, "Soeren Kierkegaards Sokratesauffassung," *PhA*, IV (1930), 27ff. Eduard Schwartz, *Charakterköpfe aus der antiken Literatur* [IV³¹], p. 51, appropriately characterizes the Socratic irony as "the individual variation of a genuine Attic plant cultivated on the soil of democracy." Perhaps this is the reason why the best recent analysis of irony came from the country of "understatement"; see James A. K. Thomson, *Irony* (London, 1926). / See also Jaspers, *Philosophie* [II¹⁴], II, 284ff.;* Schaerer, *La Question platonicienne* [V²⁸], ch. I, 4: "La Sincérité et l'ironie," also pp. 16, 176, 258; de Vries, *Spel bij Plato* [V²⁸]. How badly irony can be misunderstood is apparent in Richard Robinson, *Plato's Earlier Dialectic*² (Ithaca, N. Y., and Oxford, 1953), pp. 8ff.; see my review in *CP*, XL (1945), 253–59.

4. Theophrastus is of special value because he seems to have eliminated the image of Socrates completely, i.e., deliberately; only when we realize

this can we understand him correctly. It becomes particularly apparent when contrasted with Aristotle's description of the *eiron* (*Nicomachean Ethics* IV 13 1127a 22 *et seq.*, 1127b 22 *et seq.*) and with that of Ariston in Philodemos, "Περὶ κακιῶν" (ed. Christian Jensen, Leipzig, 1911), p. 38. See Leopold Schmidt, *Commentatio de* εἴρωνος *notione apud Aristonem et Theophrastum* (Marburg, 1873); Wilhelm Büchner, "Über den Begriff der Eironeia," *Hermes*, LXXVI (1941), 339ff.*

5. "Precisely because it is the nature of irony never to take off its mask, and because, Proteuslike, irony constantly changes its mask, it necessarily inflicts so much suffering upon any loving youth. (Note: The ironist raises the individual above his immediate existence—this is the act of liberation—to keep him suspended just as, according to the legend, Mohammed's coffin is suspended between two magnets, one that attracts and one that repels.) In this way, irony has something repellent about it but, at the same time, something extremely seductive and bewitching." Kierkegaard, p. 48; tr. Schaeder, p. 39.

6. *Werke* (19 vols., Berlin, 1832-87), XIV, 59ff. Following Hegel, e.g., is Wilhelm Windelband, *Lehrbuch der Geschichte der Philosophie*[5] [I[10]], p. 78. Hegel's polemic against the concept of irony in romantic literature actually hits only the nihilistic exaggerations. See *Briefwechsel zwischen Wilhelm Dilthey und dem Grafen Paul Yorck von Wartenburg, 1877-97* (Halle, 1923), p. 216: "The iteration of Socratic 'ignorance' [by Plato] is not irony—contrary to the romanticist view—but pure truth, since knowledge, according to the natural bent of the Greeks, is ontically determined." The opposition of irony to truth in this remark is particularly striking. For—in spite of Aristotle—what would be truer than irony? See also Friedrich Ast, *Platons Leben und Schriften* (Leipzig, 1816), p. 100, where we sense the proximity of romanticism. Max Brod, *Heinrich Heine* (Amsterdam, 1934), pp. 289ff., deals with the romanticist's view of irony as both related and opposed to the Socratic-Platonic view.*

7. "Maximen und Reflexionen," *Jahrbuch der Goethe-Gesellschaft* (Weimar), XXI (1907), no. 1198.

8. "Plato, or the Philosopher," in *Representative Men* (1850).

9. *Prosaische Jugendschriften*, ed. Jakob Minor (2 vols., Vienna, 1882-1906), II, 392.

10. "Lyceumsfragment" 108, ibid., II, 199. See also Schlegel's essay on "incomprehensibility," ibid., II, 386ff. / Hermann Gundert, "Enthusiasmos und Logos bei Platon," *Lexis*, II (1949), 46, discussing philosophical discourses, says, "Enthusiasm becomes apparent only in a statement that is itself enthusiastic, but it is true only in the irony, with which the *logos* of that statement withdraws again from its own assertion."

11. εἰ μὲν ἔστιν ἃ θρυλοῦμεν ἀεί, καλόν τέ τι καὶ ἀγαθὸν καὶ πᾶσα ἡ τοιαύτη οὐσία, 76D. εἶμι πάλιν ἐπ' ἐκεῖνα τὰ πολυθρύλητα, 100B.

12. See ch. III.

13. See Otto Apelt, "Die Taktik des platonischen Sokrates," *Platonische Aufsätze* (Leipzig, 1912), pp. 105f.; *re* irony, see his essay on Plato's humor, ibid., 72ff. Harald Höffding, *Humor als Lebensgefühl*, tr. H. Goebel (Leipzig, 1918), also speaks of Plato's humor; so does Erich Bethe, *Die griechische Dichtung* (Potsdam, 1924), p. 258. But humor implies a different concept of personality; see the end of Kierkegaard's essay (German tr., p. 275); also Rudolf Bultmann, *Glauben und Verstehen* (2 vols., Tübingen, 1933-52), II, 208ff., on humor as "secularization of the Christian understanding of suffering."*

14. On Diotima, see Walther Kranz, "Diotima," *Antike*, II (1926), 313-32; and "Diotima von Mantineia," *Hermes*, LXI (1926), 437-44. Gerhard Krüger, *Einsicht und Leidenschaft* [II²²], pp. 142ff.: "Diotima is incomparably more than Socrates, as certainly as mystical wisdom is more than the act of questioning." We should not overlook the fact, however, that Plato shows us Diotima only through the ironical speech of Socrates, and that Socrates died for the sake of questioning. / Kranz believes that Diotima was a historical person; the report on her activity in delaying the pestilence (*Symposium* 201D) reads indeed like a historic fact (Krüger). But even in that case "the real person of the priestess is of no significance for the dialogue" (Kranz).* / The Attic relief (about 420 B.C.) of a priestess in Gustave Fougères, "Stèle de Mantinée," *BCH*, XII (1888), pl. iv and pp. 376ff., has been interpreted as Diotima by Hans Moebius, "Diotima," *JDAI*, XLIX (1934), 45-60, esp. p. 58, and Karl Schefold, *Die Bildnisse der antiken Dichter*, [VI⁶], p. 66. / Worth while reading though fanciful is R. Godel, "Socrate et Diotime," *Bulletin de l'Association Guillaume Budé*, 4th ser., XIII (1954), no. 4, 3ff.

15. See new note in Addenda to the Second Edition, p. 401, below.

CHAPTER VIII

1. Herman Grimm, *Goethe*⁵ (Berlin, 1894), p. 322: "The ancients knew the landscape only as a background for human actions; they lacked the concept of solitude as such." Georg Simmel, *Rembrandt* (Leipzig, 1917), p. 77: "In classical art, the particulars are so represented as to produce in a typical spectator the most favorable impression in respect to characteristics, beauty, and clearness. . . . Perhaps a very common trait of the Mediterranean peoples is revealed here too: to accommodate their behavior to the presence of a spectator." / See also Hermann Schmalenbach, "Zur Genealogie der Einsamkeit," *Logos*, VIII (1920), 62-96, and his *Leibniz* (Munich, 1921), pp. 152ff. On Sophocles see my "Die griechische Tragödie und das Tragische," *Antike*, I (1925), 303, 314; II (1926), 94.

2. *Phaedo* 73A. See my *Der Grosse Alcibiades*, II, 29.

3. See Walther Kranz, "Das Verhältnis des Schöpfers zu seinem Werk in der althellenischen Literatur," *Neue Jahrbücher für das klassische Altertum* (Leipzig, 1924), pp. 65ff.

4. On the general context see Rudolf Hirzel, *Der Dialog* (2 pts., Leipzig, 1895); Karl Joël, *Geschichte der antiken Philosophie* (Tübingen, 1921), pp. 773f.; the chapter "Dialog" in Wilamowitz' *Platon* [I¹⁷], II; and Hans-Georg Gadamer, *Platos dialektische Ethik* (Leipzig, 1931), ch. I § 5: "Der sokratische Dialog."

5. On the following see Karl Justi, *Die ästhetischen Elemente der platonischen Philosophie* (Marburg, 1860), pp. 9f.

6. *Charmides* 154DE, *Alcibiades* I 132A, *Theaetetus* 169AB. The myth of the *Gorgias* 523C *et seq.* contains an elaboration of the same motif.

7. Remember the metaphorical use of light and darkness in Plato, e.g., *Phaedrus* 261E: εἰς φῶς ἄγειν, *Laws* 663B: τὸ σκότος ἀφελών, 788C: φῶς—σκότος, furthermore, *Letter VII* 341D: ἐξαφθὲν φῶς and the simile of the cave.

8. Proclus, *In Alcibiadem, Procli Opera Inedita*², ed. Victor Cousin (Paris, 1864), p. 308, ll. 24ff. τὰ προοίμια τῶν Πλατωνικῶν διαλόγων συνᾴδει πρὸς τοὺς ὅλους αὐτῶν σκοπούς, καὶ οὔτε δραματικῆς ἕνεκα ψυχαγωγίας μεμηχάνηται τῷ Πλάτωνι. . . . οὔτε τῆς ἱστορίας στοχάζεται μόνης. . . . ἀλλ' ὥσπερ καὶ τοῖς ἡμετέροις δοκεῖ καθηγεμόσι καὶ ἡμῖν καὶ ἐν ἄλλοις μετρίως ὑπέμνησται [where?] τῆς ὅλης τῶν διαλόγων ἐξήρτηται καὶ ταῦτα προθέσεως.

9. Wilamowitz-Moellendorff, *Platon*, I, 181 = I², 183.

10. See my *Der Grosse Alcibiades*, I, 2.

11. Deussen, *Sechzig Upanischaden* [III²⁸] p. 426, contains the comparison with Socrates. On the literary form of the Indian dialogues, see Hermann Oldenberg, *Die Lehre der Upanischaden* (Göttingen, 1915), pp. 148ff.

12. K. E. Neumann, tr., *Die Reden Gotamo Buddho's aus der Mittleren Sammlung* (3 vols., Munich, 1896–1902), esp. vol. III. See Karl Fries, *Das philosophische Gespräch von Hiob bis Platon* (Tübingen, 1904), pp. 75ff.

13. Julius Stenzel, "The Literary Form and Philosophical Content of the Platonic Dialogue," *Plato's Method of Dialectic*, tr. D. J. Allan (Oxford, 1940), pp. 1–23, has this problem thoroughly worked out. See also Hirzel, I, 240.

14. Thus, e.g., K. F. Hermann, *Geschichte und System der platonischen Philosophie* [IV³²], p. 354; Hirzel, pp. 240f. (concerning the *Republic*); Wilamowitz, *Platon*, I, 555 = I², 561 (on the *Sophist*). Opposed: Paul Wendland, "Die Aufgaben der platonischen Forschung," *NGG*, 1910, p. 112.

15. See ch. V.

16. *The Will to Power*, tr. A. M. Ludovici, 2 vols. (Complete Works, vols. 14 [originally 9] and 15, Edinburgh and London, 1909–10), II,

378, § 980. See W. A. Kaufmann, "Nietzsche's Admiration for Socrates," *JHistId*, IX (1948), 472ff.*

17. *Pensées*, no. 203 (ed. J. Chevalier, Paris, 1936, p. 875).

18. See Wilhelm von Scholz, "Das Schaffen des dramatischen Dichters," *Kongress für Ästhetik und allgemeine Kunstwissenschaft* (Stuttgart, 1914), 377ff.; Marino Gentile, "Platone autore di drammi filosofici," *Rivista di Filosofia Neo-scolastica*, XXII (1930), 427ff. The essay by F. W. von Thiersch, "Über die dramatische Natur der platonischen Dialoge," *AbhMun*, 1837, tries to read the five acts of the drama into the Platonic dialogues and thus does not get beyond a mechanical speculation. On Plato's relation to tragedy, see Helmut Kuhn, "The True Tragedy," *HSCP*, LII (1941); LIII (1942); Dorothy Tarrant, "Plato as Dramatist," *JHS*, LXXV (1955), 82ff. / The old work by James Geddes, *An Essay on the Composition and Manner of Writing of the Ancients, Particularly Plato* (Glasgow, 1748), continues the method of the ancients in the criticism of style, and even today has some charm as evidence of the author's love of the artist-philosopher Plato. / According to the formulation by Friedrich Gundolf, *Goethe* (Berlin, 1925), p. 488, "The dialogue is the appropriate literary form for the discussion of human antagonisms, the drama for their embodiment," one would classify a great part of Plato's written work as drama. In the same way, of Goethe's two opposites, "poet" and "writer of dialogues" (*Die guten Weiber, Werke*, 1827–34, XV, 265), Plato would be the former as well as the latter, and often more the former than the latter.

19. Ferdinand Dümmler, "Prolegomena zu Platos Staat IX," *Kleine Schriften* [I⁹], I, 158, says in reference to *Republic* VI 491 E, "Without a certain amount of sympathy the imposing artistic perfection of design in this character would not be understandable." Alain, *Idées* [VI⁶], p. 17, is still better: "Plato paints himself here as he might have been, as he feared to be."*

20. Dionysius of Halicarnassus, *Epistula ad Pompeium* (ed. Usener et Radermacher), II, 228: καὶ πολὺς ὁ τελέτης ἐστὶν ἐν τοῖς τοιούτοις [in such features of style] παρ' αὐτῷ, ὡς καὶ Δημήτριος ὁ Φαληρεὺς εἴρηκέ που καὶ ἄλλοι συχνοί· οὐ γὰρ ἐμὸς ὁ μῦθος. Another version in *De Demosthene*, ibid., I, 138, however, reads: καὶ πολυτέλειά τις ἐν τοῖς . . . συχνοὶ πρότερον· . . . The word πρότερον, which fits only into this second version, suggests that Dionysius wrote differently in the two places, contrary to the opinion of Usener and Radermacher, as of Felix Jacoby, *Die Fragmente der griechischen Historiker* (Berlin and Leiden, 1923–54), II, B, 964, frag. 11.

21. "Vorarbeiten zu einer Physiologie der Pflanzen," *Werke* (Weimar edn. [I²³]), II, VI, 302.

22. See ch. VI.

23. See ch. VII.

CHAPTER IX

1. The passages in Plato where *mythos* and similar words occur have been collected by Couturat, *De Platonicis mythis* [VI¹¹], pp. 3ff.; and Walter Wili, *Versuch einer Grundlegung der platonischen Mythopoiie* (Zurich diss., 1925) 9ff., reviewed by Julius Stenzel, *DLZ*, XLVII (1926), cols. 1139-42. On the theme of this chapter see also John Alexander Stewart, *The Myths of Plato* (London and New York, 1905); Karl Reinhardt, *Platons Mythen* (Bonn, 1927); R. Wiggers, *Beiträge zur Entwicklungsgeschichte des philosophischen Mythos der Griechen* (Rostock diss., 1927); Perceval Frutiger, *Les Mythes de Platon* (Paris, 1930); Paul Stöcklein, "Über die philosophische Bedeutung von Platons Mythen," *Philologus, Suppl.* 30 (1937); H. W. Thomas, *Epekeina* (Würzburg diss., 1938); Krüger, *Einsicht und Leidenschaft* [II²²]; M. P. Nilsson, *Geschichte der griechischen Religion* [II¹⁷], I, 772ff.; Pierre-Maxime Schuhl, *Études sur la fabulation platonicienne* (Paris, 1947); Ludwig Edelstein, "The Function of the Myth in Plato's Philosophy," *JHistId*, X (1949), 463ff.

2. Nevertheless, the myth is still a kind of *logos* in the fullest sense of the word. Socrates' words, *Republic* 501E: ἡ πολιτεία ἥν μυθολογοῦμεν λόγωι, ἔργωι τέλος λήψεται, seem to indicate that the *Republic* is both mythical and logical in character.

3. *Republic* 377A: τοῦτο δέ που ὡς τὸ ὅλον εἰπεῖν ψεῦδος, ἔνι δὲ καὶ ἀληθῆ.

4. The polemic of Kolotes against Plato's mythical poetry is instructive, as is the defense of the master by the Neoplatonists. See Macrobius, *In Somnium Scipionis* I 2; Proclus, *In Rem publicam Platonis Commentarii*, ed. W. Kroll (2 vols., Leipzig, 1899-1900), II, 105ff.

5. This sense is especially clear in *Statesman* 268D-69C, 271A, 272CD; also in *Timaeus* 21D, 22C, and *Symposium* 190B.

6. This remains correct, even though primitive man is quite generally designated as γυμνὸς καὶ ἀνυπόδητος καὶ ἄστρωτος καὶ ἄοπλος in the *Protagoras* 321C 5, and γυμνὸς καὶ ἄστρωτος in the *Statesman* 272A 5. The relationship is strange: is Socrates to be characterized as the original human being? On the Socratic features of Eros, see Robin, *La Théorie platonicienne de l'amour* [II¹⁸], p. 154.

7. That this myth as found in Plato goes back to Protagoras has not been proved by Dickerman's penetrating and learned dissertation, *De argumentis quibusdam . . . e structura hominis et animalium petitis* (Halle, 1909). It has only been proved that the Platonic tale has its place within a sphere of broad discussions of the manifold and purposeful forms of creatures and of human civilization. But the myth bears features that are decidedly not Protagorean. We might admit with Woldemar Uxküll-Gyllenband, *Griechische Kulturentstehungslehren* (Archiv für Geschichte der Philosophie, XXXVI, pts. 3 and 4,

Suppl., Berlin, 1924), p. 20—who takes over and extends Dickerman's exposition—that the mythical raiment is potentially Protagorean; but we can figure out, to a certain extent, how the story of
the origin of religion must have looked if Protagoras had written
it. Now we read in Plato that on account of his relationship with
the deity (!) man is the only living being that believes in gods
and erects altars and statues of the gods (322A). Once we realize how
un-Protagorean that is, we must doubt whether the garb of the myth
really is solely responsible for the divine origin of ἔντεχνος σοφία and
πολιτικὴ ἀρετή, which, by way of ἐπειδὴ δὲ ὁ ἄνθρωπος θείας μετέσχε
μοίρας, is connected with the origin of religion. Thus there is little
left for Protagoras of what Uxküll-Gyllenband attributes to him,
least of all the "founding of the science of human pre-history." / The
myth is attributed to Protagoras by Wilhelm Nestle, *Vom Mythos
zum Logos* (Stuttgart, 1942), pp. 282ff., and by Gregory Vlastos,
introd. to *Plato's Protagoras*, B. Jowett's tr., rev. Martin Ostwald, ed.
Gregory Vlastos (New York, 1956), p. ix *et seq.* / Against Protagorean origin: Harold Cherniss, *AJP*, LXXI (1950), 87. See Kurt v.
Fritz, "Protagoras," *RE*, XX, cols. 917f.

8. *Vorsokr.* 28 [18] A 35.

9. ἐπειδὴ καὶ τούτοις χρόνος ἦλθεν εἱμαρμένος γενέσεως, *Protagoras* 320D ∼
ἐπειδὴ γὰρ πάντων τούτων χρόνος ἐτελειώθη, *Statesman* 272D.   γυμνόν
τε καὶ ἀνυπόδητον καὶ ἄστρωτον, *Protagoras* 321C ∼ γυμνοὶ δὲ καὶ
ἄστρωτοι, *Statesman* 272A.   πόλεις οὐκ ἦσαν, *Protagoras* 322B ∼
πολιτεῖαι οὐκ ἦσαν, *Statesman* 271E.   ἀπώλλυντο ὑπὸ τῶν θηρίων,
Protagoras 322B ∼ διηρπάζοντο ὑπ' αὐτῶν (*scil.* τῶν θηρίων),
Statesman 274B.   Ζεὺς οὖν δείσας περὶ τῷ γένει ἡμῶν μὴ ἀπόλοιτο
πᾶν, *Protagoras* 322C ∼ θεός. . . . κηδόμενος ἵνα μὴ χειμασθεὶς
ὑπὸ ταραχῆς . . . , *Statesman* 273D.   Προμηθεύς. . . . κλέπτει
Ἡφαίστου καὶ Ἀθηνᾶς τὴν ἔντεχνον σοφίαν σὺν πυρί, *Protagoras* 321C
∼ πῦρ μὲν παρὰ Προμηθέως, τέχναι δὲ παρ' Ἡφαίστου καὶ τῆς συντέ-
χνου, *Statesman* 274C. Uxküll-Gyllenband notes the conformity of
the last two passages (p. 18), but interprets it erroneously to mean
that Plato used the same work of Protagoras in both dialogues.

10. Justice is done to this myth neither if we find in it only anti-Platonic
traits, with Friedrich Schleiermacher (*Platos Werke*², 6 vols., Berlin,
1807–28, I, 233) and many others, nor if we say that it is "even
superior to any other fable of Plato," with the Sophists' friend George
Grote (*Plato and the Other Companions of Socrates*, 3 vols., London,
1865, II, 47). Olof Gigon, "Studien zu Platons Protagoras," *Phyl-
lobolia für Peter von der Mühll* (Basel, 1946), pp. 124ff., discovers
"enclosed in the myth fragments of very different origin," and attempts to make everything appear as disparate as possible.

11. From the literature on the myth of Aristophanes, and on Orphic,
Babylonian, and Indian parallels and their possible influence upon it,

see Konrat Ziegler, "Menschen und Weltenwerden," *Neue Jahrbücher für das klassische Altertum* (Leipzig, 1913), pp. 529ff.; Albrecht Goetze, "Eine orphisch-arische Parallele," *ZBud*, IV (1922), 170–89; Wilamowitz, *Platon* [I¹⁷], I, 370 = I², 373; Bidez, *Eos* [IV¹⁵], ch. 5; Jula Kerschensteiner, *Platon und der Orient* (Stuttgart, 1945), pp. 147ff.

12. See ch. III, pp. 64ff., above.

13. Frank, *Plato und die Pythagoreer* [I³], pp. 90f., 298ff.; Ivan Mortimer Linforth, "Soul and Sieve in Plato's Gorgias," *University of California Publications in Classical Philology*, XII, no. 17 (1944), 295ff.; Eric Robertson Dodds, *The Greeks and the Irrational* (Sather Classical Lectures 25, Berkeley and Los Angeles, 1951), pp. 209, 225.

14. Couturat proves that anamnesis is a half-mythical conception, not a rational dogmatic concept, as which it is mostly understood in the history of philosophy, e.g., by Zeller, *Philosophie der Griechen* [II³], II, 1, 835. However, as to the rationalistic dissolution of the mythical which Couturat offers later, I refer to Hegel, *Werke*, XIV, 211f.: "We realize here [in the *Phaedr.*] in what sense Plato speaks of scientific insight as recollection. He states explicitly that this is said only in similes and comparisons." This does not prevent us from interpreting the anamnesis "logically"; it is indeed the presupposition of all λέγειν. See, e.g., Richard Hönigswald, *Die Philosophie des Altertums* [I²¹], p. 180. But the interpreter must beware of dismissing the mythical as a "questionable shift from the logical to the psychological," Natorp, *Platos Ideenlehre* [I²¹], p. 36. In reference to anamnesis see Ernesto Grassi, *Il Problema della Metafisica Platonica* (Bari, 1932), ch. IV; Alexandre Koyré, *Discovering Plato*, tr. Leonora Cohen-Rosenfield (Columbia Studies in Philosophy 9, New York, 1945), p. 10. Koyré acknowledges the mythical character of anamnesis, but establishes a contrast between the mythical and the serious. / The question may be attacked by starting from the concept of "existence." See ch. XII, pp. 230ff., above.

15. Commonplace, and not very illuminating, is Olympiodoros' comparison, *In Platonis Phaedonem commentaria*, ed. Wilhelm Norvin (Leipzig, 1913), pp. 228, 25ff.: τριῶν δὲ οὐσῶν νεκυιῶν. . . . ἥδε μὲν (the *nekyia* of the *Phaedo*) περὶ τῶν τόπων μᾶλλον ποιεῖται τὸν λόγον, ἡ δὲ ἐν Γοργίᾳ περὶ τῶν δικαζόντων, ἡ δὲ ἐν Πολιτείᾳ περὶ τῶν δικαζομένων.

16. The expression "doctrine of metempsychosis" should be avoided, since our discussion has shown at least that Plato has no "doctrine" of anything like the migration of souls. It is a widespread view that the *Gorgias* contains no reference at all to this "doctrine"; see, e.g., Hans von Arnim, *Platos Jugenddialoge und die Entstehungszeit des Phaidros* (Leipzig, 1914), p. 163. We tried to refute this view in our text, but contrary argument has made no impression on H. W. Thomas, *Epekeina*, p. 71.

17. Proclus, *In Rem publicam* II 105 2 (ed. Kroll): τούτων δὲ ἐφ' ἑκάτερα τῶν λόγων τεταγμένων ἡ περὶ τῆς κοσμικῆς τάξεως θεωρία τὴν μέσην ἀπείληφε χώραν.

18. See chs. IV and XV.

18a. See J. S. Morrison, "Parmenides and Er," *JHS*, LXXV (1955), 59ff.

19. Plato: ἐπειδὴ ἀγένητόν ἐστιν καὶ ἀδιάφθορον αὐτὸ ἀνάγκη εἶναι ~ Parmenides: ὡς ἀγένητον ἐὸν καὶ ἀνώλεθρόν ἐστι. οὔποτε λήγει κινούμενον ~ Empedokles: ἀλλάσσοντα διαμπερὲς οὐδαμὰ λήγει. οὔτε ἀπόλλυσθαι οὔτε γίγνεσθαι δυνατόν ~ Parmenides: οὔτε γενέσθαι οὔτ' ὄλλυσθαι ἀνῆκε Δίκη. πᾶσαν γένεσιν συμπεσοῦσαν στῆναι ~ Parmenides: τὼς γένεσις μὲν ἀπέσβεσται. Alkmaion: see Wilamowitz, *Platon*, I, 456, 459. "These ideas are derived from pre-Socratic conceptions," says Stenzel, *Über zwei Begriffe der platonischen Mystik: ΖΩΙΟΝ und ΚΙΝΗΣΙΣ* [I³⁸], p. 13. See Reinhardt, *Mythen*, pp. 83f. Schweitzer, *Platon und die bildende Kunst* [I¹¹], pp. 63f., refers for the myth of *Phaedrus* to a golden ear pendant at Boston (pl. 37); it is in fact but one of the many instances of winged charioteers, horses, and chariots in Greek art.

20. *The Thirteen Principal Upanishads*, tr. Robert Ernest Hume (Oxford, 1934), p. 351. / Arthur Berriedale Keith, *The Religion and Philosophy of the Veda and Upanishads* (Harvard Oriental Series, XXXII, Cambridge, Mass., 1925), pp. 609, 613, refers to "the interesting parallel" but is in favor of independence, since "the details are perfectly distinct."

21. These relations have been worked out most thoroughly by Arnim, *Jugenddialoge*, pp. 156ff., and differently but surely not correctly by Rogers, *The Socratic Problem* [VI⁶], App. C. For the comparison of the soul with a chariot see Pseudo-Isokrates, *Demonicea* 32. As early as ancient times the relationship was felt between the team of the soul striving toward the supraheavenly sphere and that of Parmenides driving up to the goddess of truth. (See Natorp, *Ideenlehre*, p. 74.) For Sextus, *Adversus mathematicos* VII 112, interprets Parmenides' proem with Plato in mind. See Reinhardt, *Parmenides* [I³¹], p. 33.

22. Formerly I called these verses "Orphic" because of Plato's reference to "secret poems." That cannot be proved. Schleiermacher, *Platons Werke*, I, 1² (Berlin, 1812), p. 385, even makes Plato the author of these verses.*

23. On the astronomical element in the *Phaedrus*, whereby a move toward the *Timaeus* is indicated, see Stenzel, *ΖΩΙΟΝ und ΚΙΝΗΣΙΣ*. Also Wilamowitz, *Platon*, I, 456 = I², 461; Arnim, pp. 174ff. A. Boeckh, *Philolaos des Pythagoreers Lehren nebst den Bruchstücken seines Werkes* (Berlin, 1819), pp. 105ff., had interpreted this peculiarity of the *Phaedrus* as due to the vague personality "Philolaos." If one disregards the name, there is still something right in this view. Carl Kerényi, "Astrologia

Platonica," *ArchRW*, XXII (1923), 24, understands the word ἄρχοντες in an astrological sense, and the twelve gods as those of the Zodiac. Kerschensteiner, *Platon und der Orient*, pp. 183ff., opposes this view.* / Arnold von Salis, "Die Gigantomachie am Schilde der Athena Parthenos," *JDAI*, LV (1940), 160ff., considers the motif of the chariots in Plato's myth as inspired by the shield of Pheidias' Athena. The comparison is important, and one cannot doubt that Plato was familiar even with the details of the monument. The error in von Salis' construction is that he interprets such terms as ἡγεμών, τάξις, κοσμεῖν, etc., in a military sense. There is no war in Platos' myth.

24. James Adam (*The Republic of Plato* [IV¹⁴]), discussing *Republic* 615A, rightly calls attention to the fact that in the *Republic* the period of a thousand years does not include the lifetime of a hundred years, while in the *Phaedrus* the whole interval from birth to rebirth is summed up as a thousand years. This difference, though Plato may not have taken it into consideration, may be relevant to our discussion. In reference to this and to the following see Arnim, pp. 168ff.

25. On the connection between these degrees and those of the constitutions of states and souls in the *Republic* see Arnim, p. 167.

26. See Arnim, pp. 211ff., who is mistaken only in taking this motif in the *Phaedrus* to be an external addition. For it is the ἐρωτικὴ μανία whose highest steps lead to the εἶδος, and the φιλόσοφος is ultimately identical with the φιλόκαλος or μουσικὸς καὶ ἐρωτικός, 248D; cf. μουσικῶς ἐρᾶν, *Republic* II 403A.

27. Here the text must be emended: ὁ δὲ ἀρτιτελής, ὁ τῶν τότε πολυθεάμων 251A 1 cannot be correct. For not every ἀρτιτελής need be πολυθεάμων and vice versa, just as 250E 1 reads ὁ μὴ νεοτελὴς ἢ διεφθαρμένος. In our passage too ἢ would be most appropriate instead of the second ὁ. And that is the reading of the Papyrus of Oxyrhynchus 1016.*

28. On the connection of Eros and soul, both of which are "intermediates," see Ernst Hoffmann, "Platons Lehre von der Weltseele," *Sokrates*, 1915, pp. 187–211; and "Methexis und Metaxy bei Platon" 1919, pp. 48–70. See also ch. II, 41ff.

29. On the systematic classification concealed here see Arnim, pp. 215f.

30. On the following see ch. I, esp. 22ff.

31. See Reitzenstein, *Synkretismus* [I³⁸], esp. chs. I and IV; Bidez, *Eos*, ch. X.

32. On the myth of the *Timaeus* see the commentators and Hoffmann, *Platonismus und Mittelalter* [II⁸], pp. 60ff.

33. That the participant in the dialogue is not the "tyrant" Kritias but his grandfather has been shown by John Burnet, *Greek Philosophy* (London, 1914), I, 338. See also Alfred E. Taylor, *A Commentary on Plato's Timaeus* (Oxford, 1928), pp. 23ff.

34. Marsilio Ficino, instead, in *Divi Platonis opera* (Venice, 1561), p. 422 remarks on the *Critias*, "*Plato noster officiosissimus patriae suae filius*

laudavit eam in Menexeno ex rebus contra orientales, laudat rursus in Critia ex rebus contra occidentales. Atque utrobique. . . . commonefacit omnes ne patriae sint ingrati." / What was once said by Niebuhr is now said by George Sarton, *A History of Science* (Cambridge, Mass., 1952), I, 408ff. Against Sarton, see my chapters "Crito," "Menexenus," and "Critias" in vols. 2 and 3 of the present work.

35. See ch. XVII.

36. Kerschensteiner, pp. 187ff.

37. *Critias* 109B: θεοὶ ἅπασαν γῆν ποτε κατὰ τοὺς τόπους διελάγχανον. ∼ *Statesman* 271D: κατὰ τόπους. . . . ὑπὸ θεῶν ἀρχόντων παντ' ἦν τὰ τοῦ κόσμου μέρη διειλημμένα. *Critias* 109B: κατοικίσαντες, οἷον νομῆς ποίμνια, κτήματα καὶ θρέμματα ἑαυτῶν ἡμᾶς ἔτρεφον. ∼ *Statesman* 271D: τὰ ζῷα κατὰ γένη καὶ ἀγέλας οἷον νομῆς θεῖοι διειλήφεσαν δαίμονες. *Critias* 109C: ἐκ πρύμνης ἀπευθύνοντες οἷον οἴακι πειθοῖ ψυχῆς ἐφαπτόμενοι κατὰ τὴν αὐτῶν διάνοιαν οὕτως ἄγοντες τὸ θνητὸν πᾶν ἐκυβέρνων. / *Statesman* 272E: ὁ κυβερνήτης οἷον πηδαλίων οἴακος ἀφέμενος. *Critias* 121A: ἐπεὶ δ' ἡ τοῦ θεοῦ μὲν μοῖρα ἐξίτηλος ἐγίγνετο ἐν αὐτοῖς πολλῷ τῷ θνητῷ καὶ πολλάκις ἀνακεραννυμένη, τὸ δὲ ἀνθρώπινον ἦθος ἐπεκράτει, τότε ἤδη τὰ παρόντα φέρειν ἀδυνατοῦντες ἠσχημόνουν ∼ *Statesman* 273B: τοῦτων αὐτῷ τὸ σωματοειδὲς τῆς συγκράσεως αἴτιον. . . . ὅτι πολλῆς ἦν μετέχον ἀταξίας πρὶν εἰς τὸν νῦν κόσμον ἀφικέσθαι. . . . σμικρὰ μὲν τἀγαθά, πολλὴν δὲ τὴν τῶν ἐναντίων κρᾶσιν ἐπεγκεραννύμενος ἐπὶ διαφθορᾶς κίνδυνον ἀφικνεῖται.

38. Lewis Campbell, *The Sophistes and Politicus of Plato* (Oxford, 1867), p. xxviii, stresses these traits of the myth: "The chief motive of the fable is to recall the mind from resting in a mere abstract ideal. 'We are not living in the golden age': i.e., in forming our conception of true statesmanship, we must take account of the imperfect conditions of the actual world." Correct, though somewhat one-sided.

39. Cf. 270B: τὸ τὴν τοῦ παντὸς φορὰν τοτὲ μὲν ἐφ' ἃ νῦν κυκλεῖται φέρεσθαι, τοτὲ δὲ ἐπὶ τἀναντία. ∼ Empedokles frag. 17:1 τοτὲ μὲν γὰρ ἓν ηὐξήθη μόνον εἶναι ἐκ πλεόνων, τοτὲ δ' αὖ διέφυ. . . . 269C: οὐδεὶς εἴρηκεν, νῦν δὲ δὴ λεκτέον. ∼ Empedokles frag. 17, 25: τὴν οὔτις. . . . δεδάηκε θνητὸς ἀνήρ· σὺ δ' ἄκουε. . . . 272D ἐπειδὴ γὰρ πάντων τούτων χρόνος ἐτελειώθη ∼ Empedokles frag. 30: αὐτὰρ ἐπεὶ μέγα νεῖκος ἐνὶ μελέεσσιν ἐθρέφθη ἐς τιμάς τ' ἀνόρουσε τελειομένοιο χρόνοιο. . . . The last two passages were compared by Campbell. On possible Oriental models of this myth, see Reitzenstein, *Synkretismus*, esp. ch. 2; Bidez, *Eos*, ch. 9; Kerschensteiner, p. 103ff. The idea that *Statesman* 270A, μήτ' αὖ δύο τινὲ θεὼ φρονοῦντε ἑαυτοῖν ἐναντία στρέφειν αὐτόν, as well as *Laws* 896E were written with reference to Persian dualism is very plausible. But as to the factual conformity with such eschatological conceptions as Reitzenstein adduces—following Axel Olrik, *Ragnarök* (Berlin and Leipzig, 1922), pp. 385ff.—from the *Mahabharata*, the Persian *Bahman-Yast*, and Oriental and Nordic fairy tales, the following is to be

said from Plato's standpoint: in those eschatologies the distortion of all standards and the approaching end of the world are made manifest by the fact that the size and the life span of men diminish. Reitzenstein seems to have rightly referred Hesiod, *Erga* 181 to this chain of thought: εὖτ' ἂν γεινόμενοι πολιοκρόταφοι τελέθωσι. Plato, however, differs perceptibly from all this. For he characterizes just the time of perfection, when the god held the rudder of the world, by the fact that everything was the reverse of what it is today: men came into the world full grown and kept growing younger. One should therefore make it clearer than Reitzenstein does that if there is a connection Plato has at least completely reversed the sense of these things. For as far as I can see neither the motif nor its application are in accord. At most one might perhaps relate the great periods quite generally to the Orient. / On the four Indian Yugas (world periods) see Christian Lassen, *Indische Altertumskunde*[3] (2 vols., Leipzig, 1867-74), I, 2, 499. But according to the (oral) judgment of Geldner, "it cannot at all be maintained that the system was current before Alexander's time." / However, in order to get beyond "influences" and "dependencies," the first question is what sense this periodicity makes in Occident and Orient.

40. See p. 39; Paul Kucharski, "Observations sur le mythe des 'Lois' 903b–905d," *Bulletin de l'Association Guillaume Budé*, 4th ser., XIII (1954), no. 4, 31–51.

41. Hegel, *Werke*, XIV, 189.

42. See as example of the Neoplatonic polemic against Kolotes (n. 4, this chapter) Macrobius, *In Somnium Scipionis* I 2 17: "*De diis autem et de anima non frustra se nec ut oblectent ad fabulosa convertunt, sed quia sciunt inimicam esse naturae apertam nudamque expositionem sui. Quae sicut vulgaribus hominum sensibus intellectum sui vario rerum tegmine operimentoque subtraxit, ita a prudentibus arcana sua voluit per fabulosa tractari.*" See also the Neoplatonist Sallustius, in A. D. Nock (ed.), *Concerning the Gods and the Universe* (Cambridge, 1926), ch. 3: (Περὶ μύθων): ἔξεστι δὲ καὶ τὸν κόσμον μῦθον εἰπεῖν, σωμάτων μὲν καὶ χρημάτων ἐν αὐτῷ φαινομένων, ψυχῶν δὲ καὶ νοῶν κρυπτομένων.

43. Stewart, *Myths*, pp. 18ff., refers in a similar connection to Dante's letter and to the corresponding discussion of the *Convito*, principally in order to differentiate Plato's myths from allegories.

44. *Phaedrus* 229B *et seq.*, *Republic* 378D. What is called ὑπόνοια there is ἀλληγορία later on; cf. Plutarch, *De audiendis poetis* 19E. / There is need for a history of interpretation, with a comprehensive view of at least classical, Jewish, and Christian literature. See Rudolf Bultmann, "Das Problem der Hermeneutik" (1950) in *Glauben und Verstehen*, II, 211ff.

45. Dante, *The Latin Works*, tr. Philip H. Wicksteed and A. G. Ferrers Howell (London, 1904), pp. 347, 348, 360.

CHAPTER X

1. Henri Bergson, *La Pensée et le Mouvant*[5] (Paris, 1934). Of the two papers here quoted, "Introduction à la Métaphysique" has been published in English: *An Introduction to Metaphysics*, tr. T. E. Hulme (London, 1913).

2. Georges M. A. Grube, *Plato's Thought* (London, 1935). Paul Shorey, "The Question of the Socratic Element in Plato," *Proceedings of the Sixth International Congress of Philosophy* (New York, 1927), p. 577.

3. Friedrich Ueberweg and Karl Praechter, *Grundriss der Geschichte der Philosophie*, I[14] (Berlin, 1926), p. 262; Sir David Ross, *Plato's Theory of Ideas* (London, 1951), p. 174.

4. J. A. Stewart, *Plato's Doctrine of Ideas* (Oxford, 1909); Heinrich Friedemann, *Platon. Seine Gestalt* (Berlin, 1914); R. S. Bluck, *Plato's Phaedo* (London, 1955), pp. 180ff.

5. Harold Cherniss, "The Philosophical Economy of the Theory of Ideas," *AJP*, LVII (1936), 145ff.; Wilhelm Windelband, *Lehrbuch der Geschichte der Philosophie*[5], pp. 76ff.

6. Wincenty Lutoslawski, *The Origin and Growth of Plato's Logic* (London, 1897).

7. W. R. Inge, *The Philosophy of Plotinus* (2 vols., London and New York, 1918).

8. *The World as Will and Idea*, tr. Haldane and Kemp, I, 230.

9. Richard Hönigswald, *Philosophie des Altertums*, pp. 139ff.

10. Julius Stenzel, *Studien zur Entwicklung der platonischen Dialektik*, p. 13 (Eng. edn., 36f.); "Metaphysik des Altertums" in A. Baeumler und M. Schröter (eds.), *Handbuch der Philosophie* (Munich, 1929), p. 101; "Der Begriff der Erleuchtung bei Platon," *Antike*, II (1926), 235ff. = *Kleine Schriften zur griechischen Philosophie*[2] (Darmstadt, 1957), 151ff.

11. W. Dilthey, *Gesammelte Schriften*, I (Leipzig, Berlin, 1922), pp. 182ff.

12. Tr. Haldane and Kemp, I, 230, 231, 240.

CHAPTER XI

1. Chapter XI has been substantially revised for this second edition.

2. For discussion, see the Addenda, n. 2, p. 402, below. / On this and the following etymologies, cf. Boisacq's *Dictionnaire*. Also *Etymologicum Magnum*: τὸ μὴ λήθη ὑποπῖπτον. *Etymologicum Gudianum*: παρὰ τὸ λήθω. Hesychios: ἀληθεῖς οἱ μηδὲν ἐπιλανθανόμενοι. Sextus Empiricus, *Adversus logicos* VIII § 8: ὅθεν καὶ ἀληθὲς φερωνύμως εἰρῆσθαι τὸ μὴ λῆθον τὴν κοινὴν γνώμην. Olympiodoros, *In Platonis Phaedonem* (Norvin) 156, 15: (ἐκ τῶν τοῦ Χαιρωνέως) ὅθεν καὶ ἡ ἀλήθεια τὸ ὄνομα δηλοῖ λήθης ἐκβολὴν εἶναι τὴν ἐπιστήμην. See Rufus M. Jones, *The Platonism of Plutarch* (Chicago diss., 1916), p. 101, n. 68.

3. On the etymology in Hesiod, *Theogony* 233, and the emphasis on the meaning "not-forgetting," see new n. 3 in the Addenda to the Second Edition, below, p. 403.

4. See the articles ἀληθής, ἀλήθεια etc., in H. G. Liddell and R. Scott, *A Greek-English Lexicon*, rev. H. S. Jones and R. McKenzie (2 vols., Oxford, 1940); Franz Passow, *Wörterbuch der griechischen Sprache*, ed. Wilhelm Crönert (Göttingen, 1912-13), cols. 261-64; and the excellent article in Gerhard Kittel, *Theologisches Wörterbuch zum Neuen Testament* (6 vols. published, Stuttgart, 1933ff.), I, 239f. Wilhelm Luther, *Wahrheit und Lüge im ältesten Griechentum* (Göttingen diss., 1935), is thorough.*

5. On *Iliad* XII 433: γυνὴ χερνῆτις ἀληθής or ἀλῆτις see Walter Leaf (ed.), *The Iliad*[2] (2 vols., London, 1900-1902), I, 555; Hermann Fränkel, *Die homerischen Gleichnisse* (Göttingen, 1921), pp. 58f.; Luther, p. 24. The variant ἀλῆτις seems improbable on account of the rhyme χερνῆτις ἀλῆτις. ἀληθής would fit in with ἐπὶ ἶσα (cf. ἰσάζουσα), whereas ἀλῆτις would be a mere ornament.

6. Parmenides, *Vorsokr.* 28 [18] B 3: τὸ γὰρ αὐτὸ νοεῖν ἐστίν τε καὶ εἶναι. "For the same is thinking and being": Diels-Kranz; similarly, Kurt Riezler, *Parmenides* (Frankfort, 1934), p. 29. "For it is the same thing that can be thought and that can be": Cornford, *Parmenides* [I[31]], pp. 31ff.; similarly, Hölscher in "Der Logos bei Heraklit," *Varia Variorum* [V[2]], pp. 79f. See also Gadamer in *Varia Variorum*, p. 64; and Fränkel, *Dichtung und Philosophie des früheren Griechentums* [VI[1]], pp. 457f. It seems certain to me that Parmenides the ontologist wants ἔστιν or ἐστίν to mean "is," not "can." On the other hand, ἐστίν is probably weakened if taken as a copula. Perhaps thus: "Thinking is, and being is, and both are the same." (The position of τε is necessitated by the meter.)

7. On this and the discussion that precedes in the text, see Heidegger's *Sein und Zeit*, p. 219.

8. The page numbers in the following refer to Martin Heidegger, *Platons Lehre von der Wahrheit* (Bern, 1947). See Gerhard Krüger, "Martin Heidegger und der Humanismus," *Studia Philosophica* (Basel), IX (1949), 93ff.; Dario Faucci, "Una recente interpretazione Heideggeriana del mito della caverna," *Leonardo* (Milan, 1946).

9. Three kinds of things are carried past: tools or implements, figures of men, and figures of animals. I would like to follow up Heidegger's translation in detail; though it has real merits, it contains features which are not only strange but wrong. / According to Krüger, p. 115, the figures, not the shadows, symbolize "the visible and tangible objects of experience." This interpretation is both right and wrong. The shadows as well as the figures symbolize these objects, the shadows to those still in chains, the figures to those who are freed from the chains and have completed part of the ascent.

10. Heidegger, "Vom Wesen des Grundes," *Festschrift für Edmund Husserl* (Halle, 1929), pp. 71ff., esp. p. 98: "Transcendence is explicitly stated in Plato's phrase ἐπέκεινα τῆς οὐσίας." / See also chs. I and III in the text, above, pp. 3ff., 59ff.

11. On the difficulties of Aristotle, *Metaphysics* IX 10, see Jaeger, *Studien zur Entstehungsgeschichte der Metaphysik des Aristoteles* [VI³], pp. 50ff.; and Ross, *Aristotle's Metaphysics* [VI⁹], II, 273ff.

CHAPTER XII

1. *Procli Opera Inedita*, ed. Victor Cousin² (Paris, 1864), pp. 308ff.

2. For comments on dialogue and existence see Erich Frank's remarks in *Philosophical Understanding and Religious Truth* (London and New York, 1945), p. 22, and "Die Philosophie von Jaspers," *Knowledge, Will and Belief* (Zurich and Stuttgart, 1955), p. 276, as also Julius Stenzel, "Zum Aufbau des platonischen Dialogs," *Festschrift für Karl Joël* (Basel, 1934), p. 234 = *Kleine Schriften* [X¹⁰], p. 335. Stenzel, who does not use the word "existence," writes, "By admitting that he never attains truth, and by compelling his partners in the dialogues to recognize that truth is always beyond our intellectual grasp, he [Socrates] conveys a stronger sense of the power of philosophic truth than does any later form of philosophizing." René Schaerer, *La Question platonicienne* [V²⁸], p. 202: "The pure artist creates closed works. . . . The dialogues, on the contrary, are open works."

3. On play and seriousness see chs. V and VII.

4. On the following see Kierkegaard [VII³]; also Étienne Gilson, *Being and Some Philosophers* (Toronto, 1949), pp. 142ff.

5. *A Fragment of Philosophy*, by Johannes Climacus, "responsible for publication": S. Kierkegaard, tr. David F. Swenson (Princeton and New York, 1936).

6. Gilson, p. 146.

CHAPTER XIII

1. Eduard Meyer, *Geschichte des Altertums* [IV²⁷], III, § 166; V, § 987ff.; Wilamowitz, *Platon* [I¹⁷], II, ch. 21; Richard Stanley Harold Bluck, *Plato's Life and Thought* (London, 1949), p. 189.* / In connection with this chapter see Johannes Geffcken, *Griechische Literaturgeschichte* (2 vols., Heidelberg, 1926-34), II, 159ff. and nn. 56ff., 134ff.; Hans Leisegang, "Platon," *RE*, XX (1950), col. 2522.

2. Franz Dornseiff, *Echtheitsfragen antik-griechischer Literatur* (Berlin, 1939), pp. 51ff. Some years before, Dornseiff in "Platons Buch Briefe," *Hermes*, LXIX (1934), 223ff., had attributed the epistolary novel to Plato himself.

3. Gerhard Müller, "Die Philosophie im pseudoplatonischen VII. Brief," *AfP*, III (1950), 251ff., owing to misinterpretations of *Letter*

VII 341AB, 345A-C, and failure to grasp its irony, finds that it "expresses a psychology to which we are not accustomed in Plato," basing his criticism of 342E upon a doubtful textual variant: ἀμῶς γέ πως instead of ἄλλως γέ πως. He holds that skepticism concerning the elements of thinking has no place in Plato's philosophy, despite the fact that Luigi Stefanini in *Platone* (2 vols., Padua, 1932), I, "Introduzione," §§ III, IV explains how deep was the foundation of this "skepticism" in Plato's thinking. The *"logos,"* despite Müller, is something quite different from a "mere phenomenon of sound"; the third stage (εἴδωλον) is not necessarily higher than the second (λόγος), but both are required to attain the fourth—the science, e.g., of the circle. Instead of finding an "inexcusable omission of the dianoetic sphere" in 342B, one should point out that the letter differs from Book VI of the *Republic* in not separating sharply the four stages of cognition. Moreover, Müller attributes the affecting passage in the *Letter* (328B *et seq.*), in which the inner struggle to reach a final decision is portrayed, to the workings of a "military mind." We have touched upon only a few points and say nothing of Müller's rejection of parts of Books V and VII of the *Republic*. / For detailed criticism of Müller's arguments see Bertha Stenzel, "Is Plato's Seventh Epistle Spurious?" *AJP*, LXXIV (1953), 383ff. See, moreover, Julius Stenzel, "Über den Aufbau der Erkenntnis im VII. Platonischen Brief," *Kleine Schriften* [X¹⁰], pp. 85ff.*

4. Paul Shorey, *What Plato Said*; Robin, *Platon* [IV⁴]. Shorey's view has had a remarkable influence. See Ronald Bartlett Levinson, *In Defense of Plato* (Cambridge, Mass., 1953), p. 38. Otherwise one would not understand how Cherniss could write (*The Riddle of the Early Academy* [IV⁴], p. 5), ". . . . and for the sake of those who, like Professor Burnet, believe the *Epistles* to be genuine. . . ." followed by quotations from *Letters VI* and *VII*. Or see George Boas, "Fact and Legend in the Biography of Plato," *PR*, LVII (1948) 439–57, esp. 453ff.; with the reply by Bluck, ibid., LVIII (1949), 503–9. In France, Robin's skepticism apparently continues to be an active influence: see P. Chantraine's review of Dornseiff's *Echtheitsfragen*, *RevPhil*, 3d ser., XVIII (1944), 210f. On the other hand, Victor Goldschmidt, *Les Dialogues de Platon* (Paris, 1947), takes the philosophical passage of *Letter VII* as the starting point of his interpretation. Gigon, *Sokrates* [VI⁶], would not have entirely omitted Plato's autobiography if he had recognized the authenticity of *Letter VII*. On the other hand, Georges Méautis, *Platon vivant* (Paris, 1950), calls it *"un document d'une valeur unique."* Festugière, *Contemplation et vie contemplative* [III⁴⁰], considers *Letters VII* and *VIII* genuine, but holds that *Letter II* is certainly spurious.* / Johannes Lohmann, *Gnomon*, XXVI (1954), 453, asserts that the "ill-famed" *Letter VII*,

because of its theory of language and cognition, "cannot have been written before the Hellenistic period."

5. See Zeller, *Philosophie der Griechen* [II³], II, 1, 474ff.

6. See Franz Joseph Egermann, *Die platonischen Briefe VII und VIII* (Berlin diss., 1928), reviewed by Wilamowitz in *Gnomon*, IV (1928), 361ff.; John Harward, "The Seventh and Eighth Platonic Epistles," *CQ*, XXII (1928), 143–54; Günther Hell, *Untersuchungen und Beobachtungen zu den platonischen Briefen* (Berlin diss., 1932) and "Zur Datierung des siebenten und achten platonischen Briefes," *Hermes*, LXVII (1932), 295–302; R. S. Bluck, *Plato's Seventh and Eighth Letters* (Cambridge, 1947), pp. 14ff. and Appendix III.

7. See Heinrich Gomperz, *Platons Selbstbiographie* (Berlin and Leipzig, 1928), reviewed by Egermann in *Gnomon*, V (1929), 629ff.; Heinrich Weinstock, *Platonische Rechenschaft* (Berlin, 1936).

8. *Letter II* is considered to be spurious by Wilamowitz (1919), Howald (1925), Souilhé (1926), R. G. Bury (1929), Günther Hell (1932), A. K. Rogers (1933), Glenn R. Morrow (1935), Pasquali (1938), Theiler (1938), and Festugière (1950); and to be authentic by Salin (1921), A. E. Taylor (1926), P. Friedländer (1928), F. Novotny (1930), Harward (1932), Bluck (1947), L. Wishart (1949), and H. Leisegang (1950). A scholar of G. C. Field's circumspection (*Plato and His Contemporaries* [IV¹], pp. 197ff.) confesses that he "cannot stomach" the passage in *Letter II* 312D–313A.

9. The same theme had been previously touched on in 312B, and occurs again in *Letter VII* 345B. Joseph Souilhé, *Platon* (Edition Budé XII, part I; Paris, 1926), I, lxxx, interprets it as "irony" in *Letter VII* but thinks it is meant "seriously" in *Letter II*, which must be false for that reason.

10. See the quotations from ancient literature in František Novotny (ed.), *Platonis Epistulae* (Brno, 1930), p. 91. / Perhaps καλὸς καὶ νέος was a current combination of words somewhat like νέος καὶ ἁπαλός. See Friedrich Ast, *Lexicon Platonicum* (3 vols., Leipzig, 1835–38) s.v. Regarding the closeness in meaning of νέος and καλός see *Phaedrus* 278E, referred to by Howald, *Die Briefe Platons* [I⁵], p. 188. Hermippos, in *Athenaeus* XI 505E, furnishes an even better analogy: Gorgias had called Plato καλὸν καὶ νέον τοῦτον 'Αρχίλοχον. Concerning this passage of *Letter II* and the authenticity of the letter see Edgar Salin, *Platon und die griechische Utopie* (Munich, 1921), p. 268.

11. Stefanini, *Platone*, I, xxx; Souilhé, p. lxxix; Morrow, "Studies in the Platonic Epistles" [IV²⁷], p. 106.

12. The authenticity of *Letter VI* was upheld by A. Brinckmann in "Ein Brief Platons," *RhM*, LXVI (1911), 226–30, and Jaeger, *Aristotle*, p. 111. I am convinced that they are right; but when Jaeger states that "Brinckmann's presentation of conclusive evidence firmly established

its authenticity," I should say by way of reservation that only un-authenticity can be conclusively proved. / Paul Shorey's denial of the authenticity of *Letter VI*—"Notes on the Sixth Platonic Epistle," *CP*, X (1915), 87f.—is indicative of the occasional hastiness of judgment displayed by this outstanding scholar. φημ' ἐγὼ καίπερ γέρων ὢν (322D) obviously belongs with what follows, not what precedes. For the sentence reads: Ἐράστῳ δὲ καὶ Κορίσκῳ. . . . φημ' ἐγώ. . . . προσδεῖν σοφίας. Therefore γέρων ὢν has nothing whatever to do with σοφίᾳ τῇ καλῇ, and Shorey read "senile eroticism" into this passage. This may assist us in evaluating his "silly sentence" and "foolish equivocation." To the textual changes made by Jaeger, *Aristotle*, p. 173, and Novotny, *Epistulae*, pp. 131ff., we may object that the participle makes good sense if it is read in conjunction with the words following it: "Old as I am, I know and say that one must be realistic in politics, cautious and capable of self-protection." There is more irony in the sentence than Apelt, Howald, Souilhé, or Post (see Novotny, p. 131) seem to appreciate. See Rudberg, *Platonica Selecta*, p. 73.

13. Giorgio Pasquali, *Le Lettere di Platone* (Florence, 1938), pp. 178f.
14. Moritz H. E. Meyer, G. F. Schömann, and J. H. Lipsius, *Der attische Prozess* (2 vols., Leipzig, 1883–87), I/II, 628ff.
15. Aristotle, *Nicomachean Ethics* V 3 1129b 222, contains similarly brief and general provisions: assault and evil talk are prohibited, μὴ τύπτειν μηδὲ κακηγορεῖν.
16. According to Post, Novotny, and Pasquali, these were the Olympic games of 364 B.C.; that is, the letter was written prior to the third journey. E. Meyer, *Geschichte des Altertums*, V, § 988, and John Harward, *The Platonic Epistles* (Cambridge, 1932), p. 167, assert that the letter was written in 360. At any rate, it cannot have been written much later than that.
17. Field, *Plato and His Contemporaries*, p. 201; Rogers, *The Socratic Problem* [VI⁶], pp. 181ff. On the following cf. Plotinus, *Enneades* V i 8, VI vii 42 ("here as everywhere else, Plotinus is quoting from memory," Paul Henry, *Études Plotiniciennes*, Paris, 1938, I, 137). Proclus, *In Rem publicam* [IX⁴] I 287, 11; idem, *In Timaeum*, ed. E. Diehl (2 vols., Leipzig, 1899–1900), I 356, 8; 393, 19.

CHAPTER XIV

1. Chapter XIV is a revised version of "Structure and Destruction of the Atom According to Plato's Timaeus," *University of California Publications in Philosophy*, XVI, no. 11 (1949). Much that is said here is anticipated in Paul Shorey, "Platonism and History of Science," *Proceedings of the American Philosophical Society* (Philadelphia), LXVI (1927), 159ff. See also Vittorio Enzo Alfieri, *Atomos Idea, l'origine del concetto dell' atomo nel pensiero greco* (Florence, 1953); Walther Kranz, "Die

Entstehung des Atomismus," *Convivium, Beiträge zur Altertumswissenschaft* (Stuttgart), 1954, pp. 14ff. It is manifest how much every venture of this kind owes to the interpreters of Plato's *Timaeus:* Martin, Archer-Hind, Taylor, Cornford, Rivaud. Many more specific references could have been made, especially to Taylor, *Timaeus*, and Francis M. Cornford, *Plato's Cosmology* (London and New York, 1937). / For special problems see Eva Sachs, *Die fünf platonischen Körper* (Berlin, 1917), ch. III; Léon Robin, "La Place de la physique dans la philosophie de Platon" (1918) in *La Pensée hellénique* (Paris, 1942), pp. 231ff.; and the important ch. III in Ahlvers' *Zahl und Klang* [IV¹⁴].*

2. Kurt Riezler, *Physics and Reality* (New Haven, Conn., and London, 1940), pref.: "the widening cleavage between nature and man"; George Sarton, *The Study of the History of Science* (Cambridge, Mass., 1936), p. 10: "the chasm which is cutting our culture asunder and threatening to destroy it"; Herbert McLean Evans, *Ideals in Medicine* (Berkeley, Calif., 1951), p. 14: "The greatest rift of all, surely, is that Grand Canyon cut across the mind's high plateau which now bids fair to separate forever students of the sciences from those of the humane letters." See also Sarton, *The History of Science and the New Humanism* (Cambridge, Mass., 1931), pp. 7ff.

3. R. G. Collingwood, *The Idea of Nature* (Oxford, 1945), p. 177; Pierre Rousseau, *Histoire de la science* (Paris, 1945). Comte's remark is a variant of Hegel's well-known saying that history of philosophy is philosophy itself.

4. W. C. D. Dampier-Whetham, *A History of Science* (Cambridge, 1929), p. 28, "the best single volume available today" according to Sarton's *Study* (1936), p. 65; James Jeans, *The Growth of Physical Science* (Cambridge, 1947), pp. 47ff.: "while physics was still in this primitive stage of its development, it met with two major disasters in the attitude of two great thinkers, Plato and Aristotle"; Charles Singer, *A Short History of Science* (Oxford, 1941), pp. 64ff.; Rousseau, p. 52; Aldo Mieli, *Panorama general de historia de la ciencia* (Buenos Aires, 1945), pp. 52ff.; Henry Smith Williams, *A History of Science* (5 vols., New York and London, 1904–10), I, 181: Plato "apparently had no sharply defined opinions as to the mechanism of the universe, no tangible idea as to the problems of physics, no favorite dreams as to the nature of matter"; Floyd Karker Richtmyer, *Introduction to Modern Physics*² (New York and London, 1934), p. 9: Plato "did not make contributions to physics such as are of interest in connection with the present discussion. Quite the opposite, however, is true of Aristotle"; Ferdinand Rosenberger, *Die Geschichte der Physik* . . . (Brunswick, 1882–90), p. 15: "Plato's physics is of slight importance."

5. Werner Heisenberg, "Ideas of the Natural Philosophy of Ancient Times in Modern Physics," in *Philosophic Problems of Nuclear Science*,

tr. F. C. Hayes (London, 1952), pp. 53–59; Abel Rey, *La Science dans l'antiquité* [IV¹⁴], III, 277ff.; Alfred North Whitehead, *Process and Reality* (Cambridge, 1929), pp. 142ff.

6. Bertrand Russell, *A History of Western Philosophy* (London, 1945), p. 165: Plato's *Timaeus* "contains more that is simply silly than is to be found in his other writings." Russell seems to echo Whitehead as Jeans echoes Dampier-Whetham. J. E. Boodin [I³⁹] instead calls the *Timaeus* "Plato's immortal cosmological dialogue." *

7. Whitehead, *The Concept of Nature* (Cambridge, 1920), p. 11.

8. See Hermann Bonitz, *Index Aristotelicus* (Berlin, 1870), p. 462; José Ortega y Gasset, "Las dos grandes metáforas," *El Espectador* (Madrid), IV (1925), 153.

9. Plutarch, *De defectu oraculorum* ch. 10. Aristotle, *Physics* IV 2 209b 11, identifies his ὕλη with the χώρα of the *Timaeus*. See Léon Robin, *La Théorie platonicienne des idées et des nombres d'après Aristote* (Paris, 1908), pp. 418ff; Sir David Ross, *Plato's Theory of Ideas* (Oxford, 1951), pp. 125f. A modern understanding of what Plato meant is often defective by virtue of the fact that, from the variety of his metaphors and terms, this concept of χώρα is singled out in isolation— why? (1) Because Plato himself, at the end of this discussion (52A 8), uses the word χώρα as a brief summary of, but not as an exclusive substitute for, all the preceding metaphors: ". . . the Receptacle" (this again but one metaphor among many) "now identified ultimately" (but not in such a way that all previous descriptions are wiped out) "with space" (Cornford). (2) Because Aristotle identifies his ὕλη with Plato's χώρα as the most rational among the metaphors in the *Timaeus*. (3) Because only χώρα corresponds (or seems to correspond) to a concept in modern scientific terminology.

10. Not all aspects of the problem of χώρα can be discussed here. See Clemens Baeumker, *Das Problem der Materie in der griechischen Philosophie* (Münster, 1890), pp. 126ff.; Taylor, *Timaeus*, p. 312, follows Baeumker, rightly opposed by Cornford, *Cosmology*. See also Robin, *La Pensée hellénique*, 272ff.; Stenzel, *Zahl und Gestalt* [IV¹⁸], pp. 84ff.; Cherniss, "The Sources of Evil According to Plato," *PAPS*, XCVIII (1954), 23ff.; Festugière, *La Révélation d'Hermès Trismégiste* (4 vols., Paris, 1949–54), II, "Le Dieu cosmique," 114ff.

11. Cherniss, "War-time Publications Concerning Plato," *AJP*, LXVIII (1947), 257, reviewing Pierre Louis, *Les Métaphores de Platon* (Paris, 1945).

12. Is this not very different from Descartes' "*seule qualité dont j'aie une idée claire et distincte*" which Gaston Milhaud, *Les Philosophes géomètres de la Grèce* (Paris, 1934), p. 293, quotes as an analogy? In order to save something of this analogy, Milhaud omits the word ἀπορώτατα.

13. Collingwood, p. 147.

14. Werner Heisenberg, *The Physical Principles of the Quantum Theory*, tr. Carl Eckart and F. C. Hoyt (Chicago, 1930); Paul A. M. Dirac, *The*

Principles of Quantum Mechanics (Oxford, 1930), pp. 4ff.; Pascual Jordan, *Physics of the 20th Century*, tr. Eleanor Oshry (New York, 1944), pp. 134ff.; Erwin Schrödinger, *Science and the Human Temperament* (London, 1935), pp. 52ff.: "Indeterminism in Physics."

15. Diels, *Elementum* [IV¹⁹], p. 14.

16. Ibid., p. 20; Cornford, *Cosmology*, pp. 220f. See above, p. 95.

17. Heinrich Gomperz, "Problems and Methods of Early Greek Science," *JHistId*, IV (1943), 161ff. On the polarity of speculation and empirical research in Greek biology, see Olof Gigon, "Die naturphilosophischen Voraussetzungen der antiken Biologie," *Gesnerus, Vierteljahrsschrift der Schweizerischen Gesellschaft für Geschichte der Medizin und der Wissenschaften* (Aarau), III (1946) 35ff.

18. Heiberg, *Geschichte der Mathematik und Naturwissenschaften* [IV¹⁵], p. 12: "In the *Timaeus* Plato used the atomic theory of Demokritos in not exactly an improved form." Howald, "Εἰκὼς λόγος," *Hermes*, LVII (1922), 74, calls it "comic" that anyone considers the theory of elements in the *Timaeus* to be founded on mathematics. Ernst Gegenschatz, *Platons Atlantis* (Zurich diss., 1943), p. 21, says that "the carelessness with which Plato makes use of Theaitetos' discovery is unparalleled." See in opposition Hans-Georg Gadamer's penetrating analysis, "Antike Atomtheorie," *ZgN*, I (1935–36), 81ff.

19. Robin, *La Pensée hellénique*, p. 271, ascribing to necessity the construction of the four elementary corpuscles, seems to confuse mathematical necessity with the blind necessity which Plato here calls *Ananke*. Robin, arguing against Brochard (p. 274), does not grasp Plato's thought when he says that matter expresses itself in geometrical determinations before having known the persuasive activity of the intelligence. Nor does he do so when he makes an inaccurate reference to Aristotle, *De generatione et corruptione* 329a 21ff., and conceives of Plato's matter as consisting of promiscuously whirling triangles. On the passage in Aristotle see Cherniss, *Aristotle's Criticism of Plato* [III¹], I, 147ff.*

20. Émile Meyerson, *De l'explication dans les sciences* (2 vols., Paris, 1921), I, 298ff.

21. In reference to crystallography see R. Heinicke in *ZgN*, II (1936–37), 152ff. / On atomic structure in general see Hans Reichenbach, *Atom and Cosmos* (London, 1932), pp. 244ff.; William Lawrence Bragg, *Atomic Structure of Minerals* (Oxford, 1937), passim; H. A. Kramers and Helge Holst, *The Atom and the Bohr Theory of Its Structure*, tr. R. B. Lindsay and Rachel T. Lindsay (London, 1923), pp. 19ff.; Schrödinger, *Science*, pp. 148ff.: "Conceptual Models in Physics." On the following see Heisenberg, *Philosophic Problems of Nuclear Science*, pp. 30ff., 57.

22. Whitehead, *Process and Reality*, p. 145: "Newton would have been surprised at the modern quantum theory and the dissolution of quanta into vibrations: Plato would have expected it."

23. Cornford, *Cosmology*, pp. 230ff.

24. Taylor, *Timaeus*, p. 384.

25. Ancient science did not even lack experiments; this is shown by William Arthur Heidel, *The Heroic Age of Science* (Baltimore, 1933), ch. "Experimentation." Contrary to Heidel, Cornford, *Principium Sapientiae* (Cambridge, 1952), stresses "the neglect of experiment and indulgence in speculative dogmas." See the review of Cornford's book by Gregory Vlastos in *Gnomon*, XXVII (1955), 68. See also Ludwig Edelstein, "Recent Trends in the Interpretation of Ancient Science," *JHistId*, XIII (1952), 573ff.; D. J. Furley, "Empedocles and the Clepsydra," *JHS*, LXXVII (Part 1, 1957), 31ff.*

26. Gadamer, "Atomtheorie," p. 94. I hope that the dispute concerning the meaning of these triangles which began—for us—with Aristotle has now come to an end.

27. Taylor, *Timaeus*, pp. 401ff.; Cherniss, *Aristotle's Criticism of Plato*, I, 128ff., 444ff.*

28. The scientist who treats historical matters runs an analogous risk. It may suffice to select three sentences from James Jeans's books: "Plato tells us that Anaxagoras claimed to be able to explain the workings of nature as a machine" (*Physics and Philosophy*, Cambridge, 1942, p. 13); "We have seen how his [Plato's] picture of the world consisted of forms which exist only in our minds, and of sensible objects" (ibid., p. 195); "in his only scientific dialogue—the *Timaeus*, the weakest of them all—he tries to discover the plan of the universe from the wholly gratuitous assumption that the structure is like that of a man—the macrocosm must, he thinks, resemble the microcosm" (*Growth*, p. 64). It is easy to imagine what physicists would say if historians made similarly inaccurate assertions in the field of natural science—as we probably do.

29. Schrödinger, *Science*, pp. 39ff.; Hans Reichenbach, *The Rise of Scientific Philosophy* (Berkeley, Calif., 1951), pp. 156ff.: "The Laws of Nature."*

30. Kurd Lasswitz, *Geschichte der Atomistik vom Mittelalter bis Newton* (2 vols., Hamburg and Leipzig, 1890), I, 60ff.; *The "Opus majus" of Roger Bacon*, ed. J. H. Bridges (Oxford, 1897), pt. IV. ch. XII. Raymond Klibansky, *The Continuity of the Platonic Tradition During the Middle Ages* (London, 1939), shows how much is still unknown or half known, and how much is still to be done in this respect.

31. Leonardo Olschki, *Geschichte der neusprachlichen wissenschaftlichen Literatur* (3 vols., Heidelberg, Leipzig, Halle, 1919–27), I, 216ff.; Charles Ravaisson-Mollien, *Les Manuscrits de Léonard de Vinci* (Paris, 1889), MSS. F and I, fol. 27, "Figura Delementi."

32. *Joannis Kepleri Astronomi Opera Omnia*, ed. C. Frisch (8 vols., Frankfurt a. M. and Erlangen, 1858–71), vol. I, *Prodromus dissertationem cosmographicarum*, pp. 95ff. (see front.); vol. V, *Harmonices mundi libri*, pp. 85ff.; vol. VII, *Strena seu de nive sexangula*, pp. 715ff.

33. Ernst Cassirer, "Die Antike und die Entstehung der exakten Wissenschaft," *Antike*, VIII (1932), 276–300, esp. 281.

34. Walter Charleton, *Physiologia Epicuro-Gassendo-Charletoniana.* . . . (London, 1654), p. 307: "It cannot impugne, at least, not stagger the reasonableness of this conjectural Assignation of a Tetrahedrical figure to the Atoms of Cold, that Plato (in Timaeo) definitely adscribeth a Pyramidal Figure to Fire, not to the Aer, i.e., to the Atoms of Heat, not to those of Cold."

35. Ralph Cudworth, *The True Intellectual System of the Universe* (London, 1678), p. 53: "Plato . . . did but play and toy sometimes a little with Atoms and Mechanism. As where he would compound the Earth of Cubical, and Fire of Pyramidical Atoms, and the like."

36. Emanuel Swedenborg, *Opera quaedam aut inedita aut obsoleta De Rebus Naturalibus*, ed. A. H. Stroh, under the auspices of the Royal Academy of Sciences of Sweden (3 vols., Stockholm, 1907–11).*

37. M. Matter, *Emanuel de Swedenborg* (Paris, 1863), p. 39; Frank Washington Very, *An Epitome of Swedenborg's Science* (2 vols., Boston, 1927), passim. See also the introductions to the three volumes of Swedenborg's *Opera quaedam*.

38. William Hyde Wollaston in *Philosophical Transactions* (1808), pp. 96ff.; "Lettre de M. Ampère," *Annales de Chimie* (Paris), XC (1814), 43ff. Both are readily accessible in Friedrich Wilhelm Ostwald's *Klassiker der exakten Wissenschaften* (Leipzig, 1921).

39. Goethe, *Maximen und Reflexionen*, in the Jubiläums-Ausgabe (40 vols., Stuttgart and Berlin, 1902–7), XXXIX, 80. The name of the physicist André Marie Ampère occurs in Goethe's *Nachträge zur Farbenlehre, Naturwissenschaftliche Schriften* (Weimar edn. [I²³]), V, 1, 412. Jean-Jacques Ampère, the physicist's son, visited Goethe in 1827. He wrote to Mme Récamier, "*Il* [Goethe] *m'a entretenu des découvertes de mon père qu'il connaît très bien.*" See *Goethes Gespräche*, ed. Flodoard Waldemar von Biedermann (5 vols., Leipzig, 1909–11), III, 381, no. 2487. How familiar Goethe was with the *Timaeus* is shown by his *Materialien zur Geschichte der Farbenlehre.* "Plato's Bläue," in *Maximen und Reflexionen*, no. 1148, refers to *Timaeus* 68c. See Ernst Grumach, *Goethe und die Antike* (2 vols., Berlin, 1949), II, 762ff.

Goethe read the *Timaeus* in 1801, again in 1804 when he received a copy of the translation by K. J. Windischmann: *Platon's Timaeos; Eine echte Urkunde wahrer Physik* (Hadamar, 1804), and once more in 1827/28 when he received a copy of *Platons Lehren auf dem Gebiete der Naturforschung und der Heilkunde* (Leipzig, 1826) by J. R. Lichtenstaedt. Windischmann's translation is dedicated to "Professor Schelling, the restorer of the oldest and truest physics"; and Lichtenstaedt, too, refers to Schelling, because of whom "Plato's name is held again in honor even among natural scientists and physicians."

CHAPTER XV

1. Chapter XV first appeared in the *Jahrbuch des deutschen Archäologischen Instituts*, XXIX (1914), 99ff. Erich Frank, *Plato und die sogenannten Pythagoreer* (Halle, 1923), pp. 184ff., arrived independently at essentially the same results as to the myth in the *Phaedo*. On this chapter see also Friedrich Gisinger, "Geographie," *RE*, Suppl. IV, col. 577; Abel Rey, *La Science dans l'antiquité* [IV¹⁴], II, 425ff.; James Oliver Thomson, *History of Ancient Geography* (Cambridge, 1948), pp. 110ff., and the review of the latter by A. W. Gomme, *JHS*, LXXI (1951), 261f., from which we quote: "On some points I am inclined to doubt his [Thomson's] judgment, as on 'Plato's positive contempt for observation upon which natural science rests.' " Similarly, only stronger, A. E. Taylor, *A Commentary on Plato's Timaeus* [IX³³], p. 417.
2. See pp. 27f. and 186ff.
3. The following objections may be made to Frank's view (*Plato und die Pythagoreer*, app. V and VI) that Parmenides did not hold the theory of the earth as a sphere (a view shared by William Arthur Heidel, *The Frame of the Ancient Greek Maps*, New York, 1937, pp. 70ff.):
   (1) Theophrastus uses the expression στρογγύλος (*Vorsokr.* 28 [18] A 444) in referring to Parmenides' conception of the earth. When Aristotle refers to bodies, this expression always describes a sphere or a spheroid form. See Rodolfo Mondolfo, "Platone e la Storia del Pitagorismo," *AeR*, 1937, pp. 235ff.
   (2) According to Theophrastus, Parmenides was the first to ascribe this shape to the earth. That does not agree with an earth thought to have the form of a disk.
   (3) The expression σφαιροειδής used by Diogenes (*Vorsokr.* 28 [18] A 1) fits in with (1) and (2).
   (4) Poseidonios credited Parmenides with the theory of zones; even if we share Karl Reinhardt's skepticism of this attribution (*Parmenides* [I³¹], p. 147; *Kosmos und Sympathie*, Munich, 1926, p. 361), we are still faced with the fact that it presupposes a spherical form of the earth in Parmenides. See also Rey, II, 431f.; Rehm and Vogel, "Exakte Wissenschaften" in Gercke and Norden, *Einleitung in die Altertumswissenschaft* [IV¹⁵], II, 5, 11f. Even if Parmenides held the theory, he had no need to produce "serious proof" (Frank, p. 187). In the history of the sciences, imagination is often far in advance of empirical research, and we know the symbolical significance of the sphere for Parmenides' "pure being." Likewise, Parmenides could speak of the spherical earth in his poem without giving rise to scientific inferences drawn from it for a century to come.*
4. See Rohde, *Psyche* [I³⁷], pp. 55ff., 59ff., 571ff.; Ludolf Malten, "Elysion und Rhadamanthys," *JDAI*, XXVIII (1913), 35–51, esp. 49.

5. This illusion is quite understandable, since we do not by any means live at the end of our inhabited world, but at its approximate center. From this location we are as unlikely to see the remote walls of our hollow as, for example, an inhabitant of the North Sea coast to see the Alps. The illustration does not do this idea justice.

6. Hermann, *Geschichte und System der Platonischen Philosophie* [IV³²], p. 688. For a comparison of the *Phaedrus* and the *Phaedo* see Max Pohlenz, *Aus Platos Werdezeit* (Berlin, 1913), p. 333f.

7. Eugen Oder, "Ein angebliches Bruchstück Demokrits," *Philologus*, Suppl. VII (1899), 275 (a reference I owe to Diels): "In order to achieve a certain effect, Plato did not hesitate to combine disparate elements; for his αἰώρα is a mechanical principle which would not fit the vitalistic conception of an earthly animal inhaling and exhaling." In opposition it must be said that Plato uses this "vitalistic conception" merely as comparison (ὥσπερ, 112в), and that the geographic theory presented above is uniformly mechanistic.

8. The theory of the porosity of the earth and of subterranean basins and watercourses occurs in Anaxagoras (*Vorsokr.* 59 [46] A 42, 5; A 90) and in Diogenes of Apollonia (*Vorsokr.* 64 [51] A 17f.). We may be inclined to see in them, as do Oder and Hermann Diels, "Über die Genfer Fragmente des Xenophanes und Hippon," *SBBerl*, 1891, p. 581, predecessors of Plato's theory. But even then we must not forget that Plato explained a much larger number of phenomena by means of a uniform geophysical construction.

9. Diels, "Wissenschaft und Technik bei den Hellenen," *Neue Jahrbücher für das klassische Altertum*, XXXIII (Leipzig, 1914), 5 = *Antike Technik²* (Leipzig, 1920), p. 10, contrasts the practical map of the earth with the theoretical achievements of the philosopher Anaximander. Its scientific character, nevertheless, lies in those of its aspects which go beyond practical questions. See James A. K. Thomson, *The Greek Tradition* (London and New York, 1927), pp. 5f., "On an Old Map": "Was Anaximander's really the first map? The first scientific map it no doubt was." / "The mathematicizing trend" (Jaeger, *Paideia* [IV⁴], I, 155f.) was certainly very strong in Anaximander's conception of the earth. But it is obvious that it dominated his geography less than his cosmology, in which he is a precursor of the Pythagoreans. Ernst Hugo Berger, *Geschichte der wissenschaftlichen Erdkunde der Griechen²* (Leipzig, 1903), p. 250, appears to reverse the actual state of affairs when he describes the development by saying that in the fourth century lists of harbors and descriptions of coasts had replaced general maps of the earth.

10. See Bruno Meissner, "Babylonische und griechische Landkarten," *Klio*, XIX (1925), 96ff.; Thomson, *Ancient Geography*, p. 39 and pl. I; Gustav Hölscher, "Drei Erdkarten," *SBHeid*, 1944–48, pp. 32ff.

11. The remark that "the sun is invisible" on the northernmost of these

"islands" may recall the Cimmerians in the *Odyssey* XI 15ff. In an inscription of Assurbanipal, to be sure, Lydia, which was quite close, is placed at a fantastic distance: "Gu-ug-gu, the king of Lu-ud-di, a realm beyond the sea, a distant land whose name my fathers' kings had never heard."

12. Herodotus IV 36: γελῶ δὲ ὁρῶν γῆς περιόδους γράψαντας πολλούς ἤδη καὶ οὐδένα νόον ἐχόντως ἐξηγησάμενον. οἳ Ὠκεανόν τε ῥέοντα γράφουσι πέριξ τὴν γῆν ἐοῦσαν κυκλοτερέα ὡς ἀπὸ τόρνου καὶ τὴν Ἀσίην τῇ Εὐρώπῃ ποιεύντων ἴσην. Aristotle, *Meteorology* II 5 362b 12: διὸ καὶ γελοίως γράφουσι νῦν τὰς περιόδους τῆς γῆς· γράφουσι γὰρ κυκλοτερῆ τὴν οἰκουμένην. Gemini, *Elementa Astronomiae*, ed. Carolus Manitius (Leipzig, 1898) ch. 16, 4: οἱ δὲ στρογγύλας γράφοντες τὰς γεωγραφίας πολὺ τῆς ἀληθείας εἰσὶ πεπλανημένοι. / The doubts as to this tradition which Heidel expresses in *The Frame of the Ancient Greek Maps*, pp. 11f. are unjustified.

13. *Vorsokr.* 68 [55] A 94, B 15; in conjunction with the latter, see the introductory remarks of the Scholia on Dionysios Periegetes, *Geographi Graeci Minores*, ed. Karl Müller (2 vols., Paris, 1855–61), II, 428; ultimately derived from Eratosthenes.

14. Cleomedes, ed. Ziegler, I, 8, 40. Similarly, Martianus Capella VI 590: "*Formam terrae non planam, ut aestimant, positioni qui eam disci diffusioris assimilant, neque concavam, ut alii, qui descendere imbrem dixerunt telluris in gremium* [the reasoning is formulated somewhat differently and impresses us as archaic], *sed rotundam globosam.*" In a later passage: "*si emersi solis exortus concavis subductioris terrae latebris abderetur.*" / Demokritos, *Vorsokr.* 68 [55] A 94: (περὶ σχήματος γῆς) Δημόκριτος δισκοειδῆ μὲν τῷ πλάτει, κοίλην δὲ τῷ μέσῳ. Archelaos, *Vorsokr.* 60 [47] A 4 § 4: κύκλῳ μὲν οὖσαν ὑψηλήν, μέσον δὲ κοίλην. σημεῖον δὲ φέρει τῆς κοιλότητος ὅτι ὁ ἥλιος οὐκ ἀνατέλλει τε καὶ δύεται πᾶσιν. See *Vorsokr.* 59 [46] A 87: ὅτι οὔτε κοίλη ἡ γῆ ὡς Δημόκριτος οὔτε πλατεῖα ὡς Ἀναξαγόρας. Anaximenes *Vorsokr.* 13 [3] A 7 6: κρύπτεσθαί τε τὸν ἥλιον οὐχ ὑπὸ γῆν γενόμενον, ἀλλ' ὑπὸ τῶν τῆς γῆς ὑψηλοτέρων μερῶν σκεπόμενον.

15. Compare also Thomson, *Ancient Geography*, p. 114: "The basin is really the old concave disc, but now put on the surface of a huge globe." According to Frank's construction, *Plato und die Pythagoreer*, pp. 25 and 189, a shift from concave to convex eventually resulted in the theory of the sphere.

16. The dominating role of the eschatology is not open to doubt. But does this justify Rehm, "Exakte Wissenschaften" [IV¹⁵], II, 5, 12, Hans Werner Thomas, *Epekeina* (Würzburg diss., 1938), pp. 83ff., and Richard S. H. Bluck, *Plato's Phaedo* (London, 1955), p. 200, in dismissing the geophysical foundation as "not seriously meant"? Briefly stated, here are the objections:

   (1) The picture of the earth presented in the *Phaedo* shows features

unrelated to the mythical superstructure, but significant as parts of a geophysical construction.

(2) As the myth of the *Phaedo* is based on a geophysical foundation, that of the *Republic* rests on a cosmological construction; the myth changed some of the cosmology but did not produce it.

(3) Like the myth of the *Phaedo*, that of Atlantis is based on a picture of the earth. The two pictures are related, and that of the *Timaeus* is not only chronologically but developmentally later, as is shown in sec. III of this chapter. Rehm and Thomas did not even discuss the second and third of these arguments. To support the independence of the geophysical element in the myth of the *Phaedo* one might refer to Aristotle, who criticized it in detail and purely from the standpoint of natural science (*Meteorology* II 2 355b 32). His criticism yields no proof other than the result of our own analysis. Rehm's and Thomas' view is also shared by Frutiger, *Les Mythes de Platon* [IX¹], pp. 61ff.

17. It is easy to understand that Proklos (*In Platonis Timaeum* I 180) did not recognize the contrast. But even E. H. Berger, "Die Grundlagen des marinisch-ptolemäischen Erdbildes," *BerLeipz*, 1898, pp. 91ff.; and Gegenschatz, *Platons Atlantis*, still mingle the contraries. The sphere of the *Timaeus* has no κοῖλα. On the picture of the earth in the legend of Atlantis see Bidez, *Eos, ou Platon et l'Orient* [IV¹⁵], app. II, "L'Atlantide"; Thomson, *Geography*, pp. 90ff.

18. Thomas Henri Martin, *Études sur le Timée* (2 vols., Paris, 1841), I, 312; Berger, "Grundlagen," p. 98. The exterior land mass, which surrounds Okeanos on the map of Kosmas Indikopleustes, also forms part of this line of thought; see *The Christian Topography of Cosmas Indicopleustes*, ed. Eric Otto Winstedt (London, 1909), pp. 129, 26 (= 185A) and pl. VII.

19. Berger's view ("Grundlagen," p. 104) that the concept of the "true land" is "entirely mythical" is open to doubt. It is a strange error that he considers this true continent to be a preliminary stage of the picture of the earth developed by Marinus and Ptolemy—which shows the Indian Ocean as a closed sea and includes a land bridge between eastern Asia and eastern Africa.

20. Felix Jacoby, *Fragmente der griechischen Historiker* [VIII²⁰], II, B, no. 115, frag. 75. See Erwin Rohde, *Der griechische Roman und seine Vorläufer*² (Leipzig, 1900), p. 219.

21. Plutarch's observations regarding the "true land," *De facie in orbe lunae*, ch. 26, p. 941, also go back to Plato; the same is true of Μάρκελ-λος ἐν τοῖς Αἰθιοπικοῖς in Proclus, *In Timaeum* I 177. / The number of modern works which may be considered successors of the legend of Atlantis is too large to permit enumeration. The most recent survey is by Hans Herter in *RhM*, n.s., XCII (1944), 236ff. Sources of the kind quoted by Pierre Benoît in his novel *L'Atlantide*, tr. Arthur

Chambers as *The Queen of Atlantis* (London, 1920), may become the object of further research: "the *Journey to Atlantis* of the mythographer Denys de Milet" and "the fascinating story of the Gorgon according to Procles of Carthage, quoted by Pausanias."

22. We can give the name and date of an advocate of this view: "*Athinagoras Arimnisti inquit unum esse mare quod rubrum et quod extra Eracleas columpnas*": Aristotle, "Περὶ τῆς τοῦ Νείλου ἀναβάσεως," *Aristotelis Fragmenta*, ed. V. Rose (Leipzig, 1886), p. 194, l. 23. Athenagoras defended this theory before Artaxerxes Ochos some time between 357 and 349 B.C. See Joseph Maria Partsch, "Über das Steigen des Nils," *AbhLeipz*, 1909, p. 572 [22] 7.

23. The shorelines outside the temperate zone are carried through, although, according to the theory of the time, they were inaccessible to empirical knowledge.

24. Strabo I 56 says in an entirely different context, which however presents the same linguistic problem: τὸ δὴ "τεναγίζειν τὸν λεχθέντα τόπον συνάπτοντα τῷ τῆς Ἐρυθρᾶς κόλπῳ" ἀμφίβολόν ἐστιν, ἐπειδὴ τὸ συνάπτειν σημαίνει καὶ τὸ συνεγγίζειν καὶ τὸ ψαύειν. See Friedrich G. G. Sorof, *De Aristotelis geographia* (Halle diss., 1886), p. 8.

25. Simplicius—*Simplicii in Aristotelis Physicorum Libros Commentaria*, ed. H. Diels (2 vols., Berlin, 1882–95), p. 548—comments on the argument: οὐ γὰρ ὁμοιότητα τῶν τόπων ἐπιδεῖξαι βούλεται ὡς οἶμαι διὰ τούτων ἀλλὰ γειτνίασιν. However, neighboring areas are not necessarily connected by land. Alexander von Humboldt, *Kritische Untersuchungen über die historische Entwicklung der geographischen Kenntnisse von der Neuen Welt* (2 vols., Berlin, 1836), I, 120, expresses an interesting view: "The meaningful argument which Aristotle derives from the existence of elephants on the opposite coasts of Africa and India is based upon the small distance between the two land masses, since it is assumed that the same type of products must be found at the two extreme points of the inhabited world." Therefore it is not correct to conclude from the argument about the elephants that a land bridge existed. See Berger, *Erdkunde*, p. 318; Thomson, *Geography*, p. 119.

26. A broader interpretation of the expression "Red Sea," such as that given by Partsch, p. 569 [19], does not change the results at which we have arrived.

27. Berger, *Erdkunde*, pp. 305, 320.

28. Berger, ibid., and "Grundlagen," p. 121, finds in the *Phaedo* a preliminary development of Krates' theory of the circling oceans crossing each other. This is due to misunderstandings of both language and subject matter.

29. Sorof, *Geographia*, p. 14; Berger, *Erdkunde*, p. 321; Paul Bolchert, *Aristoteles' Geschichte der Erdkunde von Asien und Libyen* (Quellen und

Forschungen zur alten Geschichte und Geographie XV, Leipzig, 1908), p. 44.

30. By ἡ ἔξω θάλαττα Aristotle means east or west. *Meteorology* I 13 350b 13: Χρεμέτης. . . . εἰς τὸν ἔξω ῥεῖ θάλατταν. 362b 28: τὰ δὲ τῆς Ἰνδικῆς ἔξω καὶ τῶν στηλῶν τῶν Ἡρακλείων.

31. See Partsch, op. cit. The text is contained in *Aristotelis Fragmenta*, ed. Rose, pp. 188ff. / Diels, *Doxographi* [II¹], pp. 226ff., was of the opinion that the treatise originated at least with the older Peripatetics (whereas, according to an oral communication, he later adopted Partsch's view). I believe I can invalidate one argument of his against Aristotle's authorship. If the author of *De inundacione Nili* expresses complete agreement with Herodotos in his polemic against Thales, we should bear in mind that Herodotos' objections to the circular map are repeated by Aristotle almost verbatim. Hence another similarity is probably not accidental either: Herodotus I 203: τὴν μὲν γὰρ Ἕλληνες ναυτίλλονται πᾶσα καὶ ἡ ἔξω στηλέων [why should we wish to add Ἡρακλέων?] θάλασσα ἡ Ἀτλαντὶς καλεομένη καὶ ἡ Ἐρυθρὴ μίη ἐοῦσα τυγχάνει. Aristotle, *De caelo* 298a 9: τοὺς ὑπολαμβάνοντας συνάπτειν τὴν περὶ τὰς Ἡρακλείους στήλας τόπον τῷ περὶ τὴν Ἰνδικὴν καὶ τοῦτον τὸν τρόπον εἶναι τὴν θάλατταν μίαν. The element giving rise to suspicion thus turns into an argument in favor of Aristotle's authorship. / Albert Rehm, "Nilschwelle," *RE*, XVII, cols. 572ff., defends the authenticity of the treatise.

32. August Forbiger, *Handbuch der alten Geographie* (3 vols., Hamburg, 1877), I, 112; Berger, *Erdkunde*, p. 247; Friedrich Gisinger, *Die Erdbeschreibung des Eudoxos von Knidos* (Stoicheia VI, Heidelberg, 1921); Heinrich Karpp, *Untersuchungen zur Philosophie des Eudoxos von Knidos* (Würzburg, 1933), pp. 1ff.; Thomson, *Geography*, pp. 116ff.; Erich Frank, "Eudoxos," *Knowledge, Will and Belief* (Zurich and Stuttgart, 1955), pp. 138ff.

33. Diels, *Doxographi*, p. 386. / The report in the Scholium δ 477 is inaccurate. / Referring to Hermann Diels, "Seneca und Lucan," *AbhBerl*, 1885, p. 17, and in opposition to Friedrich August Ukert, *Geographie der Griechen und Römer* (3 vols. in 6 pts., Weimar, 1816–46), I, 2, 216, I find it unthinkable that the fully developed theory of the sphere and the climatic zones originated with the Egyptian priests, although Diodoros I 40 also ascribes Eudoxos' view to "some philosophers in Memphis." It seems that Eudoxos liked to refer to his sojourn in Egypt and to his relations with the priests. See also Diogenes Laërtius VII 89 regarding the "Dog Dialogues" allegedly translated from the Egyptian.

34. In this context, Nikagoras is credited with a bare assumption and not with the scientific theory of the zones. The latter is formulated as a basis by Aristotle, who introduces it with the words, "*Non plane*

autem hoc determinat, videtur enim nichil negociatus esse circa hoc quod dicitur." When thus Nikagoras' view is raised to the status of a scientific hypothesis, it agrees with Eudoxos' theory, and we are surprised to find no mention of the latter in Aristotle.

35. It is no proof but noteworthy that Simplicius 547, in commenting on this passage, mentions Canopus as an example. For other passages relating to this see Berger, *Erdkunde*, p. 247, n. 5.

36. Ukert, *Geographie*, holds a different view.

37. *Agathemeros* I 2 (*Geographi Graeci Minores*, II, 471): Εὔδοξος δὲ τὸ μῆκος διπλοῦν τοῦ πλάτους.

38. See E. H. Berger, "Die Stellung des Poseidonius zur Erdmessungsfrage," *BerLeipz*, 1897; Thomson, *Geography*, pp. 158ff., 212ff., 229ff.

39. For nn. 39 and 40 see the Addenda, p. 404, below.

CHAPTER XVI

1. This essay is part of a chapter from the book *Legal Philosophy from Plato to Hegel* (Baltimore, 1949). It was originally published under the title "Plato's Theory of Law," *Harvard Law Review*, LVI (1942), 359–87. An account of pre-Socratic legal ideas and a discussion of Plato's view of the nature of law have been omitted here in the interests of space.

   Note on the Translations. I have in general, for the quotations appearing in the text, followed the translations of Bury, Shorey (for the *Republic*), Jowett, and Taylor, though sometimes in combination or with modifications. My debt to the felicitous translations which England occasionally ventures to append to his edition of the *Laws* and to his notes will be readily apparent. My obligations to the commentaries of Grote, Shorey, Taylor, Nettleship, and Ritter will also be obvious.

   [The notes in this chapter are, of course, Mr. Cairns's. They and the text have been edited only for technical conformity. All the references are to Plato's *Laws* unless otherwise indicated.—P.F.]

2. *Autobiography* (London, 1926), II, 442.

3. Jacques Cujas, *Opera Omnia* (Naples, 1722), V, 666, where instances in the *Digest* of specific borrowings from Plato are cited.

4. Cf. *Republic* 472c. Strictly, Platonic *Ideas* are not abstractions from sense-data since sense-data are only approximations of *Ideas*.

5. The doctrine plainly needs a defense since it led even Mill to assert that it postulated infallibility, or something near it, in the rulers of the state, "or else ascribes such a depth of comparative imbecility to the rest of mankind, as to unfit them for any voice whatever in their own government, or any power of calling their scientific ruler to account." J. S. Mill, *Dissertations and Discussions* (Boston, 1868), IV, 325.

6. *Apology* 17D; *Laches* 196B; *Phaedrus* 272DE; *Republic* 492BC; *Theaetetus* 172CE.

7. *Statesman* 295AB. Plato again brings in the idea of equity in *Laws* 875D.

8. *Apology* 24; *Laws* 862E, 874E *et seq.*; *Protagoras* 326D.

9. Plato believed that law was unknown in primitive society (680A).

10. *Gorgias* 482E; *Laws* 889D *et seq.*; *Republic* 551B.

11. Sophocles, *Antigone* 454, *Oedipus Tyrannus* 865; Xenophon, *Memorabilia* IV IV 19.

12. *Laws* 838B, 841B, 680A, 793A–C, 890E; *Republic* 563D; *Statesman* 294C, 299A, 300A, 301A, 302A.

13. Plato observes that our statesmen, who are sometimes contemptuous of authors, are most fond of writing (*Phaedrus* 257–58). When a statesman produces a composition he insists upon signing it at the beginning, thus: "Be it enacted by the senate, the people, or both, on the motion of a certain person" who is the statesman (ibid., 278D).

14. For the full distinction in Attic law, see Karl Friedrich Hermann, *A Manual of the Political Antiquities of Greece* (Oxford, 1836), p. 268.

15. Cujas refers to Plato's proposed law on injury to a neighbor's land by the obstruction of the outflow of floodwaters or by permitting them to flow out too violently as the source of the rule in *Digest* I.13.I. See n. 3 above.

16. Plato's desire to treat contributions to benefit associations as an imperfect obligation is perhaps influenced by Attic law, which allowed recovery against citizens in good circumstance, but not otherwise.

17. Cf. *Gorgias* 480B; *Laws* 934AB; *Republic* 380B. At this point Plato did not attempt to meet the argument on which the reformation and deterrent theories break down. Both theories justify the punishment of innocent men; the deterrent theory if he is believed to be guilty by those likely to commit the crime in the future; and the reformation theory if he is a bad man, but not guilty of the offense charged.

18. "A man named Chaong An-ching, aided by his wife Chaong Wong-shee, flogged his mother. Upon the circumstances being made known to Tungchee, in whose reign the crime was perpetrated, an imperial order was issued, to the effect that the offenders should be flayed alive, that their bodies should then be cast into a furnace, and their bones, gathered from the ashes and reduced to a powder, should be scattered to the winds. The order further directed that the head of the clan to which the two offenders belonged, should be put to death by strangulation; that the neighbours living on the right and left of the offenders should, for their silence and non-interference, each receive a flogging of eighty blows, and be sent into exile; that the head or representative of the graduates of the first degree (or B.A.), among whom the male offender ranked, should receive a flogging of eighty blows and be exiled to a place one thousand li distant from his home; that the

granduncle of the male offender should be beheaded; that his uncle and his two elder brothers should be put to death by strangulation; that the prefect and the ruler of the district in which the offenders resided, should for a time be deprived of their rank; that on the face of the mother of the female offender four Chinese characters expressive of neglect of duty towards her daughter should be tattooed, and that she should be exiled to a province, the seventh in point of distance from that in which she was born; that the father of the female offender, a bachelor of arts, should not be allowed to take any higher literary degrees, that he should receive a flogging of eighty blows, and be exiled to a place three thousand li from that in which he was born; that the mother of the male offender should be made to witness the flaying of her son, but be allowed to receive daily for her sustenance a measure of rice from the provincial treasurer; that the son of the offenders (a child) should be placed under the care of the district ruler, and receive another name; and, lastly, that the lands of the offender should for a time remain fallow." John Henry Gray, *China: A History of the Laws, Manners, and Customs of the People* (London, 1878), II, 237–38.

19. *Apology* 26A; *Gorgias* 466A; *Hippias Minor* 376B; *Laws* 731C; *Meno* 77–78; *Protagoras* 345D; *Republic* 589C; *Timaeus* 86E.

20. Plato's penal principles are most fully set out in *Laws* bk. IX.

21. Similarly, in the *Euthyphro*, before the invention of a grammatical vocabulary, Plato seems to be attempting a philosophical distinction between the active and the passive voice of a verb. From that point of view to us today the argument appears unnecessarily complex.

22. *Republic* 405; *Theaetetus* 175–77. The scholiast advised that the passage from the *Theaetetus*, which in its entirety contrasted the man of affairs and the lawyer with the philosopher, be memorized in full.

23. Kant, *Critique of Pure Reason*, tr. N. K. Smith (New York, 1933), p. 47.

CHAPTER XVII

1. See Hans Herter, "Platons Atlantis," *Bonner Jahrbücher*, CXXXIII (1928), 28–47, and *RhM*, n.s., XCII (1944), 236ff.; XCVI (1953), 1ff.; these papers helped to correct or formulate details more clearly here. Robert S. Brumbaugh, "Note on the Numbers in Plato's *Critias*," *CP*, XLIII (1948), 40ff. = *Plato's Mathematical Imagination* [IV^{14}], pp. 47ff. merits consideration; but his constantly reiterated opinion that Plato intended to express disorder or confusion by means of these figures cannot be correct. The danger for Atlantis lies precisely in the opposite direction, that is, in a trend toward exaggerated mathematicizing.*

NOTES: PAGES 308-20395

2. Despite the great lapse of time, this may recall Roman bridges such as that of Saint-Chamas in Provence.

3. In 116c 3, τὰ βασίλεια stands like a title of everything that follows up to 117A; in 117A τὰ βασίλεια designates, in a more limited sense, the palace.

4. On this chapter and figs. 10, 11, and 12, see the concurring remarks of A. E. Taylor, tr. and ed., *Plato: Timaeus and Critias* (London, 1929), p. 8. The three plates in R. G. Bury, tr. and ed., *Plato: Timaeus, Critias . . .* (LCL, 1929), show a great deal of agreement with my reconstructions (of 1928). Bury's map of the coastal plain appears to be erroneous in only one detail: the main canal surrounding the plain looks as if it were fifty stadia wide instead of one stadium; consequently, an incomprehensible double line (bridge?) has been drawn through this canal in the main axis of the circular town.

5. Compare *Critias* 115c *et seq.* with Herodotus I 98 181-5; Diodorus I 48, II 7-9. In the history of the *ekphrasis*, which I have previously outlined (*Johannes von Gaza und Paulus Silentiarius*, Berlin and Leipzig, 1912, Introd.), the *Critias*, oddly enough, is missing. It would have been most appropriately discussed in the chapter on the novel (ch. 4), and it is connected with much that is dealt with in the chapter on historiography (ch. 3). Thus this example confirms again the significance of Ionian historiography for the history of the *ekphrasis*. The *Critias* may also be cited as an example of what is said about the alternation of descriptive and narrative elements.

6. See for example Stephen Langdon, *Building Inscriptions of the Neo-Babylonian Empire* (Paris, 1905), Pt. I, 88, no. 9, 29: "The holy chamber where his royal presence abides with bright gold like a shining wall I made, Kahilisug with gold I clothed." There are many similar references. Cf. Solomon's temple, I Kings 6 : 20ff. (gold covering), I Chronicles 29 : 4 (gold and silver covering). A remote similarity with the many colors of the stone buildings may be found in the town wall of Erythrai, in which three layers each of white chalk blocks alternate with one layer of dark-red trachyte blocks. See G. Weber, "Erythrai," *AM*, XXVI (1901), 103-18, esp. 105.

7. This regularity may again be observed in the city plan of Robert Koldewey, *Das wiedererstehende Babylon* (Leipzig, 1925), ill. 256. Herodotos implies that this regularity would be even more obvious if the section of the city situated on the west bank were as well known as that on the east.*

8. See Walter Otto, ed., *Handbuch der Archäologie* (Handbuch der Altertumswissenschaft, sec. 6, 3 vols., Munich, 1939-50), I, 705; E. Herzfeld and F. Sarre, *Archäologische Reise im Euphrat- und Tigrisgebiet* (4 vols., Berlin, 1911-20), II, 106ff., ill. 180; W. Andrae, "Hatra I-II," *WVDOG*, IX and XXI (1908, 1914); Felix von

Luschan (ed.), *Ausgrabungen in Sendschirli* (Berlin, 1893–1911 and 1943), II, pl. 29. For the Assyrian camps, see Johann Hunger and Hans Lamer, *Altorientalische Kultur im Bilde* (Die neue Wissenschaft, vol. 103, Leipzig, 1911), ill. 139. For Tepe Gawra, see W. F. G. Knight in *Vergilius* (Bulletin of the Vergilian Society), Jan. 1939, p. 9.

9. Reference to this agreement was made by Hellmut Bossert, "Zur Atlantisfrage," *Orientalische Literatur-Zeitung*, XXX (1927), cols. 649–55, esp. 654. Bossert does not inquire into Plato's imaginative plan, to be sure, but is concerned with the ghost of the "real" Atlantis. / For bibliographical data in this chapter I am indebted to Paul Jacobsthal.

10. Armin von Gerkan, *Griechische Städteanlagen* (Berlin and Leipzig, 1924), pp. 30f., denies any connection. See Ernst Fabricius, "Hippodamos," *RE*, VIII, cols. 1731ff.; "Städtebau," *RE*, III A, cols. 1992ff. See *Vorsokr.* 39, [27]. Martin Erdmann, "Hippodamos," *Philologus*, XLII (1884), 206 n. 40, is inclined to assume that such an influence existed; so is W. L. Newman, *The Politics of Aristotle* (4 vols., Oxford, 1887–1902), I, 382.

11. See Fabricius, p. 1734; Erdmann, p. 204.

12. Albert Rivaud, in his introduction to the *Critias, Platon, Œuvres complètes* (Paris, Collection Budé X), p. 250, writes with reference to Hippodamos, "Plato could find all the essential elements of his narration almost without leaving Athens." A glance at a map of the Athenian harbors (e.g., in Judeich, *Topographie von Athen* [IV¹], Plan 3) suffices to refute this thesis.

13. See Hans Herter, "Die Rundform in Platons Atlantis und ihre Nachwirkung in der Villa Hadrians," *RhM*, XCVI (1953), 1ff.

14. See *Israel Exploration Journal*, VII (Jerusalem, 1957), 29ff. with figs. 12 and 18 and plates 6 and 7.

15. Albert Erich Brinckmann, *Platz und Monument* (Berlin, 1923), p. 41; *Stadtbaukunst* (Berlin, 1920); "Antonio Avelino Filarete's Tractat über die Baukunst. . . ," ed. W. von Dettingen, in R. von Eitelberger von Edelberg, *Quellenschriften für Kunstgeschichte* (Vienna), n.s., VIII (1871).

CHAPTER XVIII

1. Chapter XVIII appeared, under this heading, in *AJP*, LXVI (1945), 337ff. The fourth part of the paper is omitted here; it is concerned with the similarity between Plato, *Alcibiades* I 133A *et seq.*, and Aristotle, *Eroticus* (*Aristotelis Fragmenta*, ed. V. Rose, Leipzig, 1886) frag. 96, and concludes that Aristotle had the Platonic passage in mind.

2. Polybius, *Historiae* XXXI 23-30, ed. Büttner-Wobst, ed. Paton (LCL) = XXXII 9-16, ed. Bekker, ed. Hultsch = *Excerpta Historica iussu Imperatoris Constantini Porphyrogeniti confecta*, ed. Boissevain et al., II, 2 (ed. Roos), 187ff. See Edward Kennard Rand, *The Building of Eternal Rome* (Cambridge, Mass., 1943), ch. I.

3. τὴν ἐπ' εὐταξίᾳ καὶ σωφροσύνῃ δόξαν Polybius (*Excerpta Historica* II 2, p. 190, l. 7). Diodorus (*Excerpta Historica* II 1, p. 287, l. 11) gives a careless excerpt: τὴν ἐπ' εὐταξίᾳ σωφροσύνην.

4. See Hans von Arnim, *Stoicorum veterum Fragmenta* (3 vols., Leipzig, 1903-24), III, 5, frag. 12; 48, frag. 197; 63, frag. 262; 72, frag. 293.

5. Theodor Mommsen, *The History of Rome*, tr. W. P. Dickson (5 vols., London, 1913), IV, 197.

6. Rand, p. 30.

7. It is worth mentioning that the very word συνεργός occurs in a similar context in another passage of the *Symposium* 212B: ὅτι τούτου τοῦ κτήματος τῇ ἀνθρωπείᾳ φύσει συνεργὸν ἀμείνω Ἔρωτος οὐκ ἄν τις ῥᾳδίως λάβοι. συνεργός is Eros here, not Socrates. But it must be remembered that Diotima's Eros has many traits of Socrates.

8. David Sachs drew my attention to Iamblichus, *De Pythagorica Vita* § 24, where the pupil says to Pythagoras, ἑαυτῷ ἀρχήσει πρῶτον τινά See Zenobius, I 94, *Corpus paroemiographorum Graecorum*, ed. Leutsch-Schneidewin (1839), I, 30.

9. See Arnim, III, 64.

10. Rudolf von Scala, *Die Studien des Polybios* (Stuttgart, 1890), pp. 97ff.

11. See the survey in Scala, p. 122. T. R. Glover's statement in *Cambridge Ancient History* (12 vols., Cambridge, 1923-39), VIII, 4f., "His references to Plato do not suggest great sympathy" might be applied just as well to many passages in Aristotle. Would it not be misleading in one case as well as the other?

12. Scala, p. 201. See also J. B. Bury, *The Ancient Greek Historians* (New York and London, 1909), p. 204, although Plato does not have the place in the picture to which he is entitled.*

13. See for example F. W. Walbank, "Polybius on the Roman Constitution," *CQ*, XXXVII (1943), 73-89, esp. 86.

14. Polybius, XXXVI 15, ed. Büttner-Wobst = XXXVII 2, ed. Bekker.

15. In Eduard Schwartz's chapter on Polybios in *Charakterköpfe* [IV[31]], p. 79, one excellent and very pertinent sentence ("Polybios owed it to Hellenic philosophy. . . .") is followed by an analysis which is refuted by Polybios' own account ("he will educate his young friend not as a philosopher, but as a man of practical life"—"not to become virtuous or wise, but to become a Roman nobleman").

16. See the introduction to Proklos' and Damaskios' commentaries: *Procli Opera Inedita*, ed. Victor Cousin, 281ff.; *Initia Philosophiae ac Theologiae ex Platonicis Fontibus Ducta*, ed. Georg Friedrich Creuzer (4

vols., Frankfurt a. M., 1820–25), II, 3ff. It is perhaps not inappropriate to mention that Lucilius had read the *Charmides* when he wrote the twenty-ninth book of his *Satires*, i.e., between 132 and 123 B.C. See *Lucilii Carminum Reliquiae*, ed. Friedrich Marx (2 vols., Leipzig, 1904–5), I, vv. 830–33, with commentary, II, 288; Conrad Cichorius, *Untersuchungen zu Lucilius* (Berlin, 1908), pp. 68ff., 177.

17. W. Warde Fowler, *The Religious Experience of the Roman People* (London, 1911), p. 363. For reference to ch. XVIII, see Richard Harder, "Die Einbürgerung der Philosophie in Rom," *Antike*, V (1929), 291–316.

Addenda to the Second Edition

The revised and additional notes that comprise this section are indexed on pp. 430 f., below.

CHAPTER I

3. In contrast to the view expressed by McKeon (p. 339, n. 3, above), see Werner Jaeger, *Aristotle*, tr. R. Robinson (2d edn., Oxford, 1948), p. 3: "Aristotle was the first thinker to set up along with his philosophy a conception of his own position in history." Aristotle is in fact the founder of doxography and thus—in a certain sense—of the history of philosophy. However, are not the beginnings already noticeable in Plato? Cf. *Sophist* 242B *et seq.*, and my remarks in *Plato 3*, p. 263. It is clear that no single hypothesis agrees with the complexity of facts.

11. On metaphors of vision for mental processes, see C. J. Classen, *Sprachliche Deutung als Triebkraft platonischen und sokratischen Philosophierens* (Zetemata, XXII, Munich, 1959), pp. 43ff.

16. On the contact of Greece with the East, cf. the following (from India): *Bhagavad-Gita*, XI, 8 (tr. Mohini M. Chatterji, Boston and New York, 1896, p. 170): "But thou art not able to see Me with these thine own eyes. I shall give thee the eye divine; behold my power as God." The *Bhagavad-Gita* is quoted also by Dhan Gopal Mukerji, *Thy Brother's Face* (New York, 1924), p. 138f.: "Behold Me, thy true Self, with the eye of thy Spirit . . . that our soul-eye may soon open wide and behold him who is waiting to become visible."

17. On *Eidos* and *Idea*, see also Werner Jaeger, *Paideia* [IV⁴], III, 24.

21. Only in the interpretation of a passage of Plato are we later able to show that Plato is interpreted too much through Plotinos. [*Original note continues, above, p. 342.*]

31. In favor of παλίντροπος are P. Wheelright, *Heraclitus* (Princeton, 1959), pp. 153f., and W. Kranz, in *RhM*, C (1958), 250ff. Wilamowitz, *Griechisches Lesebuch* (Berlin, 1902), II/2, 129, prints παλίντροπος but interprets παλίντονος. If παλίντονος is the correct reading, it follows, incidentally, that Diels in his edition of the pre-Socratics put Parmenides in the wrong place (as noted above, p. 343).

CHAPTER II

5. On the demonic, see also *Goethe im Gespräch, Eine Auswahl von E. Grumach* (Fischer Library, Frankfurt a. M. and Hamburg, n.d.), pp. 168ff.

6. Wilamowitz, *Platon* (Berlin, 1919), II, 362, considers the phrase τὸ δαιμόνιον τε καὶ to be "a miserable interpolation." Codex Laurentianus IX 85 does not have the second τὸ. Ast (see p. 345, n. 6, above) remarks: *Articulum expunximus, quia ειωθὸς cum articulo τε significanti cohaeret et* δαιμόνιον *adjective positum est.*"

9. See Plutarch, *De genio Socratis*; Apuleius, *De deo Socratis*; cf. Maximus, in *Maximi Tyrii Philosophumena*, ed. H. Hobein (Leipzig, 1910), Orations 8, 9. For Proklos, see p. 345, n. 9, above.

20. On the intermediary, see also N. Cooper, "The Importance of ΔΙΑΝΟΙΑ in Plato's Theory of Forms," *CQ*, n.s., XVI (1966), 65ff.

22. Among the references cited on p. 347, n. 22, above, the following should be included: Georg Simmel, "Der platonische und der moderne Eros," *Fragmente und Aufsätze* (Munich, 1923), pp. 125ff.

CHAPTER III

5. On the simile of a way, see also Karl Jaspers, *Die grossen Philosophen* (Munich, 1957), I, 274ff.

6. Harald Höffding, *Bemerkungen über den platonischen Dialog "Parmenides"* (Berlin, 1921), ch. 3, "Der Begriff des Plötzlichen in Platons Philosophie"; E. Bickel, "Μεταχρηματίζεσθαι, Ein übersehener Grundbegriff des Poseidonios," *RhM*, C (1957), 98. See also F. M. Cornford, as cited above, p. 348, n. 6.

31. As to the agreement of passages, Fritz Heinemann's objection—see "Ammonios Sakkas und der Ursprung des Neuplatonismus," *Hermes*, LXI (1926), 17—is appropriate only for the comparison with Thessalos of Tralleis: μόνωι μοι πρὸς μόνον ὁμι λεῖν (*Catalogue astrol. codices [graec.]* VIII 3 4).

39. See also E. R. Dodds, "Tradition and Personal Achievement in the

Phlosophy of Plotinus," *Journal of Roman Studies*, L (1960), 1ff. Dodds (p. 7, n. 16) believes that I overestimate the "difference of outlook between Plotinus and Plato."

40. Among the references cited on p. 351, n. 40, above, the following works of Ernst Hoffmann should be included: "Die Sprache und die archaische Logik" [III²], pp. 64ff., and *Platonismus und Mystik im Altertum* (Heidelberg, 1935).

CHAPTER IV

4. Additional recent literature on the Academy is listed, for 1945–55, in T. G. Rosenmeyer, *CW*, L/13 (1957), 176, and for 1950–57 in H. Cherniss, *Lustrum*, IV (1959), 27ff.

12a. In reference to geometry, see also Athenaeus XI 508E. / τὸ Πλάτωνος ἀγαθόν was well enough known that comedy could play with it; for example, see Amphis, in Diogenes Laërtius III 27.

14. For recent literature on Plato's mathematics, see Rosenmeyer, *CW*, L/14 (1957), 194; Cherniss, *Lustrum*, V (1960), 388.

20. On spherical geography see, in addition to ch. XV (pp. 261ff., above): A. Rehm, "Exakte Wissenschaften" [IV¹⁵], II, 12; H. W. Thomas, *Epekeina* (Würzburg, 1938), pp. 83ff.

21. The National Museum of Athens preserves a complicated mobile model—first dated 65 B.C., now 82 B.C.—of the stars and system of chronometry that was fished out of the sea near Antikythera; see D. J. de Solla Price, "An Ancient Greek Computer," *Scientific American*, CC/6 (June, 1959), 60ff. Cf. R. S. Brumbaugh, "Plato and the History of Science," *Studium Generale* (Berlin, Göttingen, Heidelberg), XIV (1961), 520ff.

30. The passage is *Gorgias* 468E–481B. / [*Original note continues, above, p. 355.*]

31. To the references cited on p. 356, n. 31, above, these should be added: Helmut Berve, *Dion* (Abhandlungen Mainzer Akademie, 1956), and also in *Gnomon*, XXXV (1963), 375ff.; Hermann Breitenbach, *Platon und Dion* (Zurich, 1960); J. B. Bury, *A History of Greece* (Modern Library, New York, n.d.), pp. 652ff.

CHAPTER V

11. The scholion on *Letter II* 314c was omitted by Greene because it is extant only in one fifteenth-century manuscript. (See L. Edelstein, "Platonic Anonymity," *AJP*, LXXXIII, 1962, p. 7, n. 17.) Even if the scholion is late, it is correct.

20. To the references in n. 20, pp. 358–59, above, this should be added: Hans Joachim Krämer, *Arete bei Platon und Aristoteles* (Abhandlungen Heidelberger Akademie, 1959). [*Original note continues, p. 359.*]

CHAPTER VI

2. Ps-Hippokrates, Περὶ Τέχνης § 1: εἰσί τινες οἳ . . . ἐμοὶ δὲ . . .
3. The latest and most thorough analysis is that of H. J. Krämer, *Arete bei Platon und Aristoteles* (Heidelberg, 1959), chs. 3, 4. Krämer shows that we are dealing not with an isolated lecture "On the Good" by the aged Plato, as is often assumed, but rather "with a typical occurrence." It may, however, be doubtful whether Plato regularly offered such a series of discussions. And should one speak strictly of the "esoteric Plato" here? Does it not seem, rather, that the esoteric and the exoteric are ironically interwoven? The account in Aristoxenos' *Harmonics* (at 44 5 *et seq.* [*M*]; see Krämer, p. 405, n. 44), τοὺς πλείστους τῶν ἀκουσάντων . . . προσιέναι γὰρ ἕκαστον, makes a "public lecture" more probable, although such a lecture would then decidedly have led into the esoteric.
6. Even more radical than Gigon—who himself restrained his radicalism in his review of the Magelhães-Vilhena work cited on p. 361, n. 6, above—is A. H. Chroust, *Socrates, Man and Myth* (Notre Dame, Ind., 1959), pp. ??? ????? ????? ?? ????, to be honest with ourselves and frankly admit that we possess no knowledge whatever about the historic Socrates." / To the references cited on p. 361, above, Karl Joël's *Geschichte der antiken Philosophie* [VIII⁴], I, 271ff., should be added.

CHAPTER VII

1. Goethe's remark is printed also in E. Grumach, *Goethe und die Antike* (Berlin, 1949), II, 762.
2. On irony see also Thomas Mann's *Nachlese* (Stockholm, 1956), pp. 166ff., "Humor und Ironie."
3. Cf. also Karl Jaspers' *Die grossen Philosophen* (Munich, 1957), I, 267f. [*Original note continues, above, p. 363.*]
4. On Ariston see also *Hermes*, XLVI (1911), 393ff.
6. On romanticism and irony, see also O. F. Walzel, *Deutsche Romantik* (Leipzig, 1908), pp. 32ff.
13. Cf. Mann's *Nachlese*, pp. 166ff.
14. On Diotima see also L. Robin, *Le banquet* (*Platon Budé*, IV/2, 1949), pp. xxii ff.
15. See ch. V in the text, above; also, F. Schleiermacher, *Platos Werke* [IX¹⁰], II/2, 252f.; F. Susemihl, *Die genetische Entwicklung der platonischen Philosophie* (Leipzig, 1855–60), I, 292; H. Bonitz, *Platonische Studien* (3d edn., Berlin, 1886), p. 183. / Wilamowitz, *Platon* [I¹⁷], I, 554 (2d edn., 1920, p. 560), reconstructs what the *Philosopher* should have contained. Edgar Salin, *Platon und die*

griechische Utopie (Munich, 1921), p. 57, interprets the fact that Plato did not write the *Philosopher* as proof that the essential had already been said. The *Philosopher* "abandoned" for the *Timaeus*: W. Theiler, in *MusHelv*, IX (1952), p. 66, n. 7. Cf. my remarks in *Plato 3*, p. 281, also p. 525, n. 5. See, finally, the clever (sometimes too clever) remarks on the *Philosopher* in Krämer, *Arete bei Platon und Aristoteles* (Heidelberg, 1959), pp. 247ff., 316f. Krämer did not take into consideration my thesis of the "wordless irony." / Recent literature on the *Philosopher* is listed by Cherniss in *Lustrum*, IV (1959), 146.

CHAPTER VIII

16. Perhaps Aristotle, *Metaphysics* II 3 994b 32 *et seq.* also belongs here.

19. In contrast, G. J. de Vries, *Spel bij Plato* (Amsterdam, 1949), p. 277, expresses this opinion on the author: "niet geheel onjuist, maar met een gevaarlijke afdwaling naar psychologisme en een populair sort psychoanalyse."

CHAPTER IX

22. Schleiermacher (see original n. 22, above, p. 371) is right in saying that "every translation of ἔπη ἀπόθετα is actually only guesswork." He even makes Plato the author of the verses on the winged love.

23. On the astronomical element of the *Phaedrus*, see further W. J. W. Koster, *Le Mythe de Platon, de Zarathoustra et des Chaldéens* (*Mnemosyne*, Suppl. III, Leyden, 1951), 4ff.

27. On *Phaedrus* 251A *et seq.*, see further E. Salin, "Platon Dion Aristoteles," in *Robert Boehringer: Eine Freundesgabe* (Tübingen, 1957), pp. 525ff. The connection of the word ἀρτιτελής with 'Αριστοτέλης (Salin, pp. 533ff.) is clever but most doubtful. *1*) ἀτελής and νεοτελής belong to the language of the mysteries; this is quite possible also for ἀρτιτελής, which need not have been coined by Plato. *2*) 'Αριστοτέλης and ἀρτιτελής have a different accent, and must therefore have sounded very different. *3*) Aristotle does not bear "the promising name: the one consecrated as the best"; rather, the name signifies him who accomplishes the best. One should compare such names as Καλλιτέλης, Δημοτέλης, Πραξιτέλης, 'Οδοιτέλης. / That Διὸς δῖον in 292E 1 points to Dion of Syracuse (Salin, p. 532) cannot be proved but is very possible.

CHAPTER XI

2. Compare, for instance, two semantically not very different words, ἀτρεκής, ἀτρέκεια and ἀκριβής, ἀκρίβεια, both of which mean some-

thing like "accurate" or "determinate," and are often synonymous with "true" or "correct." Neither is etymologically clear, and whether they derive from Indo-European roots remains uncertain despite all searching efforts by etymologists. Also ψεῦδος, ψευδής, since Homer the usual opposite to ἀλήθεια, ἀληθής, and another opposite, ἀπάτη, "deceit" or "deception," are apparently non-Indo-European. Thus ἀληθής, which belongs to the same semantic domain, is perhaps not at all ἀ-ληθής, just as the interpretation ἀ-τρεκής, ἀ-κριβής and ἀ-πάτη would impose upon these words an alpha privative that hardly belongs to them and that seemingly does not even help us in understanding them. / See Émile Boisacq, *Dictionnaire étymologique de la langue grecque* (4th edn., Heidelberg, 1950).

3. In the same verse, 233, of the *Theogony*, Hesiod assigns to the sea god Nereus the two honorific attributes α-ψευδής, without deceit, and ἀληθής. (See Karl Deichgräber, *Hesiod Theogonie 80–103*, Göttingen, 1947, printed as ms., 6 pp.) From this conjunction it is likely that Hesiod wanted his audience to understand ἀληθής as ἀ-ληθής. In addition, a passage immediately preceding shows Eris (Strife) apparently in intentional contrast to Nereus. Perhaps Hesiod even thought that the contrast was suggested by the two names, i.e., he understood *Nereus* as *non-Eris*. But even if this similarity of sound was accidental, it can be no accident that Lethe is among the children of Eris. It is not clear why—until, shortly afterward, Nereus is characterized as ἀ-ληθής. Finally, and most importantly, there is Hesiod's praise of Nereus: he is "not-erring and mild, and he does not forget or neglect what is right (οὐδὲ θεμιστέων λήθεται), but he knows how to give just and mild counsel." He does not forget: that is precisely the verb that Hesiod wished to impress upon his listeners as going with ἀληθής.

4. On the history of the term, Ernst Heitsch, "Die nichtphilosophische ΑΛΗΘΕΙΑ," *Hermes*, XC (1962), 24ff., also is important. Heitsch lists the more recent literature, following it back to Johannes Classen (1851). Note esp. W. Luther, "Der frühgriechische Wahrheitsgedanke im Lichte der Sprache," *Gymnasium*, LXV (1958), 75ff., and C. J. Classen, *Sprachliche Deutung als Triebkraft platonischen und sokratischen Philosophierens* (Munich, 1959), pp. 94ff.

CHAPTER XIII

1. Bluck's survey of research on the Platonic letters, however, notes almost exclusively the opinions of those who have edited, translated, or commented on the letters. Even so, this survey—which extends from Constantin Ritter (1910) to Giorgio Pasquali (1938)—omits the translations of G. Rudberg (1921) and W. Andrae (1923), as well as the edition of R. G. Bury (1929). / To the references sug-

gested for this chapter these should be added: L. Wickert, "Platon und Syrakus," *RhM*, XCIII (1950), 27ff., 383f.; L. Edelstein, "Platonic Anonymity," *AJP*, LXXXIII (1962), 1ff. For a bibliography of literature 1945–55, see Rosenmeyer, *CW*, L/13 (1957), 179; for 1950–57, see Cherniss, *Lustrum*, IV (1959), 88ff.

3. On *Letter VII*, see also G. Rudberg, *Platonica Selecta* (Stockholm, 1956), pp. 72ff.

4. On *Letter II*, see also W. Theiler, in *Gnomon*, XIV (1938), 625ff. For *Letter VII*, W. G. Runciman (*Plato's Later Epistemology*, Cambridge, 1962, pp. 54f.) believes that genuineness cannot be proved.

CHAPTER XIV

1. Additional works to be consulted are Wolfgang Schadewaldt, "Das Welt-Modell der Griechen," in *Hellas und Hesperien* (Zurich and Stuttgart, 1960), pp. 426ff.; Werner Heisenberg, *Physik und Philosophie* (Stuttgart, 1959), ch. 4.

6. Concerning the *Timaeus*, see further A. F. Braunlich, "Plato on Twentieth Century Physics," in *Studies Presented to D. M. Robinson*, II (St. Louis, 1953), pp. 1072ff.

19. On Aristotle and Plato, see also G. S. Claghorn, *Aristotle's Criticism of Plato's "Timaeus"* (The Hague, 1954), p. 8.

25. For a caricature of an experiment, see Aristophanes, *Clouds* 144 *et seq.*

27. On Aristotle, see further Sir Thomas Heath, *Mathematics in Aristotle* (Oxford, 1949), pp. 169ff.

29. On law and chance, see further Moritz Schlick, "Die Kausalität in der gegenwärtigen Physik" (1931), in *Gesammelte Aufsätze* (Vienna, 1938), pp. 41ff.

36. On Swedenborg, see also K. Lasswitz, *Geschichte der Atomistik* [XIV[30]], II, 372f.

CHAPTER XV

3. T. G. Rosenmeyer (in *CQ*, n.s., VI, 1956, 193ff.) wants to prove that Plato in the *Phaedo* did not think of the earth as a sphere. For discussion of Rosenmeyer's view, see Cherniss, *Lustrum*, IV (1959), 131f., §§ 660, 661. Rosenmeyer's thesis that *Phaedo* 111c 4 – 113c 8 presupposed a flat earth is wrong, as a glance at Fig. 7 (p. 268, above) proves.

39. See Alexander von Humboldt, *Kosmos* (5 vols., Stuttgart and Tübingen, 1845–62), II, ch. 6.

40. On the chronicles, see Ida Rodriguez Prampolini, *La Atlántida de Platón en los Cronistas del Siglo XVI* (Mexico, 1947).

CHAPTER XVII

1. For the more recent literature on the *Critias*, esp. on Atlantis, see Rosenmeyer, *CW*, L/13 (1957), 178; Cherniss, *Lustrum*, IV (1959), 79ff. / On what follows in the text, the circular harbor of Carthage should be mentioned among Plato's models (see *Plato* 3, p. 554, n. 4).

CHAPTER XVIII

12. On Panaitios, see also É. des Places, "Le Platonisme de Panétius," in *Mélanges de l'École française de Rome* (1956).

INDEX

geography/geophysics (*continued*)
262–64, 269–70, 272–73,
274, 276, 278 (fig., 263);
Parmenides, 262, 386[3]; in
the *Phaedo*, 95–96, 97, 199,
261–73, 274, 277; subterranean
streams, 266–68, 387[8]; Theopompos, 276–77; in *Timaeus*,
273–77, 280, 285, 389[16];
true earth, 263–66, 268; true
ocean and true continent, 96–
97, 201–2, 274–76, 389[19 21];
water and land, distribution
of, 284; winds, origin and
course of, 281; zones, theory
of, 271, 278–82, 283, 391[33 34];
see also cosmos / cosmology
geometry, 27, 92–93, 102
Gercke, Alfred, 353[15], 362[8], 386[3]
Gerkan, Armin von, 396[10]
Gestalt, 16
Ghazali, al-, 74
Gigon, Olof, 361–62[6], 369[10],
378[4], 383[17]
Gillespie, R. C. M., 341[17]
Gilson, Etienne, 235, 346[20], 377[4 6]
Gisinger, Friedrich, 386[1], 391[32]
Glaukon, 8, 24, 148, 166
Glover, T. R., 397[11]
Godel, R., 365[14]
Goethe, 5, 27, 40, 73, 144, 167,
169, 260, 339[2], 367[18]; and
the demonic, 33–34, 35, 36, 38,
44, 345[5 11]; and *Eros*, 44, 50;
on irony, 137, 363[1]; on light
and darkness, 63–64, 348[3];
and Schiller, 20–21, 342[23];
and the *Timaeus*, 385[39]; the
Urpflanze of, 20–21
Goetze, Albrecht, 344[38], 370[11]
Goldbeck, Ernst, 349[13]
Golden Age, 39, 206, 208, 308
Goldschmidt, Victor, 344[35], 378[4]
Gomme, A. W., 386[1]
Gomperz, Heinrich, 379[7], 383[17]
Gomperz, Theodor, 340[11 12],
341[16], 351[1], 357[6]
Gorgias, 7, 13, 22, 111, 128, 141,
340[12], 357[6], 379[10]
GORGIAS, 60, 159, 168, 178, 195,

216; *cited:* 27, 28, 85, 103,
155, 156, 175, 181, 186, 190,
296, 366[6], 393[10 17], 394[19];
see also eschatology
Grassi, Ernesto, 370[14]
Gray, John Henry, 394[18]
Greene, William Chase, 357[11],
360[28]
Grimm, Herman, 365[1]
Grimm, Jakob, 341[16]
Grimm, Wilhelm, 341[16]
Grote, George, 236, 362[9], 369[10],
392[1]
Grube, Georges M. A., 347[22],
375[2]
Grumach, Ernst, 385[39]
guardians of the state, *see*
Republic
Gundert, Hermann, 345[1], 351[40],
364[10]
Gundolf, Friedrich, 367[18]
Gyges, ring of, 297
gymnastics, 159

Hadrian, Villa of, 321–22
Haliste, Pärtel, 355[26]
Hambruch, Ernst, 354[18]
Harder, Richard, 356[4], 398[17]
Hardy, Edmund, 349[12]
harmony of the universe, 188
Harward, John, 379[6 8], 380[16]
Hatra, 320
Hegel, Georg W. F., 234, 348[9],
370[14], 374[41], 381[3]; interpre-
tation of Plato's myths, 209;
on irony, 144, 364[6]
Heiberg, J. L., 253, 353[15], 383[18]
Heidegger, Martin, 136; and
aletheia, 221–29, 376[7 8 9], 377[10]
Heidel, William Arthur, 384[25],
386[3], 388[12]
Heinicke, R., 383[21]
Heinze, Richard, 346[18], 354[19]
Heisenberg, Werner, 247, 251,
254, 381[5], 382[14], 383[21]
Hekataios of Abdera, 319
Hekataios of Miletus, 96, 127,
276
Helbig, Wolfgang, 359[22]
Helikon of Kyzikos, 91, 353[15]

Addenda to the Second Edition

BIBLIOGRAPHY OF THE WRITINGS OF
PAUL FRIEDLÄNDER

1905

Argolica: Quaestiones ad Graecorum historiam fabularem pertinentes. Berlin diss., 1905.

1907

Herakles: Sagengeschichtliche Untersuchungen. Philologische Untersuchungen, XIX. Berlin, 1907.

"Zum Plautinischen Hiat," *Rheinisches Museum,* LXII (1907), 73–85.

1909

"Zur Entwicklungsgeschichte griechischer Metren," *Hermes,* XLIV (1909), 321–51.

"Persona," *Glotta,* II (1909), 164–68.

"Zur Frühgeschichte des argivischen Heraions," *Athenische Mitteilungen* (Archäologisches Institut), XXXIV (1909), 69–79.

1912

Johannes von Gaza und Paulus Silentiarius: Kunstbeschreibungen Justinianischer Zeit. Leipzig and Berlin, 1912. (Reprinted, Hildesheim, 1969).

"Die Chronologie des Nonnos von Panopolis," *Hermes,* XLVII (1912), 43–59.

"Prometheus-Pandora und die Weltalter bei Hesiod," *Zeitschrift für das Gymnasialwesen,* LXVI (1912), 802–3.

"Entwicklung des Chores in der nacheuripideischen Tragödie," *Zeitschrift für das Gymnasialwesen,* LXVI (1912), 806–8.

1913

"Hypothekai," *Hermes,* XLVIII (1913), 558–616. Part I, "Hesiod," pp. 558–72 (reprinted in *Wege der Forschung,* Vol. XLIV, *Hesiod,* Darmstadt, 1966, pp. 223–38); Part II, "Theognis," pp. 572–603; Part III, "Demokrit," pp. 603–16.

1914

"Kritische Untersuchungen zur Geschichte der Heldensage," *Rheinisches Museum,* LXIX (1914), 299–341.

"Das Prooemium der Theogonie," *Hermes,* XLIX (1914), 1–16. (Reprinted in *Wege der Forschung,* Vol. XLIV, *Hesiod,* Darmstadt, 1966, pp. 277–94.)

"Die Anfänge der Erdkugelgeographie," *Jahrbuch des Deutschen Archäologischen Instituts,* XXIX/2 (1914), 98–120.

Review of *Hesiods Theogonie mit Einleitung und Kommentar,* by Wolf Aly. *Sokrates. Zeitschrift für das Gymnasialwesen,* n.s., II (1914), 288–90.

Review of *Homerische Aufsätze*, by Adolf Römer. *Deutsche Literaturzeitung*, 42/43 (1914), cols. 2264–68.

1921

Der Grosse Alcibiades: Ein Weg zu Platon. Part I. Bonn, 1921. Review of *Griechische Verskunst*, by Ulrich von Wilamowitz. *Deutsche Literaturzeitung*, 30/31 (1921), cols. 409–16.

1922

"Die Aufgaben der klassischen Studien an der Universität," in *Schule und Leben*, No. 6 (Berlin, 1922), pp. 21–34.

Review of *Der Kranz des Meleagros von Gadara*, selections trans. by August Oehler. *Deutsche Literaturzeitung*, 29 (1922), cols. 623–27.

1923

Der Grosse Alcibiades: Ein Weg zu Platon. Part II, *Kritische Erörterung*. Bonn, 1923.

1925

"Die griechische Tragödie und das Tragische," Parts I and II. *Die Antike* (Berlin), I (1925), 5–35, 295–318.

1926

"Die griechische Tragödie und das Tragische," Part III. *Die Antike*, II (1926), 79–112.

Review of *Altionische Götterlieder unter dem Namen Homers*, tr. R. Borchardt. *Gnomon*, II (1926), 344–49.

1927

"Die Philipps-Universität zu Marburg 1527–1927," *Zur Geschichte des Altphilologischen Seminars* (Marburg, 1927), pp. 695–701.

1928

Platon. Vol. I, *Eidos, Paideia, Dialogos*. Berlin, 1928.

"Die Entdeckung der Erde durch die Griechen," *Mitteilungen* (Marburg, Universitätsbund), No. 11 (1928), pp. 23–30.

1929

"Retractationes, I," *Hermes*, LXIV (1929), 376–84.

1930

Platon. Vol. II, *Die platonischen Schriften*. Berlin, 1930.

1931

"Vorklassisch und Nachklassisch," in *Das Problem des Klassischen und die Antike*, ed. W. Jaeger (Berlin, 1931), pp. 33–46. (Reprinted, Stuttgart, 1961.)

Review of *Hesiodi Carmina*, ed. Felix Jacoby. *Göttingische gelehrte Anzeigen* (Göttingen, 1931), pp. 241–66. (Reprinted in *Wege der Forschung*, Vol. XLIV, *Hesiod*, Darmstadt, 1966, pp. 100–30.)

1932

"Retractationes, II," *Hermes*, LXVII (1932), 43–46.
"Statius: *An den Schlaf*," *Die Antike*, VIII (1932), 215–28.
"Aristophanes in Deutschland," Part I. *Die Antike*, VIII (1932), 229–53.

1933

"Aristophanes in Deutschland," Part II. *Die Antike*, IX (1933), 81–104.

1934

"Lachende Götter," *Die Antike*, X (1934), 209–26.
"Polla ta deina," *Hermes*, LXIX (1934), 56–63.
Review of *Die Dionysiaka des Nonnos*, tr. Thassilo von Scheffer. *Deutsche Literaturzeitung* (1934), cols. 683–87.
Review of *Platons "Symposion,"* tr. and ed. J. Sykutris. *Göttingische gelehrte Anzeigen* (Göttingen, 1935), No. 9.
Die Melodie zu Pindars Erstem Pythischen Gedicht," *Berichte über die Verhandlungen der Sächsischen Akademie der Wissenschaften zu Leipzig*, Phil.-hist. Kl., LXXXVI/4 (1934), 1–53.

1935

"Pindar oder Kircher?" *Hermes*, LXX (1935), 463–72.
"Zur New Yorker Nekyia," *Archäologischer Anzeiger* (1935), cols. 20–33.

1937

"Athanasius Kircher und Leibniz: Ein Beitrag zur Geschichte der Polyhistorie im XVII. Jahrhundert," *Rendiconti della Pontificia Accademia Romana di Archeologia*, XIII (1937), 229–47.

1938

"Geschichtswende im Gedicht: Interpretationen historischer Epigramme," *Studi italiani di filologia classica*, XV (1938), 89–120.
"Dis kai tris to kalon," *Transactions of the American Philological Association*, LXIX (1938), 375–80.

1939

Spätantiker Gemäldezyklus in Gaza: Des Prokopios von Gaza Ekphrasis Eikonos. Studi e testi della Biblioteca Vaticana, LXXXIX, 1939. (Reprinted, together with *Johannes von Gaza und Paulus Silentiarius: Kunstbeschreibungen Justinianischer Zeit*, Hildesheim, 1969.)
"The Epicurean Theology in Lucretius' First Prooemium," *Transactions of the American Philological Association*, LXX (1939), 368–79.

1941

"Pattern of Sound and Atomistic Theory in Lucretius," *American Journal of Philology,* LXII (1941), 16–34.
"Plato, *Phaedrus* 245A," *Classical Philology,* XXXVI (1941), 51–52.

1942

"A New Epigram by Damagetus," *American Journal of Philology,* LXIII (1942), 78–82.
"Heracliti fragmentum 124," *American Journal of Philology,* LXIII (1942), 336.
Review of *Plato's Theology,* by Friedrich Solmsen. *Philosophical Review,* LII (1942), 507–9.

1944

"The Greek Behind Latin," *Classical Journal,* XXXIX (1944), 270–77.

1945

Documents of Dying Paganism. Textiles of Late Antiquity in Washington, New York, and Leningrad. Berkeley and Los Angeles, 1945.
"Socrates Enters Rome," *American Journal of Philology,* LXVI (1945), 337–51. (Printed also in *Platon* I, 2d and 3d edns., and in both edns. of *Plato* I.)
Review of *T. Lucreti Cari De rerum natura,* ed. W. E. Leonard and S. B. Smith. *American Journal of Philology,* LXVI (1945), 318–24.
Review of *Plato's Earlier Dialectic,* by Richard Robinson. *Classical Philology,* XL (1945), 253–59.

1948

Epigrammata. Greek Inscriptions in Verse from the Beginnings to the Persian Wars. With the collaboration of H. B. Hoffleit. Berkeley and Los Angeles, 1948.
Review of *Pindari Epinicia,* ed. Alexander Turyn. *American Journal of Philology,* LXIX (1948), 214–17.

1949

"Structure and Destruction of the Atom According to Plato's *Timaeus,*" *University of California Publications in Philosophy,* XVI (1949), 225–48.

1952

"Erinnerung an Georg Loeschcke," *Bonner Jahrbücher,* CLII (1952), 13–16.

1953

Rhythmen und Landschaften im Zweiten Teil des Faust. Weimar, 1953.

1954

Platon. Vol. I, *Seinswahrheit und Lebenswirklichkeit.* 2d edn., Berlin, 1954.

1957

Platon. Vol. II, *Die platonischen Schriften. Erste Periode.* 2d edn., Berlin, 1957.

1958

Plato 1. *An Introduction,* tr. Hans Meyerhoff. New York (Bollingen Series LIX:1) and London, 1958.

1959

"Noch einmal zur Echtheit der Pindar-Melodie," *Hermes,* LXXXVII (1959), 385–89.
Adnotatiunculae: "Die Melodie zu Pindars Erstem Pythischen Gedicht" and "Hestia Polyolbos," *Hermes,* LXXXVII (1959), 389–92.

1960

Platon. Vol. III, *Die platonischen Schriften. Zweite und dritte Periode.* 2d edn., Berlin, 1960.
"Akademische Randglossen," in *Die Gegenwart der Griechen im neuren Denken* (Festschrift für H.-G. Gadamer). Tübingen, 1960, p. 317.

1963

Plato 1. *An Introduction,* tr. Hans Meyerhoff. Harper Torchbook reprint, 1963.

1964

Platon. Vol. I, *Seinswahrheit und Lebenswirklichkeit.* 3d edn., Berlin, 1964.
Platon. Vol. II, *Die platonischen Schriften. Erste Periode.* 3d edn., Berlin, 1964.
Plato 2. *The Dialogues, First Period,* tr. Hans Meyerhoff. New York (Bollingen Series LIX:2) and London, 1964.

1969

Plato 3. *The Dialogues, Second and Third Periods,* tr. Hans Meyerhoff. Princeton (Bollingen Series LIX:3) and London, 1969.
Plato 1. *An Introduction,* tr. Hans Meyerhoff. 2nd edn., Princeton (Bollingen Series LIX:1) and London, 1969.
Studien zur antiken Literatur und Kunst. Berlin, 1969.

PAUL FRIEDLÄNDER
A NOTE ON HIS LIFE AND WORK

Dr. Friedländer's writings on Plato, known in German to two generations of scholars and now available to the English reader, have had a major influence on Plato studies in modern times. First published in German in two volumes, and in subsequent editions revised and developed into three volumes which have been translated and again expanded, the *Plato* of Paul Friedländer is recognized as the "first resolute attempt to understand Plato's dialogues entirely on the basis of their ancient presuppositions." Other works of Dr. Friedländer's cover a broad range of interest, beginning with the origins and development of legendary or mythical heroes. His main effort, however, was given to the study of Greek literature. His articles on Hesiod brought a new understanding of this archaic poet and made it clear that archaic poetry as such cannot be judged by the criteria of subsequent times.

Dr. Friedländer was also interested in the style that developed in late antiquity. His work on John of Gaza and Paul Silentiarius and on Procopius combines an exact interpretation of the texts with an archaeological reconstruction of the poetic descriptions. He later wrote a widely regarded series of essays on the height of classical literature, tragedy, and the nature of the tragic. Another of his concerns was metrics and in particular the authenticity of a controversial specimen of Greek music. In his effort to ascertain the genuineness of this melody, Dr. Friedländer searched through the vast correspondence of Kircher, a famous Jesuit of the seventeenth century. Here he discovered a hitherto unknown letter written to Kircher by the young Leibniz. The relation of the two men, and an analysis of the history of ideas, became the focus of additional writings by Dr. Friedländer. He also wrote several articles on Latin literature, including some passages of Lucretius with their characteristic blend of poetic and philosophic elements.

Typically, Dr. Friedländer's commentary on Statius' poem "To Sleep" opens vistas of a particular theme in various literatures and in art. His keen interest in art and archaeology is evident also in his *Documents of Dying Paganism*, in which textiles representing goddesses much revered in late antiquity are interpreted and co-ordinated with the background of religious and cultic change. Dr. Friedländer's thorough knowledge of German literature and its penetration by the literature of antiquity is apparent especially in two studies, one on Aristophanes and the other on the second part of Goethe's *Faust*. The Goethe study shows the synthesis of elements from Dante and Shakespeare, as well as from antiquity, in the various aspects of the German drama.

Paul Friedländer's life work is remarkable for the broad field it covers, for the multiplicity of themes, and for the fullness of knowledge which he perseveringly sought not for its own sake but for clarification and deeper understanding. At the time of his death in December, 1968, he had just completed revisions and additional work on a volume of collected studies. In this as in all his efforts he had the constant and scholarly aid of his wife, Dr. Charlotte Friedländer, who now so ably carries on the responsibility for publications.

Born in Berlin in 1882, Paul Friedländer received his doctorate in classics from the University of Berlin in 1905. He held professorships at the universities of Berlin and Marburg, and at Halle until his compulsory retirement by the Nazi government in 1935. In 1939 he was able to come to the United States to accept a lectureship at The Johns Hopkins University, and in the following year he joined the faculty of the University of California in Los Angeles. Appointed there as full professor of classics in 1945 and honored as faculty research lecturer for 1949, Dr. Friedländer was professor emeritus of classics at his death in his eighty-sixth year.

CITATION FROM THE BAVARIAN ACADEMY
Munich
March, 1967

Honored colleague,

The Bavarian Akademie der Wissenschaften finds it a pleasure and a privilege to congratulate you on the occasion of your eighty-fifth birthday.

Your scholarship has extended to a wide range of classical studies. As a young man you investigated the origin and development of Greek legends in their manifold variants; in this domain you struck out on paths very different from those taken by your famous teachers Hermann Usener and Ulrich von Wilamowitz. In the following years, while still pursuing your studies on the early period of Greek culture, you turned your attention to the late years of classical antiquity, providing an interpretation of the art descriptions of John of Gaza and Paul Silentiarius. And in the same period you published an important contribution to the history of Greek metrics.

The second decade of your scholarly activity began with work on the text and interpretation of Hesiod's poems. Here your patient efforts to explain seemingly strange, incomprehensible, or contradictory passages and sections in the work of the archaic peasant poet led certain scholars to attack you as a "harmonist" bent on preserving the tradition at all costs. You, however, met the often dictatorially arrogant attacks of your opponents with a charming blend of conciliation in tone and firmness in substance, and in the end, in the universal opinion of your colleagues, carried off a victory which is scarcely contested today.

The same decade was marked by your penetrating—and widely noticed —essays on Greek tragedy and the tragic, and by the first publications bearing witness to your concern with Plato, which was to culminate in your chief work, your *Plato*, published first in two, then in three volumes. In contrast to earlier books on Plato, which had either treated his philosophy more or less from the standpoint of modern philosophical views or systems, or, like the two-volume work of Wilamowitz, dealt with Plato the man without going very deeply into his philosophy, your book was the first resolute attempt to understand Plato's dialogues entirely on the basis of their ancient presuppositions.

You were driven out of Germany by the regime of injustice, but soon after your arrival in the United States you established a splendid new sphere of activity in which you exerted an ever-widening influence not only on your students but on your American colleagues as well. Your collection of Greek verse inscriptions, which appeared soon after World War II, has become a valuable instrument for the discussion of the history of the Greek epigram. In the last few years your book on Plato has run into many editions, and has appeared in English translation. Meanwhile your scholarly activity has extended to the most varied fields, from earliest to latest antiquity, from philosophy to the interpretation of ancient works of art in terms of the history of religions. Last but not least, every meeting with you has been a source of personal profit to your colleagues and to your visitors from Europe. We wish you a long continuation of your fruitful efforts.

The President
—The Secretary of the Philosophical-Historical Section